Trees of Santa Barbara

Dombeya cacuminum

Eucalyptus cladocalyx

TREES
of
SANTA BARBARA

Robert N. Muller and J. Robert Haller

Santa Barbara Botanic Garden

Copyright © Santa Barbara Botanic Garden 2005
Second printing, 2015

Second Edition of revised and expanded version.

Previous versions published by the Santa Barbara Botanic Garden:
Katherine Muller, Richard Broder, and Will Beittel, *Trees of Santa Barbara*, 1974
Maunsell Van Rensselaer, *Trees of Santa Barbara*, 1948
Maunsell Van Rensselaer, *Trees of Santa Barbara*, 1940

All rights reserved. No part of this book may be reproduced in any form or by any electronic or mechanical means without written permission of the publisher. Request for permission to make copies of any part the work should be mailed to: Santa Barbara Botanic Garden, 1212 Mission Canyon Road, Santa Barbara, CA 93105-2126.

All photographs J. Robert Haller and Robert N. Muller: Copyright © Santa Barbara Botanic Garden.

Editorial Assistant: Katey O'Neill
Graphic Design and Production: Katey O'Neill

Library of Congress Control Number: 2004098691

ISBN 978-0-916436-07-0

Front Cover: Canary Island palm surrounded by young Senegal date palms at the Santa Barbara County Courthouse. Robert N. Muller.
Back Cover: African tulip tree. J. Robert Haller.

This edition is dedicated to
Santa Barbara Beautiful
*In honor of their 50th Anniversary
and with deep appreciation to their commitment to tree planting in Santa Barbara.
Many of the trees described in this book would not exist if not for
their street tree planting efforts.*

Contents

Preface . . . . Page ix
Acknowledgements x
Introduction 1
The Joy of Identifying Trees 11
Organization of This Book 19

GYMNOSPERMS
    Araucariaceae 20
    Cupressaceae 25
    Ginkgoaceae 48
    Pinaceae 49
    Podocarpaceae 77
    Taxaceae 81

ANGIOSPERMS
Dicots
    Aceraceae 83
    Anacardiaceae 90
    Annonaceae 98
    Apocynaceae 99
    Aquifoliaceae 101
    Araliaceae 104
    Betulaceae 108
    Bignoniaceae 111
    Bombacaceae 120
    Boraginaceae 121
    Caprifoliaceae 122
    Casuarinaceae 124
    Celastraceae 127
    Ebenaceae 128
    Elaeocarpaceae 130
    Ericaceae 131
    Euphorbiaceae 133
    Fabaceae 139
    Fagaceae 192
    Flacourtiaceae 206
    Hamamelidaceae 207
    Hippocastanaceae 210
    Hydrophyllaceae 213
    Juglandaceae 214

Contents

Lauraceae 218
Loganiaceae 226
Lythraceae 227
Magnoliaceae 228
Malvaceae 232
Meliaceae 236
Menispermaceae 240
Moraceae 241
Myoporaceae 257
Myricaceae 258
Myrtaceae 259
Oleaceae 326
Phytolaccaceae 334
Pittosporaceae 335
Platanaceae 343
Proteaceae 344
Rhizophoraceae 350
Rosaceae 351
Rutaceae 365
Salicaceae 373
Sapindaceae 379
Scrophulariaceae 388
Simaroubaceae 389
Sterculiaceae 390
Tamaricaceae 398
Thymelaeaceae 399
Tiliaceae 400
Ulmaceae 401
Verbenaceae 405

Monocots

Agavaceae 408
Arecaceae 410
Asphodelaceae 438
Dracaenaceae 439

Glossary 440
Bibliography 444
Latin/Common Name Index 446

Preface

Santa Barbara and its surrounding communities are indeed special places. Their reputation for lush, even opulent, gardens is by no means an accident. Through much of its history Santa Barbara has lain at the intersection of an ideal climate and the reverence of its citizens for the beauty of nature. It is from this juncture that Santa Barbara's reputation as the "Riviera of the West" developed. The loamy alluvial soils of Santa Barbara and the Goleta Valley supported the nurseries of the early plantsmen, while the eroded rocky marine terraces of Montecito, the Riviera, and Hope Ranch provided likely settings for the secluded estates favored by the wealthy, who sought unique and exotic species for their landscapes. Today, the rich horticultural offerings in Santa Barbara are a legacy that residents and visitors, alike, enjoy and appreciate.

This book is also built on a legacy. The first *Trees of Santa Barbara* was published by the Santa Barbara Botanic Garden in 1941. Written by Maunsell Van Rensselaer, this first book listed 550 species and varieties. It was revised and republished in 1948 with the addition of almost 200 new species and varieties. Twenty-six years later Katherine Muller (Van Rennselaer's successor as Director of the Santa Barbara Botanic Garden), Richard E. Broder (Herbarium Botanist at the University of California, Santa Barbara), and Will Beittel (former City Arborist and Senior Nurseryman at the University of California, Santa Barbara) teamed to completely rewrite the book. Many of the original species had been lost and numerous others had been added. Thirty-one years have passed since publication of the previous volume, and numerous changes in the trees of Santa Barbara have occurred. The present volume includes over 400 species. Of the 600 species included in the previous volume, almost 100 were lost to drought or development. Over 40 new species have been added to the Santa Barbara flora. Over 70 species in the previous version occurred only in private gardens and were not available to the public. These have been excluded from this work.

In this edition of *Trees of Santa Barbara,* we have expanded the descriptions of each species to provide a consistent basis of comparison of key features (*i.e.* habit, leaves, bark, twigs, flowers, and fruit). In this regard, the book has the feel of a taxonomic flora. However, we have tried to minimize botanical jargon and have focused on characteristics most useful in identification of a species. We have also expanded the pictorial coverage of important characteristics. While it was impossible to provide complete photographic coverage of each species, all are represented by at least one photograph of a useful feature to assist with identification.

ACKNOWLEDGEMENTS

This book builds upon the legacy left by many horticulturists and conservators whose love for Santa Barbara created the richly varied urban landscape that surrounds us today. The efforts of early plantsmen such as Joseph Sexton, Francesco Franceschi, A. Boyd Doremus, E. O. Orpet, and many others are seen every day in the parks and along the streets of Santa Barbara and neighboring communities. These early horticulturists' passion for plants from far-off lands paved the way for plant enthusiasts drawn to Santa Barbara by its near-idyllic setting and weather.

Previous volumes of *Trees of Santa Barbara* by Maunsell Van Rensselaer (1940, 1948), and Katherine Muller, Dick Broder, and Will Beittel (1974) documented the diversity of Santa Barbara's rich arboreal legacy. Those volumes and Will Beittel's *Santa Barbara's Street and Park Trees* (1972) set the stage for this revision.

Many individuals and organizations have made this project possible. Most especially, we are grateful to Bob and Marlene Veloz and Virginia L. T. Gardner whose support carried this project from initiation to completion. The Santa Barbara Botanic Garden provided the initial sponsorship of the project while Bob Muller was on sabbatical leave from the University of Kentucky. The Santa Barbara County Horticultural Foundation and Santa Barbara Beautiful contributed financial support towards the book's final production. The support of all of these individuals and organizations is gratefully acknowledged. During the course of writing, several individuals provided encouragement, critique, and, most especially, information on new trees and new locations of old trees. Dan Condon, Bruce Van Dyke, and Carol Terry were always ready to "talk trees." Avis Keedy was a constant source of support and enthusiasm. Finally, the encouragement of the many people for whom this book is intended has been a continuing inspiration. To all we are deeply grateful and indebted.

Syagrus romanzoffiana

INTRODUCTION

Trees have been important to inhabitants of the Santa Barbara region for longer than recorded history. Certainly, for Native American Chumash people, the deep shade provided by coast live oaks was a welcome respite from an intense summer sun. Those same oaks provided abundant crops of edible acorns, as well as fuel for cooking and warmth. However, other species of trees were also important for the Chumash. California bay *(Umbellularia californica)*, holly-leaved cherry *(Prunus ilicifolia)*, gray pine *(Pinus sabiniana)*, and willows (*Salix* spp.) provided food and building materials. The establishment of Mission Santa Barbara in 1786 brought horticulture to Santa Barbara, and with it the introduction of new species. Most of these were brought for purposes of food, and in 1793 Captain George Vancouver observed almonds, apples, apricots, cherries, lemons, limes, oranges, peaches, pears, and pomegranates in the Mission's gardens. Larger plantations of olives and vineyards were established near Jalama where climate and soils were found to favor both crops. A cursory look at the gardens associated with the missions today might suggest that the Fathers maintained a lush setting of floristic diversity for their contemplation. However, it is likely that little beyond foodstuffs was introduced during the Mission period. California pepper (*Schinus molle*—neither Californian nor a pepper) is known to have been introduced by the Spanish, and there is some suggestion that chinaberry *(Melia azedarach)* was introduced for its corrugated seeds that were used to make rosaries. Palms (likely the Mexican fan palm, *Washingtonia robusta*) were brought to support the traditions of Palm Sunday. But there is no evidence that horticultural aesthetics were a motivation for introduction of any woody species during the Mission era.

The first nurseries in California came with the political stability of statehood, and during the 1850s several nurseries were established in San Francisco. Joseph Sexton is credited with establishing the first nursery in the Santa Barbara area in 1867, and within ten years his catalog was described in a local newspaper as containing "62 pages, descriptive of all the rarest shrubs and plants." His ten-acre nursery lay on the corner of what is now Hollister Avenue and Ward Memorial Highway, and the original Sexton garden, now on the grounds of a local motel, contains many of the trees he originally planted. Although complete lists of his introductions no longer exist, Sexton is credited with popularizing cork oak *(Quercus suber)*, dragon tree *(Dracaena draco)* and Lombardy poplar *(Populus nigra* 'Italica'). Thus began a long tradition of horticulture that continues today. Sexton also unwittingly contributed to what has become a major concern of horticulture today—the introduction of aggressive exotic species that can outcompete native species and dominate large tracts of disturbed land. By 1889 he was harvesting plumes from 5,000 hills of pampas grass (*Cortaderia selloweana*), which has since become an invasive weed. During the same period, Ellwood Cooper bought 2,000 acres of the Dos Pueblos Ranch west of Glen Annie, in a canyon that bears his name today. He planted olives, walnuts, and almonds; but, more importantly, Cooper was a champion of a then little known genus from Australia—*Eucalyptus*. He planted over 50,000 trees of the Tasmanian blue gum (*Eucalyptus globulus*) that were intended to be used for wharf pilings. While these never met their expectations, Cooper's enthusiasm for the genus led him to introduce over 50 species of *Eucalyptus*, many of which are attractive horticultural components of Santa Barbara's streets and parks.

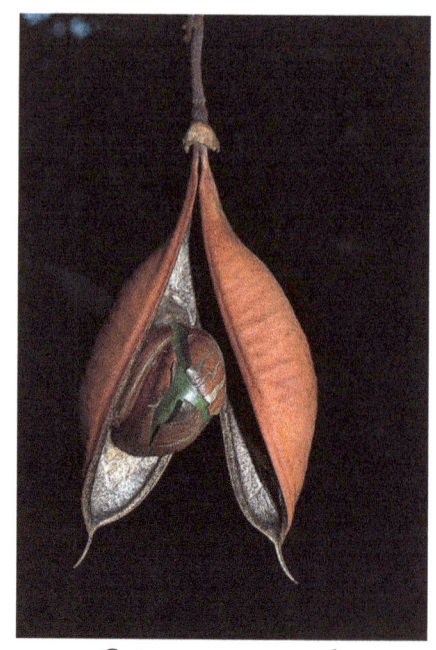

Castanospermum australe

During the period from 1880 to 1910, four plantsmen had significant impacts on Santa Barbara horticulture. Kinton Stevens established a nursery in 1883 at the Montecito site that was to become Madame Ganna Walska's Lotusland. Stevens started his business by cultivating popular fruit trees, prunes, olives, and lemons; but he also developed a strong interest in tropical plants for use as ornamentals. He was commissioned to collect palms from Hawaii for use in San Francisco's Golden Gate Park. His love for palms led to the planting of California fan palms (*Washingtonia filifera*) along Cabrillo Boulevard. He also introduced the Chilean wine palm (*Jubaea chilensis*) and a host of tropical species that now grace Santa Barbara's streets. Stevens' son, Ralph, carried on the family tradition in a number of capacities, serving briefly as Park Superintendent following the retirement of Boyd Doremus. However, most of his contributions were in the private sector. He restored and enhanced the magnificence of Lotusland and added immensely to the plantings of Santa Barbara's streets and parks.

Francesco Franceschi (born E. O. Fenzi) came to Santa Barbara in 1893 at the age of 50 and brought with him a lifelong love and knowledge of plants. Within two years he had published a small book cataloging nearly 600 species of introduced plants in the Santa Barbara area: *Santa Barbara Exotic Flora: A Handbook of Plants From Foreign*

Countries Grown at Santa Barbara, California. Even at that time, Santa Barbara's unique combination of equable climate and horticultural enthusiasts was evident. Franceschi established the Southern California Acclimatizing Association in 1895, based on the false Lamarckian concept that with each generation, species of plants would become progressively better-adapted to the environment of their parents. Although the premise of the Association failed, its activities did not. A nursery was established on the southwest corner of State and Gutierrez Streets and by 1895 had "500 specimen trees and shrubs belonging to about 300 different genera and never grown here before." All that remains of the former nursery today is the Sexton flame tree *(Brachychiton* x *roseus)* facing State Street. In 1905, Franceschi purchased 40 acres of barren, rocky landscape on Mission Ridge Road that he called Montarioso. Here he built a three-story residence and started an ambitious botanic garden. He desired a "permanent and instructive demonstration for landscape architects, horticulturists, gardeners, and all persons who take an interest in plants and flowers." Today, the remnants of this once stately collection are preserved as Franceschi Park. Franceschi left Santa Barbara in 1913 to return to his native Italy. He is credited with having introduced over 2,000 species that he propagated for sale in his nurseries. Many of these have since been lost. However, his legacy remains not only in Franceschi

Syzygium jambos

Park but also in several successful introductions about town. His successful propagation of Montezuma bald cypress *(Taxodium mucronatum)* is seen in trees planted in West Alameda Plaza and Plaza del Mar by Dr. A. B. Doremus, Santa Barbara's first Superintendent of Parks.

Dr. Augustus Boyd Doremus came to Santa Barbara in 1882 at the age of 40 with his family and a prognosis for a life shortened by kidney disease. However, he lived another 55 years, and his accomplishments shaped much of the future look of Santa Barbara. In 1902, Santa Barbara established its first Parks Commission to which Doremus was appointed. The appointment was appropriate, as he was well-known for his love of plants, exemplified by the spectacular gardens around his home on Anapamu Street above Santa Barbara High School. The other two members of the Parks Commission shouldered administrative responsibilities and left the ground work to Doremus. He first addressed the abandoned Alameda Plaza that had become little more than a weed patch. Through the years, he plowed, developed water lines, and planted both blocks of the Plaza with lasting results that can be seen today. Plaza del Mar was at that time a wetland lying at the base of the Mesa (formerly Diblee Hill). Doremus led the effort to fill it in with sand and soil, thereby creating this park and Pershing Park. His plantings of Moreton Bay fig *(Ficus macrophylla)*, rusty-leaf fig *(Ficus rubiginosa)*, and yate *(Eucalyptus cornuta)* still grace the grounds of this former swamp. Doremus and his colleagues are credited with saving Oak Park from development and creating the palm-lined Cabrillo Boulevard, known today as Chase Palm Park. On the streets of Santa Barbara, Doremus developed a vision of palm-lined

Lophostemon confertus

Erythrina lysistemon

promenades and horticultural diversity. He planted the original queen palms *(Syagrus romanzoffiana)* on State and Santa Barbara Streets, the Brazilian cedarwoods *(Cedrela fissilis)* along Gutierrez Street, the Mexican fan palms *(Washingtonia robusta)* along East Haley, the camphor trees *(Cinnamomum camphora)* on Chapala Street, and the California bay trees *(Umbellularia californica)* on West Alamar Avenue. However, Doremus' best known plantings are the distinctively crowned Italian stone pines *(Pinus pinea)* that were placed along East Anapamu Street between Milpas and Olive Streets in 1908. Those between Olive and Garden Streets were planted in 1929 by Ralph Stevens, Doremus' successor as Superintendent of Parks. Dr. Doremus' energy and accomplishments belie the dire medical situation with which he came to Santa Barbara. During the first 6 of his 18-year tenure as unpaid "park superintendent," he introduced no fewer than 326 species to grace Santa Barbara's streets and parks.

Peter Reidel immigrated from his native Netherlands at the age of 20 and arrived in Santa Barbara in 1905. He brought with him a lifelong love of plants and training from a gardening trade school and the agricultural and horticultural college at Wageningen. He briefly joined Franceschi's Southern California Acclimatizing Association, but that business relationship failed when Franceschi returned to Italy. He became associated with the Montecito Nursery and, as a landscape contractor, developed many of the fine estates in Montecito. In 1935, he began teaching high school, college, and evening classes. After retiring in 1942, he began preparing the manuscript for "Plants for Extra-Tropical Regions," which was three-quarters complete at the time of his death and was published privately by the California Arboretum Foundation. However, perhaps his most important contributions were in educating homeowners, for he recognized that the beauty of a city such as Santa Barbara depended as much on individual homeowners as on streets and parks.

Following Doremus' retirement as Superintendent of Parks, the position was filled briefly by Ralph Stevens, son of Kinton Stevens; however, his longterm replacement was E. O. Orpet, who held the position from 1921 to 1930. Orpet came to Santa Barbara in 1920 at the age of 57 with a full career's experience in both his native England and the eastern United States. Within six months he was appointed the city's third Superintendent of Parks, an effort that he combined with a private nursery practice. Orpet's energy, enthusiasm, and knowledge seemed boundless, and he added considerably to Santa Barbara's horticultural flora. He corresponded widely and maintained an active trade with plantsmen in other parts of the world. At one time he had a collection of over 800 species of succulents, including over 30 aloes that he propagated for use in plantings around Santa Barbara. As Superintendent of Parks, he was responsible for many of the city's street plantings, including the olive trees *(Olea europaea)* along the length of Olive Street, the cork oaks *(Quercus suber)* in Samarkand Heights, and the Southern magnolias *(Magnolia grandiflora)* on San Andres Street. One of Orpet's most significant contributions was the creation of Hillside Park, today known as Orpet Park. There, in little more than a barren pile of rock and rubble, he planted a diversity of plants from around the world. The Great Depression and subsequent droughts have reduced the grandeur of the original collection at Orpet Park; however, it still retains many unique species that can be seen nowhere else in Santa Barbara. Orpet experimented with numerous other plants that were not successful. He grew over 300 seedlings of *Protea* spp., but found that they could not survive the alkaline water used in irrigation. Among his successful introductions were white elder *(Nuxia floribunda)* and peumo *(Cryptocarya alba)*. After ten years as Superintendent of Parks, Orpet resigned in 1930 to devote his energies to his nursery business. When he died in 1956 he was one of the most respected horticulturists in the country. In recognition for his lifetime's achievements, he was awarded the *Florens de Bevoise* medal of the Garden Club of America.

Will Beittel was city arborist from 1956 to 1963, then nurseryman at the University of California at Santa Barbara. He had the unique history of coming to horticulture from a career as a music arranger and producer in Los Angeles. He was a coauthor of the previous edition of this book and wrote his own *Santa Barbara's Street and Park Trees*. Just as Reidel did, Beittel taught adult education classes on woody plants.

Many others have contributed to the horticultural diversity and appreciation of Santa Barbara's street and park trees. Finlay MacKenzie (Superintendent of Parks from 1938 to 1962), Bruce Van Dyke (horticulture teacher in Santa Barbara City College's

Adult Education classes for over 40 years and News Press horticultural writer for 32 years), and, more recently, Dan Condon (city arborist for over 20 years) have all nourished the "urban forest" of Santa Barbara and enabled the city to maintain its place as one of the premiere garden spots of the world, known for its unusual plantings and picturesque landscapes.

The Santa Barbara Environment

Horticultural development in Santa Barbara has depended greatly on its citizens and the love of plants that they brought with them from other regions. The area's natural beauty, however, attracted many settlers to the area. Certainly the setting of Santa Barbara on the narrow coastal shelf below the Santa Ynez Mountains and the picturesque views of the Channel Islands created a balmy ambience that was difficult to resist. However, equally important was the combination of climate and soils that favored a variety of plant species found in few other places in the world.

Southern California enjoys a Mediterranean climate, which is generally characterized by ocean-moderated temperatures and annual precipitation of 10 to 40 inches that occurs primarily during the winter months. In Santa Barbara, the long-term average annual precipitation for the 122-year period of 1867 to 1989 is 17.9 inches, and rains occur primarily during the winter and spring months of November through April. Daily maximum temperatures for the period 1951 to 1980 average 76°F during July, the hottest month, and daily minimum temperatures average 43°F in December and January, the coldest months of the year. Although temperatures as high as 105°F have been recorded (September 1978)[1], on average Santa Barbara experiences temperatures above 90°F only two days per year. Similarly, the lowest temperature recorded was 29°F, and on average only one day per year experiences temperatures as low as 32°F. However, these data are averages from climatic stations located near the coast. Local topography strongly influences actual temperatures experienced. For instance the Riviera, the Mesa, and the "banana belt" of Hope Ranch, all at slightly higher elevations, are essentially frost-free. On the other hand, cold air drainage in lowland areas away from the coast, such as

---

[1] On June 17, 1859 a freak event occurred that has not been repeated. Near the end of the noon hour a blast of superheated air blew off the desert and raised morning temperatures in the upper 70s to 133º by 2 pm. Later in the afternoon the wind died and by 7 pm temperatures were back to where the day had started, in the upper 70s. Reports of the time indicated that livestock "died on their feet," birds fell out of the sky, and, of course, vegetable gardens and fruit crops were destroyed. This event, a *simoon*, set a record high for any location on the continent that stood for 75 years.

Hidden Valley and Goleta Valley, experience frequent winter frost. These microclimatic differences can strongly influence the suitability of species for some locations.

Very similar climatological patterns can be found in Ventura, Laguna Beach, and even coastal San Diego; however, nearby cities that lie away from the moderating influence of the ocean experience extremes that are unexpected in Santa Barbara.

Liriodendron tulipifera

San Luis Obispo, for instance, which lies ten miles from the coast behind the San Luis Hills, is much warmer with an average of 12 days per year over 90°F and an extreme temperature of 112°F recorded in September 1971. Lompoc, which also lies ten miles from the coast but is not protected from the ocean, is both warmer and colder, with temperatures below 32°F occurring 14 days out of the year. To the south of Santa Barbara, cities inland from the coast are significantly warmer. Pasadena experiences 54 days above 90°F annually, and Burbank experiences this condition 57 days each year. In addition to warmer temperatures, the amount of precipitation declines south of Santa Barbara. Annual rainfall in Laguna Beach is 12.3 inches compared to Santa Barbara's 17.9 inches. Santa Monica receives 13.7 inches, and even Oxnard, only 30 miles to the southeast, receives much less rainfall—14.5 inches annually.

The coastal outline of Southern California is another feature that significantly influences the climate of Santa Barbara. The Catalina eddy is created by strong atmospheric movement down the West Coast. When the coastline turns to the east starting at Point Conception, the north-south axis of this air movement carries its trajectory out to sea, resulting in an eddy that reaches as far south as Santa Catalina Island. This counter-clockwise circulation brings warm, moisture-laden air that condenses on salt particles to create the "marine layer" of which Santa Barbarans are so aware. The fog and overcast skies of the Catalina Eddy persist during the hot, dry summer months and reduce the drying potential of the intense summer sun.

The soils of Santa Barbara are seldom limiting to plant growth. Almost all of the soils along the coastal shelf from Goleta to Summerland are of sedimentary origin, having been derived from either old marine terraces or alluvium that washed down from the marine sandstones and mudstones of the Santa Ynez Mountains. The low rainfall has done little to leach nutrients from these soils and much of the area is reasonably alkaline or, at most, modestly acidic. These relatively benign soils support a vast range of plant requirements and have helped foster the diversity of species grown here. Santa Barbara has successfully grown trees from the tropical regions of the world, the subalpine zones of Tasmania and Asia, the grasslands of eastern Africa and South America, and, of course, the Mediterranean regions of Europe, South Africa, Australia, and South America. One group of plants in particular is encouraged by the basic soils of Santa Barbara; palms (Arecaceae) are globally known to be restricted to basic soils, regardless of climatic condition. Over 25 species of palms currently grow on the city's streets and parks, and numerous others grow on private estates, attesting to the success of this group in the Santa Barbara area. In direct contrast, species of the heath family (Ericaceae) are universally recognized to require acidic soils for optimal growth. The success of so few Ericaceous species in our flora reflects the lack of acidic soils in our landscapes. Indeed, *Arbutus unedo* and its cultivar *Arbutus* 'Marina' derive from the limestone regions of the western Mediterranean region and seem to be the only ericaceous trees that thrive in the Santa Barbara environment.

A Conservatory of Global Biodiversity

The many species of trees in Santa Barbara are ambassadors from nature of their native lands. Some have unique biological features, such as *cherimoya (Annona cherimola)* whose flowers increase in temperature by as much as 6°F when they open, thereby releasing a variety of odors that attract pollinating beetles and flies. Others reflect the cultures of native peoples from many different regions of the world. The seeds of the broad-leaved lucky bean tree *(Erythrina latissima)* were worn in necklaces and charms to ward off evil by native peoples of southern Africa. The bark of Hindu laurel *(Cocculus laurifolius)* contains alkaloids that were used by indigenous peoples of the Malay Peninsula to poison their arrows and darts. Other species are simply best known for their natural beauty.

Santa Barbara's streets and parks are an outdoor conservatory for the display and conservation of an important element of the biotic wonder of our world. Many of the trees described in this book come from very restricted distributions and are subject to the devastating effects of conflicting land use policies. Others are indeed endangered and exist primarily or solely in horticulture. As a conservatory, Santa Barbara's streets and parks present an unsurpassed opportunity to educate its citizens and visitors about the wonders of the natural world. It is the purpose of this revision to bring that world a little closer to ourselves each time we step out the door.

One of the realities of today's global travel and transport is that plants introduced to new areas may become very aggressive colonizers, invading disturbed and natural landscapes alike. Fortunately, this occurs only with a very small number of the many plants that have been intentionally or accidentally introduced; yet, the impacts of those few invaders can be substantial. The reasons for these invasive tendencies are variable, but generally result from lack of natural controls (e.g. competitors, herbivores, plant diseases). Aggressive competitive abilities of exotic species may result in loss of native species with lesser competitive ability, loss of habitat that supports a diverse array of native species, and fundamental change in ecosystem function. Most often successful invasion occurs on lands that have been disturbed by grazing, agriculture, or other human activity, and usually the invading species are herbaceous. However, a number of trees have been found to be invasive in California's landscapes. One of the more common of Santa Barbara's trees, the California pepper *(Schinus molle),* is also an aggressive invader of landscapes throughout much of Southern California. Several species of *Tamarix* are aggressive invaders of riparian habitats in desert lands and have significantly lowered the water tables of these regions. *Tamarix aphylla,* the tamarisk found at Coal Oil Point on the West UCSB Campus, is the least aggressive of these species; however, its potential threat as an invasive species is currently being reevaluated. In the Santa Barbara region, other invasive species include *Ailanthus altissima, Robinia pseudoacacia,* and *Eucalyptus globulus.* The threats of introduced species raise important questions regarding plant introduction programs. During the days of Sexton, Franceschi, Orpet, and others, exotic species were given little thought except for their horticultural value and ease of propagation. We now recognize that plant introduction must be undertaken with more care. It is particularly important to recognize that many of the features that are the basis for horticultural selection (e.g. ease of propagation, success in a variety of environments) are also important attributes of successful invaders. Screening of potential invasive exotic species has become a high priority for the horticultural industry and must be a consideration for any new trees introduced to Santa Barbara's urban forest.

The Joy of Identifying Trees

Identifying strange plants can be a daunting task for the uninitiated, involving new terms and features of plants not previously observed. However, the satisfaction of learning a new species and its unique characteristics can bring a whole new world to life. Accessing that world depends on a suite of skills that enable accurate identification. The following discussion presents and defines characteristics of trees that are used in their identification.

Life Form

One of the first attributes of a tree that is noticed by the informed observer is its growth habit. Broadly speaking, two growth forms are readily recognized. **Excurrent growth** occurs when the central axis of the tree remains the dominant point of stem elongation, and the branch elongation remains secondary to this central axis. The net result is a pyramidal growth form that is obvious to even the most casual observer. Most conifers, such as bunya-bunya *(Araucaria bidwillii*[2]*)* and Canary Island pine *(Pinus canariensis)*, are strongly excurrent in their growth pattern. Sweet gum *(Liquidambar styraciflua)* and tulip tree *(Liriodendron tulipifera)* are also characterized by the "Christmas tree" form of excurrent growth. **Decurrent growth** occurs when the central axis of the tree looses dominance, and dividing branches each assume a more or less equal share of growth. This growth pattern results in a rounded spherical crown, such as seen in coast live oak *(Quercus agrifolia)* and African fern pine *(Afrocarpus gracilior)*. Crowns of either growth form can be additionally characterized by the density of their foliage. Trees with open crowns allow considerable sunlight to pass through and can be identified by the amount of "sky" that can be seen through the foliage *(Corymbia citriodora)*. Others have much more dense crowns that block almost all of the sky *(Acacia melanoxylon)*.

While deciduousness is often considered an attribute of the leaf, it characterizes the habit of the overall tree as well. **Deciduous** trees lose most or all of their leaves at some point during the annual growing cycle. In temperate zones of the world this may be synchronized with "winter" conditions and serve as a measure of protection against freezing temperatures. On the other hand, for plants originating in subtropical, seasonally arid zones, leaf loss may be more directly related to dry conditions and may serve as a means of

---

[2] In this discussion, species are named as typical examples of characteristics being discussed.

avoiding drought damage to the plant. Many angiosperms from colder or drier climates are deciduous. Not many of our Santa Barbara trees are deciduous; however, ginkgo *(Ginkgo biloba),* native to eastern Asia, is winter-deciduous, and the native California buckeye *(Aesculus californica)* is drought-deciduous. **Evergreen** trees, of course, retain their leaves year-round. Leaves may last only one year, in which case they are lost as soon as the new year's leaves have completed growth. In other evergreen species, leaves may last for several years. In trees from tropical regions, it is impossible to age individual leaves because growth is continuous and there is no means to recognize the end of one year's growth and the beginning of the next. However, in trees from temperate zones, for example silver maple *(Acer saccharinum),* the accumulation of scars from the scales protecting dormant buds provides a ready means for determining twig age.

Pseudotsuga macrocarpa

Reproduction

All of our trees are true seed plants and can be divided into two broad groups based upon characteristics of reproduction. Reproduction in the **gymnosperms** is considered to be primitive, in that the production of pollen and ovules occurs separately on the surfaces of individual modified leaves called **sporophylls.** This necessarily creates a physical separation between pollen and ovule production. **Monoecious** species have both pollen and ovule production on the same individual, although in separate structures *(Abies bracteata).* **Dioecious** species have pollen and ovule production on separate individuals *(Juniperus californica).* The sporophylls are frequently clustered into a woody or somewhat fleshy **cone** (for example, *Pinus* spp. or *Juniperus* spp.). In other gymnosperms, the sporophylls are not clustered into a cone. Instead, they become fleshy **arils** that envelope the seed *(Afrocarpus gracilior).*

The **angiosperms** are flowering plants and are characterized by the production of ovules in an enclosed and protective ovary. They are also frequently pollinated by insects or birds. Two common classes of living angiosperms are recognized today. The **monocots** are characterized by flower parts in threes, a single cotyledon or seed leaf, and a parallel pattern of leaf venation. **Dicots,** on the other hand, have flower parts usually in fours or fives, two cotyledons, and a complex net-like pattern of leaf venation.

The evolution of a true flower has led to development of a profusion of floral structures and fruiting characteristics. The flowers of a tree are clustered into an **inflorescence** (all flowers and components above the last leaf) whose structure is often distinctive. The inflorescence may, in fact, be **simple** (consisting of only a single flower). A **compound inflorescence** contains multiple flowers clustered beyond the last leaf. Within the inflorescence, the individual flower may occur on a **pedicel** (stalk) or it may be **sessile** (stalkless). **Spikes** contain sessile flowers along a central axis that open first at the top or bottom *(Schefflera actinophylla)*. **Racemes** contain flowers on a pedicel along a central axis with the bottom individuals usually opening first *(Acacia melanoxylon)*. **Panicles** are branched inflorescences in which the basal flowers open first *(Aesculus californica)*. **Cymes** are branched inflorescences in which the terminal flowers open first, usually leading to a flattened top *(Lophostemon confertus)*.

A **perfect flower** contains both pollen and ovule production in the same structure *(Spathodea campanulata)*. However, monoecy and dioecy may occur in angiosperms as well. The outermost portion of the flower is the **calyx,** which is a whorl of green leaf-like structures called **sepals.** Prior to opening, the calyx serves to protect the young bud of the

Ceiba insignis

developing flower. Inside the calyx there is usually another whorl called the corolla, which is composed of several to many **petals.** The petals are often bright-colored and showy and serve to attract insect pollinators. Collectively, the calyx and the corolla are referred to as the **perianth.** In some cases, the petals and sepals cannot be distinguished and are referred to as **tepals.** Inside the perianth, **pollen** is produced in one or more **anthers** which are supported by a stalk or **filament,** all of which is referred to as the **stamen.** Finally, at At the center of the flower is the female structure, referred to as the **pistil,** that consists of a swollen **ovary** containing one or more ovules, a **stigma** on which pollen lands, and a usually elongate **style** through which the pollen grows to reach the ovule.

Koelreuteria bipinnata

Successful reproduction in the angiosperms culminates with the production of mature **fruit** and viable seed. The nature of the fruit serves to both protect the developing seed and to assist with dispersal to new habitats. Most fruit are **simple** in that they are the product of a single pistil; however, **compound** fruit contain an **aggregate** of individual fruits *(Platanus racemosa)*. Fruits may be partially or wholly fleshy or they may be dry. Fleshy fruits are attractive to birds and other animals which aid in dispersal of their seeds. **Berries** are fleshy throughout with scattered individual seeds that are not otherwise encased separately within *(Sambucus mexicana)*. A **drupe** consists of a fleshy exterior with a single seed that is encased in a woody "stone" *(Olea europea)*. **Pomes** contain a fleshy exterior with several seeds encased in a thin papery shell *(Pyrus kawakami)*.

Dry fruits may have wings (**samaras**) that serve to catch the wind and aid in dispersal *(Acer saccharinum)*. Among wingless dry fruits, **nuts** are characterized by a hardened shell that does not open to release the seed *(Carya illinoensis)*. Multiple-seeded dry fruits include **legumes** that open along two seams *(Ceratonia siliqua)*, **follicles** that open along a single seam and are the product of a simple ovary *(Brachychiton acerifolius),* and **capsules** that open along two or more seams and are the product of a compound ovary that contains multiple chambers *(Chiranthodendron pentadactylon)*.

Bark

The bark of a tree can be one of its most distinctive features; yet, bark is often seen as a featureless structure of little interest. With the exception of the palms, the bark of all trees in this book is a product of secondary growth, the process by which expansion of the girth occurs. A cross section of a tree's trunk will show two general areas—the wood, which makes up most of the surface area of the section, and the bark, which is an outer shell to the wood. Secondary growth occurs in the **vascular cambium** that separates these two regions. Dividing cells of the cambium produce new wood cells to the inside (**xylem**) which function both in increasing the strength of the tree and in transporting water and nutrients from the soil to the canopy. To the outside, the cambium produces the **phloem** which carries food from the photosynthesizing tissues to the roots. A close look at the bark of a tree will reveal that it actually consists of two layers—the inner bark, where active food transport occurs, and the outer bark, which consists of dead phloem and corky material and serves to protect the tree from damage. In contrast to the accumulating layers of wood, this outer bark gradually sloughs off thereby limiting its thickness. Also, as the tree grows in girth, its expanding circumference results in cracking and fissures in the outer bark. The patterns of sloughing off and cracking are often distinctive to individual species and can be key aids in identification.

Twigs

The growing shoots of the canopy become the twigs that support its foliage. Technically, a twig is the current year's shoot growth; however, in this book indentifying characteristics of twigs may include the previous two- to four-years's growth as well. Many features of

Dais cotinifolia

twigs are useful in identification. Most twigs are rather elongated; however, some species are characterized by very short **spur shoots** in which there is very little extension from year to year *(Ginkgo bioloba)*. Color and shape are obvious characteristics of all twigs. Other characteristics are variable in occurrence. **Buds** are rudimentary shoots and flowers and may occur in the axils of leaves or at the terminal end of a shoot. The preformed leaves and flowers are protected by a series of scales that may be overlapping in a shingle-like pattern (**imbricate**; *Liquidambar styraciflua*) or may meet at the edges (**valvate**; *Alnus rhombifolia*). In trees that are seasonally dormant, these scales fall away at the beginning of growth, leaving an obvious series of scars on the twig that mark the beginning of that year's growth. In these same trees, leaves that are seasonally deciduous leave a **leaf scar** sometimes showing internal scars from the **vascular bundles** that transported food and nutrients *(Radermachera sinica)*.

The surface of the twig is often marked by corky **lenticels** that serve in the exchange of gasses with the atmosphere *(Ailanthus altissima)*. These lenticels may be minute, even unobservable to the unaided eye, or they may be obvious with unique shapes and patterns of distribution. Lenticels are important because most twigs carry on some measure of photosynthesis during their first year. Some twigs are obviously green from their chlorophyll content *(Maytenus boaria)*. In others, the chlorophyll is hidden beneath a gray or brown layer of **epidermis.** Another internal feature of twigs is the **pith,**

Nerium oleander

the central core of the stem. The pith may be solid with a core of spongy white or brown tissue. It may be hollow, or it may be **chambered** or **diaphragmed** in which the hollow core is divided by solid partitions *(Juglans regia)*.

Many trees have spines, thorns, or prickles that may occur on the twigs or even on the trunk. **Spines** are modified leaf structures that frequently occur along the twig at the base of the leaf *(Acacia farnesiana)*. These have evolved from parts of leaves or from **stipules,** leaf-like appendages at the base of the leaf petiole. **Thorns** have evolved from twigs and may be single projections or multiply-branched

Hibiscus rosa-sinensis

(Parkinsonia aculeata). Thorns do not occur in association with leaves and are found independently on the stem. **Prickles** are developed from the outer epidermal layer of the stem only and do not involve vascular tissues *(Ceiba speciosa)*. They can usually be readily identified by the ease with which they can be broken off of the stem.

Leaves

One of the most obvious and lasting features of a tree is the leaf, which is often its most diagnostic characteristic. Leaves come in a multitude of shapes and sizes. Sometimes there may be considerable variation on a single tree; however, this variability usually centers on a common theme. Leaves may be connected to the stem by a **petiole** (leaf stalk) or they may be **sessile** (without a petiole). **Simple** leaves are not divided along the midrib into separate components *(Catalpa speciosa)*. Simple leaves may be deeply divided or **lobed;** however, that division does not extend to the midrib *(Morus alba)*. Leaves in which the lobing has extended all the way to the midrib to create separate **leaflets** are **compound. Palmately compound** leaves have the leaflets clustered around a central point in a fan-shaped pattern *(Tabebuia chrysotricha)*. **Pinnately compound** leaves have the leaflets (**pinnae**) arranged in rows along either side of the central axis or **rachis** *(Cassia leptophylla)*. In some cases, the leaf may not have a terminal leaflet, resulting in an even number of leaves. In others, a terminal leaflet is present creating an odd number of leaflets. In extreme cases, the leaf may be divided again into a **bipinnately compound** leaf *(Koelreuteria bipinnata)*.

Hibiscus elatus

Simple leaves and leaflets come in a variety of shapes and forms. Long, very narrow leaves are referred to as **linear** *(Afrocarpus gracilior)*, while round leaves are **orbicular** *(Eucalyptus cephalocarpa)*. Leaves may be **lanceolate** (lance-shaped; *Eucalyptus cinerea*); **elliptical** *(Quillaja saponaria)*; **ovate** (egg-shaped; *Ligustrum lucidum*); **oblong** (longer than wide with parallel sides; *Banksia integrifolia*); or **deltoid** (shaped like an equilateral triangle; *Erythrina lysistemon*). The **apex** (tip) of the leaf or leaflet may be **acute** (pointed at a sharp angle; *Sophora japonica*), **obtuse** (rounded at a broad angle; *Cryptocarya alba*), or **acuminate** (with an elongated sharply tipped apex and concave sides; *Inga pilosula*).

Leaf and leaflet **margins** are also diagnostic. **Entire** margins are smooth, without teeth or lobes *(Plinia edulis)*. **Serrate** margins have forward-pointing teeth *(Eriobotrya deflexa)*, while teeth of dentate margins point straight out. **Undulate** margins are wavy *(Pittosporum undulatum)*.

The surfaces of leaves and their petioles may be covered with a variety of **pubescence** (hairs). **Tomentose** leaves are covered with a mat of interwoven hairs *(Vitex agnus-castus)*. Leaves without pubescence are **glabrous** *(Casuarina glauca)*. In other cases leaves may be only lightly hairy or have hairs restricted to the veins or **axils** (junctures) of the veins.

Finally, leaf color can be an important diagnostic feature. We all know that leaves are green; however, close examination will uncover several shades of green from deep forest green to light yellow-green. Leaves can be glossy or dull. The density and length of hairs on the surface of a leaf can alter its color to make it appear whitish. Some leaves are covered with a **glaucous** whitish waxy layer that can be rubbed off *(Cupressus arizonica)*.

Organization of This Book

The following descriptions are arranged taxonomically in that genera are grouped within their respective plant families. Gymnosperms and the two classes of the angiosperms (dicots and monocots) are segregated in Parts I, II, and III of the species descriptions. Within each part, plant families, their respective genera, and species within genera are arranged alphabetically. Any other scientific name which has been recently applied to the genus or species is indicated beneath the currently correct scientific name.

Each description includes, as far as possible, common names, geographic location, information on inflorescence, flowers, fruit, twigs, bark, and leaves. Ecological, cultural or taxonomic information of interest is provided, along with notes on locations in the Santa Barbara area where the species can be observed. Since this book is limited to publicly accessible trees (street and park trees and those in publicly accessible gardens), locations cited will always be available for personal observation. Botanical descriptions are often laden with scientific terminology that more precisely defines a characteristic. For this book, botanical terminology has been minimized to the extent possible; however, in several situations this terminology could not be avoided. An extensive glossary is provided at the end of the text to assist in navigating these often obscure terms.

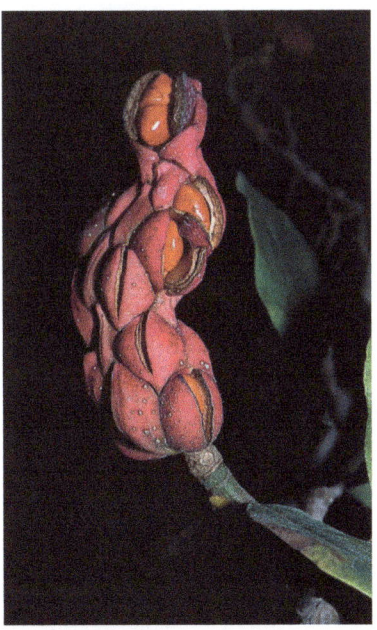

Magnolia x *soulangeana*

GYMNOSPERMS
Araucariaceae

Members of the Araucaria Family are restricted to the Southern Hemisphere, excluding South Africa. However, its earliest fossil records are solely from the Northern Hemisphere. Today, the family includes three genera and about 32 species (including the newly discovered Wollemia Pine), and includes some of the most important timber trees of the Southern Hemisphere. It is unique in producing seed cones with one seed per scale and no distinct bracts embracing the scales.

Agathis

Agathis is a genus of about 16 evergreen species extending from Malaysia and the Phillipines to Australia and New Zealand. The resin of some species is used by native peoples for varnish and pottery glaze. *Agathis* is the Greek name for a ball of thread which the female catkins resemble.

Agathis robusta
Queensland kauri-pine, Australian dammar pine

Found in isolated populations in coastal southern and northern Queensland, Australia.

Habit An evergreen tree with a clean bole; to 80 feet tall.

Inflorescence Monoecious; male cones axillary, cylindrical, 1 1/2–3 1/2 x 1/3 inches.

Fruit Seed cones ovate, 4–5 x 3–4 inches; scales numerous, strongly overlapping, 1–1 1/2 inches wide.

Twigs Yellow-green, becoming stout and dull gray.

Bark Thin, gray-brown; scaly, exfoliating to reveal tan patches.

Leaves Opposite, simple; ovate or elliptical, 2–5 x 3/4–2 inches; leathery, glossy dark green above, paler beneath, with parallel venation; margins somewhat thickened; tapering to a wide, flat petiole.

Notes *A. robusta* is one of several Southeast Asian trees yielding dammar resin that was used variously in caulking boats and creating varnishes. The species name *robusta* means strong, robust.

Top: Characteristic narrow crown of Agathis robusta. *Bottom: Distinctive mottled bark and opposite placement of broad leaves.*

Locations A tree in East Alameda Plaza and street trees in the 1100 block of East Indio Muerto. Five trees in the lawn east of the Student Services building at Santa Barbara City College.

Araucaria

Araucaria is a genus of 18 species confined to the Southern Hemisphere from South America to Australia and New Guinea. Thirteen of these are restricted to the South Pacific islands of New Caledonia. Its species are marked by the symmetry of young trees and the branchless lower boles of older trees with ragged, flattish-topped crowns. The genus is named for the Araucani Indians of central Chile.

Araucaria bidwillii
Bunya-bunya tree, bunya-bunya pine

A native primarily of coastal regions of southeastern Queensland, Australia.

Habit An evergreen tree with a distinctive open, dome-shaped crown; the foliage seemingly clustered at the ends of horizontal or drooping branches; to 100 feet tall.

Inflorescence Usually dioecious; male cones 6–7 x $1/2$ inches, erect, borne on upper branches of the tree.

Fruit Seed cones erect, borne at top of the tree; elliptical or globose, to 12 x 9 inches; scales numerous, 4 x 3 inches, with a sharp point.

Twigs Initially green, becoming stout and brown.

Bark Thick, resinous, peeling in thin layers; appearing to have large warts where old branches have been trimmed off.

Leaves Spirally arranged, of two forms; on sterile branches lanceolate, 2 inches long, stiff, very dark green; denser, shorter (less than 1 inch) and stiffer on fertile branches.

Notes The seeds have an excellent food value and are used by native peoples of Queensland. The seed crop is, however, not continuous. Some seed are produced every year, but a full crop is not obtained until the third year. The species name *bidwillii* honors John Carne Bidwill (1815–1853), gardener and cattle-dealer in Australia and New Zealand, and collector of New Zealand plants.

Locations West Alameda Plaza and on the southwestern side of the Courthouse along Anacapa Street. Several trees southeast of the Performing Arts Building at the University of California, Santa Barbara. Other mature trees

Top: The rounded crown of Araucaria bidwillii *is a common skyline sight.*
Bottom left: The short stiff leaves are spirally arranged on the twig and are interspersed with male cones.
Bottom right: The massive seed cone can weigh up to 15 pounds.

Araucaria columnaris
New Caledonian pine

Native to New Caledonia, Polynesia, and the Isle of Pines.

Habit An evergreen, columnar tree with dense foliage; to 70 feet tall.

Inflorescence Monoecious; male cones 1–2 1/2 inches long, surrounded at the base by a dense cup of leaves.

Fruit Seed cone ellipsoid, to 6 x 4 1/2 inches; scales numerous, 1 1/4 inches across with a terminal spine.

Twigs To 18 inches long, arranged horizontally and somewhat pendulously on the stout branches.

Bark Outer bark shedding off in papery layers.

Leaves Spirally arranged, of two forms; ovate, broad, 1/4 x 1/8 inch; curved inward and closely overlapping; appearing like a woven rope; more triangular on juvenile shoots, to 1/2 inch long.

Notes The columnar form emerges from the unique characteristic of shedding lower branches when they have grown long, and growing short shoots from adventitious buds in their place. In preparation for an earlier version of this book, Dr. Reid Moran made the interesting observation that all of the specimens of this species in Santa Barbara lean strongly to the southeast, similar to observations of the species in India. However, in Hawaii this phenomenon is unknown. The species name *columnaris* means columnar.

Locations A single tree in the Cabrillo Ball Park, two others in East and West Alameda Plaza, and one in MacKenzie Park. A street tree on Calle Cedro at San Roque School.

The characteristic lean of Araucaria columnaris *to the southeast is common throughout Santa Barbara.*

Araucaria cunninghamii
Hoop pine, colonial pine, Moreton Bay pine

Native to the coastal regions of Queensland and northeastern New South Wales, Australia.

Habit An evergreen tree, with dense clusters of foliage at the ends of horizontal branches; to 80 feet or more tall.

Inflorescence Monoecious; male cones terminal, cylindrical, 1 1/2–3 inches long.

Fruit Seed cones terminal at the end of short shoots, globose, to 4 inches in diameter.

Twigs Green, becoming stout and gray.

Bark Rough, in horizontal hoops and peeling off in thin layers; dark brown or black.

Leaves Spirally arranged, lanceolate, sharply pointed, keeled, incurved, to 1/2 inch long; dark green, crowded and overlapping; on younger trees less dense, spreading, not appressed.

Notes The species name *cunninghamii* honors Allan (1791–1839) and Richard (1793–1835) Cunningham—British brothers, Kew collectors, and colonial botanists in New South Wales, Australia.

Locations A nice tree at the Music Academy of the West in Santa Barbara. Another in lower Orpet Park is in decline. Young trees are on the grounds of El Camino and Hollister Elementary Schools in Goleta.

Top: The needles on Araucaria cunninghamii *are short and spreading on younger stems.*
Bottom: The common name, hoop pine, derives from the bark, which peels in thin hoops around the trunk.

Araucaria heterophylla
Norfolk Island pine, star pine

Native to Norfolk Island, Australia.

Habit A tall, symmetrical evergreen tree with a typical flat-topped crown; to 160 feet tall.

Inflorescence Monoecious; male cones 1/2 x 1 1/2–2 inches.

Fruit Seed cones often broader than long, 3–4 x 3 1/2–4 1/2 inches.

Twigs Up to 2 feet long on vigorous individuals; oriented to point towards the sky in two ranks.

Bark Peeling in thin layers with vertical curls; blackish-brown.

Leaves Spirally arranged, of two forms; mature leaves flattened, stiff, dark green, 1/4–1/3 inch long, incurved and overlapping to give a braided appearance; juvenile leaves narrower and extending away from the stem.

Notes As individual tees of *A. heterophylla* reach maturity, height growth ceases and they develop a flat-topped appearance. The species name *heterophylla* means different-leaved.

Locations West Alameda Plaza and on the southwestern side of the Courthouse along Anacapa Street. Other mature trees obvious in the skyline about Santa Barbara. A famed tree is on the corner of Chapala and Carrillo Streets. Several trees at the University of California, Santa Barbara.

Top: The characteristic star shape of the Araucaria heterophylla *becomes flat-topped with age.*
Middle: Although not as large as those of bunya-bunya tree, the seed cones are still quite large.
Bottom: The braided appearance of the foliage on the twig is distinctive.

Cupressaceae

The Cypress Family includes 20 genera and 125 species and is of nearly worldwide distribution. It includes important timber trees and many species that supply resins and flavorings. The long-recognized Taxodiaceae has recently been combined with this family.

Callitris

Callitris is a genus of 19 species native to Australia and New Caledonia. All of its species are adapted to arid regions and are considered to be among the most useful of the Australian conifers for horticultural purposes. The name is derived from the Greek words *kalli* (beautiful) and *treis* (three) and refers to the beautiful arrangement of plant parts in threes.

Callitris rhomboidea
Oyster Bay pine

Native to coastal regions of Australia, except Western Australia and the Northern Territory; naturalized in New Zealand.

Habit A small evergreen tree with a narrow, dense crown; to 40 feet tall.

Inflorescence Monoecious; male and female cones axillary on terminal portions of twigs. Pollen shed in January.

Fruit Seed cones several to a cluster, remaining on the tree for several years; globose, $1/3$–$1/2$ inch across, shiny red-brown; scales 6, diamond-shaped, thick, the three smaller scales half the size of the larger; umbo prominent, thick, erect, armed with a short prickle.

Twigs Becoming light gray with dark maroon rectangles marking old leaf scars.

Bark Dark gray, thick, tight, furrowed in a spiral.

Leaves In opposite pairs, small, $1/12$–$1/8$ inch long; closely appressed to the twig, keeled on the lower half, sharply pointed at the apex; bright green to glaucous.

Notes The species name *rhomboidea* means diamond-shaped.

Locations County Administration Building parking lot, near the Victoria Street entrance.

Top: The yellow pollen cones of Callitris rhomboidea *stand out against the dark foliage.*
Bottom: The wispy foliage and prominent umbo of the seed cone are characteristic. Like those of the related genus Cupressus *in the Northern Hemisphere, the seed cones open fully and release their seeds when exposed to the heat of fire.*

Calocedrus

Calocedrus is a genus of three species that, like so many other coniferous genera, is found in western North America and Southeast Asia (Myanmar (Burma) to southwestern China). *Calocedrus* is a name derived from Greek, meaning beautiful *(kalos)* cedar *(cedrus)*.

Calocedrus decurrens
Incense cedar

Common in mixed evergreen and mixed conifer forests from southern Oregon through California and western Nevada (near Lake Tahoe) to northern Baja California, at elevations ranging from about 2,000 to 7,500 feet.

Habit   An evergreen tree with an uneven and raggedly branched crown; to 90 feet tall.

Inflorescence   Monoecious; male and female flowers solitary, terminal, usually on different branches of the same tree; male cones square in cross section. Pollen shed January to February.

Fruit   Seed cone ovoid, 3/4–1 inch long; with six scales; pendulous; yellowish- to reddish-brown.

Twigs   Strongly flattened into a dense, fan-like spray.

Bark   Thick, deeply furrowed; cinnamon-red, with a silvery gray overtone.

Leaves   Opposite; scale-like, strongly appressed except at the tip; about 1/8 inch long on ultimate twigs, 1/2 inch long on main shoots; light green with whitish margins; with a strong resin odor when crushed.

Notes   The species name *decurrens* means running down the stem.

Locations   Trees in the Santa Barbara Botanic Garden in the Arroyo and Meadow Sections. One in San Roque Park on Canon Drive. A large tree near the Anacapa Street entrance to City Hall. Small trees on the south side of the library at the University of California, Santa Barbara.

Top: Calocedrus decurrens *is dense and conical as a young tree, but develops a more irregular, open crown with age.*
Middle: The yellow pollen cones are square at the ends of the twigs, which are arranged in dense fan-like sprays.
Bottom: The six scales of the seed cone are arranged in opposite pairs that do not overlap. The fully open cone is shaped very much like a fleur de lys.

Cryptomeria

Cryptomeria is a genus composed of a single species, but containing over 200 varieties and cultivars. Its name is from the Greek *krypto* (hidden) and *meris* (part) referring to the hidden reproductive parts.

Cryptomeria japonica
Japanese cedar, goddess of mercy fir, peacock pine

This single species of the genus is found in Japan and southern China.

Habit A graceful evergreen conifer with a straight bole; to 60 feet tall.

Inflorescence Monoecious; pollen cones clustered in groups of 20 or more, 1/4–1/3 inch long, orange or reddish when mature.

Fruit Seed cones solitary, terminal on the ends of short shoots, round, 1/2–3/4 inch across, composed of 20–30 scales, each with 2 or 3 points on the apex; dull brown; maturing in the first year, but persistent on the stem for several months after seed dispersal.

Twigs Green, glabrous, sometimes prolonged from the apex of the seed cone.

Bark Reddish-brown, fibrous, exfoliating in long strips.

Leaves Spirally arranged in five columns; awl-shaped, 1/4–1/2 inch long; pointed forward on the twig and curved inwards; laterally compressed, but keeled on both sides giving a four-sided appearance in cross section; stiff; dark green with stomata on both surfaces.

Notes Because of its size in its native habitat, this is an important timber tree. However, it is best known for its ornamental value in mild regions. A cultivar, *C. japonica* 'Elegans' (plume cryptomeria) is distinguished by its bushy habit (but reaching 30 feet) and its soft leaves which turn from bright green in summer to reddish-bronze in winter. The species name *japonica* means from Japan.

Locations Lotusland and the campus of Westmont College, just south of the circle.

Top: The sharp-pointed needles of Cryptomeria japonica *are arranged in five spiral columns on the twig; pollen cones are clustered at the ends of the twigs.*
Bottom: The reddish-brown seed cones are solitary on short shoots and are composed of twenty to thirty scales that end in two or three points.

Cupressus
Cypress

This genus consists of about 20 species scattered in the temperate zones of all continents in the Northern Hemisphere. Many of the taxa exist as small, disjunct populations that vary primarily in superficial morphological characteristics, leading to much disagreement concerning taxonomic identity. The wood is extremely decay-resistant due in part to its strongly odorous nature, making it repellent to insects. For this reason it is attractive for furniture and lining closets used in storing clothing and other insect-susceptible materials. The genus name is the Latin name for the Italian cypress *(C. sempervirens)*.

Cupressus abramsiana
Santa Cruz cypress

Found in mixed forest and chaparral stands in the Santa Cruz Mountains, California, usually on sandy, nutrient-poor soils.

Habit An evergreen tree with a conical form; to 25 feet tall.

Inflorescence Monoecious; pollen cones $1/6$ x $1/12$ inch, with 10–16 scales, more or less four-sided.

Fruit Seed cones globose to elliptic, $2/3$–$1 1/4$ inches long, shiny gray-brown, scales 8-10 with a small prickly umbo.

Twigs Yellow-green becoming brownish-red then reddish-gray.

Bark Thin, fibrous, broken and peeling in thick vertical strips or plates, gray.

Leaves Opposite; acute but blunt-pointed, bright green, $1/6$ inch long, gland absent, aromatic when crushed.

Notes The species name *abramsiana* honors LeRoy Abrams (1874–1956), American botanist at Stanford University.

Locations Santa Barbara Botanic Garden along the Porter Trail in the Ceanothus and Cupressus Sections.

The seed cones of Cupresssus abramsiana *are shiny gray-brown, and the twigs are coarse with small, opposite scale-like needles.*

Cupressus arizonica
Smooth-bark Arizona cypress

Found in central Arizona, Southern California, and Baja California, and extending to central Mexico at elevations of 1,500 to 5,000 feet.

Habit A dense, irregularly branched tree; to 50 feet tall.

Inflorescence Axillary or terminal; pollen cone yellow, round to angular, to $1/5$ inch long.

Fruit Seed cones globose, $3/4$–$1 1/4$ inches; glaucous becoming reddish-brown to gray-brown at maturity; scales 5–10 (usually 8), umbos prominent.

Twigs Very slender, four-sided.

Bark Highly variable; frequently deciduous, leaving a smooth, cherry-red surface, or fibrous and furrowed, gray-brown.

Leaves Opposite; scale-like, $1/16$–$1/12$ inch long, finely toothed, acute, keeled; grayish-green or blue-gray, usually glaucous; with a conspicuous resin-exuding gland on the back; strongly lemon-scented when crushed.

Notes *C. arizonica* has been considered to be composed of five geographic varieties (sometimes given subspecies status) based on external features, particularly bark. However, because of the complete intergradation of the distinguishing features throughout their range, a recent revision of the genus has considered the five varieties to simply reflect broad variation within the species. *C. arizonica* has been used effectively in the recovery of degraded lands in southern Europe and northern Africa. The species name *arizonica* means from Arizona.

Locations Several trees in the Santa Barbara Botanic Garden along the Porter Trail in the Cupressus Section.

Top: Young trees of **Cupressus arizonica** *are narrow and conical. With age they become more open and irregularly shaped.*
Bottom: Blue-gray, scale-like needles on twigs that become tan in the second year.

Cupressus funebris
Chamaecyparis funebris

Mourning cypress, Chinese weeping cypress

Found in mountainous districts of central China usually below 3,000 feet.

Habit A conical to rounded evergreen tree, with multiple stems from the base and pendulous branchlets; to 30 feet in height.

Inflorescence Terminal or axillary; pollen cones solitary, ellipsoid or ovoid, to $1/5$ inch long, with 10–14 scales, yellow.

Fruit Seed cones globose, $1/3$–$2/3$ inch across; blue-green turning dark brown; scales 8, with a stout curved blunt umbo; often on short curved stalks.

Twigs Flattened.

Bark Gray-brown or brown, smooth, finely broken into long thin strips, somewhat fibrous.

Leaves Opposite; deltoid-ovate, $1/12$ inch long, lateral pairs folded around the flattened stem, facial pairs flattened; acute, keeled, closely appressed but the apex free and pointed; glands obscure; pale green or bluish-green with a blackish spot near the apex.

Notes After it was first discovered by western science in 1793, the species was found planted throughout higher elevations of the Himalayas near tombs and temples. That tradition has been carried on throughout the world today and gives the species its common name. The species name *funebris* means relating to a funeral.

Locations Santa Barbara Cemetery; Westmont College north of the Student Center.

Top: The rounded compact crown of Cupressus funebris *is often seen near temples and cemeteries. Bottom: The blue-green cones with recurved umbos stand out against the green foliage.*

Cupressus goveniana
Gowen cypress

Found in closed-cone pine forests (Bishop Pine) of the north and central coast of California (Mendocino, Sonoma, and Monterey Counties), usually below 1,500 feet.

Habit An evergreen conical tree becoming broader with age; to 50 feet in height.

Inflorescence Monoecious; terminal or axillary; pollen cones 1/8–1/6 inch long, four-sided, yellow.

Fruit Seed cones often in dense clusters; globose or oblong, 1/2–3/4 inch long; dark brown or dull gray, often green beneath; 6–10 scales with a small, warty umbo; ripening in second year.

Twigs Dull reddish-gray.

Bark Pale, gray-brown, shallowly furrowed and flaky on older trees; brighter reddish-brown, scaly on younger stems.

Leaves Opposite; light yellowish-green, becoming dull dark green; ovate, but with a somewhat acute apex, 1/12 inch long; glands usually absent.

Notes A species described in the 1974 version of this book, *C. pygmaea*, has been recently included as a subspecies of *C. goveniana*. Its original description was based primarily on the observation that in its native habitat (Mendocino County), it rarely exceeds six feet in height. However, when grown on more fertile soils (such as one at the Santa Barbara Botanic Garden along the Porter Trail), it readily achieves the height described here. The species name *goveniana* honors James Robert Gowen, 19th-century British horticulturist, secretary of the Royal Horticultural Society 1845 to 1850.

Locations Santa Barbara Botanic Garden, in the Meadow Section and along the Porter Trail in the Cupressus Section.

A cluster of large, round seed cones of Cupressus goveniana *will mature in the second year.*

Cupressus guadalupensis
Guadalupe cypress

Endemic to Guadalupe Island off the west coast of Baja California and in scattered populations on both sides of the California/Baja California border.

Habit An evergreen bushy tree often with multiple ascending branches and an irregular, spreading and open crown; to 30 feet in height.

Inflorescence Monoecious; terminal; pollen cones with 10–14 scales.

Fruit Seed cones irregularly globose, 3/4–1 inch in diameter; green, turning brownish-gray, never white-glaucous; scales 3–5 pairs, with an irregular surface; umbos inconspicuous or prominent.

Twigs Green, becoming reddish, then gray; foliage somewhat sparse.

Bark Smooth; gray or reddish-brown, scaly and exfoliating, sometimes peeling in thin irregular plates, leaving a smooth, glossy, reddish-brown to dark red to gray or green surface.

Leaves Opposite; bright green to blue-gray, sometimes glaucous, 1/12 inch long, acute; resin gland absent or small and depressed; lemon-scented or turpentine-scented when crushed.

Notes *C. guadalupensis* includes two varieties: *C. guadalupensis* var. *guadalupensis* (Guadalupe cypress) from Guadalupe Island and *C. guadalupensis* var. *forbesii* (Tecate cypress) from the mainland. The latter was first described by Willis Linn Jepson in 1907. Its peeling bark and smooth red surface make it an attractive addition to the landscape. The species name *guadalupensis* means from Guadalupe Island.

Locations Both varieties can be found at the Santa Barbara Botanic Garden, along the Porter Trail in the Ceanothus and Cupressus Sections. The Tecate cypress is also at Westmont College east of the baseball field.

Top: *The multiple shiny stems of the tecate cypress* (**Cupressus guadalupensis** *var.* forbesii) *are attractive in the landscape.*
Bottom: *Foliage, seed cones, and twigs.*

Cupressus lawsoniana
Chamaecyparis lawsoniana

Port Orford cedar, Lawson false cypress

Native to the coastal regions of southwestern Oregon and northwestern California, often on serpentine soils.

Habit An evergreen tree with an acute conical crown and short, horizontal or drooping branches that ascend abruptly at the end; to 80 feet tall.

Inflorescence Monoecious; male cones terminal on the twigs, pink to purple, 1/8 inch long. Pollen shed in May.

Fruit Seed cones numerous; globose, 1/3 inch in diameter, initially blue-green, becoming brown; scales 8, with compressed umbos, arranged in 4 rows.

Twigs Pendulous, held in a flat plane.

Bark Reddish-brown, with rounded scaly plates.

Leaves Opposite; green, glaucous; tightly appressed in two ranks; keeled, with a distinct tip, gland visible along the keel.

Notes The species tends to "throw" considerable variation in its seedlings, lending it to selection for widely different cultivars. To date, well over 150 cultivars have been developed. The species name *lawsoniana* honors Charles Lawson (1794–1873), English botanical author and nurseryman whose nursery first introduced *C. lawsoniana*.

Locations A large tree at the north end of the Santa Barbara Street wing of the County Courthouse. Others in the Santa Barbara Botanic Garden in the Arroyo, Manzanita, and Redwood Sections.

Top: This cultivar of Cupressus lawsoniana *has become a handsome addition to the Santa Barbara County Courthouse.*
Bottom: The foliage lies in a flat, pendulous plane and often has a pale blue-green cast.

Cupressus macrocarpa
Monterey cypress, California mountain cypress, fragrant cypress, white cedar

Native only to the Monterey Peninsula and Point Lobos, California, this species has been planted widely throughout the world.

Habit A tall evergreen tree, with a generally irregular, flat-topped crown in older age; to 75 feet tall.

Inflorescence Monoecious; terminal; pollen cones 1/4–1/8 inch, yellow, more or less four-sided, with 12–14 scales.

Fruit Seed cones almost globose, 1–1 1/2 inches in diameter; scales 8–12, somewhat shiny brown, flat, with a short, central umbo.

Twigs As wide as scales, green becoming reddish-brown, scales falling in the second and third years.

Bark Thick, fibrous, resinous; rich brown initially, aging to white-gray; furrowed, leaving flat ridges.

Leaves Opposite; scale-like, triangular, less than 1/8 inch long, blunt and slightly swollen at the apex, sometimes furrowed on the back; bright green, or dark in older trees, not glaucous, without whitish margins.

Notes Monterey cypress exists naturally in only two groves within a few hundred yards of the Pacific Ocean, near Monterey, California. However, fossil evidence indicates that it was much more widespread. This seems likely as it has been successfully planted extensively from Southern California to Washington and in warm and subtropical regions throughout the world. The species name *macrocarpa* means large fruit.

Locations Common throughout town. Trees along East Cabrillo Boulevard, Channel Drive, at the Douglas Preserve, and in Hope Ranch and Montecito.

Top: The several stems from near the base of the tree and the open, flat-topped crown are characteristic of Cupressus macrocarpa.
Bottom: Almost round seed cones and dark-green foliage.

Cupressus sargentii
Sargent cypress

Found in closed forests and chaparral, usually on serpentine soils, in the Coast Ranges of California, from Mendocino County to Santa Barbara County.

Habit An evergreen tree with a pyramidal crown; to 50 feet tall.

Inflorescence Monoecious; pollen cones small $1/6 \times 1/12$ inch, angled or cylindrical, with 10–12 scales.

Fruit Seed cones globose, $2/3$–$1 1/4$ inches, glossy brown becoming dull brown to gray, scales 6–10, rough with a conspicuous stubby umbo.

Twigs Green, becoming reddish-gray.

Bark Fibrous, thick, dark gray or brown, furrowed to leave interlacing flat-topped ridges; sometimes peeling from the upper branches, leaving a smooth red surface; faintly smelling of turpentine when crushed.

Leaves Opposite; dull, dusty green to grayish-green, glaucous or not, $1/12$ inch long, broad, bluntly acute, with a small, dark, non-functional resin gland.

Notes The seed cones of *C. sargentii* are strongly serotinous and only open when exposed to the heat of a fire. Consequently, stands of this species are even-aged and generally of the same size. The species name *sargentii* honors Charles Sprague Sargent (1841–1927), American dendrologist, first director of the Arnold Arboretum.

Locations Several trees in the Santa Barbara Botanic Garden on the Porter Trail in the Ceanothus and Cupressus Sections.

Top: The crown of **Cupresus sargentii** *retains its conical form in maturity.*
Bottom: The seed cones remain closed until exposed to the heat of a fire.

Cupressus sempervirens
Italian cypress, Mediterranean cypress

Originally native to the eastern Mediterranean, northern Iran, Asia Minor, Crete, and Cypress, this species was introduced to Italy in ancient times and is now widely spread throughout the Mediterranean region.

Habit An upright evergreen tree, becoming spreading with age; to 50 feet tall.

Inflorescence Monoecious; pollen cones small $1/10$–$1/12$ inch long, with 12–14 scales.

Fruit Seed cones globose, about 1 inch in diameter; glossy brown to gray; scales 8–14, arranged in 4 rows; umbo small with a prickly tip.

Twigs Gray-brown, flaky.

Bark Thin, smooth, somewhat fissured, gray-brown; becoming fissured and fibrous on older stems.

Leaves Opposite; scale-like, arranged in densely overlapping opposite pairs forming 4 vertical rows on the twig; individual scales less than $1/16$ inch long; apex blunt; dull dark gray-green; giving an overall very fine texture to the twig.

Notes Wood from this species was used to carve sarcophagal ornaments in Egypt and statues of Greek gods; extracts were used in foot baths and are still used to scent soaps. Two forms of *C. sempervirens* are now recognized: *C. sempervirens* f. *sempervirens* is a narrow, conical to columnar form planted extensively in formal gardens; *C. sempervirens* f. *horizontalis* is more cedar-like in habit with a spreading, horizontal crown. The species name *sempervirens* means always green.

Locations Of four original trees at Franceschi Park, only one remains. Two very columnar trees by the Santa Barbara Public Library entrance on Anapamu Street. Street trees on Pueblo Street from Santa Barbara Street to De la Vina Street, and on Richland Drive and Broadmoor Plaza in the San Roque area.

Top: **Cupressus sempervirens** f. **sempervirens**, *commonly found as a landscape feature in formal gardens, has a crown that can vary from the narrow conical form shown here to an extremely narrow cylindrical form. Bottom: The shiny scales of the seed cones are arranged in four rows.*

X *Cuprocyparis*
X *Cupressocyparis*

The genus is composed of a single species originating in England as a hybrid between cultivated individuals of *Cupressus macrocarpa* and *Xanthocyparis (Chamaecyparis) nootkatensis*. The genus name has recently been changed to reflect the inclusion of the former *Chamaecyparis nootkatensis* in the new genus *Xanthocyparis*.

X *Cuprocyparis leylandii*
X *Cupressocyparis leylandii*

Leyland cypress

A horticultural hybrid of *Cupressus macrocarpa* and *Xanthocyparis nootkatensis* (formerly *Chamaecyparis nootkatensis*).

Habit A dense, columnar evergreen tree; to 100 feet tall.

Inflorescence Monoecious; pollen cones terminal and solitary, grayish-brown.

Fruit Seed cones round, 1/2–3/4 inch across; scales 8, dark shiny brown with a small central umbo.

Twigs Yellow-green to green, becoming reddish- to grayish-brown, angular from basal portions of leaf scales.

Bark Reddish-brown, peeling in vertical flakes on older stems, resinous.

Leaves In opposite pairs at right angles to each other and tightly appressed; scale-like, with a sharp-pointed apex, 1/16 inch long; the lateral leaves keeled; dark blue-green, yellowish-green at the ends of sprays; somewhat malodorous when crushed.

Notes Almost all plantings of Leyland Cypress have been cloned by propagation of cuttings from three known crossings of *Cupressus macrocarpa* and *Xanthocyparis nootkatensis*. The species name *leylandii* honors C. J. Leyland, plant propagator who created the hybrid in the 1890s.

Locations Several trees along the south side of La Mesa Park. Others in Willowglen Park and Mount Calvary Cemetery.

Top: The dense, dark green crown of X Cuprocyparis leylandii, *and its several stems, are characteristic.*
Middle: The yellow-green twigs become reddish, then gray-brown.
Bottom: The tightly appressed, small scale-like leaves are arrayed on irregular twigs that give an overall unkempt appearance to the crown.

Juniperus
Juniper

A genus of about 50 species, all in the Northern Hemisphere with the exception of one, *J. procera,* which is found in the mountains of East Africa. Its species are well-known as indicators of calcareous soils. *Juniperus* is the Latin name for juniper.

Juniperus californica
California juniper

Native to dry, rocky slopes of the Inner Coast Ranges, the southern Sierra Nevada, and the higher elevations of the Mojave and Colorado Deserts in California, extending to Arizona, Nevada, and Baja California.

Habit A small, multi-stemmed evergreen tree or large shrub with a dense, rounded crown; to 25 feet.

Inflorescence Dioecious, rarely monoecious; pollen cones and seed cones terminal.

Fruit Globose, 1/4–1/2 inch; bluish-green then reddish-brown with a glaucous bloom, with small prickles on the scales, containing 1–2 seeds.

Twigs Usually round, as wide as scale leaves are long.

Bark Gray, shreddy, peeling in thin strips; smooth on smaller branches.

Leaves Opposite; scale-like, 1/16 inch long; with a conspicuous abaxial gland; closely appressed, not overlapping; light yellowish-green, becoming dark green.

Notes Used for fence posts where locally abundant. The species name *californica* means from California.

Locations Santa Barbara Botanic Garden, in the Meadow Section.

Top: Juniperus californica *is a small tree or large shrub with sprawling appearance. Its many stems make an attractive climbing tree for children.*
Bottom: The many glaucous seed cones ("berries") are attractive to birds.

Juniperus chinensis
Chinese juniper

Widely spread in China and Japan.

Habit A dense conical or cylindrical evergreen tree with ascending branches; to 45 feet tall.

Inflorescence Usually dioecious; male cones bright yellow, usually on adult branchlets.

Fruit Roundish, 1/3 inch in diameter; conspicuously silver-gray glaucous; maturing in 2 years.

Twigs Round, wider than the length of the scales.

Bark Reddish-gray, shreddy, flaking in small scaly plates.

Leaves Opposite; juvenile leaves paired, spreading from the branchlet, awl-shaped, 1/3 inch long with a green midrib and 2 white bands of stomata above, sharp-pointed; adult leaves four-ranked, 1/16 inch long, with an inconspicuous glandular depression on the back; closely appressed, overlapping.

Notes One of the most common species in cultivation, this species is quite variable and numerous cultivars have been described. One, the Hollywood juniper (*J. chinensis* 'Torulosa'), is quite common in Santa Barbara and is characterized by an irregular crown composed of long, twisted, whip-like branches with terminal tufts of branchlets. The species name *chinensis* means from China.

Locations A single tree of the species in West Alameda Plaza. The 'Torulosa' cultivar can be seen on the Anacapa Street side of the County Administration Building and in the Santa Barbara Cemetery.

Above left: The mature crown of the Juniperus chinensis *retains a dense conical form.*
*Above right: In the Hollywood juniper (*J. chinensis *'Torulosa'), the long thin branches give the appearance of waving arms.*
Left: The very glaucous seed cones are usually found on separate plants from the pollen cones.

Juniperus occidentalis
Western juniper

Found on dry, rocky slopes in foothills and mountains of eastern California, Nevada, Oregon, Washington, and Idaho, from 1,000 to 10,000 feet.

Habit A small, single-stemmed evergreen tree with a rounded to conical crown; 15–40 feet tall.

Inflorescence Monoecious or dioecious; pollen cones oblong, to 1/8 inch long.

Fruit Seed cones of two distinct sizes, 1/4–1/2 inch, ovoid, blue to blue-black, fleshy and resinous, containing 2–3 seeds, maturing in two years.

Twigs Erect, three- to four-sided in cross section, about 2/3 or less as wide as length of scale-like leaves.

Bark Red-brown to brown, exfoliating in thin strips

Leaves Opposite, of two forms; awl-shaped leaves 1/8–1/4 inch long, scale leaves less than 1/8 inch long, not overlapping, tightly appressed; all leaves green with an ovate to elliptic abaxial gland exuding conspicuous yellow or white resin lending a blue-green color to the entire plant; finely toothed margins.

Notes Two varieties of *J. occidentalis* are recognized. *J. occidentalis* var. *occidentalis* is found mostly below 6,000 feet in eastern Oregon and Washington, Idaho, Nevada, and northeastern California, has brown bark and smaller seed cones, and is often monoecious. *J. occidentalis* var. *australis* is found mostly within California (Sierra Nevada, Panamint Range, San Gabriel Mountains, and San Bernardino Mountains) at elevations of 5,000 to 10,000 feet, has reddish bark and larger seed cones, and is mostly dioecious. The abundant resin production lends a dotted appearance to the younger twigs and foliage. The species name *occidentalis* means western.

Locations Santa Barbara Botanic Garden near the northeast corner of the Meadow.

Top: The small scale-like leaves of Juniperus occidentalis *have a depressed gland on the back that exudes a grayish resin.*
Bottom: The red shreddy bark is a common feature to many, but not all, species of Juniperus.

Juniperus osteosperma
Utah juniper

Widely distributed on dry, rocky soils through most of the southwestern United States; from east of the Sierra Nevada and the eastern Mojave Desert in California throughout Nevada and Utah, and extending into Idaho, Wyoming, Colorado, New Mexico, and Arizona.

Habit Shrubs or small evergreen trees with single or, less commonly, multiple stems and a rounded crown; to 25 feet tall.

Inflorescence Monoecious; pollen cones cylindrical, 1/8 inch long.

Fruit Seed cones globose, 1/3 inch across, bluish-brown, maturing red-brown or tan, fibrous, peduncles straight, maturing in 1–2 years.

Twigs Erect, three- to four-sided in cross section, about as wide as length of scale-like leaves.

Bark Thin, gray-brown, becoming ash white, exfoliating in thin shreddy strips on larger stems.

Leaves Opposite; scale-like, 1/12 inch long, opposite in 4 ranks, light yellow-green, tightly appressed, glands embedded and inconspicuous, resinous exudate absent, margins finely toothed.

Notes Appropriate for its common name, *J. osteosperma* is the dominant juniper in Utah. The species name *osteosperma* means hard seed.

Locations Trees in the Santa Barbara Botanic Garden near the entrance, in the Desert Section, and in the Pinyon-Juniper Woodland.

Large blue-green seed cones and minute scale-like leaves of Juniperus osteosperma.

Metasequoia

Metasequoia includes only a single species. Its name is from the Greek *meta* (beyond, above) and *Sequoia,* which it resembles.

Metasequoia glyptostroboides
Dawn redwood

Although widespread across the Northern Hemisphere over 65 million years ago, *M. glyptostroboides* is naturally found today in five populations occurring within an eleven-mile radius in central China.

Habit A deciduous tree with a conical crown, becoming rounded; to 50 feet tall.

Inflorescence Monoecious; pollen cones arranged in perpendicular pairs on long spikes or panicles.

Fruit Seed cones roundish, ³/₄–1 inch across, terminal, solitary and hanging on lateral twigs; scales 20–30, woody, reddish-brown, arranged in opposite pairs alternating with one another, the uppermost and lowermost scales sterile.

Twigs Usually green, the lateral ones often deciduous with the leaves.

Bark Reddish-brown, becoming grayish, peeling off in thin strips, reddish in the furrows.

Leaves Opposite in a pinnate arrangement; linear, flattened, apex pointed, ¹/₂ x ¹/₁₆ inch, larger on young trees; bright green above with a narrowly grooved midrib, yellow-green below, turning rusty-brown before abscission.

Notes The genus *Metasequoia* was originally described as representing several species from the Tertiary; however, in 1945 the first living specimens of the genus were collected from an isolated region of central China. The public interest in this "living fossil" has led to a wide horticultural distribution today. The genus has characteristics close to *Sequoia* (cone morphology) and *Taxodium* (deciduous twigs); however, it differs from both in having opposite leaves on the twigs. The species name *glyptostroboides* means carved cone.

Locations Two young trees in West Alameda Plaza. Another in Lower Orpet Park between the lawn and Pedregosa Street.

Top: This young tree of Metasequoia glyptostroboides *is deciduous during the winter months, as are all individuals of this species.*
Bottom left: The pale green foliage turns brown in fall and drops while still attached to the twig.
Bottom right: The pale gray bark is underlain by a reddish-brown tint.

Sequoia

The genus *Sequoia* includes only one species. Its name is the Cherokee name given to George Gist (1770–1843), the inventor of the Cherokee alphabet. Gist was the son of an American Indian woman and an American-German merchant. In Cherokee, *sequoia* means opossum and was used to refer to a child of such an interracial relationship.

Sequoia sempervirens
Coast redwood

Native to the fog zone of the Pacific coast from southwestern Oregon to Central California.

Habit A narrowly conical evergreen tree with an open crown of horizontal or drooping branches; recently measured at 369 feet tall in its native habitat.

Inflorescence Monoecious; terminal, appearing with the flush of new growth. Pollen usually shed in April.

Fruit Seed cone ovoid, 3/4–1 1/8 x 1/2–7/8 inches, reddish-brown, pendulous, maturing in one year, persistent following seed shed; scales wrinkled, leathery, attached at the center.

Twigs Pendulous, frequently shedding with the leaves, dark green initially, becoming ridged from the scale leaves, turning gray; winter buds on persistent twigs protected by overlapping brown scales.

Bark Reddish-gray on the surface, darker red beneath, very fibrous, deeply fissured.

Leaves Opposite, of two forms; scale-like leaves, in several ranks on leaders and shoots, loosely appressed, with an incurved point; needle-like leaves, 1/4–1 x 1/10 inch, with a sharpened apex, dark green with 2 broad stomatal bands below, appearing to be arranged in a two-ranked, pinnate formation on lateral branches.

Notes Redwood trees live to 2,200 years of age. The thick fibrous bark protects it from fire and it sprouts naturally following a burn. The association of the species with the coastal fog zone involves an important adaptation. The large surface area of the foliage acts to strip water out of the fog and increases the actual precipitation reaching the ground. This additional moisture figures prominently in the survival of redwoods in these areas. It is one of the few conifers to reproduce through stump sprouts. *S. sempervirens* is the state tree of California along with *Sequoiadendron giganteum*. The species name *sempervirens* means always green.

Locations Santa Barbara Botanic Garden in the Redwood Section, on the grounds of the County Courthouse, West Alameda Plaza, the Sexton House on Hollister Avenue, Stow House, and the Santa Barbara Genealogical Society.

Top: A very narrow crown of Sequoia sempervirens. *Bottom: Terminal seed cones and needles in two ranks.*

Sequoiadendron

The genus *Sequoiadendron* includes only the following species. The name is a combination of *Sequoia* and the Greek *dendron* (tree).

Sequoiadendron giganteum
Giant sequoia

Native to the western slopes of the Sierra Nevada in Central California at elevations from 4,300 to 8,000 feet, where winter snows reach a depth of two to ten feet.

Habit An evergreen, narrowly conical tree, with drooping branches; to 310 feet tall in its native habitat.

Inflorescence Monoecious; pollen cones terminal, nearly round, 1/4–1/3 inch across.

Fruit Seed cones terminal, solitary, ovoid, 2–3 x 1 1/2 inches, reddish-brown; scales 35–40, apex woody, the outer face four-sided, almost diamond-shaped; maturing in the second year and persistent after seed shed.

Twigs Green from attached leaf bases, becoming brown; winter buds small, without scales, hidden by late leaves.

Bark Thick, to 2 feet, bright reddish-brown, fibrous, deeply furrowed.

Leaves Scale-like or needle-like, the flat base adhering to the twig and the tip free, 1/8–3/16 inch long, sharp-tipped, spirally arranged in 3 rows; persisting about 4 years.

Notes Because of its location in the Sierra Nevada, *S. giganteum* was not discovered until late in California's history when an Englishman named John Bidwell explored the headwaters of the Sacramento River. The tree is known for its large size and great age. Most individuals of the species are 400 to 1,500 years of age. However, individuals have been estimated to be 3,000 to 3,500 years old. This is neither the tallest, nor the oldest tree in the world, those attributes going to *Eucalyptus amygdalina* and *Pinus longaeva*, respectively. *S. giganteum* is the state tree of California along with *Sequoiadendron sempervirens*. The species name *giganteum* means giant.

Locations Three trees on the Santa Barbara County Courthouse grounds near the corner of Anapamu and Santa Barbara Streets.

Top: This **Sequoiadendron giganteum** *has retained its conical form; however, the crowns become more rounded in older trees.*
Middle: Seed cones begin dispersing their seeds in the second year; however, the partially serotinous cones release most of their seed following fires.
Bottom: The sharp-tipped needles are spirally arranged in three rows.

Taxodium

Taxodium includes one species from eastern North America and the highlands of Mexico and Guatemala. Its name is a combination of the Greek words *taxus* (yew) and *eidos* (resembling), referring to the similar leaf shapes.

Taxodium mucronatum
Montezuma bald cypress, Mexican swamp cypress, Mexican cypress

Native to the central mountains and tablelands of Mexico and Guatemala, from 1,500 to 7,000 feet, also found in southwest Texas.

Habit A semi-evergreen or evergreen tree with a rounded crown and pendulous branchlets; to 150 feet tall.

Inflorescence Monoecious; pollen cones in three- to six-inch-long branched spikes at the end of the previous year's shoots; female flowers solitary, scattered along the twigs.

Fruit Seed cones round, 1/2–1 1/4 inches across, resinous, purplish, on short stalks; scales coarse and few, with a spreading apex.

Twigs Those at the ends of shoots persistent, lateral twigs shed with the leaves; buds rounded with overlapping sharp scales.

Bark Reddish-brown to dark gray, fibrous, furrowed into elongate flakes.

Leaves Spirally arranged, but twisted to appear two-ranked, narrow, pointed, 1/3–3/4 inch long, dull light green, usually persistent but sometimes turning yellow or brown in the spring and fall at the time of new growth.

Notes *T. mucronatum* is very similar to the fully deciduous bald cypress *(T. distichum)* of the southeastern United States and differs primarily in its almost evergreen habit, long, arching twigs, and geographic distribution. The species name *mucronatum* means with a small point.

Locations East Alameda Plaza. Trees in Vera Cruz Park, Plaza del Mar, and the 200 block of West Yanonali Street were all planted by Dr. A. B. Doremus.

Top: The pendulous twigs of Taxodium mucronatum *are evident from a distance.*
Bottom: Twigs with seed cones, foliage, and pollen cones all display pendulous character.

Thuja

A genus of six species from North America and eastern Asia. Its name derives from the Greek name *thuia* for a type of juniper.

Thuja orientalis
Oriental arbor-vitae, Chinese arbor-vitae

Native to northern and western China, and cultivated early in Japan and Korea. Now widely cultivated throughout the world with about 30 named varieties.

Habit A large shrub or small bushy evergreen tree, often many-stemmed from the base; ascending branches and foliage arranged in flat vertical sprays; to 25 feet tall.

Inflorescence Monoecious; pollen cones terminal, small.

Fruit Seed cones ovoid, $2/3$ inch long; fleshy, glaucous before ripening; 6 scales, each with a large woody hook at the apex, the apical two of the cone narrow and sterile, opening widely when mature.

Twigs Reddish-brown, fibrous, scaly.

Bark Thin, grayish-red, peeling in fibers.

Leaves Opposite; triangular scales, smaller than the other species, less than $1/12$ inch long; with a distinct groove on the back; green or light green; giving a slight odor of turpentine when crushed.

Notes The name arbor-vitae comes from the eastern North American *Thuja occidentalis,* the foliage of which contains a high concentration of vitamin C. The French explorer Jacque Cartier and his crew drank cedar tea along the St. Lawrence River in 1535 to fend off scurvy. Upon hearing this, King Francis I named the tree arborvitae, the "tree of life." The species name *orientalis* means eastern.

Locations Three small trees in the 1400 block of Laguna Street.

Twigs of **Thuja orientalis** *exhibiting terminal pollen cones, solitary seed cones, and flattened display of foliage.*

Thuja plicata
Western red cedar, western arbor-vitae

Native to coastal regions of western North America from Alaska to Northern California and in the wetter parts of the northern Rocky Mountains.

Habit A slender, conical evergreen tree; larger trees may be buttressed at the base; branches in flat, horizontal sprays, frequently pendulous at the ends; to 45 feet tall.

Inflorescence Monoecious; pollen cones minute, reddish.

Fruit Seed cones ovoid, 1/2–3/4 inch long; erect and green when young, becoming brown when mature; scales 10–12, each with a thickened point near the apex.

Twigs Shiny green, becoming orange and then reddish-gray.

Bark Thin, grayish-brown; shiny and flaky when young, shredding with age into elongate strips.

Leaves Opposite; shiny yellowish-green; scale-like on ultimate divisions of the spray, ovate, 1/4 inch long, with an inconspicuous resin gland on the back; triangular on vigorous upright shoots, 1/8 inch long, often without glands; all with a strong aromatic odor when crushed.

Notes In Santa Barbara *T. plicata* gives no evidence of the immense size (to 200 feet tall) it attains in its native habitat. This tree has an important role in the cultures of native peoples of the American northwest. Its strong, decay-resistant and lightweight wood was used in creating shelter, totem poles, and the special war canoes of the region. The species name *plicata* means folded, like a fan.

Locations Trees in the Arroyo and Redwood Sections of the Santa Barbara Botanic Garden.

Top: Thuja plicata *retains its foliage to the ground when grown in the open.*
Bottom: The flat, horizontal sprays of foliage and dense clusters of upright seed cones are characteristic.

Ginkgoaceae

The Ginkgo Family is the only remnant from an isolated order of the gymnosperms with no close living relatives. During the Jurassic Period, the family probably contained at least six genera.

Ginkgo

Ginkgo is an ancient genus that dates to the Jurassic Period, some 150 million years ago. Although it consists of only one species today, as many as six have been identified from the fossil record. *Ginkgo* gets its name from the 17th-century Chinese words *gin* (silver) and *kyo* (apricot).

Ginkgo biloba
Ginkgo, maidenhair tree

A relic of eastern China.

Habit A deciduous tree with a loose, unkempt-looking crown; to 50 feet tall.

Inflorescence Dioecious; axillary; solitary; male reproductive structures catkin-like; female structure long-stalked, with two ovules at the end of each stalk. Pollen shed in March.

Fruit A hardened seed inside a fleshy outer shell; to 1 inch in diameter; yellow-orange with a silvery sheen; with a strong unpleasant odor.

Twigs Of two forms; long shoots containing alternate leaves, short spur shoots containing clusters of 3–5 leaves; light creamy gray; buds chestnut brown, 1/4–1/3 inch across.

Bark Gray to creamy gray; deeply furrowed on older trees.

Leaves Clustered on short spur shoots, fan-shaped, 2–3 inches across (larger on young vigorous trees), the apical margin often divided into two large, irregular lobes; with numerous branching parallel veins originating from the base, no midrib; light green when young, becoming dark green in midsummer, turning bright yellow by late autumn in mild climates or with the first frost in colder climates; petioles to 3 inches.

Notes *Ginkgo biloba* is an ancient tree with fossils dating back 225 million years. It is a sacred tree in the Orient and may owe its survival to centuries of cultivation by Buddhist priests. It probably no longer occurs in a truly natural state. This species is unique among seed plants in its fertilization by motile male sperm.

Top: Brilliant yellow foliage of **Ginkgo biloba** *in the fall. Bottom left: Male flowers and foliage on short spur shoots. Bottom right: Leaves in fall and summer.*

Because of the unpleasant odor of the fleshy-covered seeds, considerable effort has been put into determining criteria for distinguishing sexes in young plants. To date, no reliable morphological basis for this distinction has been developed, although male trees tend to have narrower crowns and drop their leaves earlier than females. The species name *biloba* means two lobes.

Locations Trees in lower Orpet Park, West Alameda Plaza, Willowglen Park, and Alice Keck Park Memorial Gardens. Street trees in the first block of East Quinto and on La Cumbre Lane. Several trees in front of the Performing Arts Building at the University of California, Santa Barbara.

Pinaceae

The Pine Family is perhaps the most important family of timber trees in the world. Its 12 genera and 220 species are primarily found in the Northern Hemisphere and around the equator in the Americas and Indonesia. Its commercial products include solid wood products, pulp, and resins (e.g. turpentine). Many of the genera are characterized by pollen grains that are subtended by two air-filled sacs. This reduces the density of the pollen and increases wind dispersion during the pollination process.

Abies
Firs

Abies includes 49 species, which are almost exclusively found in the cooler climates of the North Temperate Zone. However, species do occur at higher elevations in lower latitude regions of Vietnam, Central America, and northern Africa. The genus is readily distinguished from *Picea* (the spruces) by the flattened needles that cannot be rolled between the fingers, cones that are upright when mature and disintegrate on the tree following seed dispersion, resin blisters on the bark of young stems, and large circular or elliptic leaf scars that are flush with the twig. *Abies* is the classical Latin name for fir.

Abies bracteata
Abies venusta
Santa Lucia fir, bristlecone fir

Native only to the Santa Lucia Mountains of Monterey County, California. Restricted to moist canyon bottoms, north-facing steep rock faces, and dry rocky summits.

Habit An attractive narrowly conical evergreen tree; to 160 feet tall.

Inflorescence Monoecious; pollen cones yellow to yellow-green at maturation.

Fruit Seed cones 3–4 x 1 1/2–2 inches; scale bracts with long protruding spines, 1–2 inches long, frequently tipped with resin drops.

Twigs Tan, glabrous; buds unlike any other fir, spindle-shaped, sharp-pointed, to 3/4 inch long, without resin.

Bark Thin, light reddish-brown, slightly fissured; dull gray with resin blisters when young.

Top: Sharp-pointed needles of Abies bracteata *arranged in two ranks.*
Bottom left: Striking gray color of stomata on lower surface of needles.
Bottom right: Elongate bracts and resinous seed cone.

Leaves Needles somewhat spreading horizontally into 2 ranks; needles flattened with sharp, spine-like points, to 2 x 1/8 inches; upper surface dark green, slightly concave or grooved; lower surface with 8–10 rows of stomata.

Notes The thin bark and disjunct distribution of this species to moist canyon bottoms and rocky outcrops suggests that it is extremely intolerant of fire and survives only in those locations where fire effects are minimized. The species name *bracteata* means with bracts.

Locations Trees in the Redwood Section of the Santa Barbara Botanic Garden.

Abies concolor
White fir

Broadly distributed in the mountainous regions of the western United States from Idaho to northern Baja California.

Habit An evergreen tree with a rounded crown when mature; to 160 feet tall.

Inflorescence Monoecious; pollen cones red, purple, or green at maturation.

Fruit Seed cones cylindrical, 3–5 x 1 1/4 inches; greenish or purple when growing, brown when mature; scales broader than long, 1/2 x 1 inch, bracts concealed.

Twigs Orange-brown to olive, becoming grayish or silvery; buds large, broadly conical, blunt, covered with resin.

Bark Thick with deep furrows; gray-brown to black with alternating light and dark layers; light gray with resin blisters on younger stems.

Leaves Needles two-ranked on lower branches, almost vertically arranged on upper branches; flattened, 1 1/2–3 1/2 inches long, usually not grooved on the top, apex rounded or slightly pointed; glaucous on both surfaces, with several lines of stomata visible on the lower surface; yielding an odor of oranges when crushed.

Notes The species is widely variable and has been described as a catchall for western firs with green seed cones and glaucous leaves. A recent revision of the genus has described individuals from the Sierra Nevada and Coast Ranges of California as *A. lowiana;* however, the distinction is not fully accepted. The species name *concolor* means uniformly colored.

Locations A small tree in the Redwood Section and another in the Yellow Pine Forest Section of the Santa Barbara Botanic Garden.

Flattened, round-tipped needles of Abies concolor *with glaucous waxy coating on upper surface.*

Abies grandis
Grand fir

Native to the Pacific states from Vancouver Island to Northern California, and also found in Idaho and western Montana.

Habit A tall evergreen tree with a rounded crown; the largest of the firs, reaching almost 250 feet in its native habitat.

Inflorescence Monoecious; pollen cones bluish-red, purple, orange, yellow, or greenish at maturation.

Fruit Seed cones cylindrical but narrowed towards the apex, blunt or sunken at the apex, 2–4 x 1–1 1/4 inches; green to purplish, becoming brown when mature; scales crescent- to fan-shaped, much wider than long, densely pubescent; bracts much shorter than scales.

Twigs Slender, olive-green to dark orange-brown; buds ovoid, blunt-tipped, 1/4 inch long, purple or bluish-brown, covered with resin.

Bark Deep brown, thick and scaly with furrows separating flat gray ridges; smooth grayish-brown with numerous horizontal resin blisters (not to be confused with lenticels) when young.

Leaves Needles two-ranked, alternating shorter with longer on each side of the twig; flattened, 1–2 inches long, notched at the apex; upper surface dark shiny green, grooved; lower surface with several lines of white stomatal dots; with an odor of oranges when crushed.

Notes In contrast to *A. concolor,* this species exhibits little variation throughout its geographic range. The species name *grandis* means large, noble.

Locations Trees in the Redwood Section of the Santa Barbara Botanic Garden.

Top: Sap-covered, upright seed cone of Abies grandis. *Bottom: Flattened needles with notched apex. Longer needles tend to alternate with shorter ones along the stem. Note the gray lines of stomata on the lower surface.*

Abies pinsapo
Spanish fir

Found principally in three isolated forests in the mountainous region around Ronda in southern Spain.

Habit An evergreen tree with a dense conical crown; to 60 feet tall.

Inflorescence Monoecious; pollen cones dark red.

Fruit Seed cones cylindrical, tapering to the apex, 4–5 x 1 3/4 inches; scales triangular, bracts concealed; cone exuding large drops of resin.

Twigs Reddish brown; buds ovoid, resinous.

Bark Smooth initially, becoming rough and furrowed on older trees.

Leaves Needles not twisted to form 2 ranks, foliage spreading around the twig much like that of a spruce; flattened, 1/2–3/4 inch long, apex blunt or slightly pointed; upper surface convex, not grooved; both surfaces with distinct lines of stomata.

Notes The species name *pinsapo* is an old Spanish word combining *pino* (pine) and *sapino* (fir) and meaning pine-fir, or possibly short for *Pinus saponis,* soap-fir, since twigs crushed in water yield a kind of soap.

Locations A straggly specimen at Stow House. Another at Westmont College on the northwest side of the circle.

Flattened needles of Abies pinsapo *arranged around the stem, with upright seed cones. Note the central core of an older cone in the lower center. The scales of* Abies *cones fall off when the seeds are dispersed.*

Cedrus
Cedar

A genus of four species in the mountains of North Africa, the eastern Mediterranean and the western Himalayas. *Cedrus* is the classical Latin name for cedar.

Cedrus atlantica
Atlas cedar

Endemic to the Atlas Mountains of Algeria and Morocco.

Habit An evergreen tree, with an open, loose pyramidal crown; main branches frequently steeply ascending, secondary branches horizontal and twigs pendulous; central leader stiff, erect; to 50 feet in height.

Inflorescence Monoecious; solitary, terminal, on short twigs; pollen-bearing cones cylindrical, 2 inches long, erect. Pollen shed August to September.

Fruit Seed cones erect, ovate to cylindrical, 2–3 inches long, flat or slightly concave at the apex; glossy light brown; ripening in 3rd season, disintegrating upon seed dissemination; scales less than $1\frac{1}{2}$ inches wide.

Twigs Light tan in current year's growth, becoming darker and duller with age.

Bark Light gray, smooth on young stems and branches; dark gray, scaly and fissured on older stems.

Leaves Needles held in dense clusters of 20–30 on short shoots usually on the upper sides of the twigs; $\frac{1}{2}$–$1\frac{1}{4}$ inches long, stiff, four-angled in cross section; green to gray-green.

Notes *C. atlantica* was introduced to Europe from seed collected by Lord Somers in the Atlas Mountains of Algeria and Morocco in 1845. One specimen planted as a seedling in 1847 reached a height and diameter of 110 x $4\frac{1}{2}$ feet in 90 years. Several varieties have been introduced, including the densely crowned var. *glauca* which is noted for its glaucous, blue-green color that is especially intense on new growth. Some authors consider *C. atlantica* to be a subspecies of *C. libani,* and have revised the genus to include only two species. However, this has not become commonly accepted. The species name *atlantica* means from the Atlas Mountiains.

Top: The dense, rounded crown and blue-green foliage of Cedrus atlantica *var.* glauca *are distinctive; however, the crown becomes more open and asymmetrical with age. Bottom: Clusters of short needles and a flat-topped or dimpled cone.*

Locations Three individuals of the *C. atlantica* var. *glauca* are planted in the circle at Calle Rosales and Vista de la Cumbre. One tree on the east side of Centennial House at the University of California, Santa Barbara.

Cedrus deodara
Deodar cedar, Himalayan cedar

Native to the Himalayas above 4,000 feet from Afghanistan to Garhwal, India.

Habit An evergreen tree with an open tapering crown, the flexible branches and leader noticeably drooping even from a distance; to 80 feet tall.

Inflorescence Monoecious; however, frequently occurring as dioecious. Pollen shed August to September.

Fruit Seed cones 1 or 2 together; barrel-shaped, apex rounded; 3–4 inches long; bluish-glaucous when young, reddish-brown when mature; scales numerous, fan-shaped, large, 1 1/2–2 inches wide.

Twigs Pubescent with very short hairs, flexible, light tawny to gray.

Bark Grayish-brown, broken into irregular elongated scales, with obvious horizontal lenticels on smaller stems and branches.

Leaves Needles grouped in whorls of 15–20, usually at the ends of short spur shoots; 1–1 1/2 inches long, sharply pointed; bluish-green.

Notes Like *Cedrus atlantica*, *C. deodara* has numerous cultivars. It was introduced to Britain between 1822 and 1831 and has been used extensively in gardens in southern and western England. The deodar is an important timber tree in its native habitat. Although it grows best in native habitats receiving 40 to 70 inches of rain per year, it also thrives in areas receiving less than 30 inches if the soils are good. The species name *deodara* means tree of the gods in Hindi.

Locations Planted throughout town. Specimens in East and West Alameda Plaza. Street trees on Canon Drive, from State Street to Stevens Park.

Top: The open crown and drooping leader of Cedrus deodara.
Bottom: Long needles and rounded or conical cone.

Picea
Spruces

Picea is a genus of about 40 species from the cool temperate and boreal regions of the Northern Hemisphere. It is distinct from *Abies* in several respects, including persistent raised leaf bases, pendulous cones with persistent scales, and four-angled needles that "roll" between the thumb and forefinger. *Picea* is the Latin name for pitch-pine and is derived from *pix* (pitch).

Picea abies
Norway spruce

Broadly spread in northern, central, and eastern Europe; reaching to Greece and the Balkans only in higher mountainous regions.

Habit An evergreen tree, frequently with pendulous branches; to 70 feet tall.

Inflorescence Monoecious; pollen cones axillary, 1 x 1/2 inch, seed cones terminal.

Fruit Seed cones pendulous, cylindrical, 4–6 inches, light brown when ripe; scales thin, flexible, often diamond-shaped, 1–1 1/4 x 5/8–3/4 inches, usually toothed at the apex.

Twigs Reddish-brown or orange-red; buds conical, apex rounded, 1/4 inch long with reddish-brown scales.

Bark Gray-brown, broken into small round or square plates by shallow fissures.

Leaves Needles bent away from the lower side of the twig; straight, rigid, sharp-pointed, 1/2–1 inch, attached to a small peg on the twig; four-sided, dark green with 2 or 3 stomatal lines on all sides.

Notes *P. abies* has many uses in its native lands. In addition to its timber and pulp values, its resins are used in wound dressings, its leaves are used to make spruce beer, and the resonance of its wood has made it ideal for stringed instruments. In North America it is extensively used in forest plantations in Canada and the northeastern United States. It has been suggested that the distinct pendulous branches noted so much in the eastern United States and Canada may be a result of general vigor loss due to air pollution. However, with more than 140 varieties and cultivars, this characteristic may be part of the genetic variation in the species. The species name *abies* means fir.

Locations A tree at Westmont College, south of the circle, planted just west of the *Picea smithiana*.

Sharp-pointed, squared needles and pendulous cone of Picea abies.

Picea sitchensis
Sitka Spruce, tideland spruce

Occurs in coastal forests of western North America from Northern California to Anchorage, Alaska.

Habit An evergreen tree with a narrow conical crown; to 50 feet tall.

Inflorescence Monoecious; pollen cones axillary, in clusters, yellow to purple.

Fruit Seed cones 2–4 inches long, pale yellow to reddish-brown; scales papery thin, narrowly diamond-shaped, the apex appearing irregularly eroded away.

Twigs Somewhat stout, not drooping, orange to reddish-brown, glabrous; buds reddish-brown, rounded, to 1/4 inch long.

Bark Grayish-brown to orange-brown.

Leaves Needles bent away from the lower side of the twig; straight, rigid, sharp-pointed, 1/2–1 inch, attached to a small peg on the twig; flat or with a rounded top, dark or yellow-green with 8–12 stomatal lines on the bottom.

Notes *Picea sitchensis* is the largest species of this genus, occasionally exceeding 320 feet tall with trunk diameters of 14–16 feet. It is restricted to the narrow fog belt in the coastal Pacific Northwest and may spend over 240 days each year in the clouds. The wood of old-growth trees has been prized for its narrow, but exceedingly uniform, growth rings and has been used to produce soundboards for high quality harps, pianos, and violins. The species name *sitchensis* refers to the city of Sitka, Alaska.

Locations Three young trees in the Redwood Section of the Santa Barbara Botanic Garden.

Top: Wispy foliage and light tan twigs of Picea sitchensis *grown in the shade. Sun-grown foliage is much more dense on the twig.*
Middle: Twigs of all Picea *species retain a pedicel to which the needle was attached.*
Bottom: Pendulous cones with thin, rough-margined scales.

Picea smithiana
Picea morinda

West Himalayan spruce, Morinda spruce

Native to the high elevations of the Himalayan Mountains from 7,000 to 12,000 feet, extending from Tibet to Afghanistan.

Habit A tall, broadly conical evergreen tree with distinctive pendulous branches; to 40 feet tall.

Inflorescence Monoecious; pollen cones axillary cylindrical, $1\frac{1}{2} \times \frac{2}{3}$ inches, female cones terminal.

Fruit Seed cones cylindrical with tapered ends, $4\text{--}7 \times 1\frac{1}{2}\text{--}2$ inches; bright green when young, turning bright brown; scales roundish, not toothed, margins wavy.

Twigs Pale brown or grayish, shiny, hairless; buds spindle-shaped, $\frac{1}{2}$ inch long, reddish-brown.

Bark Gray-brown, broken by shallow fissures into small round or square plates.

Leaves Needles sparely spread around the shoot and curved forward; $1\frac{1}{2}$ inches long, slender, sharply pointed, four-sided, with 5 stomatal lines on each side.

Notes This is one of the most important softwood timber species of eastern Asia. The species name *smithiana* honors Sir James Edward Smith (1759–1828), first president of the Linnean Society of England.

Locations A tree at Westmont College south of the circle, planted just east of the *Picea abies*.

Top: Sparse, somewhat curved needles of Picea smithiana.
Bottom: Cone with thin, broad scales.

Pinus
Pines

This genus includes approximately 95 species native to the Northern Hemisphere throughout North America, Europe, and Asia. It is distinguished by having its needles held in fascicles surrounded by a membranous sheath. Several species have significant timber value and have been planted extensively in plantations for that purpose. Among the species planted in Santa Barbara, *P. radiata* and *P. sylvestris* have been used in timber programs throughout the world. The name derives from the Greek *pinos,* meaning pine-tree, or from the Celtic *pin* or *pyn,* meaning mountain or rock and referring to the habitat of the tree.

Pinus attenuata
Knob-cone pine, narrow-cone pine

Occurring naturally in the Cascade Range of southern Oregon and Northern California, the Sierra Nevada, the Coast Ranges of Oregon and California, and the San Bernardino Mountains in Southern California, usually below 6,000 feet.

Habit A sometimes several-trunked evergreen tree with an open crown from the sparse placement of needles on the branches; to 50 feet tall.

Inflorescence Monoecious; pollen cones orange-brown, 1/2–2/3 inch long.

Fruit Seed cone conic-oblong, usually asymmetric at base; 4–6 inches long, on a short peduncle; scales lustrous, light brownish-yellow; umbo prominent with a short, sharp prickle; on young trees cones may be clustered in whorls on main stem, on older trees whorls clustered on branches; serotinous, lasting for many years.

Twigs Slender, flexible, grayish-brown; initially rough from leaf bracts, becoming smooth; winter buds narrow and pointed with resinous scales.

Bark Dark brown on older trunks and quite smooth; fissured only on lower trunk.

Leaves Needles in fascicles of 3 (rarely 2); 5 inches or more long; pale yellowish- or bluish-green; stomata present on both surfaces; thick and more or less rigid; basal sheath brown, persistent.

Notes *P. attenuata* is a fire-dependent species of chaparral vegetation. Its long-lived cones sometimes become imbedded in the trunk. The species name *attenuata* means narrowing to a point.

Locations Individuals in the Ceanothus Section and at the upper part of the Meadow Section of the Santa Barbara Botanic Garden.

Top: Needles in fascicles of three and pollen cones of Pinus attenuata.
Bottom: Curved, sessile cones with knob-like scales.

Pinus canariensis
Canary Island pine, Canary pine

Endemic to the Canary Islands and naturally occurring on dry, exposed volcanic mountain slopes between 3,500 and 6,500 feet.

Habit A single-stemmed evergreen tree, with branches beginning low on trunk and becoming spreading in upper crown; to 100 feet tall.

Inflorescence Monoecious; male cones clustered below the needles.

Fruit Seed cones 4–8 inches long, oval-oblong when closed, conical with a flat base when open; scales with a prominent apophysis and a well-developed transverse keel; umbo blunt at the tip.

Twigs Stout and ascending; winter buds large with reflexed and fringed scales.

Bark Deeply fissured with rough, large reddish-brown ridges, orange between.

Leaves Needles in bundles of 3 with long persistent sheaths, 8–10 inches long, thin, gracefully curved, clustered at the ends of twigs; dark green with blue-gray lines from stomata on inner side; primary leaves continue to occur with secondary leaves (needles) on shoots of mature trees.

Notes *P. canariensis* has a strong tendency towards sprouts along the lower trunk of mature trees resulting in juvenile foliage on young twigs. Epicormic sprouting is strongly stimulated by fires of moderate intensity. This is one of the few pine species with such a response. The species has a close and interesting relationship with *P. roxburghii*, which is native to the foothills and lower slopes of the Himalayas. The species name *canariensis* means from the Canary Islands.

Locations Common about town. Trees in West Alameda Plaza, others in the east end of MacKenzie Park. Street trees on Los Pinos Drive and 3900 State Street. Many on the campus of the University of California, Santa Barbara.

Top: Narrow, open crown of **Pinus canariensis** *with foliage somewhat clustered at the ends of branches.*
Middle: Dark green needles and large terminal cluster of brown pollen cones.
Bottom: Seed cones with large, somewhat recurved apophyses.

Pinus cembroides
Pinyon pine, Mexican nut pine, Mexican stone pine

Widely distributed in the Sierra Madre Oriental and the Sierra Madre Occidental of northern Mexico and their extensions into Arizona and Texas; between 4,500 and 8,500 feet, usually in the transition between desert and higher, more humid forest. Also in the mountains of the Cape Region of southern Baja California.

Habit   A small evergreen tree with an irregularly shaped, open crown; young trees pyramidal in form; to 30 feet tall.

Inflorescence   Monoecious; pollen cones single or in groups of 2–5, ellipsoid, yellow.

Fruit   Seed cones globose, symmetrical, 1–1½ x 1–2 inches when open; lustrous reddish- to yellowish-brown, resinous; scales few, those in center of cone larger than those at either end, thick with thinner margins; apophysis pyramidal with a transverse keel; umbo slightly raised with a small, deciduous prickle; opening and falling in two years.

Twigs   Slender, grayish, rough.

Bark   Thin and smooth on young trees and upper stem and branches of older trees; dark brown and divided into irregularly shaped plates by deep furrows on lower trunk of older trees.

Leaves   Needles in bundles of 2–3, mostly 3, stiff, often curved, 1–3 x $1/16$ inches; stomata on both surfaces; usually dark green above, glaucous beneath; fascicle sheath $1/4$ inch long, shed early.

Notes   The seeds are edible and have formed a significant part of diets of numerous people living in the region. The species name *cembroides* means similar to *Pinus cembra*.

Locations   A single tree in Franceschi Park above the driveway to the house.

Needles of **Pinus cembroides** *in groups of two or three without an apparent fascicle sheath.*

Pinus coulteri
Coulter pine, big-cone pine

Found in the Coast Ranges of California from Mt. Diablo, east of San Francisco, to Santa Barbara County, then south through the mountains of Southern California to northernmost Baja California, at elevations of 1,000 to 7,500 feet.

Habit An evergreen tree with an open crown and spreading, downwardly curved branches; to 70 feet tall.

Inflorescence Monoecious; pollen cones ovoid to cylindrical, to 1 inch long, light purple-brown becoming orange-brown.

Fruit Seed cones largest and heaviest of all pines, up to 14 x 8 inches, may weigh as much as 4½ pounds, hanging on branches, mature cones have a unique pale yellow color; scales thick with massive, woody, light brown apophysis ending in a long, sharp, curved, forward-pointing spine.

Twigs Thick, rough, reddish-brown; scale leaves large, decurrent and persistent, lending a roughened appearance to the twig.

Bark Dark gray-brown with rough, irregular reddish-orange plates and ridges, and deep fissures.

Leaves Needles in bundles of 3, 6–12 inches long, stout, sharp-pointed, margins finely serrate, stand out stiffly from branches in curved whorls; stomata persistent in numerous fine lines on all 3 sides of needle; bundle sheath to 1½ inches long, pale brown, persistent.

Notes Within its range, Coulter pine naturally occurs in dry mountainous locations and appears to establish following fire. It is most common in transitional vegetation between chaparral or oak woodland and higher-elevation conifer forest. Of the pines planted in Santa Barbara, it is most closely related to *P. torreyana*. The species name *coulteri* honors Thomas Coulter (1793–1843), Irish botanist who collected in Mexico and California.

Locations A declining tree of moderate size on the corner of Bath Street and West Alamar Avenue. Smaller trees in the Santa Barbara Botanic Garden. Naturally occurring trees on La Cumbre Peak and the crest of the Santa Ynez Mountains behind Santa Barbara.

Large, stout needles of Pinus coulteri *with massive seed cone, the heaviest of the genus* Pinus. *The cones are semi-serotinous, opening gradually over a period of years.*

Pinus edulis
Two-needle pinyon pine, nut pine

Widely distributed in the southwestern United States (principally Arizona, Utah, Colorado, and New Mexico). Found in foothills and on mesas at elevations from 5,000 to 8,000 feet in the transition from desert to more humid locations at higher elevations.

Habit A small evergreen tree with a short trunk and a many-branched rounded compact crown; to 30 feet tall.

Inflorescence Monoecious; pollen cones ellipsoid, 1/4 inch long, yellowish- to reddish-brown.

Fruit Seed cones globose, symmetrical, 1–2 x 1 1/2–3 inches when open, orange to reddish-orange, resinous; on a very short peduncle (1/4 inch) that is deciduous with the cone; scales few, those in center of the cone larger and bearing seeds, thickened by broad, conical apophysis; umbo dorsal with a small, deciduous prickle.

Twigs Light gray, stout, rough.

Bark Thin and smooth on young trees and upper stems of mature trees; on lower stems of mature trees less than 1/2 inch thick, covered with thin, brownish-gray, scaly plates.

Leaves Needles mostly in fascicles of 2 (occasionally 1 or 3), incurved, thick, stiff, 1–2 inches long, dull-green; stomata on both surfaces; bundle sheaths thin, recurved and early deciduous.

Notes *P. edulis* has been considered to be a variety of *P. cembroides*. It is distinguished principally by having most needles in fascicles of two, instead of three, and by its geographic distribution centered in the southwestern United States, instead of northern Mexico. As in the other nut pines, the seeds are edible and have provided sustenance for wildlife and people. The species name *edulis* means edible.

Locations A tree in West Alameda Plaza. Another in the Pinyon-Juniper Woodland Section of the Santa Barbara Botanic Garden.

Top: Short, curved needles of **Pinus edulis** *in pairs, with no apparent fascicle sheath.*
Bottom: Short seed cone with few scales.

Pinus halepensis
Aleppo pine

Originating in the dry mountains surrounding the Mediterranean Sea and eastward into Azerbijan in western Asia, from sea level to an elevation of 5,500 feet.

Habit An evergreen tree, often with a divided trunk halfway up, with a densely branched dome-shaped or flat-topped crown, often directed away from the prevailing wind, branches more or less horizontal with twigs projecting up; to 100 feet tall.

Inflorescence Monoecious; pollen cones clustered at the ends of twigs.

Fruit Seed cones ovoid, 2–5 x 2–3 inches, pendulous, on a short stout pedicel; initially light brown, turning gray; scales with a transverse ridge; umbo gray, flattened, without a prickle; may be grouped in whorls of 2–3; persistent on the tree for many years after seed dispersal.

Twigs Smooth and gray-green; winter buds small with reflexed scales.

Bark Light to dark brown, with light brown grooves and narrow plates.

Leaves Needles in fascicles of 2 (sometimes 3), to 3$^{1}/_{2}$ inches long; thin and often twisted; fascicle sheath persistent, but fragile; thinly set on twigs; remaining up to 2 years, two-year-old needles may develop pale yellow bands.

Notes The occurrence of *P. halepensis* along the African coast of the Mediterranean is unique for the genus, and the species reaches its maximum elevation in Morocco. It is very drought resistant and is adapted to dry summers. It is one of the few pines, including *P. pinea*, whose seeds take three years to mature. The species name *halepensis* refers to the city of Aleppo, Syria.

Locations Common about town. Street trees on Pesetas Lane. Others in upper Orpet Park and MacKenzie Park.

Top: Full, but light, crown of Pinus halepensis. *Middle: Thin needles with a young seed cone. Bottom: Maturing seed cones with characteristic light brown color.*

Pinus jeffreyi
Jeffrey pine

Distributed throughout the higher mountains of California and extending into Oregon, Nevada, and Baja California, usually at elevations between 5,000 and 9,000 feet, but extending downward to much lower elevations on serpentine soils in the northern portion of its range.

Habit A potentially stately evergreen tree; to 90 feet tall.

Inflorescence Monoecious; pollen cones narrow cylindrical, 3/4–1 1/2 inches long, yellow to purple-brown.

Fruit Seed cones ovoid-conical, 6–12 inches long, light red-brown, nearly sessile; apophysis of the scale slightly raised, not keeled; umbo with a short reflexed prickle.

Twigs Stout, gray- to purple-brown, becoming roughened with age from persistent primary leaves; buds ovoid, 3/4–1 1/4 inches long, tan, not resinous, scales conspicuously fringed.

Bark Dark cinnamon-red, often tinged with purple on older trunks, typically deeply furrowed and narrow, broken into elongate plates, but highly variable.

Leaves Needles in bundles of 3, stout, 4–9 inches long, slightly twisted, usually gray-green, all surfaces with fine stomatal lines, persisting 4–6 years; fascicle sheath 1/2–1 inch long, persistent.

Notes *P. jeffreyi* is superficially similar to *P. ponderosa*. However, it has very different resin chemistry from the latter and is usually distinguished by its strong smell of vanilla from the fissures of the bark. It is usually found in higher-elevation forests, above the zone of *P. ponderosa*. The species name *jeffreyi* honors John Jeffrey (1826–1854), Scottish gardener at the Royal Botanical Garden, sent to British America in 1850 to complete the explorations of David Douglas.

Locations Young trees at the Santa Barbara Botanic Garden in the Ceanothus and Meadow View Sections.

Stout needles and large, compact cone of **Pinus jeffreyi**.

Pinus monophylla
Singleleaf pinyon pine

Broadly distributed in lower mountain and foothill regions of the southwestern United States, including California, Nevada, Utah, Arizona, and Idaho, and south into Baja California.

Habit A small evergreen tree, with a much-branched, rounded crown and foliage seemingly clustered at the ends of branches; to 40 feet tall.

Inflorescence Monoecious; pollen cones yellow, about 1/2 inch long.

Fruit Seed cones ovoid before opening, becoming almost globose when seed shed, 1 1/2–2 1/2 inches long, pale yellow-brown, nearly sessile; apophysis of scale thickened and slightly raised, with a strong transverse keel; umbo with a short, sharp, and flexible point; seeds disseminating in two years and cones dropping shortly after.

Twigs Stout, gray-brown; buds resinous, light orange-brown, 1/4 inch long, with thin scale margins.

Bark Red-brown, scaly, with irregular furrows and cross-checking.

Leaves Needles 1 per fascicle (rarely 2), ascending and often curved, 3/4–2 1/4 inches long, round or grooved; gray-green or blue-green, all surfaces with stomatal lines; fascicle sheath 1/4–1/2 inch long, shed early.

Notes *P. monophylla* is usually found on desert-facing slopes from 3,300 to 7,600 feet (to 9,500 feet in the White and Inyo Mountains of eastern California) in the transition between arid high desert and more moist montane forests. It hybridizes readily with *P. edulis* and *P. quadrifolia;* however, its range is generally to the west and north of *P. edulis.* It is the state tree of Nevada. The species name *monophylla* means single leaf. This is the only species in the genus *Pinus* characterized by single-needle fascicles.

Locations A single tree at the Santa Barbara Botanic Garden in the Manzanita Section.

Top: Single needles and large resinous buds of Pinus monophylla. *This is the only pine species characterized by single-needle fascicles.*
Bottom: *Seed cones with open, cup-like scales.*

Pinus muricata
Bishop pine

Occurring in isolated populations along the coast of California and into northern Baja California; also occurring on the Santa Barbara Channel Islands and south to Cedros Island.

Habit A short evergreen tree with a dome-shaped or irregular crown; less than 40 feet tall.

Inflorescence Monoecious; pollen cones densely produced along new growth below the foliage, ellipsoid, less than 1/4 inch long, orange.

Fruit Seed cones ovoid, 2–4 x 2 1/2–3 inches; held in whorls of 2–5 almost at right angles to the stem, almost parallel to it, or at intermediate angles; scales more strongly developed on the side opposite to the branch, giving a variably asymmetrical shape, shiny red-brown in the first year, becoming dull gray; umbo with a sharp, curved, 1/4-inch-long spine; sessile and persistent on branches; serotinous, may remain on the tree unopened for many years.

Twigs Somewhat stout, stiff, grayish-brown, initially rough from leaf bracts; winter buds large, 1 inch long, conical, pointed, and resinous.

Bark Dark gray with purplish-brown scales; wide, deep, vertical fissures creating long plates.

Leaves Needles in bundles of 2, 3–6 inches long, rigid, erect, margins finely serrate, dark green, in dense clusters at ends of twigs; bundle sheaths 1/2 inch long, becoming shorter with age until they appear almost deciduous.

Notes This species is highly variable and several varieties have been described, including *Pinus muricata* var. *remorata* (the Santa Cruz Island Pine). The species name *muricata* means pointed, full of sharp points.

Locations Santa Barbara Botanic Garden, along the Porter Trail, and in the Island and Arroyo Sections. One tree in the parking lot of Monroe School.

Dark, stout needles in bundles of two and asymmetric seed cones with enlarged, sharp-pointed scale tips of Pinus muricata.

Pinus pinea
Italian stone pine, umbrella pine

Occurring in coastal areas of the northern Mediterranean region from Spain to Cyprus and along the southern shore of the Black Sea.

Habit A picturesque evergreen tree, with a distinct umbrella-shaped crown formed by the branching pattern and prolific twigs, trunk frequently dividing into several stems at mid height; to 70 feet tall.

Inflorescence Monoecious; pollen cones yellow.

Fruit Seed cone 4 x 5 inches; apophysis shiny, pale brown, convex with 5 radial ribs; umbo distinct, without a prickle; cones usually solitary, remaining closed and attached to the branches for years.

Twigs Twisted, pale green to yellowish; winter buds light brown with reflexed and fringed scales, 1/2 inch long.

Bark Strikingly reddish-brown to orange, with deep gray furrows, forming large plates on larger trees.

Leaves Needles in bundles of 2, clustered at the ends of current twig growth, rigid, twisted, 5–6 inches long, dull green; fascicle sheath persistent, 1/8 inch long, dull gray.

Notes *P. pinea* is well-known for its nut production and has been cultivated for that purpose for over 6,000 years. Most of the world's supply of pine nuts is produced in Italy. The species name *pinea* means pine cone.

Locations Common about town. Street trees on East Anapamu Street between Milpas and Olive Streets were propagated by Dr. Franceschi and planted by Dr. Doremus in 1908. Those between Olive and Garden Streets were planted by Ralph Stevens in 1929. A large tree at the entrance to Cottage Hospital.

Top: Characteristic rounded crown and multiple trunks of Pinus pinea.
Middle: Dull green needles in bundles of two and somewhat flattened seed cones.
Bottom: Characteristic bark with flat, reddish-brown plates.

Pinus ponderosa
Ponderosa pine, western yellow pine

Broadly distributed in western North America from British Columbia to Southern California, through the Rocky Mountains into Mexico, and even extending east into the badlands of Nebraska and South Dakota.

Habit An evergreen tree, with a broadly cone-shaped to rounded crown on a straight bole; to 200 feet tall in its native habitat.

Inflorescence Monoecious; pollen cones yellow or red.

Fruit Seed cones generally ovoid, 2–6 inches long, dull to lustrous reddish-brown, nearly sessile; scales of closed cones set in steep spirals; apophysis raised, with a transverse keel; umbo with a prickle that curves outward when the cone is open.

Twigs Stout, orange-brown, becoming roughened with age from persistent primary leaves; buds ovoid, 1/3–3/4 inch, red-brown, very resinous, scales light brown.

Bark Yellow- to red-brown, broken into large elongate plates.

Leaves Needles generally in bundles of 3, stout, 3–10 inches long, slightly twisted, deep yellow-green, all surfaces with fine stomatal lines, persisting 3–6 years; fascicle sheath 1/2–1 1/4 inches long, persistent.

Notes *P. ponderosa* is highly variable; three varieties have been described, and additional geographic variants have been informally recognized. The northern and central Rocky Mountain populations are generally distinguished by needles in bundles of two. The species is the most economically important of the western pines and has a wood very similar to the white pines. The species name *ponderosa* means heavy.

Locations Trees at the Santa Barbara Botanic Garden in the Yellow Pine Forest and Meadow View Sections.

Top: Rounded crown of a young Pinus ponderosa.
Bottom left: Light tan mature seed cone, which is smaller, has fewer scales, and is less compact than the cone of P. jeffreyi.
Bottom right: Needles in bundles of three of P. ponderosa. *For comparison, a twig with needles of* P. jeffreyi *is shown on the right.*

Pinus quadrifolia
Parry pinyon pine, four-leaved pinyon pine

Known only from isolated locations in Southern California: the San Jacinto Mountains in Riverside County and near the Mexican border in the Cuyamaca Mountains of San Diego County; more common in the mountains of northern Baja California. Found on rocky sites between 4,000 and 6,000 feet.

Habit A small evergreen tree, with a many-branched stem and a dense rounded crown; to 30 feet tall.

Inflorescence Monoecious; pollen cones ovoid, yellow, about 1/2 inch long.

Fruit Seed cones ovoid before opening, becoming globose when open, 1 1/2–3 1/2 inches long, pale yellow-brown, mostly sessile; apophysis strongly thickened, raised, diamond-shaped and transversely keeled; umbo blunt, frequently exuding pitch; seeds disseminating after two years and cones dropping shortly thereafter.

Twigs Slender, pale orange-brown, with fine gladular hairs, becoming brown to gray-brown.

Bark Gray to red-brown, broken into irregular scaly plates.

Leaves Needles often 4 per fascicle, but commonly with 3 needles and occasionally with five-needled fascicles as well, 1 1/4–2 1/2 inches long, curved, stiff, green to blue-green, adaxial surface strongly whitened with stomatal bands; fascicle sheath 1/4 inch long, sheds early.

Notes *P. quadrifolia* is the rarest of the pinyon pines reaching the United States. It hybridizes readily with *P. monophylla,* and many of the trees in wild populations may contain genetic material from that species. The species name *quadrifolia* means four-leaved.

Locations Trees in the Meadow and Desert Sections of the Santa Barbara Botanic Garden. One by the original entrance steps from the parking lot to the meadow, planted in 1951.

Short, stiff needles in bundles of four and pitch-covered seed cone with very stout scales of Pinus quadrifolia.

Pinus radiata
Monterey pine

Naturally rare, occurring in three isolated populations along the coast south of San Francisco.

Habit An evergreen tree with one to several trunks and a wide rounded to flattened crown containing numerous stout horizontal branches; to 90 feet tall.

Inflorescence Monoecious; pollen cones ellipsoid to cylindrical, 1/2–2/3 inch long, orange-brown.

Fruit Seed cone ovoid, asymmetrical, 2–6 x 2–3 inches; shiny, light brown; scales with a transverse ridge, umbo flat and without a prickle, basal scales thickened and rounded on side away from the stem; usually borne in whorls of 4 or 5 and turned back along the stem.

Twigs Gray and densely set with needles; winter buds short, brown, very resinous.

Bark Rough, with deep fissures and thick, flat, vertical ridges; dark gray to black, or reddish-brown.

Leaves Needles in bundles of 3, 4–6 inches long, twisted, dark green with a persistent bundle sheath.

Notes During portions of the Pleistocene Epoch (11,000 to two million years ago), *P. radiata* was broadly spread throughout California, including the Santa Barbara area. Today its nearest natural occurrence is in Cambria in San Luis Obispo County. Because of its rapid growth rate, it has been planted extensively in forest plantations in the Southern Hemisphere, especially in New Zealand and Chile. The species, however, is particularly susceptible to several diseases, including pitch canker and Armillaria root rot. In the Santa Barbara area, many of the plantings of *P. radiata* have succumbed to these ailments, as have many trees in the wild populations. The species name *radiata* means radiating, in reference to the whorls of cones about the branches.

Locations Two trees in MacKenzie Park on the slope above the ball fields. Others at Oak Park, in the Douglas Family Preserve, and several at the University of California, Santa Barbara. Street trees on Cathedral Oaks Road between Stow Grove County Park and Los Carneros Road. Another on Cabrillo Boulevard at Corona del Mar.

Top: Dark, open crown of Pinus radiata.
Bottom left: Whorled clusters of recurved, moderately serotinous seed cones.
Bottom right: Needles in bundles of three and immature seed cones.

Pinus roxburghii
Chir pine, long-leaved Indian pine, *sula*

Found in the foothills and mountain slopes of the Himalayan Mountains from 1,300 to 7,500 feet.

Habit An evergreen tree with a straight, erect trunk and open crown, with many long, wide-spreading branches; to 130 feet tall.

Inflorescence Monoecious; male cones persistent on the twigs below clustered needles.

Fruit Seed cone ovoid to oval, 4–6 inches long, shiny gray-brown or nut-brown; scales with thick, woody, and reflexed apophyses; umbo small, without a prickle; borne singly or in pairs on very short peduncles; either hanging or extending laterally from the branch.

Twigs Pale gray or light brown, covered with bract-like primary leaves which remain for several years; winter buds small, with no resin.

Bark Dark, gray-brown, with scaly plates; fissures showing orange beneath.

Leaves Needles in bundles of 3, 8–12 inches long, clustered near the ends of the twigs, flexible, yellow-green, persisting for 1–3 years; bundle sheaths long, 1 inch or more.

Notes Chir pine is closely related to *P. canariensis* from the Canary Islands, yet the two species are separated by over 6,000 miles. They differ primarily in the cones, which do not have reflexed apophyses in *P. canariensis*. *P. roxburghii* also appears to have a broader crown and more yellow-green foliage. It is believed that the close relationship of these two species results from the more or less continuous distribution of their common ancestor along the shores of the Tethys Sea, a truly "mediterranean sea," which was continuous (or almost so) from the Atlantic to the Indian Ocean, separating Africa from Eurasia, from about 90 to 10 million years ago. As the Tethys Sea closed and the climate dried, the pines became restricted to the relatively moist western and eastern ends of the former seaway. Most of the differences between modern *Pinus canariensis* and *P. roxburghii* may have evolved since their geographic separation. The species name *roxburghii* honors William Roxburgh (1751–1815), Scottish doctor and Superintendent of the Royal Botanic Garden at Calcutta (1793–1814).

Top: Somewhat rounded crown with yellow-green foliage of Pinus roxburghii.
Bottom left: Dense clusters of pollen cones with yellow-green needles in bundles of three.
Bottom right: Seed cones with stout reflexed apophyses.

Locations Trees in MacKenzie Park and Franceschi Park east of the cottage. Street trees in the 1500–1600 blocks of De la Vina Street.

Pinus sabiniana
Gray pine, foothill pine

Found in the dry foothills and mountains surrounding the Sacramento-San Joaquin Valley of Central California, at elevations of 500 to 6,000 feet. Extending west almost to the coast in the Santa Lucia Mountains near Big Sur and south to northern Santa Barbara and Los Angeles Counties

Habit A medium-sized evergreen tree, with a very open, often repeatedly-forked crown and ascending branches; to 75 feet tall.

Inflorescence Monoecious; pollen cones 1/2–2/3 inch long, yellow.

Fruit Seed cones massive, heavy, ovoid, 6–10 inches long, dull red-brown, resinous; apophysis elongated and curved, continuous with the umbo into a long upcurved claw; shedding seed in the second year, but remaining on the tree for up to seven years.

Twigs Slender, pale purple-brown and glaucous, becoming gray, rough.

Bark Irregularly furrowed into rectangular or blocky plates; dark brown to nearly black, inner bark orangish.

Leaves Needles in fascicles of 3, 6–12 inches long, relatively slender for their length, often drooping, stout, dull blue-green, with pale stomatal lines on all surfaces, persisting 3–4 years; sheath one inch long, persistent.

Notes The large seeds of *P. sabiniana* were an important food source for Native Americans living within its range. However, an earlier common name, digger pine, was a pejorative reference to these early inhabitants who also dug roots for food. The species name *sabiniana* honors Joseph Sabine (1770–1837), English barrister and horticulturist, founder of the Transactions of the Royal Horticultural Society.

Locations Several trees at the Santa Barbara Botanic Garden.

Top: Open crown with several stems of **Pinus sabiniana**.
Bottom left: Drooping blue-green needles in bundles of three, with terminal pollen cones.
Bottom right: Massive seed cones with stout, curved apophyses.

Pinus thunbergii
Japanese black pine, *kuro-matsu*

Occuring in the coastal regions of southern Japan and South Korea, from sea level to 3,200 feet.

Habit A small evergreen tree, often with the look of a an overgrown bonsai; to 30 feet tall.

Inflorescence Monoecious; pollen cones 1/4–1/3 inch long, yellow.

Fruit Seed cones small; may occur singly or in groups of 2–20 to a shoot; brownish-gray; base flattened when mature; apophysis of scales with a transverse keel; umbo armed with a minute prickle.

Twigs Light brown; containing many bracts which are deciduous after 3–4 years; winter buds 2/3 inch long, with pointed apex and tight gray scales with white fringes.

Bark Dark gray or purplish-gray, with deep vertical fissures; outer layers scaly and peeling.

Leaves Needles in fascicles of 2, rigid, dark green, somewhat twisted and densely set on twigs, 3–5 inches long; basal sheath 2/3 inch long.

Notes Similar to the relationship between *P. canariensis* and *P. roxburghii*, *P. thunbergii* is closely related to *P. nigra*, the European black pine. Although growing to only a short stature here, in Japan *P. thunbergii* can be a very tall tree with a massive trunk, frequently divided into several stems in the dense, wide crown. The species name *thunbergii* honors Carl Peter Thunberg (1743–1828), Swedish botanist and student of Linnaeus who collected in South Africa and Japan.

Locations A tree in the east end of MacKenzie Park.

Dense, dark needles and small seed cones of Pinus thunbergii.

Pinus torreyana
Torrey pine, Del Mar pine, Soledad pine

Native to only two isolated populations: Del Mar in coastal San Diego County and on Santa Rosa Island off the coast of Santa Barbara.

Habit An evergreen tree, with a crooked, branched trunk and an irregular but somewhat rounded crown; to 100 feet tall.

Inflorescence Monoecious; pollen cones yellowish, about 1 inch long, in dense masses on the ends of twigs.

Fruit Seed cones ovoid to globose, 4–6 inches long, borne on an elongate stalk; scales woody, thickened; apophysis strongly developed, with five converging keels and a short curved tip, maturing in the third year.

Twigs Stout, with persistent primary leaves, light green becoming purplish-brown; needles clustered in tufts at the ends of twigs; terminal cluster of winter buds 1 inch long.

Bark Dark gray, flaking to show a reddish-brown undercoat, shallowly grooved, becoming scaly in older trees.

Leaves Needles in fascicles of 5, rigid, gray-green to dark green, 7–11 inches long; with many rows of stomata on all surfaces; basal sheaths up to 1 inch long, persistent.

Notes Two subspecies of *Pinus torreyana* have been recognized: subspecies *torreyana* from San Diego County with dark green needles and fully-opened seed cones that are longer than wide, and subspecies *insularis* from Santa Rosa Island with gray-green needles and seed cones wider than long. Although Torrey pine is extremely rare in nature, it does very well in cultivation and is being perpetuated in the street and park tree plantings of cities throughout California, and in New Zealand as well. The largest known specimen is the "Ward Holme Torrey Pine" on Carpinteria Avenue, Carpinteria, which was planted in 1890 and stands over 100 feet tall. The species name *torreyana* honors Dr. John Torrey (1796–1873), who co-wrote the first Flora of North America with Asa Gray.

Locations A large tree on Quinto Street at Alamar Avenue. Several large trees were planted at the west end of Oak Park by Dr. A. B. Doremus around 1910. Others in Shoreline Park, at the University of California, Santa Barbara, especially near the campus beach, and at the Santa Barbara Botanic Garden. The trees at the Botanic Garden are subspecies *insularis*. All others noted are probably subspecies *torreyana*.

Top: Open and rounded crown of Pinus torreyana *subsp.* torreyana, *which is found on the mainland.*
Middle: Elongate mainland form (left) and squat island form (right) of seed cones.
Bottom: Gray-green needles in clusters of five in P. torreyana *subsp.* insularis.

Pseudotsuga

Pseudotsuga is a genus of four species—two from North America and two from Asia. Its name alludes to its similarity to hemlock (*Tsuga*).

Pseudotsuga macrocarpa
Bigcone spruce, bigcone Douglas-fir

Native in the mountains of Southern California from Santa Barbara County to San Diego County, at elevations from 1,500 to 6,500 feet. Most of the altitudinal range of this species lies below the main conifer belt, where it occupies steep, shaded north-facing slopes and cool, moist draws.

Habit A medium-sized to large evergreen tree with long, irregularly spreading branches; to 120 feet tall.

Inflorescence Monoecious; male cones axillary, 3/4–1 inch long.

Fruit Seed cones the largest of the genus, narrowly ovoid, 3 1/2–7 x 2–2 1/2 inches, light brown; scales numerous, thick, finely ridged, to 1 inch wide; bracts only slightly exserted.

Twigs Reddish-brown, becoming grayish.

Bark Deep, dark brownish-gray, thick, deeply divided into broad ridges.

Leaves Needles two-ranked on the twig; flattened, blue-green or blue-gray, 1–1 3/4 inches, usually pointed, upper surface with a slight furrow; lower surface gray-white, with several lines of stomata; attached by a short stalk.

Notes The geographically restricted *P. macrocarpa* replaces Douglas-fir in the Coast Ranges of Southern California beginning in Santa Barbara County. It can be seen in its native habitat on the northeast side of Figueroa Mountain. The species name *macrocarpa* means large fruit.

Locations Trees at the Santa Barbara Botanic Garden and in the 2000 block of Gillespie Street.

Top: Open crown of Pseudotsuga macrocarpa *with distinct sweeping branches.*
Bottom: Resinous seed cones with short, three-pointed bracts and flattened needles.

Pseudotsuga menziesii
Douglas-fir

Broadly distributed in western North America from British Columbia to the Coast Ranges and Sierra Nevada Mountains of Central California and through the Rocky Mountains into Mexico.

Habit A large evergreen tree with drooping limbs; to 220 feet tall in its native habitat.

Inflorescence Monoecious; male cones axillary, yellow-red, 3/4–1 inch long.

Fruit Seed cones the largest of the genus, narrowly ovoid, 1 2/3–4 x 1–1 1/2 inches, light brown; scales numerous, finely ridged, to 3/4 inch wide; three-lobed bracts prominently exserted between the scales.

Twigs Slender, pubescent, becoming glabrous, buds shiny light brown and pointed.

Bark Gray and scaly, becoming deeply furrowed on large old trees.

Leaves Needles two-ranked on the twig; flattened, yellow-green to dark- or bluish-green, 1–1 3/4 inches, apex pointed or rounded, upper surface with a slight furrow; lower surface gray-white, with several lines of stomata; attached by a short stalk.

Notes Douglas-fir has historically been a significant timber tree and among its many uses it has provided framing for much of the housing in Santa Barbara. Although the species has not done particularly well in Santa Barbara, planting in cool protected locations should be successful. The species name *menziesii* honors Archibald Menzies (1754–1842), Scottish surgeon and botanist who collected plants of the Pacific region with the Vancouver expedition.

Locations A small tree that regularly bears cones can be found in the Santa Barbara Botanic Garden near the Blakesly Boulder.

Rounded needles of Pseudotsuga menziesii *and seed cones with elongate three-pointed bracts.*

Podocarpaceae

The Podocarpus Family is made up of 18 genera and 168 species primarily from the Southern Hemisphere with some representatives as far north as southern Mexico, Japan, and the mountains of equatorial Africa. The family includes important timber trees of Australasia.

Afrocarpus
Podocarpus

Afrocarpus is a genus of three species found primarily in tropical and South Africa. It has recently been separated from *Podocarpus* and is distinguished by seed-bearing structures that do not sit on a stalk or peduncle, and opposite and decussate leaves that alternate in pairs at right angles. The name reflects its geographic isolation in Africa and retains the structure of *Podocarpus* from which the genus was separated.

Afrocarpus gracilior
Podocarpus gracilior

East African yellow wood, African fern pine

Native to the higher-elevation dry forests, between 4,000 and 9,000 feet, of eastern equatorial Africa (Ethiopia, Uganda, Kenya).

Habit An evergreen tree with a cylindrical bole, but considerably branched from low on the stem when open-grown; to 100 feet.

Inflorescence Monoecious; pollen-bearing cone axillary, solitary or 2–3 together, catkin-like, 1 inch long, pinkish-purple.

Fruit Seed-bearing structures solitary, axillary, without a fleshy receptacle; fleshy and yellow while still immature, becoming green to purplish with a glaucous bloom; ovoid, 1/2–1 x 1/2–3/4 inch; hard, woody.

Twigs Green, thin, angular.

Bark Thin, pale to dark gray; broken vertically and horizontally into small rectangular scales.

Leaves Opposite, simple, with alternating pairs at right angles, clustered towards the ends of green twigs; linear to linear-oblong, 2–3 x 1/4 inches long; leathery, dark gray-green.

Notes The wood is considered to be much superior to that of European pines, to which it has been compared. This is one of the few conifers native to the African continent. This

Top: Rounded, textured crown of Afrocarpus gracilior. *Bottom: Yellow, flesh-coated seed and twigs with narrow, flattened leaves.*

species has been sold horticulturally as *Podocarpus elongatus*. The trees in Alameda Plaza were planted in 1910 from seed obtained from Africa and were among the first in California—and certainly the first in Santa Barbara. The species name *gracilior* means slender, thin.

Locations Common about town. Trees in East and West Alameda Plaza. Street trees on Hitchcock Way, in the 3000 block of De la Vina Street, the first–100 blocks of East Valerio Street, the 200–500 blocks of East Ortega Street, and the 900–1100 blocks of Milpas Street.

Podocarpus
Yellow wood

Podocarpus consists of about 100 species of evergreen shrubs and trees, including an epiphytic shrub, widely distributed through the temperate zone of the Southern Hemisphere and mountainous regions of tropical and subtropical zones. It extends north to the West Indies and Japan. As a gymnosperm it does not have true flowers, the pollen being borne in a catkin-like structure. The light green seeds develop on a dark red or purple, usually fleshy, stem (improperly termed a receptacle) formed from an infertile basal bract and are covered by a fleshy epimatium derived from the ovule-bearing scales. The genus includes some valuable timber species, and the seeds are attractive to birds and monkeys. The name combines the Greek *podos* (foot) and *karpos* (seed), referring to the fleshy stalk on which the seed are borne.

Podocarpus henkelii
Long-leaved yellow wood, Henkel's yellow wood

Found in mountain forests of the Natal and Eastern Cape Provinces of South Africa.

Habit An evergreen tree with a very dense crown; to 100 feet tall in its native habitat.

Inflorescence Dioecious; male cones solitary or in groups up to 5, pinkish, 4/5–1 3/4 inches long.

Fruit Seed solitary or in pairs, covered by a fleshy, glaucous green epimatium, globose, 1/3 inch across, borne on a fleshy glaucous green receptacle.

Twigs First year growth light green, ridged, becoming reddish-brown in fourth year.

Bark Light reddish-gray, with vertical furrows, peeling in strips.

Leaves Spirally arranged and distinctly pendulous; linear, 3 1/2–5 x 1/4–1/3 inches, midrib prominent below, glossy deep green with stomatal lines visible below; petiole very short, 1/8 inch.

Notes *P. henkelii* is an important timber tree in South Africa. The species name *henkelii* honors Dr. J. S. Henkel (1871-1962), a botanist with the South African Forestry Department and later Director of Forestry in Zimbabwe, who first recognized *P. henkelii* as a distinct species.

Locations Young trees in East Alameda Plaza.

Top: Dense, yellow-green crown of Podocarpus henkelii.
Bottom left: Drooping, elongate leaves.
Bottom right: Immature glaucous seed on a fleshy receptacle.

Podocarpus macrophyllus
Yew podocarpus, yew pine, Japanese podoberry

Native to high elevation forests of China and Japan, 8,000-10,000 feet.

Habit An evergreen tree with multiple ascending branches; to 50 feet tall.

Inflorescence Dioecious; axillary; pollen cones in bundles of 3–5 on short peduncles, with several triangular bracts at the base.

Fruit Seed solitary on a short peduncle with few basal bracts; green seed enclosed in a fleshy, purplish-black epimatium containing a white powder.

Twigs Angled, green, becoming tan.

Bark Light gray or grayish-brown, fibrous, peeling off in thin flakes.

Leaves Alternate or spirally arranged, simple; linear-lanceolate to oblong-oblanceolate, slightly curved, $2/3$–5 x $1/16$–$3/8$ inches; dark green, glossy above, paler beneath; midrib prominently raised above, slightly so beneath; sessile.

Notes The species name *macrophyllus* means large-leaved.

Locations Several street trees on San Julian Avenue.

Top: *Dense, compact crown of* Podocarpus macrophyllus.
Middle: *Spike-like clusters of pollen cones and foliage with glaucous undersurface.*
Bottom: *Glaucous, flesh-covered seed on a fleshy receptacle.*

Podocarpus totara
Totara

Widely distributed throughout New Zealand.

Habit An evergreen tree with a massive, symmetrical trunk and a dense crown; to 60 feet tall.

Inflorescence Axillary; pollen-bearing cones in groups of 1–3, $1/2$–$3/4$ inch long, on short stalks.

Fruit Seed cones grouped 1–2, on short, swollen stalks; seed borne on a fleshy crimson epimatium.

Bark Gray-brown, fibrous, thick, deeply furrowed and peeling in vertical flakes leaving a reddish-brown undertone.

Twigs Dull yellow-green, becoming gray.

Leaves Alternate, simple, dense on the twig; linear-lanceolate, $2/5$–$4/5$ x $1/8$–$1/6$ inch on older trees, somewhat larger on juvenile trees, stiff, leathery, prickly at the apex, dark green or brownish on young plants, midrib prominent beneath.

Notes The red wood of *P. totara* is one of the most important timbers of New Zealand. It is used for general building purposes as well as construction of fine furniture. In its native habitat, this species grows to great age. Trees 800 years old are common and one individual has been estimated to be 1,800 years of age. The species name *totara* is a native Maori name.

Locations A tree in East Alameda Plaza. Others in the parking lot of the County Administration Building on Victoria and Santa Barbara Streets.

Top: A small tree of **Podocarpus totara** *in East Alameda Plaza.*
Bottom: Short leaves and green flesh-covered seed sitting on a red fleshy epimatium.

Taxaceae

The Yew Family is represented in temperate zones of both the Northern and Southern Hemispheres. Its four genera and 16 species produce individual seeds that are surrounded by a conspicuous fleshy aril which aids in dispersal by birds.

Taxus

Taxus is a genus of seven species from the North Temperate Zone and extending into Mexico and central Malaysia. Its name is the classical Latin for the tree.

Taxus baccata
English yew

Widespread in Europe and extending to the Middle East (Iran) and northern Africa (Algeria).

Habit A densely branched tree or shrub with a dense crown; to 40 feet tall.

Inflorescence Usually dioecious; male cones axillary on undersides of twigs from the previous year, on short stalks, round; female cones terminal or in the axils of the uppermost leaves, solitary, green.

Fruit Seed encased in a hard bony shell which is carried in a scarlet fleshy aril or cup.

Twigs Ridged by decurrent bases of leaves; light green, reddish-brown in 2nd and 3rd years, becoming gray-brown.

Bark Thin, scaly, reddish-brown to gray-brown.

Leaves Usually appearing somewhat two-ranked, but nearly whorled on erect shoots; linear, flattened, apex spine-tipped and curved, $1/2–1 \times 1/12–1/10$ inch; shiny dark green with 2 broad pale green stripes below; persisting for 8 years.

Notes *T. baccata* is one of only three conifers which naturally occur in the British Isles. It has been the source of numerous cultivars including a compact columnar form, *T. baccata* var. *fastigiata,* which is grown in Santa Barbara. The leaves and twigs are known to contain alkaloids toxic to cattle; however, the red fleshy fruit cup is not poisonous. Extracts from *T. baccata* are now being used in the synthetic production of taxol for treatment of ovarian cancer. The previous source was strictly extracts of taxol from *T. brevifolia*. However, six trees are required to obtain a single dose, which threatens the future of this relatively rare species. The species name *baccata* means berry-like, referring to the pulpy aril enclosing the seed.

Locations A single tree in East Alameda Plaza, near the corner of Micheltorena and Santa Barbara Streets. Another in the inner courtyard of the Arts Building at the University of California, Santa Barbara.

Top: Dense crown of Taxus baccata.
Bottom: Curved, spine-tipped needles and seed enclosed in a fleshy red cup.

Torreya

Torreya is a genus of five species from North America and eastern Asia. The genus is named in honor of Dr. John Torrey (1796–1873), who co-wrote the first Flora of North America with Asa Gray.

Torreya californica
California nutmeg

Found in Northern and Central California along streams and among rock outcrops in the Coast Ranges and the Sierra Nevada, at elevations from near sea level to about 6,000 feet. Fairly common near the western borders of Yosemite and Kings Canyon National Parks.

Habit A small evergreen tree or shrub with a conical crown; to 50 feet tall.

Inflorescence Dioecious; pollen cones axillary on shoots of the previous year.

Fruit Seed ovate or oblong, 1–1 3/4 inches long, light green and purple-striped or spotted when ripe, pulp thin and woody, seed coat deeply wrinkled to appear like a nutmeg.

Twigs Green, turning red-brown in the second year; buds ovate, acute, to 1/3 inch long, with overlapping stiff brown scales.

Bark Alternate; thin, light gray-brown, faintly fissured into long narrow ridges.

Leaves Linear, thick, rigid, narrowing to a hard spiny point, 1 1/4–3 x 1/4 inches; dark green above, lighter green with two whitish lines of stomata below; strongly aromatic when crushed.

Notes The species name *californica* means from California.

Locations Santa Barbara Botanic Garden in the Redwood Section.

Spine-tipped, two-ranked leaves and immature seed of Torreya californica.

ANGIOSPERMS
Aceraceae

The Maple Family consists of two genera and 113 species, all but two of which are contained in the genus *Acer*. While the family is best known for its sugary sap, several taxa often contain milky sap. It is primarily a family of the North Temperate Zone and exhibits its greatest diversity in China.

Acer
Maples

The genus *Acer* includes 111 species from the North Temperate Zone and tropical mountains, with principal distribution centers in North America and China. Several species from North America have closely related taxa in the Orient. Interestingly, these species pairs frequently share similarly related phytophagous insects. Fossil evidence indicates that in warmer climates during the Miocene Epoch (23.8 to 5.3 million years before present) the genus was circumpolar, occurring in Alaska, Greenland, and Iceland. Subsequent cooling resulted in geographic separation and isolation of these closely related species.

The genus is distinguished by its opposite branching pattern, frequently palmate leaf structure (although sometimes entire or pinnately compound) and its fruit consisting of paired, long-winged samaras. Because of its frequently unique coloration (especially during leaf fall) and graceful form, species of the genus have been the subject of intense horticultural selection, particularly in the Orient. *Acer* was the original Latin name for the maple tree.

Acer macrophyllum
Bigleaf maple, Oregon maple

Broadly distributed in moist habitats in the coastal mountain ranges, the Cascade Range, and the Sierra Nevada of western North America, from southern Alaska to Southern California, usually below 5,000 feet in elevation.

Habit A broad-crowned deciduous tree; to 40 feet in height (although much taller in native habitats further north).

Inflorescence A many-flowered drooping raceme, 4–6 inches long, appearing before the leaves; flowers yellowish-green, to $1/2$ inch across. Blooms March to April.

Top: Opposite leaves and pendulous fruit clusters of Acer macrophyllum.
Bottom left: Flowering raceme.
Bottom right: Large paired samaras of fruit. The "wings" aid in seed dispersal.

Fruit Samaras in drooping clusters; wings slightly divergent, about $1-1 1/2$ inches long; seedcase swollen, distinctly hairy.

Twigs Light green, becoming splotched with purple in the second year, ultimately gray; terminal buds round, $1/4$ inch long.

Bark Gray to blackish-gray, furrowed with narrow, flat, vertical ridges.

Leaves Opposite, simple; very large, 6–12 inches across; with deep and narrow sinuses between five lobes, the central lobe narrowing towards the base; upper surface shiny dark-green, paler beneath, turning bright yellow or orange then light brown in autumn; petiole to 6 inches long, exuding a milky sap when broken.

Notes *A. macrophyllum* was first observed and collected by Meriweather Lewis on the Corps of Discovery expedition in 1806. It is the only tree-size maple native to the Pacific Coast. The species name *macrophyllum* means big leaf.

Locations Trees in the Santa Barbara Botanic Garden near Mission Creek. Native in moist canyons throughout Santa Barbara County.

Acer negundo
Box-elder, ashleaf maple, Manitoba maple

Widespread across temperate North America and represented by several varieties from the Atlantic seaboard to the Great Plains of the United States, extending into the lower provinces of central Canada as well as the southwestern United States, including much of California. Usually limited to riparian habitats, especially in the relatively dry western portion of its range.

Habit A broad-crowned deciduous tree, often branching within 10 feet of the ground; to 40 feet tall.

Inflorescence Dioecious; pollen flowers borne individually on long slender stalks clustered in the axils of leaves; seed flowers borne on loose racemes. Blooms February to March.

Fruit Wings of the samara broad, 1–1½ inches long, the outer margins incurved; seedcase elongated, often without mature seed; frequently remaining in dense clusters on the tree into the dormant season.

Twigs Stout, smooth, shiny greenish-purple or brown; terminal buds ovoid, ¼–⅓ inch long, with 2–3 pairs of lightly hairy scales; lateral buds of similar size, tightly appressed to the twig and located within the base of the V-shaped leaf base.

Bark Smooth, light gray when young; becoming shallowly furrowed into narrow stout ridges when older.

Leaves Opposite, pinnately compound with 3–9 leaflets; leaflets ¾–2 inches long, shallowly toothed or lobed; light green above, grayish-green beneath, yellow in autumn.

Notes This species is one of the few maples having compound leaves. Disjunct populations of *A. negundo* var. *californicum* are found scattered in California (including Santa Barbara County), typically in riparian habitats, and are characterized by no more than five sometimes deeply cut leaflets, the undersides of which are densely hairy, as are the twigs and petioles. The species name *negundo* is a Malayan name for *Vitex negundo* and was applied to *A. negundo* because of the resemblance of the leaves.

Locations Trees of *Acer negundo* var. *negundo* in the 1800 block of Robbins Street. *A. negundo* var. *californicum* at the Santa Barbara Botanic Garden near the pond and in Bohnett Park near the creek.

Pinnately compound leaves and fruit clusters of Acer negundo. *The paired samaras have narrower wings and are less spreading than those of* A. macrophyllum.

Acer oblongum
Oblong maple, flying moth tree

Located on acid soils in the mountainous Himalayan regions of Nepal, Kashmir, and western China at elevations from 2,000 to 6,500 feet.

Habit A slow-growing medium-sized tree, often evergreen; to 25 feet tall.

Inflorescence Terminal pubescent clusters of yellow-green flowers appearing with the leaves. Blooms December to January.

Fruit Samara, wings widely divergent, almost opposite, 1 inch long; nutlets hard, angular.

Twigs Initially dull green with scattered brown lenticels; becoming stout, dull gray.

Bark Gray-brown becoming light gray, peeling off in irregular plates on larger stems.

Leaves Opposite, simple; ovate-lanceolate, without lobes, apex acuminate, 2–5 x 1 1/2–2 1/2 inches; leathery, dark green above, glaucous beneath, with 3 primary veins from the base; margins entire or slightly and irregularly scalloped.

Notes *A. oblongum* was first introduced to Great Britain in 1824. It is used today as a street tree in southeastern China, Hong Kong, and San Diego. Although it originates from mountainous regions, it has a reputation in cultivation for tenderness. The species is highly variable and some tendency towards lobing of the leaves may be observed. The species name *oblongum* means oblong.

Locations Street trees in the 2000 and 2200 blocks of Santa Barbara Street, the 300 block of East Micheltorena Street, and Vista de la Cumbre adjacent to Peabody School.

Top: Compact crown of Acer oblongum.
Bottom: Unlobed leaves (unusual, but not rare in Acer*) and fruit clusters.*

Acer palmatum
Japanese maple

Widespread in mountainous regions of Japan, Korea, Taiwan, and eastern China.

Habit A small deciduous tree with an open lacy crown; 10–20 feet tall.

Inflorescence Small terminal clusters of small flowers with red-purple sepals and pinkish-white petals. Blooms in April.

Fruit Wings divergent, 1/2 inch long (although longer and deeply colored in some cultivars).

Twigs Thin, reddish-brown, becoming dull green, stout; buds small, red, pointed.

Bark Green to gray brown with light gray blotches (although variable in many cultivars), somewhat vertically striped from very shallow fissures.

Leaves Opposite, simple; 2–4 inches; with 5 to 7 (usually 5) palmate lobes and very deep sinuses, the basal pair of lobes usually directly opposed to each other; margins doubly serrate; color highly selected and variable among cultivars; petiole 3/4–2 inches long.

Notes *A. palmatum* and its many varieties are perhaps the most widely planted maples in the world. Because of the centuries of selection by Oriental horticulturists, there has been considerable confusion over the taxonomy of the species and its cultivars. Although usually considered a small tree or shrub, some very large individuals are found in gardens of Japan, Europe, and North America. The species is sometimes confused in the nursery trade with *A. japonicum,* whose sinuses extend less than halfway to the base of the leaf, and petals, like the sepals, are purple-red. The species name *palmatum* means palm-shaped.

Locations Several trees in Alice Keck Park Memorial Gardens adjacent to Garden Street. Street trees in the 1300 block of Castillo Street.

Top: Compact crown of Acer palmatum.
Middle: Young leaves and pinkish-white petals of flowers.
Bottom: Colorful fall leaves. A. palmatum, *along with* Liquidambar styraciflua *and* Pistacia chinensis, *is among the few non-native deciduous species to develop its potential for fall color in Santa Barbara's mild climate.*

Acer paxii
Evergreen maple

Found in mountain forests of southwestern China.

Habit A medium-sized evergreen tree with a rounded crown; to 45 feet tall.

Inflorescence Drooping tassel-like clusters of numerous small whitish flowers. Flowers in spring.

Fruit Samara, wings widely divergent, 1 inch long; nutlets spherical.

Twigs Of two types, short or up to 2½ feet long; initially green with numerous lenticels, flattened, becoming reddish-brown with many fine lenticels.

Bark Smooth, grayish-brown with light gray blotches, becoming furrowed and peeling in small flakes on lower trunks.

Leaves Opposite, simple; usually distinctly three-lobed, 1–2½ inches across; lobes triangular and pointing forward, the blade often pendulous on vigorous trees; base round; light to dark green above, glaucous beneath, margins entire or with small sparse teeth; petiole 1–2½ inches long.

Notes This species was named *A. buergerianum* in the previous edition of *Trees of Santa Barbara*, but it is readily distinguished from the latter by its evergreen leathery leaves. The species name *paxii* honors F. Pax (1858–1942), *Acer* taxonomist.

Locations Trees on La Cadena Street and Sutton Avenue.

Top: Rounded crown of Acer paxii.
Bottom: Leaves lacking lobes, with two lobes, or, most commonly, with three forward-pointing lobes.

Acer rubrum
Red maple

Broadly distributed throughout eastern North America, extending west to the Great Plains.

Habit A deciduous tree with an open crown; usually less than 50 feet tall in cultivation.

Inflorescence Monoecious; flowers appearing before the leaves in dense clusters, male flowers yellowish, female flowers deep red. Blooms February to March.

Fruit Samaras about 1 inch long, the outer margins held at a 60-degree angle and incurved, maturing and shedding early in the summer.

Twigs Shiny red to grayish-brown, often with short spur shoots which bear clusters of round red flower buds.

Bark Smooth and dull gray on branches and younger stems, becoming fissured into loosely attached scaly ridges on larger trees.

Leaves Opposite; 2–5 inches long with 3–5 palmate lobes, central lobe with angled sides, margins with irregular teeth, upper surface light green, lower surface whitened, turning brilliant orange or red in the fall; petiole 2–3$^1/_2$ inches, usually red.

Notes In its native range, red maple seems to occupy two different habitats: acidic bogs and wetlands, and extremely dry and acidic ridge tops. Habitats that are nutrient-rich are often occupied by sugar maple *(Acer saccharum)*. The species name *rubrum* means red.

Locations A single tree in the 400 block of Stanley Drive.

Leaves of Acer rubrum *with three to five lobes and irregularly serrate margins.*

Acer saccharinum
Silver maple, water maple

Widely distributed in the United States east of the Rocky Mountains.

Habit A fast-growing deciduous tree, the trunk frequently dividing into several near vertical stems creating an open crown; reaching 60 feet or more.

Inflorescence Monoecious; on short stalks; flowers appearing in late winter well before leaf break; male flowers with many elongate filaments which vary among trees between either red or yellow-white and provide all of the color; female flowers with extended red stigmas. Blooms February to March.

Fruit Wings of the samara 1 1/2–3 inches long, papery thin, the margins at a 90-degree angle; seedcase ribbed; green, turning yellowish-cream at maturity; often only one of the two seeds matures.

Twigs Reddish-brown, lustrous, dotted with minute lenticels, giving a strong, unpleasant odor when bruised; buds round, dark red, with 2–4 pairs of visible scales.

Bark Smooth, battleship gray when young; becoming dark reddish-brown and breaking into long narrow flakes, giving a rough, shaggy appearance.

Leaves Opposite, simple; with 5–7 lobes, 6–8 inches long, very thin and decomposing quickly; widest immediately above the base, the central lobe narrowing to the center of the leaf and separated from the lateral lobes by deep narrow notches; light green above, grayish-green beneath, turning yellow in autumn.

Notes The trunks of silver maple often become hollow providing sites for cavity-nesting and denning animals; however, the wood is quite brittle and this leads to considerable damage in high winds. The species name *saccharinum* means sugary, but this species should not be confused with the well-known sugar maple *(Acer saccharum)*, not found on Santa Barbara's streets and parks.

Locations Trees in the 300 block of East Pedregosa Street and the 700 block of West Pedregosa Street. Another in the 700 block of Chino Street. Several nice street trees in the 5000 block of Ella Lane in Goleta.

Top: Deeply lobed leaves of Acer saccharinum *with grayish-green lower surface.*
Bottom: Female flowers with barely emerging samara wings.

Anacardiaceae

The Cashew Family includes 78 genera and over 700 species and is typically found in moist to dry lowlands, mostly in the warmer parts of the world. While occurring in cool temperate zones, it does not extend into the severely cold environments found in the boreal zone or at high elevation. The sap of its species is variously clear, sticky, or milky, and is often poisonous.

Harpephyllum

Harpephyllum is a genus composed of a single species in southern Africa. Its name is derived from the Greek words for sickle *(harpe)* and leaf *(phyllon)* and refers to the shape of the leaflets.

Harpephyllum caffrum
South African wild plum

Native to the coastal forests of eastern South Africa, extending north to Zimbabwe and Mozambique. Usually found in the moist soils of river flood plains.

Habit An evergreen tree with a dense, rounded crown; to 40 feet tall.

Inflorescence Dioecious; axillary panicles; flowers in 4–5 parts, small, white. Blooms in June.

Fruit A drupe, 1 x ½ inch; the apex and point of attachment of the pedicel seemingly off-center; red when mature; with a distinctly pitted stone.

Twigs Stout, dull gray-brown, with foliage clustered at the ends.

Bark Smooth, grayish-white, with very shallow fissures and longitudinal lines of lenticels.

Leaves Alternate, pinnately compound, to 12 inches long; leaflets 4-8 pairs with a lanceolate terminal leaflet, lateral ones strongly sickle-shaped, apex long-pointed, strongly narrowing at the base, 2–4 x ½–1 inches; dark shiny green above, pale and dull beneath, turning red when senescing at the end of the second year; midrib thickened on both sides; margins entire, sometimes wavy, somewhat thickened; the rachis strongly angled, somewhat winged between upper pairs of leaflets.

Notes The fruit of *H. caffrum* is somewhat sour but is reported to make a good jelly. It is readily eaten by baboons, monkeys, and a variety of birds. The species has long been reported under the common name of "Kaffir plum." However, this common name was derived from the Arabic for unbeliever and has a long history of extremely pejorative connotations. The Latin name derives from the same source, but is not so readily changed.

Locations Scattered throughout town. Trees on Laguna Street at Valerio, in the 300 block of East Padre Street, on Garden Street north of Los Olivos. A fine tree in Franceschi Park by the entrance road. Common in several localities at the University of California, Santa Barbara.

Top: Dense, rounded crown of **Harpephyllum caffrum**. *Bottom left: Pinnately compound leaves and inflorescences of small flowers.*
Bottom right: Maturing red fruit.

Pistacia

Pistacia is a genus of 11 species distributed in southwestern North America, the Canary Islands, the Mediterranean region, and from the Caucasus to eastern Asia. Its name is from the Greek name for the nut, *pistake*.

Pistacia chinensis
Chinese pistache

Native to China, Taiwan, and the Philippine Islands.

Habit A small deciduous tree, frequently with multiple stems; to 30 feet tall.

Inflorescence Dioecious; a raceme to 6 inches long; flowers minute, reddish-yellow. Blooms March to July.

Fruit Reddish-purple, about 1/4 inch across.

Twigs Light brown on current growth, becoming gray, puberulent, appearing warty from leaf scars and vertical cinnamon-brown lenticels; buds 1/8–1/4 inch long, red-brown, with an obvious keel on the dorsal side.

Bark Grayish-brown, peeling in small rectangular flakes.

Leaves Alternate, pinnately compound, usually without a terminal leaflet, to 10 inches long, appearing clustered at the ends of twigs; rachis without wings, puberulent; leaflets 10–12, acuminate-lanceolate, strongly asymmetric at the base, if present the terminal leaflet is noticeably smaller than the laterals; turning brilliant orange to crimson in late autumn.

Notes Although not noted in the literature as having this characteristic, personal experience has demonstrated that *P. chinensis* can cause the same dermatitis for which its relative, poison oak, is well-known. The species name *chinensis* means from China.

Locations Park trees in Alice Keck Park Memorial Gardens near the east end of the pond, lower Orpet Park west of the center steps, and MacKenzie Park above the parking lot. Street trees on Fawn Place.

Top: Finely textured crown of Pistacia chinensis.
Middle left: Densely flowered inflorescences.
Middle right: Red fruit and pinnately compound leaves.
Bottom: Colorful fall foliage.

Pistacia khinjuk
Wild pistachio

Native to the mountainous regions of the Middle East, from Iraq to Punjab (northern India), found at elevations to 9,000 feet.

Habit A deciduous tree with an open crown and multiple branches; to 25 feet tall.

Inflorescence Axillary panicles of numerous small yellow and red flowers, to 5 x 3 inches. Blooms February to March.

Fruit A roundish drupe, 3/8 inch long, with slight vertical stripes.

Twigs Red-brown, with fine vertical lenticels; buds globose, to 1/2 inch long, scales pubescent with white hairs and no obvious dorsal keel.

Bark Gray-brown, broken into small rectangular flaky blocks.

Leaves Alternate, pinnately compound with a terminal leaflet, to 4 inches long; rachis without wings but with an obvious ridge between leaflet pairs; leaflets 5–7, ovate to oblong, glossy, often puberulent at the base of the midrib, terminal leaflet usually as large or larger than laterals.

Notes This species is highly variable, even on the same tree, and is frequently confused with *P. vera*. The species name *khinjuk* means from the Khinja region of Afghanistan; alternatively from the Arabic for "fruit of the terebinth tree," referring to several species of pistachio which were used to prevent wine from turning to vinegar.

Locations Franceschi Park above the entrance road.

Top: Inflorescences and emerging leaves of Pistacia khinjuk.
Bottom: Coarse, pinnately compound leaves and fruit.

Pleiogynium

Pleiogynium is a genus of two species from central Malaysia to Australia. Its name is derived from the Greek words *pleio* (full or more) and *gyn* (woman) and refers to the fruit which is nearly completely filled by the seed, leaving little of the edible flesh.

Pleiogynium timorense
Pleiogynium solandri
Burdekin plum

Native to open forests in the western Pacific region, from the Cook Islands and the Phillipines to the coast of Queensland, Australia.

Habit   A medium-sized evergreen tree; to 45 feet tall.

Inflorescence   Axillary panicles, 1–1 1/2 inches long; flowers yellow-green, 3/8–1/4 inch across on a stout yellow-green pedicel. Blooms January to February.

Fruit   A cup-shaped drupe with a flattened distal end, 3/4–1 x 3/4–1 1/2 inches, light green turning dark purple when mature.

Twigs   Stout, tan becoming gray, with obvious orange lenticels.

Bark   Light gray, smoothish, with thin flakes.

Leaves   Alternate, pinnately compound with a terminal leaflet, to 8 inches long; leaflets 5–11, lanceolate or ovate, often asymmetric, 1 3/4–4 x 3/4–2 1/4 inches, shiny green.

Notes   *Pleiogynium timorense* is frequently used as a timber tree in its native lands. The thin flesh of its fruits is edible, hence the common name. The species is highly variable and is sometimes divided into two or more taxa based on the degree of pubescence. The species name *timorense* means from Timor.

Locations   A single tree in Franceschi Park east of the cottage.

Top: Yellow-green flowers and immature fruit showing ribbed pumpkin-like appearance of Pleiogynium timorense.
Bottom: Mature purple fruit and pinnately compound leaves.

Rhodosphaera

Rhodosphaera is a genus of only one species. It is closely allied to the more common genus Rhus. *Rhodosphaera* is derived from the combination of the Greek words *rhodon* (red) and *sphairion* (sphere) in reference to the reddish round fruit of the genus.

Rhodosphaera rhodanthema
Deep yellow wood, tulip satinwood, yellow cedar

Native to a restricted area of eastern Australia, from southeastern Queensland to northeastern New South Wales.

Habit An evergreen, erect, slender tree with an open crown; to 40 feet tall.

Inflorescence Dioecious; terminal and axillary panicles, 4–8 inches long; flowers small, 3/16 inch across, pinkish-red. Blooms March to April.

Fruit A glossy brown drupe, 1/3–1/2 inch across, produced in large, persistent grape-like clusters; seed with obvious longitudinal cracks.

Twigs Rusty hairy, with red lenticels, sap milky.

Bark Brownish-gray, with longitudinal cracks on medium branches, becoming broken into rectangular plates below.

Leaves Alternate, pinnately compound with a terminal leaflet, 8–15 inches long; rachis not winged; leaflets 5–17, oblong-ovate, 1 1/2–4 x 1/2–1 1/4 inches, often asymmetric with a curved midvein, margins entire or wavy in younger individuals, with rusty hairs in the axils of the veins underneath.

Notes The wood of *R. rhodanthema* is very attractive and is sought for cabinetry. However, as a member of the Anacardiaceae, the species contains small concentrations of the irritating oils commonly found in other genera (including *Rhus*), and particularly sensitive wood workers should be cautious. The species name *rhodanthema* means red-flowered.

Locations Two female trees at Franceschi Park, one east of the cottage, the other west of the main house. A male tree adjacent to the Anacapa Street entrance to City Hall.

Top: Compound leaves and dark brown fruit of Rhodosphaera rhodanthema.
Bottom: Dense, pinkish-red flowers of inflorescence.

Rhus

Rhus is a genus of about 200 species from warm and temperate regions of the world. Well-known for the dermatitis-causing effects of some of its species, others have been used in the production of lacquers, drinks, dyes, and tanning materials. *Rhus* is the Greek name for one of the species in the genus.

Rhus lancea
Karree, willow rhus

Native in open dry landscapes of southern Africa where there is abundant ground water.

Habit   An evergreen tree with a rounded crown, drooping foliage, and a gnarled twisted trunk; to 25 feet tall.

Inflorescence   Dioecious; terminal or axillary, densely branched panicles, to 4 1/2 inches long; flowers minute, pale greenish-yellow, with a sweet fragrance that attracts honey bees. Blooms December to January.

Fruit   A roundish drupe, somewhat flattened, 1/5 inch across, green turning tan.

Twigs   Slender, initially green with reddish stripes, turning reddish-brown.

Bark   Flaky, gray with reddish-brown showing in the furrows.

Leaves   Alternate, trifoliate; leaflets sessile, very narrow, lance-shaped, 3 1/2–4 3/4 x 1/4–2/3 inches, margins entire, upper surface dark green with a densely reticulate network of veins readily visible, lower surface pale green, without petiolules; petiole 1 1/4–1 2/3 inches long, grooved.

Notes   Early settlers used the species as an indicator of accessible water. Because of the twisted nature of the trunks, the hard red-brown wood had little use other than fencing. However, the fruits were reported to make a popular local beer when pounded with water and fermented. The species name *lancea* means lance-shaped.

Locations   Common as a shrub. Individuals in Franceschi Park and Lower Orpet Park. Street trees on Lou Dillon Drive.

Top: Broadly spreading low crown of Rhus lancea. *Bottom: Thin trifoliate leaves and greenish-yellow inflorescence.*

Schinus

Schinus is a genus of 27 species from the tropical and warm-temperate Americas. The name is a variant of schinos, the Greek name for the mastic tree *(Pistacia lentiscus)*, which it resembles.

Schinus molle

Pepper tree, California pepper tree, Peruvian pepper tree, Peruvian mastic tree, Australian pepper, *molle, pirul*

Native to the Andes of Peru; however, widely introduced into the drier subtropics.

Habit An evergreen tree with a spreading, airy crown, a gnarled trunk, and pendulous twigs and foliage; to 20–30 feet tall.

Inflorescence A much-branched hanging panicle, 3–6 inches long; flowers small, 1/8 inch across, yellowish-white. Blooms in July.

Fruit A small drupe, lavender-pink, globose, 1/3 inch across.

Twigs Light green in first year, turning brownish-gray.

Bark Grayish-brown on older trunks, peeling in thick flakes (1/2 x 4 inches); younger stems and branches much lighter, with thinner flakes.

Leaves Alternate, pinnately compound, 4–12 inches long; leaflets lanceolate to linear-lanceolate, acuminate with a curved tip, frequently with 1 or more fine teeth near the apex; yellow-green when young, becoming dark green; pale with a raised midrib beneath.

Notes Because of its ease of cultivation and tolerance of drought, California pepper has been planted extensively in dry regions of the world. However, the species is an alternate host for the black scale which attacks citrus and is an aggressive invasive in some regions. The species name *molle* is a Peruvian name for the pepper tree.

Locations Common throughout town. Large trees in front of the Old Mission and in De la Guerra Plaza. Street trees in the 700 block of Santa Barbara Street and the 200 block of East Pueblo Street.

Top: *Ancient look of a mature* Schinus molle *at the Santa Barbara Mission.*
Middle: *Yellowish-white inflorescence.*
Bottom: *Red "pepper corn" fruit and fine-textured pinnately compound leaves.*

Schinus terebinthifolius
Brazilian pepper tree

Native to the Andes of Argentina, Paraguay, and Brazil

Habit A rounded evergreen tree with a twisted gnarled trunk dividing into many spreading branches; 20–30 feet tall.

Inflorescence A panicle emerging from the axils of leaves, 1–4 inches long; flowers white, small, to 3/16 inch across. Blooms in August.

Fruit A bright red drupe, clustered along the ends of twigs, 1/4 inch in diameter.

Twigs Moderately stout, light brown with small warty lenticels.

Bark Dark gray, deeply fissured into interlacing ridges with cinnamon-brown showing between.

Leaves Alternate; pinnately compound, 4–7 inches long; leaflets 7–13 (usually 9), obovate, usually entire or slightly toothed, shiny dark green above, paler beneath, midrib and almost perpendicular lateral veins yellowish-green; rachis slightly winged among first three pairs of leaflets.

Notes Although only sparsely dispersed in its native habitats, *S. terebinthifolius* has become an aggressive invader where it has been introduced in the drier tropics and Mediterranean climates. It has become particularly invasive in peninsular Florida, the Bahamas, and Hawaii and has been listed in California as an Exotic Invasive Plant of Greatest Ecological Concern by the California Exotic Pest Plant Council. The species name *terebinthifolius* means having leaves like *Pistacia terebinthus*.

Locations Common throughout town. Trees on Calle de los Amigos and the 5600 block of Cathedral Oaks. Others in the 800 block of North Nopal Street and in the 800 block of North Quarantina Street. Abundant at Goleta Beach County Park and the University of California, Santa Barbara.

Top: Rounded crown of Schinus terebinthifolius. *Middle: Compound leaves and inflorescence. Bottom: Red fruit and dark green foliage.*

Annonaceae

The Custard-Apple or Soursop Family contain 135 genera and over 2,500 species from tropical regions throughout the world. Its greatest diversity and importance is in lowland tropical rain forests. It rarely occurs at elevations above 6,000 feet in mountainous regions, but occurs in all habitats in the lowlands.

Annona

Annona is a genus of 137 species, all but eight of which are found in tropical America. The remainder are from Africa. It has the unique characteristic that the flowers of several species heat up by as much as six degrees at anthesis and release a variety of odors to attract pollinating beetles and flies. The name derives from a native *(Taino)* name for cherimoya.

Annona cherimola
Cherimoya

Believed to have been indigenous to the mountain valleys of Ecuador, Columbia, and Bolivia; however, through cultivation and naturalization, it has spread from Chile to Costa Rica.

Habit   An erect, but low-growing, evergreen tree with a rounded crown; to 20 feet tall.

Inflorescence   Axillary, solitary or in groups of 2 or 3; flowers contain 3 obvious fleshy petals to $1^{1}/_{4}$ inches long, pale cream-colored. Blooms June to July.

Fruit   A large conical or heart-shaped fruit, 4–8 x 2–4 inches; skin light green, thin or thick, covered with finger-print like markings or numerous rounded protuberances; inner flesh white, aromatic; seeds $1/_{2}$–$3/_{4}$ inch long, black.

Twigs   Purplish-gray, pliable, with raised leaf scars.

Bark   Smooth, light gray.

Leaves   Alternate, simple; ovate to elliptic, 3–6 x $1^{1}/_{2}$–$3^{1}/_{2}$ inches; green and slightly hairy on the upper surface, paler and densely pubescent below; petiole short, $1/_{2}$ inch, densely pubescent, grooved above.

Notes   The seeds, twigs, and leaves contain a number of alkaloids, many of which are poisonous. Although the crushed seeds are effective insecticides, they also cause a variety of symptoms in humans, resembling responses to atropine. The fruit is delectable, and several small orchards can be found in the Carpinteria area. The species name *cherimola* is a native name for the fruit.

Locations   This species is common in private gardens and in some local orchards. Two small trees may be seen in the Lifescape Memorial Garden at Santa Barbara City College.

Top: Unkempt appearance of Annona cherimola.
Bottom left: Broad, ovate leaves and flowers with three fleshy petals.
Bottom right: Large fruit and foliage.

Apocynaceae

The Dogbane Family includes over 250 genera and 3,100 species and are found on all continents except Antarctica. However, its greatest diversity by far is in tropical regions. The family produces an abundance of secondary compounds that have been important in the pharmaceutical industry. Recent taxonomic analysis has suggested that the family should be expanded to include most of the Asclepiadaceae in a family that would be among the ten largest of the flowering plants.

Nerium

Nerium includes only a single species. The genus name is the classical Greek name for the species.

Nerium oleander
Oleander, rose-bay

Broadly distributed in the Old World from southern Europe to northern Africa and extending east to Japan.

Habit Evergreen shrubs, becoming small trees with training; to 20 feet tall.

Inflorescence Terminal corymbs; flowers 1¼ inches across, corolla of 5 petals fused in a funnel shape with 5 spreading lobes, usually pink or white, unscented. Blooms August to October.

Fruit A two-parted follicle subtended by a persistent calyx, dark brown, 4–7 inches long.

Twigs Green, with small orange-brown lenticels, becoming more prominant in the second year.

Bark Smooth, light gray.

Leaves Whorled in threes, simple; linear-lanceolate, 4–6 inches long, leathery, dark green above, pale green below, with a strong yellow-green midrib and many fine pinnate veins, margins entire.

Notes Oleander is well-known for its poisonous qualities. All parts of the plant contain cardiac glycosides and it has been said that one leaf contains a potentially lethal dose. The species name *oleander* is from the Italian *oleandro* (olive), referring to the olive-like leaves.

Locations Common throughout town. Street trees on Ruth Avenue, in the 400 block of West Ortega Street, and on Los Olivos Street between Garden and Laguna Streets.

Top: Small street tree of Nerium oleander.
Bottom: Terminal inflorescence and narrow lanceolate foliage.

Rauwolfia

Rauwolfia is a genus of about 60 species found in tropical regions throughout the world. It is a source of many valuable medicinal alkaloids. The genus is named for Leonhart Rauwolf (d. 1569), a German physician who traveled extensively throughout the Orient.

Rauwolfia samarensis
Indian snakeroot, snakeroot

Native to the tropical rain forests of the Phillipines.

Habit A partially deciduous tree; to 50 feet tall.

Inflorescence Terminal or axillary umbels; flowers white, corolla consisting of a 1/4-inch-long tube. Blooms June to July.

Fruit Globose, 1/4 inch across, dark purple at maturity, containing a flattened seed.

Twigs Stout, light gray, with prominent leaf scars and foliage clustered at the end.

Bark Smoothish, gray-brown.

Leaves Whorled in fours, simple; oblong-elliptic, 5–8 x $1^{2}/_{3}$ x $2^{3}/_{4}$ inches, shiny dark green; midrib prominent below, white, enlarging perceptibly towards the base.

Notes As do several other species in the genus, *R. samarensis* produces the alkaloid reserpine in its stems and roots. This alkaloid has become important in western medical practice as both a tranquilizer and a treatment for high blood pressure. The species name *samarensis* means from the island of Samar in the Phillipines.

Locations Two trees in Franceschi Park east of the cottage. Street trees in the 1500 block of San Miguel and the 1900–2000 blocks of El Camino de la Luz were planted by Will Beittel.

Top: Open, rounded crown of Rauwolfia samarensis. *Bottom: Minute flowers and shiny dark green leaves.*

Aquifoliaceae

The Holly Family includes a single genus and more than 500 species. Its centers of diversity are in the tropical Americas and Asia, and only a handful of species occur in Europe, Africa, and Australia. Over 60 species have been used for teas in native cultures, and several have medicinal uses.

Ilex
Hollies

Ilex is a genus of about 500 species found throughout the world, but especially concentrated in temperate and tropical regions of Asia and the Americas. The vernacular name (holly) stems from the Anglo-Saxon *holegn* (holy tree, applied to *I. aquifolium*) and is derived from the Roman practice of sending gifts of fruiting branches to valued friends during the winter festival of Saturnalia. This tradition and the early European belief that the spiny leaves kept away evil spirits were assumed by Christians as symbols of faith and goodwill during Christmas. *Ilex* is the Latin name for *Quercus ilex*.

Ilex aquifolium
English holly

Native to Europe, western Asia, and China.

Habit An evergreen tree with a dense crown; to 30 feet tall.

Inflorescence Monoecious; axillary clusters of flowers produced on wood of the previous year's growth; flowers small, four-parted, dull white, faintly fragrant. Blooms in January.

Fruit A shiny red globose drupe, 1/3 inch across.

Twigs Green and slightly angled, becoming light gray and roughened by raised leaf scars.

Bark Dark gray, shallowly fissured on younger branches, these disappearing into a slightly roughened bark with age.

Leaves Alternate, simple; ovate or oblong-ovate, 1–3 x 3/4–2 1/2 inches; thick, leathery, shiny dark green above, pale green below; margins wavy, with several very sharp spines 1/4 inch long; petiole 1/4–3/4 inch.

Notes *I. aquifolium* was used at one time to treat smallpox, catarrh, and pleurisy. It was also shipped to the East Indies for use as an insecticide. It is one of the most variable of the hollies, with over 200 named cultivars. The species name *aquifolium* is the classical Latin name for holly, in reference to the hooked spines on the leaves.

Locations Two trees in West Alameda Plaza.

Top: Small, clustered flowers and light green lower leaf surfaces of Ilex aquifolium.
Bottom: Bright red fruit and shiny dark green upper leaf surfaces.

Ilex latifolia
Lusterleaf holly

Native to eastern China and the coastal provinces of Japan.

Habit An evergreen tree with stout twigs and a pyramidal crown that drapes the ground unless pruned, casting a dark shade; to 35 feet tall.

Inflorescence Axillary clusters of 4–10 flowers on current growth; flowers small, yellow-green, four-parted, with a square receptacle on the corners of which the stamens are inserted. Blooms in January.

Fruit Round drupes, 1/4–3/8 inch across, dull deep red.

Twigs Green, becoming grayish-brown and lenticellate in the 2nd year.

Bark Smoothish, brownish-gray.

Leaves Alternate, but appearing opposite at the ends of the twigs, simple; oblong to ovate, 3–8 x 1 1/2–3 inches; leathery, glossy dark green above, yellow-green beneath; margins with small coarse serrations, not spiny, base rounded; petiole thick, 1/2–1 inch long.

Notes The species name *latifolia* means wide-leaved.

Locations Lower Orpet Park, between the upper path and the lawn near Moreno Road.

Broad shiny leaves with small serrations and small yellow flowers of Ilex latifolia.

Ilex vomitoria
Yaupon

Native to the lowlands of the southeastern United States, from Texas to Florida and north into Virginia and Arkansas.

Habit An evergreen shrub or tree, frequently with multiple trunks; to 30 feet tall.

Inflorescence Dioecious; in axillary clusters on second year growth; male flowers numerous, females solitary or in pairs; small, 3/16 inch across, greenish-white. Blooms in January.

Fruit Globose, shiny red translucent drupes, 1/8–1/4 inch across, held close to the stem.

Twigs Initially purplish, covered with downy hair, becoming whitish-gray and glabrous.

Bark Smooth, gray to dark-gray.

Leaves Alternate, simple; narrowly oval to ovate, 1/2–1 1/2 x 1/4–3/4 inches; shiny yellow-green, margins with rounded shallow teeth to the base; petiole 1/8 inch long.

Notes *I. vomitoria* has a long history of medicinal uses by Native Americans. It has the highest caffeine content of any species native to the United States. It was used in the concoction of "black drink" as part of a cleansing ritual. The species name *vomitoria* refers to its use in a cleansing ritual by Native Americans of the southeastern United States.

Locations East Alameda Plaza near Garden Street.

Curved yellow-green leaves with shallow rounded teeth and greenish-white flowers of **Ilex vomitoria**.

Araliaceae

The Ginseng or Ivy Family includes approximately 50 genera and almost 1,500 species. It is found throughout the humid tropics with extensions into temperate zones. It is most diverse in the tropical Americas and the Indo-Pacific region.

Cussonia

Cussonia is a genus of 25 species from tropical and South Africa and extending into Madagascar. It is named for Pierre Cusson (1727–1783), a French botanist at Montpellier.

Cussonia spicata
Cabbage tree

Native to dry mountain forests and grasslands of eastern South Africa and extending into Zimbabwe.

Habit A fast-growing evergreen tree with foliage clustered near the ends of the branches; to 30 feet tall.

Inflorescence Thick terminal spikes, 8–12 closely clustered, 4–8 x 1–2 inches; flowers greenish-yellow, densely packed along the spike; peduncles stout, green, 3–4 inches long. Blooms in January.

Fruit Angular, 1/6–1/4 inch across, dark purple-black.

Twigs Very stout, green becoming yellow-gray, with closely spaced large D-shaped leaf scars.

Bark Pinkish-gray, thick, corky, becoming furrowed with age.

Leaves Alternate, bi-palmately compound, to 14 inches across; containing 5–9 leaflets, each with 3 palmate secondary leaflets subtended by a broadly winged rachis; petiole stout, green, to 15 inches long.

Notes The succulent roots have provided a food source in drought times and were also used by native peoples to treat malaria. The species name *spicata* means spike-like.

Locations Two trees located on the north side of Noble Hall at the University of California, Santa Barbara.

Top: Unusual bipinnately compound leaf of Cussonia spicata.
Bottom: Thick inflorescence spikes clustered at the end of the twig.

Oreopanax

Oreopanax is a genus of about 80 species from the tropical Americas. The genus combines the Greek roots *oreo* (mountain) with the genus name *Panax* (all-healing), meaning mountain panax.

Oreopanax capitatus
Picon

Widely spread in the lowlands from southern Mexico to tropical South America.

Habit   An evergreen tree; to 40 feet tall.

Inflorescence   An erect panicle, covered with white hairs, with heads of 4–10 flowers on short petioles. Blooms November to January.

Fruit   In heads of 2–8, globose or ovoid berries, to 1/4 inch across.

Twigs   Stout, pale green, turning gray, with obvious bud scale scars marking the initiation of each season's growth.

Bark   Smooth, tannish-gray.

Leaves   Alternate, simple; ovate to obovate, 4–6 x 1–4 inches, apex acute to slightly acuminate, glabrous, leathery, with 3–5 pale nerves from the base; petiole 4–8 inches long, pale green.

Notes   The species name *capitatus* means in a dense head.

Locations   One tree in lower Orpet Park, west of the shed.

Shiny green leaves with three palmate veins and long petioles of Oreopanax capitatus. *The inflorescences of small white flowers are shorter than the leaves.*

Schefflera

Schefflera is a genus of about 650 species from warm and tropical regions. It occurs in almost all growth forms except as herbs. The genus is named for J. C. Scheffler, a 19th-century botanist from Poland.

Schefflera actinophylla
Brassaia actinophylla

Queensland umbrella tree, Australian umbrella tree, octopus tree

Native to moist forests of Queensland and New South Wales, Australia.

Habit A multi-stemmed evergreen shrub or small tree; to 30 feet tall.

Inflorescence Terminal clusters of 5–12 narrow spikes, 12–24 inches long; flowers bright red, containing 11 sepals and stamens, petals absent, 1/4 inch across. Blooms February to March.

Fruit A small, round fleshy berry, purplish.

Twigs Stout, 1 1/2 inches thick, with persistent acuminate bud scales above the leaves; green, becoming brownish-gray, with large leaf scars.

Bark Light gray, bearing faint leaf scars, somewhat roughened by numerous lenticels.

Leaves Clustered at the ends of the branches, palmately compound on an 8- to 20-inch-long reddish petiole; leaflets 7–13, elliptic-oblong, to 12 inches long, shiny light green, margins entire or slightly toothed towards the apex, radiating around the petiole in a fashion to suggest an umbrella; petiolules 1–3 inches long.

Notes The fruit is reported to have an alcoholic content which has created navigational difficulties for birds feeding on them. The species name *actinophylla* means ray-shaped leaves.

Locations Several trees on the campus of the University of California, Santa Barbara, in the courtyard east of Ellison Hall and elsewhere.

Top: Clustered foliage and bright red flower spikes of Schefflera actinophylla.
Bottom: Palmately compound leaf with multiple ray-like leaflets.

Schefflera pueckleri
Tupidanthus calyptratus
Mallet flower

Native to India and Myanmar (Burma).

Habit An evergreen shrub or low-branching small tree; to 20 feet tall.

Inflorescence Three- to seven-flowered umbels, with stout branches; flowers to 1½ inches across, the calyx tube thickly leathery, the fused petals falling off in a cap at anthesis, stamens numerous and crowded. Blooms December to January.

Fruit A fleshy, flattened berry, to 1½ inches across.

Twigs Stout, with narrow leaf scars that extend halfway around the circumference.

Bark Smooth, tan-gray, becoming warty.

Leaves Alternate, palmately compound, petiole to 24 inches; leaflets 9–13, lanceolate, 4–12 x 1½–3½ inches, leathery, shiny green, margins entire and unusually wavy; petiolule 1–2 inches.

Notes The species name *pueckleri* honors Prince Herman von Pückler (1785–1871), German landowner and landscape gardener who created the 2,500-acre Muskau Park consisting of a town and village, areas for farming and industry, meadows, rivers, lakes, forests, and gardens.

Locations Several small trees at East Beach near the east parking lot. Others as foundation plantings at Burton and Mason Streets.

Top: Several stems and low branching form of Schefflera pueckleri.
Middle: Thickened floral receptacles and stout branches of inflorescence.
Bottom: Flattened fruit and stout twigs.

Betulaceae

The Birch Family includes six genera and about 170 species that occur primarily in the North Temperate Zone. Many of the species are wind-pollinated and the seeds likewise are wind-disseminated. Although the wood of several species is particularly dense, it frequently decays rapidly.

Alnus

Alnus is a genus of 25 species found primarily in north temperate regions and extending to Southeast Asia and into the Andes of South America. Uses of its species have ranged from manufacture of Stradivarius violins to gunpowder. However, probably its greatest significance is that the genus is capable of nitrogen fixation and has contributed to the fertility of many nutrient-poor forest ecosystems of the North Temperate Zone. *Alnus* is the classical Latin name for alder.

Alnus rhombifolia
White alder, California alder

Found along rocky stream banks and disturbed slopes from southern Washington and western Idaho, south through Oregon and California to the border with Mexico.

Top: Young seed catkins and elongate pollen catkins of Alnus rhombifolia.
Bottom: Finely serrate leaves with parallel secondary veins and old woody seed catkins.

Habit A semi-deciduous, pyramidal and somewhat open-crowned tree usually with several main trunks; to 75 feet tall.

Inflorescence Monoecious; flowers borne in cone-like catkins; female catkins in clusters of usually 3–6 on short, strongly divergent lateral sub-branches, 1/8–1/4 inch long; male catkins in clusters of 3–7 at the ends of branches above the seed-bearing catkins, 1 1/4–4 inches long. Blooms February to March.

Fruit Mature seed catkins ovoid to cylindrical, 1/2–3/4 x 1/3 inch.

Twigs Light green to red-brown; moderately glandular to densely glandular on stems bearing inflorescences, pith somewhat triangular; buds on short stalks, ellipsoid, 1/4 inch long, with 2 valvate scales, glandular and covered with a thick resinous coat.

Bark Thin; grayish, whitish, or mottled; smooth to slightly rough, broken into irregular shallow plates on older stems.

Leaves Alternate, simple; ovoid to rhombic, 1 3/4–3 1/2 x 1–2 3/4 inches; dark green and dull above, yellow-green beneath; margins flat, finely serrate, sometimes slightly doubly-serrate; veins hairy, 9–12 pairs, often branching near the margin, not impressed from above, veinlets inconspicuous.

Notes The species name *rhombifolia* means with a diamond-shaped leaf.

Locations Three trees in the demonstration garden opposite Fire Station 7 at the intersection of Mission Ridge Road and Stanwood, others along Mission Creek at the Santa Barbara Botanic Garden, and at the University of California, Santa Barbara between Kerr Hall and South Hall.

Betula

Betula is a genus of 35 species from the cool temperate and boreal regions of the Northern Hemisphere. It is closely related to *Alnus* except that the seed-bearing catkins shatter when mature. Betulinic acid, which is obtained from the bark, has been found to be successful in treating melanomas. *Betula* is the classical Latin name for birch.

Betula nigra
River birch, red birch

Broadly spread along rivers and streams in the eastern United States, from Massachusetts to Florida and west to Minnesota and Kansas.

Habit A deciduous tree with an irregular crown, frequently with several main trunks; to 35 feet tall.

Inflorescence Monoecious; flowers borne in catkins, appearing before the leaves; male catkins slender, 2–3 inches long, dark brown. Blooms March to April.

Fruit Cylindrical, pubescent, 1 1/2 x 1/2 inches, on erect stout hairy peduncles; shattering when mature in early summer.

Twigs Green, downy in the first year, becoming reddish-brown, covered with minute white lenticels.

Bark Dark reddish-brown with obvious horizontal lenticels when young; exfoliating into thin papery sheets to expose a light pinkish-tan to cinnamon-brown inner bark; becoming gray to dark brown, ridged and scaly on older trees.

Leaves Alternate, simple; somewhat ovate, 1 1/2–3 inches long; base wedge-shaped and entire, margins above the base somewhat doubly-serrate; veins 7–9 pairs, slightly impressed from above; shiny dark green above, turning pale dull yellow in the fall; petiole downy, 1/4–1/2 inch long.

Notes The species name *nigra* means darkened, black.

Locations Several trees in the 300 block of East De la Guerra Street. Others in Chase Palm Park east of the carousel.

Doubly serrate leaves of **Betula** **nigra** *with entire margins at the base. Fruit disintegrate upon dissemination of seed.*

Betula pendula
Betula verucosa

European white birch, weeping birch, silver birch

Broadly distributed in Europe and northern Asia.

Habit A deciduous tree with pendulous twigs and branches, pyramidal becoming rounded with age; to 40 feet tall.

Inflorescence Monoecious; flowers borne in catkins; male catkins 1/2–1 1/2 inches long at anthesis, usually in pairs. Blooms in April.

Fruit Mature seed catkins cylindrical, 3/4–1 1/4 x 1/3 inches; seed small, orange, with a transparent wing, shed in the fall.

Twigs Reddish-brown, smooth, with tan lenticels.

Bark Brownish-gray on very small branches, turning white with horizontal lenticels, developing blackened fissures.

Leaves Alternate, simple; small, broadly ovate, sometimes diamond-shaped, slenderly tapered at the apex, 1–3 x 3/4–1 1/2 inches; veins 5–8 pairs; margins coarsely doubly serrate, base entire; lustrous dark-green above, dotted with resin dots on both surfaces.

Notes *B. pendula* has been cultivated in Europe for over two centuries and has produced many cultivars, including ones with deeply dissected leaves and others with very pendulous branches. The species name *pendula* means hanging down.

Locations Street trees in the 400 block of East Padre Street. Also scattered in front yards on Calle de los Amigos and in the San Roque area.

Top: Several stems and weeping crown of Betula pendula.
Bottom: Diamond-shaped leaves with coarse serrations and elongate seed catkins.

Bignoniaceae

The Trumpet-Creeper Family consists of 120 genera and about 800 species. Many of the genera have particularly low numbers of species and several are monotypic. The family is almost entirely restricted to the tropics with only a few extensions into the temperate zones. Many of the species have nectaries that attract ants which in turn protect the plant from herbivores.

Catalpa

Catalpa is a genus of 11 species found in eastern Asia and North America. *Catalpa* is the North American Indian name for *C. speciosa*.

Catalpa speciosa
Catalpa, northern catalpa, cigartree, Indian-bean

Native to moist river bottoms along the Mississippi, Ohio, and Wabash rivers from Tennessee and Arkansas to southeastern Illinois and Indiana.

Habit A medium-sized, deciduous tree, with a short bole dividing into several ascending branches; to 60 feet tall.

Inflorescence Axillary panicles of few flowers, to 6 x 6 inches; flowers tubular and two-lipped composed of 5 spreading fringed lobes, 2–2 1/2 inches across the mouth; white with inconspicuous yellow and purple dots inside the tube. Blooms in June.

Fruit A long, pod-like capsule, 8–18 x 1/2–3/4 inches; persisting through the deciduous months and opening in the spring to release papery winged seeds.

Twigs Stout, green turning brown, smooth with obvious lenticels; leaf scars large, round, raised; pith large, spongy, white.

Bark Reddish-brown or gray, with deep furrows and long, flattened, interlacing ridges.

Leaves Whorled, sometimes opposite; heart-shaped with an elongated apex, 6–12 inches long; green and smooth above, hairy beneath; petiole 3–4 inches long, hairy.

Notes *C. bignonioides,* a very similar species, is found occasionally in gardens and is distinguished by very densely flowered inflorescences, flowers with many conspicuous purple spots, leaves that are malodorous when crushed and have a shortened apex, and scaly bark. Leaves of either species that are damaged by herbivorous insects are reported to produce nectar which attracts additional insects that feed upon the eggs and larvae of the original herbivores. The species name *speciosa* means showy, brilliant.

Locations Young street trees in the first block of North Salinas Street; a large yard tree in the 3000 block of Calle Noguera, another in the 700 block of Castillo Street. Three trees on the grounds of Lotusland near the pond.

Top: Tubular white flowers with purple and yellow dots of Catalpa speciosa.
Bottom: Inflorescence with large heart-shaped leaves.

Chilopsis

Chilopsis is a genus of a single species that is closely related to *Catalpa*. It differs in that its leaves are alternately placed, the flowers are more trumpet-shaped and have five instead of two stamens. *Chilopsis* is derived from the Greek words *cheilos* (lip) and *opsis* (resembling) and refers to the distinct lip in the corolla of the flower.

Chilopsis linearis
Desert willow

Native to sandy washes of desert regions of the United States, from southeastern California to Utah and New Mexico, and extending into northern Mexico.

Habit A winter-deciduous shrub or small tree, with multiple twisting trunks and a willow-like aspect; to 20 feet tall.

Inflorescence A showy terminal panicle or raceme; flowers tubular with 5 lobes spreading in a two-lipped appearance, 3/4–2 inches long, light pink to lavender with yellow ridges and purple lines, stamens not exserted, lobes of the stigma closing when touched. Blooms June to August.

Fruit A long cylindrical capsule, to 14 x 1/4 inches long; seeds flattened, 1/4–1/2 inch long, hairy at both ends.

Twigs Yellow-green, turning yellow or brown in the second year.

Bark Smooth, dark grayish-brown, becoming shallowly fissured into rectangular plates.

Leaves Generally alternate, simple; linear, curved, tapering to both ends, 4–6 x 1/4–1/3 inches; light green with a yellowish-green midrib.

Notes *C. linearis* is one of the parents, along with *Catalpa bignonioides,* of the horticultural hybrid X *Chitalpa tashkentensis,* which was created in 1964 in Uzbekistan. The hybrid combines the larger flowers of *Catalpa* with the color of *Chilopsis* and is a drought-hardy tree that can flower throughout the year. Two varieties of the cross are available in nursery trade. The species name *linearis* means lined, as in the purple lines in the flowers.

Locations Santa Barbara Botanic Garden in the Desert Section. The hybrid is increasingly planted throughout town. Street trees in the 900 and 1200 blocks of State Street.

Top: Spreading form and open crown of Chilopsis linearis.
Bottom: Tubular flowers and long, linear leaves.

Jacaranda

Jacaranda is a genus of 34 species from the New World tropics. It is known primarily for its horticultural uses and is planted extensively throughout the warm parts of the world, as well as in Santa Barbara. *Jacaranda* is derived from the Brazilian name for the genus.

Jacaranda mimosifolia
Jacaranda, tarco

Native to mountain valleys of northwestern Argentina and adjacent Bolivia.

Habit A semi-evergreen tree with a broad crown of dense foliage; to 45 feet tall.

Inflorescence A terminal panicle; flowers showy, with a curved trumpet-shaped corolla, $1^{1}/_{4}$–$1^{1}/_{2}$ x $^{1}/_{4}$–$^{1}/_{2}$ inches, purplish-blue with the tube white inside, calyx very much reduced, $^{1}/_{25}$ inch long. Blooms May to June.

Fruit A woody, flattened capsule, roundish, usually more than $1^{3}/_{4}$ inches across, apex often notched at the tip, base flat or shallowly heart-shaped, the margins somewhat wavy, drying brownish or tannish.

Twigs Stout, greenish-brown in first year becoming light brown, lenticellate.

Bark Light gray, scaly in small rectangular flakes.

Leaves Alternate, bipinnately compound, 6–18 inches long, with usually more than 12 pinnae $^{1}/_{2}$–$^{3}/_{4}$ inch apart on the rachis, each with 13–41 sessile leaflets, narrowly elliptic $^{1}/_{8}$–$^{1}/_{2}$ x $^{1}/_{25}$–$^{1}/_{6}$ inch, the venation impressed from above, glabrous or slightly pubescent along the midrib and margin, the margin slightly rolled under.

Notes Taxonomically, *J. mimosifolia* is in fact made up of two species: *J. mimosifolia* and *J. acutifolia,* which is native to the dry Andean valleys of central and northern Peru. The two species of *Jacaranda* are often confused with one another, and in the nursery trade cross-fertilization of seed trees has undoubtedly contaminated seed sources. Many of the trees in Santa Barbara appear to show characteristics that are intermediate between the two species. The true species *J. mimosifolia,* in addition to other subtle differences, is distinguished by its larger fruit, shorter calyx, and greater number of pinnae per leaf. As well, the flowers of this species are paler than the deep color of *J. acutifolia;* indeed a white form (*J. mimosifolia* 'Alba') exists in the nursery trade. The species name *mimosifolia* means with leaves like mimosa.

Locations Very common about town.

Top: Spectacular display of **Jacaranda** mimosifolia *in spring.*
Middle: Cluster of tubular lavender flowers showing the bilateral symmetry characteristic of the Bignoniaceae.
Bottom: Bipinnately compound leaves, woody fruit, and winged seed.

Markhamia

Markhamia is a genus of ten species from tropical Africa and Asia. Its name honors Sir Clements Robert Markam (1830–1916), a British explorer and author.

Markhamia lutea
Markhamia hildebrandtii

Markhamia

Found in riverine forest remnants in Kenya, in equatorial East Africa.

Habit An evergreen tree with a rounded crown and a fluted bole on older individuals; to 40 feet tall.

Inflorescence Axillary or terminal panicles, 4 inches long; flowers funnel-shaped with 5 fused petals, 2–3 1/4 inches long, bright yellow. Blooms August to September.

Fruit A twisted linear flattened capsule, 16–32 x 2/3–3/4 inches, twisted; seeds pale cream with two membranous wings.

Twigs Stout, somewhat flattened, initially olive-green, with small gray lenticels, becoming light gray-brown; leaf scars large, circular, with obvious vascular bundle scars.

Bark Light brownish-gray, finely fissured.

Leaves Opposite, pinnately compound with a terminal leaflet; leaflets 7–11, obovate, 3–7 x 1 1/2–3 inches, leathery, shiny dark green above, paler below, with tufts of hair in the nerve axils; midrib and lateral veins prominent below.

Notes Because of its drought tolerance, this species has been used extensively in reforestation projects in Africa. The species name *lutea* means yellow, referring to the flowers.

Locations Alice Keck Park Memorial Gardens near the corner of Arrellaga and Santa Barbara Streets. De la Guerra Plaza between City Hall and the News Press Building. A street tree in the 300 block of West Pedregosa and newly planted trees in the 100 and 700 blocks of State Street.

Top: Narrow crown with scattered inflorescences of Markhamia lutea.
Bottom: Flowers and pinnately compound leaves.

Radermachera

Radermachera is a genus of 15 species from Southeast Asia, some of which are cultivated for ornament or have local use for timber. The genus is named for Jacobus Cornelius Matthaeus Radermacher (1741–1783), Dutch botanist and general administrator to the Dutch East Indies in 1758.

Radermachera sinica
China doll tree

Found on lower forested slopes (1,000 to 2,700 feet) of the central Himalayas (China and India) and extending into Vietnam.

Habit   A deciduous tree with a narrow loose crown; to 30 feet tall.

Inflorescence   Terminal, erect panicles, 10–14 inches long; flowers tubular, $2^{1}/_{3}$–$3^{1}/_{4}$ inches long, white to pale yellow. Blooms July to August.

Fruit   A long thin capsule with a leathery shell, to 33 x $^{1}/_{2}$ inches.

Twigs   Stout, greenish-gray, with large circular leaf scars and vascular bundles arranged in a vertical ellipse.

Bark   Smoothish, brownish-gray.

Leaves   Alternate, bi- (or tri-) pinnately compound, about 12 inches long; leaflets ovate to ovate-lanceolate, $1^{1}/_{4}$–2 x $^{1}/_{2}$–$^{3}/_{4}$ inches, glabrous, with an entire margin; rachis and rachillae strongly channeled above; petiole $2^{1}/_{2}$–4 inches long.

Notes   The species name *sinica* means from China.

Locations   Biltmore Hotel, between Cottage #1 and Channel Drive. A small tree in the island at Modoc and Park Roads.

Top: Tubular flower and bipinnately compound leaves of Radermachera sinica.
Bottom: Curved elongate fruit.

Spathodea

Spathodea is a monotypic genus. Its name means spathe-like and refers to the cup-like flower.

Spathodea campanulata
African tulip tree, flame tree

Broadly distributed throughout tropical Africa, from Guinea to Angola and east to Sudan and Uganda.

Habit An evergreen tree with a rounded crown; to 50 feet or more.

Inflorescence Terminal racemes; flower buds conspicuous, pointed, velvet brown; flowers widely trumpet-shaped, 4 x 2–3 inches, corolla slightly two-lipped, brilliantly red-orange with a pale orange throat and yellow-fringed lobes, calyx 2¼ inches long, leathery tough, densely brown pubescent. Blooms September to October.

Fruit An oblong-lanceolate capsule, 7–8 inches long, pointed at both ends, flattish with a groove on each side, dark blackish-brown, lightly short pubescent, held upright when mature, not pendulous.

Twigs Stout, densely short rusty pubescent, with obvious warty white lenticels and large round leaf scars.

Bark Tannish-brown, lightly fissured.

Leaves Alternate, pinnately compound, with a terminal leaflet, to 15 inches long; leaflets 9–19, ovate-oblong, 2–4 x 1½ inches, dark green, glabrous, conspicuously veined, entire, petiolule very short and channeled; rachis rusty-haired, with warty lenticels near the base.

Notes *S. campanulata* is a wonderfully beautiful tree, but it is pushing its limits in Santa Barbara. Young trees are particularly susceptible to frost, and established ones in Santa Barbara are regularly deciduous. In spite of these drawbacks, the spectacular display warrants further efforts to grow the species. A variety with a pale orange to yellow flower also occurs. The species name *campanulata* means bell-shaped, as in the flower shape.

Locations Street trees on lower Alisos and Voluntario Streets. Recently planted trees, including the paler variety, in the 800 and 1000 blocks of State Street.

Top: *Spectacular display of* Spathodea campanulata *in early fall.*
Middle: *Yellow-flowered variety* (S. campanulata *var.* lutea) *with pinnately compound leaves.*
Bottom: *Uniquely structured inflorescence.*

Tabebuia

Tabebuia is a genus of over 100 species from the New World tropics. In addition to its showy flowers the genus is well-known for its extremely hardy and dense wood. Dead stems of one species are still standing in the Panama Canal, and the wood of others was used in earlier times to manufacture ball bearings. The genus has also gained considerable recognition for its pharmacological properties, including treatment of cancer. Unfortunately, these have been excessively, and erroneously, embellished in the herbal medicine literature, including statements that the flowers are carnivorous. The genus name is derived from the Brazilian name for the tree, and was based upon the native words for "ant" and "wood."

Tabebuia chrysotricha
Golden trumpet tree

Found in coastal forests and disturbed open forests of southern Brazil.

Habit A small deciduous tree with a dense crown; to 30 feet tall.

Inflorescence Terminal, a few-flowered cluster, almost sessile; flowers containing a showy yellow corolla tube with thin reddish stripes in the throat, $1^{1}/_{2}$–3 x $1^{1}/_{2}$–$2^{1}/_{4}$ inches; the calyx tubular, $2/3$ inch long and covered with rusty pubescence. Blooms in March.

Fruit A linear cylindrical capsule, $4^{1}/_{2}$–15 x $1/4$–$3/4$ inches, densely covered with reddish velvet.

Twigs Covered with rusty pubescence in first year, becoming glabrous and dull gray.

Bark Grayish-brown, shallowly fissured into interlacing ridges with orangish furrows.

Leaves Alternate, palmately compound; leaflets 5, oblong to elliptic, the terminal $3/4$–4 x $2/3$–$2^{1}/_{4}$ inches, the laterals progressively smaller, dark to olive green, margins entire, reddish pubescent, petiolules less than $1/3$ inch long; petiole $1/2$–$1^{1}/_{2}$ inches long, densely covered with reddish pubescence.

Notes The species name *chrysotricha* means with golden trichomes.

Locations Occasional. Trees in Alice Keck Park Memorial Gardens and on the southwest corner of the County Courthouse.

Top: A handsome tree of Tabebuia chrysotricha *in full flower before leaf emergence.*
Middle left: Palmately compound leaves.
Middle right: Elongate fruit with rusty red hairs.
Bottom: Cluster of bright yellow flowers.

Tabebuia impetiginosa
Tabebuia avellanedae
Tecoma ipe

Pink trumpet tree, *ipe, roble serrano*

Broadly distributed from northwestern Mexico to northwestern Argentina in seasonally dry deciduous and semi-deciduous forests, also in drier parts of Amazonia.

Habit   A deciduous tree; to 50 feet tall.

Inflorescence   Terminal panicles, flowers in clusters of three with several clusters grouped together; flowers with a cup-shaped calyx 1/4 inch long, corolla tubular, 1 1/2–3 x 1/2–2 inches, magenta with a yellow throat at anthesis, lightly wooly inside and out. Blooms April to May.

Fruit   A linear narrow capsule, 5–20 x 1/2–1 inches.

Twigs   Greenish-brown with small vertical lenticels, becoming stout and brownish-gray with fine vertical striping.

Bark   Smooth, tannish-gray, somewhat furrowed.

Leaves   Alternate, palmately compound; leaflets 5–7, ovate to elliptic, the terminal one 2–8 x 2/3–3 1/4 inches, the lateral ones progressively smaller, thin, margins serrate, somewhat scaly above and below, pubescent in the axils of the veins beneath, petiolule 1/4–1 1/2 inches long; petiole 1 1/2–5 inches long, flattened above, sparsely pubescent.

Notes   *Pau d'arco,* a medicinal derived from the bark of this species, is reputed to have been used in traditional treatments of cancer and infections. However, no clinical trials of its efficacy have been conducted, and the quinines that it contains are known for their toxic properties. The species name *impetiginosa* means skin eruption.

Locations   Trees at Alice Keck Park Memorial Gardens, La Mesa Park, and in the planter at 400 East Cota Street.

Top: Flower cluster of Tabebuia impetiginosa.
Bottom: Palmately compound leaves with thin petioles.

Tecoma

Tecoma is a genus of 13 species from tropical South Africa and the Americas. Its name is derived from the native name *tecomaxochitl*.

Tecoma stans
Stenolobium stans
Yellow elder, yellow bignonia

Native to the tropical and subtropical Americas, from Texas and Arizona to Argentina.

Habit An evergreen or semi-deciduous bushy shrub or small tree; to 25 feet tall.

Inflorescence Terminal racemes, to 2 inches long; flowers elongate, trumpet-shaped with 5 lobes, 2–2 1/2 inches long, yellow-orange, with faint red lines in throat of tube. Blooms June to July.

Fruit A pod, somewhat flattened, to 6 x 1/3 inches; the apex long and pointed, green turning light tan-brown, densely covered with lenticels; dehiscing to expose an inner septum to which are attached numerous papery-winged, overlapping seeds.

Twigs Thin, yellow-green turning grayish-tan, flattened at the nodes.

Bark Dusty grayish-tan, flaky, becoming dark gray on older stems.

Leaves Opposite, pinnately compound, with a terminal leaflet, to 6 inches long; leaflets lanceolate, 1–2 x 1/2–3/4 inches; thin, light green, margins serrate; rachis grooved on top, slightly winged, appearing slightly constricted at point of attachment of leaflets.

Notes Although a lovely addition to the ornament of our city, this species has become an aggressive invader in French Polynesia. The species name *stans* means upright, standing.

Locations Trees in Alice Keck Park Memorial Gardens along the Garden Street side and near the corner of Santa Barbara and Arrellaga Streets. Another in the inner courtyard of El Paseo. A young tree on Foothill Road between Alamar and Mission Canyon Road.

Top: Flower cluster of Tecoma stans *with pinnately compound foliage.*
Bottom: Cluster of elongate fruit.

Bombacaceae

The Baobab or Balsa-Wood Family includes approximately 18 genera and 160 species. The family is found throughout the tropics, but is most diverse in the New World tropics. Many of its species have swollen and/or spiny trunks. The lightest wood in the world, balsa-wood, is from the genus *Ochroma*. Some recent analyses have suggested that the family should be included in the Malvaceae.

Ceiba
Chorisia

Ceiba was recently expanded to include the former genus *Chorisia* and now includes 11 species from the tropical Americas, one of which is also found in Africa. In natural settings, its large showy flowers are pollinated by bats and non-flying mammals. *Ceiba* is the Latinized version of the South American name for the floss silk tree.

Ceiba speciosa
Chorisia speciosa

Floss silk tree

Native to tropical rain forests of Brazil and Argentina.

Habit A fast-growing deciduous tree with an open crown and a swollen trunk; to 50 feet tall.

Inflorescence Axillary, solitary; flowers showy, 4 inches across, with a two- to five-lobed cup-shaped calyx, the 5 petals lanceolate or oblong, usually pinkish-red, sometimes yellowish-white, brown-striped at the base, stamens fused into a long white column surrounding the pistil. Blooms September to November.

Fruit A large pear or torpedo-shaped capsule, 5–6 x 3–4 inches, dark brownish-black, containing a dense mass of black seeds with long silky white hairs.

Bark Smooth, gray to green, frequently covered with stout gray-brown prickles, 1 x 1 inch.

Twigs Green, becoming greenish-gray, moderately stout, roughened by raised circular leaf scars.

Leaves Alternate, palmately compound, 4–8 inches across, on three- to five-inch-long petioles; leaflets 5–7, lanceolate, 2–4 x 1/2–1 1/2 inches, margins toothed, petiolules 1/2–3/4 inch long.

Notes The silky hairs surrounding the seeds are characteristic throughout the genus and assist in seed dispersal. Those from *C. pentandra* are the source of commercial kapok. However, the silky hairs found in *C. speciosa* are described as being as fine as any kapok in commerce today. At one time these were used by the Matico Indians to craft arrow-proof jackets. The species name *speciosa* means showy, brilliant.

Locations Street trees in the 2400–2500 blocks of Santa Barbara Street, the 200 block of South Voluntario Street, and the 200 block of West Yanonali Street. The white silk floss tree (*C. insignis*) can be seen in the parking lot of the Santa Barbara Zoological Gardens.

Top: Ceiba speciosa *in full autumn bloom.*
Bottom left: Stout prickles on green trunk.
Bottom right, above: Showy flowers with fused elongate stamens surrounding the pistil.
Bottom right, below: Palmately compound leaf and seed mass.

Boraginaceae

The Borage Family includes 200 genera and over 2,600 species. As in the Bignoniaceae, many of the genera are monotypic. The family is found throughout tropical and temperate regions of the world, with primary centers of diversity in the Middle East and Central and South America. It is of limited distribution in very cold or very humid tropical regions. Although a large family, it has been little-used for economic or medicinal purposes.

Ehretia

Ehretia is a genus of about 50 species from Africa, southern Asia, the East Indies, and the Americas. The genus is named for Georg Ehret (1708–1770), a noted German botanical artist.

Ehretia anacua
Sugarberry, knock-away

Found in a variety of scrubby habitats in southern Texas and northeastern Mexico.

Habit An evergreen to partially deciduous shrub or small tree, frequently with several stems; to 20 feet tall.

Inflorescence A terminal inflorescence on younger leafy twigs; flowers small, 1/4 inch long, white, fragrant. Blooms in January.

Fruit An orange or dark yellow drupe, 1/3–1/2 inch across, containing 2 hemispheric stones.

Twigs Thin, brittle, reddish-brown becoming light gray-brown.

Bark Thick, furrowed, separating into thin gray or reddish scales.

Leaves Alternate, simple; elliptic to ovate, 1 1/2–2 1/2 x 1/2–1 1/2 inches, margins usually entire, upper surface very scabrous sandpapery to the touch.

Notes Although little used in California, this species readily attracts butterflies and birds, and has recently found a home in the bonsai trade. The species name *anacua* is the Native American name for the plant and gives rise to one of its common names.

Locations A cluster of stems in lower Orpet Park above the lawn and just west of the center steps.

Sandpapery leaves and flower clusters of Ehretia anacua.

Caprifoliaceae

The Honeysuckle Family includes 17 genera and about 450 species. It is primarily distributed in the Northern Hemisphere, although one species is endemic to New Zealand. Centers of diversity occur in eastern North America and eastern Asia. The family has several species of horticultural interest as well as others that have become invasive weeds. Although used to make honeysuckle wine, the family has little other economic or medicinal interest.

Sambucus

Sambucus is a small genus of nine species from temperate and subtropical regions of the Northern Hemisphere. *S. canadensis* (American elder), from eastern North America, is the source of many home-made jellies, pies, sauces, and wines. A *sambuca* is a type of harp from Roman times, the construction of which used elder wood.

Sambucus mexicana
Blue-berry elder, blue elder, blue elderberry

Broadly distributed in moist and open sites from Baja California to British Columbia and extending east into Utah and New Mexico.

Habit Large deciduous shrubs or irregularly shaped trees; to 20 feet tall.

Inflorescence Flat-topped terminal cymes with 5 branches, 3–6 inches across; flowers minute, five-parted, creamy white. Blooms in March.

Fruit A fleshy, juicy berry, $1/8$–$1/5$ inch across, nearly black covered by a dense bluish-white bloom, containing 3 seeds.

Twigs Stout on fast-growing stems, with prominent lenticels; pith large, white.

Bark Thin, light brown or reddish-gray, becoming dark gray, with shallow vertical fissures.

Leaves Opposite, pinnately compound, with a terminal leaflet, $2^{1}/_{2}$–5 inches long; petiole and rachis strongly grooved and hairy; leaflets 5–9, lanceolate, 2–6 inches long, with a somewhat elongate apex and a frequently asymmetric base, the midrib often curved, margins coarsely and sharply toothed, shiny green above, paler below,

Showy terminal inflorescence and opposite pinnately compound leaves of Sambucus mexicana.

emitting an odor reminiscent of crushed tomato leaves when bruised.

Notes The species is highly variable and includes the former *S. caerulea*. Although it is often found in wildland settings around Santa Barbara, it is also planted both for ornament and as a food source for birds. The species name *mexicana* means from Mexico.

Locations Scattered on the roadside along Mountain Drive. A large tree stands on Tallant Road near the tennis courts at Oak Park.

Viburnum

Viburnum is a genus of about 150 species from temperate and warm regions of the Northern Hemisphere. It is especially well-represented in North America and Asia. The name is derived from the classical Latin name for *V. lantanum*.

Viburnum odoratissimum
Sweet viburnum

Native to warm regions of India, Myanmar (Burma), China, Japan, and the Phillipines.

Habit An evergreen shrub or small tree with a dense rounded crown; to 25 feet tall.

Inflorescence Moderately dense terminal panicles; flowers small, 1/4 inch across, white, with a sweet odor. Blooms July to August.

Fruit A red drupe, becoming black, 1/3–1/2 inch long.

Twigs Stiff, warty, glabrous, green becoming brown in the second year.

Bark Thin, light gray, slightly roughened.

Leaves Opposite, simple; elliptic to ovate, acute at both ends, 4–8 inches long; leathery, dull olive green, becoming crimson towards senescence, with a smell of green pepper when crushed; petiole 1/2–3/4 inch long, flat on top.

Notes The species is often confused with *V. japonicum* and *V. awabuk,* the former of which has leaf veins reaching to the margin of the leaf, and the latter of which has shiny bright green leaf surfaces. The species name *odoratissimum* means highly scented.

Locations A single tree in the 2900 block of Calle Noguera, opposite Peabody School.

Terminal inflorescence and opposite leaves of Viburnum odoratissimum.

Casuarinaceae

The She Oak Family consists of four genera and about 90 species from Australia, Malesia (the former East Indies), and the southwestern Pacific. It is unique in that the apparent "leaves" are actually composed of slender, jointed branchlets, and the actual leaves are reduced to tooth-like appendages whorled around the joints. The overall effect is reminiscent of the jointed structures of horsetail. Seeds are produced in small, woody, cone-like structures. The roots of its species often harbor bacteria capable of nitrogen fixation, and members of the family are frequently used in reclamation of degraded soils.

Allocasuarina

Allocasuarina is a recently described genus into which many species formerly assigned to Casuarina have been placed. It is distinguished primarily by the functional quality of mature cones remaining unopened on the tree for many years and the enclosed seed being correspondingly long-lived. Most other features of the genus are similar to the description for *Casuarina*. Most of the 58 species are found in southern Australia and typically grow in extremely nutrient-poor sites.

Top: Branchlets and female flowers of Allocasuarina verticillata.
Bottom: Cone-like fruit.

Allocasuarina verticillata
Casuarina stricta
Drooping she oak

This species grows naturally on the coastal ranges of New South Wales, Victoria, South Australia, and Tasmania. It is an understory species of open forests and eucalyptus forests, or may form pure stands.

Habit An evergreen tree with drooping foliage; to 30 feet tall.

Inflorescence Dioecious; male spikes to $1/2$ inch long. Blooms December to January.

Fruit Cones barrel-shaped, $3/4–2 \times 1$ inches, sessile or on a peduncle $1/2$ inch long, knobby; samaras $1/4–1/2$ inch long, very dark brown.

Twigs Brownish with spreading teeth, nodes typically $1/4$ inch long.

Bark Dark brown-gray, hard, furrowed with interlacing ridges.

Leaves Branchlets alternate, drooping, to 15 inches long; segments $1/2–1 1/2$ inches long; densely pubescent in the furrows; phyllichnia slightly rounded; teeth 9–13, spreading from the next segment.

Notes The species name *verticillata* means whorled.

Locations Two trees growing closely together near the lagoon at the east end of Goleta Beach County Park.

Casuarina
Beefwood, Australian pine, she oak

Casuarina is a genus of 17 species found in Southeast Asia, the South Pacific Islands, and Australia. The genus is adapted to the dry, brackish conditions of oceanic locales. Early settlers in Australia found the wood of the species to be a reasonable substitute for the oak of Britain, hence the common name "she-oak." The name refers to the drooping branches which bear a resemblance to the feathers of the cassowary *(Casuarinus)*.

Casuarina cunninghamiana
River oak, river she oak

Found along permanent streams in the Northern Territory, Queensland, and New South Wales, Australia.

Habit An evergreen tree with an open narrow crown; to 50 feet or more.

Inflorescence Dioecious; male spikes 1/4–1 1/2 inches long; female cones solitary. Blooms October to November.

Fruit Seed cones 1/4–1/2 inch long, tannish pubescent, peduncle less than 1/2 inch long; samara 1/8 inch long.

Twigs Tannish-gray, with strongly reflexed teeth that remain from the original branchlet.

Bark Finely fissured into dark gray scales.

Leaves Branchlets alternate, drooping on healthy individuals, otherwise erect; branchlet segments 1/8–1/3 inch long; phyllichnia angular to flat with a rib; teeth on new shoot erect, 6–10.

Notes The species name *cunninghamiana* honors James Cunningham, East India Company surgeon who sent home numerous collections of plants from China between 1698 and 1702.

Locations Several trees in the 200 block of East Cota Street. Others at the Santa Barbara Municipal Airport near the corner of Hollister Avenue and Fairview Avenue.

Top: Irregular crown of Casuarina cunninghamiana. *Bottom: Branchlets and fruit.*

Casuarina glauca
Swamp oak

Found near brackish water along the coast of southeastern Queensland and northeastern New South Wales.

Habit An evergreen tree with an open narrow crown; to 50 feet tall.

Inflorescence Dioecious; male spike 1/2–1 1/2 inches long. Blooms November to December.

Fruit Seed cones red or whitish pubescent, becoming glabrous, 1/3–2/3 inch long; peduncle 1/8–1/2 inch long; samara 1/8–1/4 inch long.

Twigs Gray-brown, with strongly reflexed teeth.

Bark Gray-brown, tight, broken into short ridges on older trunks, finely broken above.

Leaves Branchlets alternate, spreading to drooping, to 15 inches long; segments 1/3–3/4 inch long, glabrous, somewhat waxy; dark green, yellow-green at joints of the segments; phyllichnia flat to slightly rounded; teeth 12–20, erect; teeth on new shoots strongly recurved.

Notes This species sprouts prolifically from expanding root systems, and in native populations often forms stands. Some evidence of this exists at Orpet Park. The species name *glauca* means covered with a fine whitish- or blue-green bloom.

Locations Until recently, the only known individuals in Santa Barbara were two male trees in Lower Orpet Park. However, two female trees have been noted growing in the median of Emerson Avenue above Roosevelt School.

Top: Cone-like fruit and branchlets of Casuarina glauca. *Bottom: Branchlets and male flowers.*

Celastraceae

The Bittersweet Family includes over 50 genera and 800 species from all regions of the world except extreme boreal zones. It is most diverse in tropical and warm temperate regions. Many species have fruit with brightly colored arils that are disseminated by birds and monkeys.

Maytenus

Maytenus is a genus of about 200 species from tropical and warm regions of the world. *Maytenus* is derived from *mantun,* the Mapuche Indian name for the species below.

Maytenus boaria
Mayten tree

Typically found in or along watercourses in arid or semiarid regions of Chile on the western side of the Andes and extending along the eastern side from Argentina to Peru.

Habit An evergreen tree with a rounded crown and strongly drooping branches; to 30 feet tall.

Inflorescence Monoecious; axillary clusters of 2–5 flowers, flowers inconspicuous, yellowish, 3/16 inch across. Blooms in January.

Fruit A capsule, 1/4 inch across, containing 2 seeds enclosed in a red fleshy aril.

Twigs Pendulous, slender, green or brown, becoming gray.

Bark Dull gray, smooth, becoming fissured into small rectangular flakes.

Leaves Alternate, simple, held perpendicular to the twig; lanceolate to narrowly ovate, 1–2 x 1/4–3/4 inches, margins finely serrate; petioles very short.

Notes In its native habitat, cattle are known for a single-minded preference for the foliage of mayten over all other fodder. Thus, Molina, in describing the species, gave it the specific epithet of *boaria* (meaning of or for cattle). The leaves were used by native peoples to reduce fevers.

Locations MacKenzie Park adjacent to State Street. Alice Keck Park Memorial Gardens near the Santa Barbara Street entry. University of California, Santa Barbara on the north side of Noble Hall. Street trees in the 500 block of West Islay Street.

Top: Weeping form and uniform lower crown of Maytenus boaria.
Bottom: Fine-textured foliage and red fruit.

Ebenaceae

The Ebony Family includes two genera and over 500 species that are found throughout the world in tropical and subtropical regions. Only a few of the species extend into cooler temperate zones. The greatest diversity of the family is in the Indo-Pacific region. The family is well-known for its hard and dark wood that has been used for carvings and other wood products. Some species have been used by native peoples as fish poisons.

Diospyros

Diospyros is a genus of approximately 450 mostly tropical trees. It includes the ebony of commerce *(D. ebenum)* as well as marblewood and zebrawood, which are favored for exotic wood products. Several species are cultivated for their fruit. The genus is named from the Greek words *dios* (Zeus or Jove) and *pyros* (grain), referring to the edible fruit.

Diospyros kaki
Japanese persimmon, *kaki*

Native to Japan, southern China, and Korea.

Habit A deciduous tree with a low-branched irregular crown; to 30 feet tall.

Inflorescence Dioecious or monoecious; axillary; male flowers in threes, bell-shaped, 2/5 inch long, with 16–24 stamens; female flowers solitary 1/2–3/4 inch long; both whitish. Blooms May to June.

Fruit Obvious and striking when mature; more or less spherical, 3–4 inches across with 4 large persistent calyx lobes, bright orange, very fleshy turning almost to jelly, with shiny seeds.

Twigs Dark brown, hairy.

Bark Grayish to dark brown, broken into rectangular blocks, with alternating dark and light layers in cross section.

Leaves Alternate, simple; ovate to oblong, 2 1/2–7 x 1 1/2–3 1/2 inches, glabrous, shiny dark green above, lighter and hairy beneath, with striking yellows, oranges, and reds in the fall; leathery and strongly veined; petiole 1/2–1 inch long, pubescent.

Notes The fruit of *D. kaki* has long been a favored source of sugar in the Orient. Its fruits may be rather astringent if not fully ripe. The species name *kaki* is the Japanese name for persimmon.

Locations Common in gardens throughout town. A small tree in Chase Palm Park east of the carrousel. Two cultivars at Lotusland.

Bright orange fruit and dark green leaves of Diospyros kaki.

Diospyros virginiana
Persimmon, possumwood

Found on disturbed, generally moist, sites throughout the eastern United States, from Connecticut to Kansas and south to Texas and Florida.

Habit A medium-sized deciduous tree with a wide rounded crown; to 40 feet tall.

Inflorescence Dioecious or monoecious; axillary; male flowers in threes on fragrant woody peduncles, bell-shaped, $1/3$ inch long, with 16 stamens; female flowers solitary $3/5$ inch long; both whitish to greenish-white. Blooms May to June.

Fruit A yellowish- to pale orange and somewhat glaucous edible berry, $1-1 1/2$ inches across, with 4 large persistent calyx lobes.

Twigs Gray to red-brown with orange lenticels, hairy or not; terminal buds absent, lateral buds solitary, with two overlapping reddish-black scales.

Bark Light to dark gray, becoming checkered with deep fissures into square blocks when young, exhibiting a rippling of alternating deep red-purple and almost black layers when cut.

Leaves Alternate, simple; ovate to elliptic, $2 1/4 - 5 1/2$ x $3/4 - 2$ inches; glabrous, shiny dark green above, lighter beneath, turning yellow-green in the fall; young leaves with translucent veins; older leaves leathery and strongly veined; petiole $1/3 - 1$ inch long, pubescent.

Notes The fruit is a favorite, if insignificant, product of Appalachian forests. It is usually eaten after the first frost when its previously astringent properties are alleviated. At that time it is a race with the possums and raccoons to see who will benefit from the year's production. Because of its hard, fine-grained characteristic, the wood of *D. virginiana* has long been favored in the manufacture of golf clubs. However, the increased usage of space-age materials (titanium) seems to have supplanted it for all but a few purists. The species name *virginiana* means from Virginia.

Locations Two street trees in the 2600 block of Orella Street.

Top: Light green lower leaf surfaces and pale orange flowers of Diospyros virginiana.
Bottom: Glossy dark green upper leaf surfaces.

Elaeocarpaceae

The Elaeocarp Family includes nine genera and about 500 species, most of which are found in Australasia and Asia. There are no natural occurrences of this family in Africa.

Crinodendron

Crinodendron is a small genus composed of four species which are geographically separated from one another in South America. The name is composed from the Greek words *krinon* (lily) and *dendron* (tree).

Crinodendron patagua
Lily-of-the-valley tree, *pataqua*

Native to the valleys of central Chile.

Habit Evergreen shrubs or small trees with a dense bushy crown; to 30 feet.

Inflorescence Axillary drooping flowers, 3/4 inch long, with 5 white lobed petals fused at the base. Blooms July to September.

Fruit A capsule with a persistent style, 1/2–1 inch long; crimson when fresh, drying to brown with tan specks; seeds small, dark purple.

Twigs Initially light green and minutely hairy, becoming gray; apical buds small, broadly triangular and with silky hairs.

Bark Rough, grayish-brown, broken into small plates.

Leaves Opposite or alternate, simple; ovate to oblanceolate, 1–3 x 1/4–1 1/3 inches; dark green and glabrous above, light green with very fine gray pubescence below, margins rolled under and somewhat serrate; petiole to 1/2 inch long, light red and minutely hairy.

Notes The species name *patagua* is the native name for the species.

Locations Street trees in the first block of North Alisos Street and in the 1500 block of San Pascual Street. Two trees in front of Franklin School in the 1100 block of East Mason Street.

Top: *Pendent flowers and young fruit of* **Crinodendron patagua**.
Bottom: *Angular crimson fruit and grayish lower leaf surfaces.*

Ericaceae

The Heath Family consists of 123 genera and approximately 4,000 species. It occurs in mild to cool regions of the world on all continents except Antarctica. The greatest diversity of the family occurs in the Andes of Columbia, Ecuador, Peru, and Venezuela. *Erica* (heather) is the largest genus, with about 665 species; of these, nearly 600 are native to the Western Cape Province of South Africa. The family is well-known for its almost singular restriction to acidic soils.

Arbutus

Arbutus is a genus of about 14 species from western North America and the western and Mediterranean regions of Europe. The genus name *Arbutus* is the Latin name for *A. unedo*.

Arbutus menziesii
Pacific madrone

Native to the coastal mountains of western North America, from southern British Columbia to the central coast of California. Rare south of Santa Barbara.

Habit A small evergreen tree; to 40 feet tall.

Inflorescence Terminal drooping panicles; flowers small, urn-shaped, about 1/3 inch long; yellowish-white or pinkish; with a strong fragrance of honey; appearing with the new leaves. Blooms March to April.

Fruit An orangish-red berry, 1/2 inch in diameter, with a rough surface covered with numerous short projections.

Twigs Stout, satiny pale green in spring becoming reddish-brown, glabrous; terminal buds 1/3 inch long, very light green.

Bark Thin, exfoliating in flakes and curled strips to expose smooth yellowish-green surfaces that become reddish-brown; on older stems accumulating in many small irregular flakes.

Leaves Alternate, simple; oval, 2 3/4–5 inches long, with 20–30 pairs of pinnate veins; thick, leathery; dark glossy green above, paler beneath; midrib and margins pale yellow-green, margins very shallowly toothed; petiole 1 inch long, pale green.

Notes *A. menziesii* is a striking member of the native flora that should receive more horticultural attention locally. However, it is susceptible to summer drought and appears to do best locally in the fog-enriched upper slopes and protected canyons of the Santa Ynez Mountains. The species name *menziesii* honors Archibald Menzies (1754–1842), Scottish surgeon and botanist who collected plants of the Pacific region with the Vancouver expedition.

Locations An excellent tree tucked in Mission Canyon behind the Weber Studio of the Santa Barbara Botanic Garden. Several small to medium-sized trees elsewhere in the Garden.

Top: Inflorescence of urn-shaped flowers of **Arbutus menziesii**.
Bottom left: Exfoliating bark, revealing the greenish photosynthetic tissue beneath.
Bottom right: Red fruit and dark green leaves with pale gray lower surface.

Arbutus unedo
Strawberry tree

Found in evergreen forests and tall maquis (chaparral), especially in rocky landscapes; occurs in Ireland, Spain, and most of the lands bordering the Mediterranean Basin.

Habit   A small evergreen tree with a dense rounded crown; to 20 feet tall.

Inflorescence   Terminal drooping panicles, 1 1/2–2 inches long; flowers small, urn-shaped, about 1/3 inch long; white tinged with green or pink. Blooming in the fall.

Fruit   A round, fleshy berry, 3/4 inch across, orange-red, with a granular surface.

Twigs   Pink-red above, pale green beneath; with dark brown glandular bristly hairs.

Bark   Light gray, shredding in thin strips to expose cinnamon-brown inner bark, becoming spirally twisted with age.

Leaves   Alternate, simple; oblong-lanceolate, 2–4 x 3/4–1 1/4 inches; margins with small forward-pointing teeth; shiny dark green above, pale beneath, glabrous; petiole 1/4 inch long, glandular hairy, reddish-green.

Notes   Although *A. unedo* has been cultivated for centuries, it is a relatively recent addition to the Santa Barbara area. The berries are edible, but rather bland; hence, its specific name—*unedo,* "I eat (only) one." Most of the trees commonly planted today are known in the horticultural industry as *Arbutus* 'Marina.' This variety was originally introduced at a 1917 horticultural exposition. However, it was lost to the public until reintroduced to the nursery trade by the Saratoga Horticultural Foundation in 1984. *Arbutus* 'Marina' is named for the Marina district of San Francisco where a long-defunct nursery had maintained the line following the exposition. *Arbutus* 'Marina' can be a striking tree and deserves more attention in Santa Barbara. In particular, its exfoliating red bark and graceful large form make it an ideal substitute for *A. menziesii.*

Locations   Increasingly common about town. Several large trees in upper Orpet Park. Another in East Alameda Plaza. A large street tree on Oramus Road.

Top: A larger **Arbutus unedo** *with multiple stems and rounded crown.*
Middle left: A young **Arbutus** *'Marina' at the Santa Barbara Golf Club.*
Middle right: Urn-shaped flowers and serrate leaves.
Bottom: Yellow and red fruit.

Euphorbiaceae

The Spurge Family includes approximately 300 genera and 9,000 species that occur worldwide. By far, the greatest diversity is found in the wet tropics and seasonally dry tropics. Species of this family are frequently opportunistic pioneers on disturbed habitats. The family is also unique in that seed dispersal for most members occurs primarily by the explosive dehiscence of the fruit. In one genus, seeds can be thrown over 80 feet from the parent plant.

Aleurites

Aleurites is a genus of five species from Indo-Malaysia and the western Pacific. The name is from the Greek word *aleurites* (floury) and refers to the young growth which appears to be dusted with flour.

Aleurites moluccana
Candlenut-tree, Indian walnut

Although the Latin name suggests an origin in the Moluccan Islands, the original distribution is not exactly known; the species has been widely cultivated throughout Southeast Asia since at least 1000 BC.

Habit A tall, evergreen tree with a whitish appearing crown; to 50 feet tall.

Inflorescence Dioecious; terminal panicles, 4–6 inches long, covered with pale white scales; flowers 1/3 inch across, with 5 pale yellowish-white petals. Blooms December to January.

Fruit In clusters of 3–6; a round drupe with 4 faint ridges radiating from the apex, 2–2½ inches across, consisting of a fleshy olive-green rind and 1–2 very hard seeds.

Twigs Covered with pale white scales.

Bark Gray, roughened with lenticels.

Leaves Alternate, simple; broadly ovate, 3–9 x 1¾–7 inches; apex tapering sharply to a point; margins entire, wavy; dark green with a silvery gloss, covered with pale white scales; peduncle 2–6 inches long, with a pair of small glands underneath near the leaf; leaves of seedlings and lower branches three- to five-lobed with a heart-shaped base.

Notes The species gets its common name from the high oil content of the seeds, which were used in candle making and were prominently

Top: Terminal inflorescence of small flowers and palmately lobed leaves of Aleurites moluccana. *Bottom: Large round fruit.*

mentioned in Charles Nordhoff's *Mutiny on the Bounty*. Today the oil is used primarily in the manufacture of soap and paint. The raw kernel is poisonous. The species name *moluccana* means from Molucca.

Locations A sapling has recently been replanted in Franceschi Park along the entry drive.

Baloghia

Baloghia is a small genus of 12 species from eastern Australia, New Caledonia, and Norfolk Island. The genus was named by Joseph Endler for Dr. Joseph Balogh, a plantsman who wrote a treatise on the plants of Transylvania in 1779.

Baloghia inophylla
Baloghia lucida
Scrub bloodwood

Widespread in coastal scrublands of eastern Australia, from central Queensland to northern Tasmania.

Habit   An evergreen shrub or small tree; to 25 feet tall.

Inflorescence   Monoecious; in terminal racemes; flowers white, with 5 spreading petals, 3/4–1 inch across, highly aromatic. Blooms November to December.

Fruit   A round, hard capsule, 3/4 inch across, splitting at maturity into 3 lobes.

Twigs   Shiny green, becoming gray brown.

Bark   Thin, smooth; dull gray-brown, stained with red sap.

Leaves   Opposite, simple; ovate or elliptical, 2 1/4–4 3/4 x 3/4–2 inches; stiff, leathery, glabrous, shiny green, margins thickened with a gland on each side just above the petiole; midrib slightly indented above, protruding below; petiole 1/4 inch, green, slightly channeled above.

Notes   When damaged, the bark and twigs release a large quantity of blood-red sap which has been used as a source of indelible paint. The species name *inophylla* means with fibrous leaves.

Locations   A single tree in lower Orpet Park below the lawn.

Leathery ovate leaves and flowers of **Baloghia inophylla.**

Bischofia

Bischofia includes only two species—one in Indo-Malaysia and the other in central and southeastern China. The genus was named to honor Gottlieb Wilhelm Bischoff (1797–1854), professor of botany at Heidelberg.

Bischofia javanica
Toog

Occurring in mixed forests or teak forests of Southeast Asia and the tropical Pacific islands.

Habit An evergreen tree with a rounded crown; to 45 feet tall.

Inflorescence Monoecious; axillary panicles, $3^{2}/_{3}$–8 inches long; flowers inconspicuous. Blooms March to April.

Fruit Globose, $^{1}/_{2}$–$^{2}/_{3}$ inch across, tannish-brown; held in grape-like bunches among the leaves.

Twigs Stout, green becoming gray, with large round leaf scars.

Bark Grayish-brown, exfoliating in silvery plates on older stems.

Leaves Spirally arranged, palmately compound, 10–12 inches long; 3 leaflets each on a petiolule, oval, to 5 x 4 inches, with an elongated apex, bases slightly unequal, leathery, margins serrate, midrib and lateral veins prominent below, lateral veins looping together near the margin; petiolule stout, to 8 inches long.

Notes The species name *javanica* means from Java.

Locations Several trees in a city parking lot at Garden Street and Cabrillo Boulevard. Street trees in the 300 block of West Junipero Street.

Compound leaves and fruit of Bischofia javanica.

Euphorbia

Euphorbia is possibly the largest genus of angiosperms. It includes about 2,000 herbs, shrubs, and trees found throughout the world, especially in warmer regions. The familiar poinsettia *(E. poinsettia)* is perhaps the most common representative. The milky sap and frequently spined stems of "woody" species are characteristic of the genus. In Africa, the succulent species fill the same ecological role that the many species of Cactaceae play in the New World. The milky latex is toxic and can cause allergic skin reactions and in some cases blindness. The name of the genus and the family is that of Euphorbus, who was the physician of Juba I, King of Numidia (49–30 BC).

Euphorbia ingens
Candelabra tree

Native to the open lands of eastern South Africa (the Natal region) and extending north to Zimbabwe and Mozambique; often associated with termite mounds.

Habit A massively branched tree with a dense rounded crown, to 30 feet tall.

Inflorescence Monoecious; axillary; a unique structure (cyathium) composed of a single female flower with a very reduced perianth, surrounded by 5 male flowers that consist of a pedicel and a single stamen, yellowish-green; the cayathia usually occur in groups of 3. Blooms in August.

Fruit A three-lobed capsule, to 1/2 inch across.

Stem Massively branched low on the trunk; the branches four- or five-winged, obviously but irregularly constricted, dark green; with pairs of very short spines on a darkened spine shield along the margins of the stem wings.

Leaves Minute, occurring along the wings of the branches, absent on flowering branches.

Notes Most of the plant's photosynthesis occurs in its stems, making the leaves almost superfluous. The sap of this species is very toxic, with contact resulting in allergic skin reactions and causing temporary or permanent loss of vision if it comes in contact with the eyes. It is used by native peoples as a fish poison causing temporary paralysis so that the fish rise to the surface. It has also been used as a purgative and to treat alcoholism and cancer. However, several fatal overdoses have been recorded. Several animals appear to be unaffected by the species—birds and the vervet monkey eat the fruit and porcupines and cane rats eat the roots. The species name *ingens* means tremendous, gigantic.

Locations Several young trees at Lotusland, south of the house.

Top: Angular stems and massive crown of Euphorbia ingens.
Bottom: Yellow-green inflorescences (cyathia) and spine shields along stem wing.

Glochidion

Glochidion is a genus of almost 300 species, most of which occur in the southwestern Pacific region. A few species are found in Madagascar and others in the New World tropics. The genus name derives from the Greek *glochidion* (barb), referring to the barbed pistil of some species.

Glochidion ferdinandii
Cheese tree, rain tree, buttonwood

Found in the rain forests of central Queensland and southeastern New South Wales, Australia.

Habit An evergreen shrub or tree; to 60 feet tall.

Inflorescence Monoecious or dioecious; compact axillary clusters of sessile flowers, flowers with 3 yellow-green sepals and petals, $1/4$ inch across, the 3–8 stamens and the 3–15 styles of the female flower fused into a column.

Fruit A green to pinkish, pumpkin-shaped capsule, $1/2$–$3/4$ inch across, splitting to expose the bright red arils of the seeds.

Twigs Light green with small white elongate lenticels, becoming tan.

Bark Grayish-brown, flaky, with linear furrows.

Leaves Alternate, simple; elliptic to broadly lanceolate, to 8 x $3^1/2$ inches, bright green and shiny above, lighter beneath, veins obvious, yellowish; petiole $1/4$ inch long.

Notes Although the leaves are simple in form, their placement on the twig appears much like a pinnately compound leaf. Many of the twigs die at the end of one year's growth but persist on the tree without leaves, giving a somewhat unkempt appearance. The species name *ferdinandii* honors Baron Ferdinand von Mueller, the first government botanist in Victoria.

Locations A single tree is located in Franceschi Park along the path directly above the main house.

Glossy green leaves and minute flower buds of Glochidion ferdinandii.

Manihot

Manihot is a genus of about 100 species from tropical and warm temperate regions of the Americas. Its name comes from the Brazilian *manioc* for cassava.

Manihot carthaginensis
Cassava, tapioca, *manioc, yuca*

Found in coastal dry scrub forests on limestone outcrops from southern Texas to Brazil.

Habit A small deciduous tree; to 15 feet tall.

Inflorescence Monoecious; terminal panicles, to 6 inches long; flowers 5/8 x 1 inch, deep maroon with yellow-tipped tepals. Blooms August to September.

Fruit A smooth round capsule, 1/2–2/3 inch, light green.

Twigs Angled, yellowish-green, leaf scars round, 1/3–1/2 inch across.

Bark Dark gray or reddish, almost glossy, spottily peeling.

Leaves Alternate, simple, but deeply palmately five-lobed; lobes themselves may be strongly lobed in the middle, 6 x 2 1/2 inches, dull blue-green above, silvery below; petiole to 8 inches long, greenish with a maroon tint or dark red throughout.

Notes All parts of the plant contain a milky sap. As implied by the name, this is a close relative of the horticultural cassava *(Manihot esculenta)*. Although not nearly as common today, its tubers were eaten by native peoples after appropriate treatment to rid the starch-laden material of its natural cyanide content. The specific epithet is an inaccurate portrayal of its geographic affinity. The species name *carthaginensis* means from Cartagena, Bolivar, Colombia.

Locations Franceschi Park below the cottage.

Top: Palmately lobed leaves and maroon and yellow flowers of Manihot carthaginensis.
Bottom: Round green fruit and drooping leaves.

Fabaceae

The Pea or Bean Family includes almost 700 genera and about 18,000 species from almost all regions of the world, especially the tropics. Many of its species are capable of nitrogen fixation and they are often found on nitrogen-poor soils. With their high protein content, the seeds have been the source of important food stuffs worldwide, and many of the species have been important forage crops. However, many species contain toxic levels of alkaloids that are harmful to human and animal health alike.

Many species of the Fabaceae contain a highly specialized structure on the petiole of the leaf, the pulvinus, that functions to adjust leaf position relative to the sun. At night the leaves hang straight down; in the morning and afternoon hours the leaves are held perpendicular to the sun so that maximum sunlight is intercepted; and at midday, when solar heat loads may be particularly high leading to desiccation, the leaves are held roughly parallel to the sun, thus minimizing solar interception.

Acacia
Wattle

Acacia is a large genus of 1,500 or more species spread throughout tropical and subtropical regions of the world, and is most abundant and diverse in relatively dry climates, especially in the Southern Hemisphere. Most species have spines or thorns, and its name derives from the Greek *akakia,* which references the Egyptian thorn *(A. arabica),* and is in turn derived from *ake* or *akis,* meaning a sharp point or thorn. Its worldwide distribution and the number of its species suggests that the genus is of ancient origin and evolved prior to the breakup of Gondwanaland leading to the present continental configuration. Its many species seem to do well in hot and dry, hot and moist, cold and dry, but not cold and moist environments. Thus, the genus is not found in boreal zones, nor typically in the highly competitive humid zones of temperate regions, such as the Pacific Northwest. Throughout its distribution the species in this genus have played an important role in the culture of native peoples, providing food, medicines, clothing, and shelter. Its common name (wattle), of Australian origin, refers to the fact that early settlers of the continent used long flexible twigs in the framing of wattle and daub huts. However, they in fact were using *Callicoma serratifolia* for that purpose. Although *Acacia* is a large genus, only 80 to 90 of its species are commonly in cultivation.

The generic name is in a state of taxonomic flux. A recent proposal to split the genus into three separate genera is likely to be adopted. If this happens, all of the Australian species will be included in a new genus, and *Acacia* will be restricted primarily to species from Africa.

Acacia decurrens

Acacia baileyana
Cootamundra wattle, Bailey acacia

A. baileyana was originally limited to a 100-kilometer range of the Cootamundra region of New South Wales, Australia. Now it is widely planted and naturalized throughout Australia and in regions of Mediterranean climate.

Habit Evergreen shrubs or small trees, initially conical with branches to the ground, then developing a distinct trunk with a dense rounded crown; to 30 feet tall.

Inflorescence Axillary racemes or panicles; rachis thin, with a waxy bloom, 2–3 1/2 inches long; flower heads globular, 1/4–3/8 inch across, bright yellow, containing 20–25 flowers. Flowers January to February.

Fruit Legume 1 1/2–4 x 1/4–1/2 inches; straight or slightly curved, flat, brown; margins straight or slightly constricted between seeds.

Twigs Somewhat ridged with intervening furrows; somewhat pubescent; usually glaucous silvery gray.

Bark Silvery gray with shallow dark furrows.

Leaves Alternate; bipinnate, containing 2–6 pairs of pinnae, each with 12–20 pairs of pinnules; rachis 1/2–1 1/2 inches long with a gland at the junction of the upper pinnae pairs, usually not the lowest; pinnules linear, 3/16 inch long, usually glaucous silvery blue-gray.

Notes *Acacia baileyana* 'Purpurea' is a variety with purplish leaves that has been increasingly planted, especially along Highway 101 near the State Street and Highway 154 overpasses. The species name *baileyana* honors Frederick Manson Bailey (1827–1915), Australian botanist and author of *Queensland Flora*.

Locations Found commonly as an invasive in the Mission Canyon area. Street trees in the 100 block of West Canon Perdido Street, 800 block of Alisos Street, and the 2000 block of Castillo Street.

Top: Rounded crown and often leaning trunk of Acacia baileyana.
Bottom: Long racemes of bright yellow flowers and shorter bipinnately compound leaves.

Acacia binervia
Acacia glaucescens
Coast *myall*

Found along the coast and limited inland locations of New South Wales.

Habit An erect or spreading evergreen tree; to 30 feet tall.

Inflorescence Axillary cylindrical racemes, 3/4–2 3/8 inches long on a peduncle 1/4–1/2 inch long; flowers golden-yellow. Flowers March to April.

Fruit Pod straight, flattened, but raised over the seeds, 2 1/2–3 1/4 x 1/4 inches; margins somewhat thickened; brown.

Twigs Angled, glaucous.

Bark Fibrous, dark gray with rusty-orange fissures.

Leaves Alternate; phyllodes somewhat to strongly sickle-shaped, 3–6 x 1/8–1/4 inches, surface covered with short gray hairs giving a glaucous appearance, with 2–3 prominent longitudinal veins.

Notes The foliage is reported to be toxic to livestock, as its leaves contains glycosides that may produce prussic acid when damaged or severed. The species name *binervia* means two-nerved.

Locations A single tree in the west end of lower planting in upper Orpet Park.

Glaucous phyllodes and elongate racemes of bright yellow flowers of Acacia binervia.

Acacia cultriformis
Knife-leaf wattle

Widely distributed on the western mountain slopes of New South Wales.

Habit A large bushy shrub to small tree, evergreen; to 15 feet tall.

Inflorescence Axillary racemes of 8–20 globular flower heads, each containing 10–35 bright yellow flowers; peduncles smooth, short, 1/4 inch. Flowers in February.

Fruit Pods in dense clusters, 2–3 x 1/4 inches, thin, smooth, dark reddish-brown; margins thin, somewhat constricted between the 2–6 seeds.

Twigs Smooth but knobby from leaf scars, angled, ribbed; light orange with a whitish waxy surface.

Bark Smooth, dark gray, becoming deeply fissured and fibrous.

Leaves Alternate; phyllodes triangular, 1/2–1 x 1/4–1/2 inch, thick, smooth, frosty blue-gray, usually crowded on the twig; upper margin angled with a raised gland; apex with a long or short point; one central curved nerve closer to the lower, straight margin.

Notes The species name *cultriformis* means shaped like a knife blade.

Locations A single small tree at the Mission Street onramp to Highway 101 North. A large shrub on Highway 101 North just west of the Ward Memorial Highway exit, and several along Ward Memorial Highway.

Top: Sprawling form of **Acacia cultriformis.**
Bottom: Triangular glaucous phyllodes and racemes of globular flower heads.

Acacia dealbata
Silver wattle

Widely distributed in southeastern Australia from Tasmania to New South Wales.

Habit An evergreen tree with a rounded feathery crown; to 50 feet tall.

Inflorescence Axillary racemes or panicles, about as long as leaves, containing 25–35 flower heads; flower heads globose, 3/16–1/4 inch across, lemon- to bright yellow, sweet-scented; peduncles lightly gray pubescent. Flowers January to February.

Fruit Pods 2–3 x 1/4–1/2 inches, straight or slightly curved, flat but swollen over seeds, margins slightly constricted between the seeds; light purplish-brown or glaucous.

Twigs Angled with slight, fine ridges, covered with fine silvery gray pubescence.

Bark Silvery gray to dark gray, with fine dark vertical fissures on older trunks.

Leaves Alternate; bipinnate containing 10–26 pairs of pinnae, each with 20–50 pairs of pinnules; pinnules silvery gray pubescent especially at the tips, 3/16 inch long; rachis 1–4 inches long, angled, with a raised gland at the junction of each pair of pinnae.

Notes A similar species, *A. mearnsii*, differs in having green foliage, narrower pods which resemble a string of beads due to the constrictions between seeds, and additional glands along the rachis between the points of pinnae insertion. *A. decurrens* is also similar, but has glabrous, dark green and more broadly spaced pinnules. *A. dealbata* is highly invasive in New Zealand, South Africa, and southern Europe. The species name *dealbata* means whitish, white-washed.

Locations Several individuals along Old Coast Highway adjacent to the Montecito Country Club golf course.

Top: A young tree of Acacia dealbata *in full flower.*
Bottom left: Long racemes of globose flower heads and bipinnately compound leaves.
Bottom right: Foliage and mature seed pods.

Acacia decurrens
Green wattle, early black wattle

Naturally occurring in scattered locations on the tablelands of New South Wales, Australia.

Habit Medium-sized evergreen tree with a dense feathery crown; to 50 feet tall.

Inflorescence Terminal racemes or panicles of 6–15 small, yellow, globular heads each containing 2–30 flowers. Flowers January to February.

Fruit Pods flat, almost straight, 2–4 x 1/4 inches, light reddish-brown; margins somewhat constricted between the seeds.

Twigs Stout, smooth, angled with ridges becoming wings up to 1/16 inch wide running down the stems from one node to the next, yellow-green.

Bark Dark gray, almost black; appearing to have large warts scattered along the lower trunk; frequently exuding a clear golden resin.

Leaves Alternate; bipinnate, consisting of 6–12 (or more) pairs of pinnae, each containing 30–40 pairs of pinnules; rachis strongly channeled above, bearing a raised gland near the base of each pair of pinnae; pinnules needle-like, 1/2 inch long, well-spaced, dark green above, pale beneath.

Notes Two species, *A. dealbata* and *A. mearnsii* are quite similar but can be distinguished by the placement of glands along the leaf rachis, or the density of pinnae on the leaf. The species name *decurrens* means running down the stem.

Locations A single tree on Lasuen Road and Moreno Road on the El Encanto Hotel property. Several others in the Cal Trans plantings on the north side of the Highway 101 interchange with Cabrillo Boulevard, near the Bird Refuge.

Top: Full crown of Acacia decurrens.
Bottom: Deep green foliage and globose flower heads.

Acacia farnesiana
Sweet acacia

Generally thought to have originated in the southern United States (western Florida to southern Arizona), Mexico, and tropical America; now naturalized throughout the tropical and subtropical regions of the world, including southern San Diego County, California.

Habit A multi-stemmed deciduous shrub or low spreading tree; to 25 feet tall.

Inflorescence Axillary simple racemes of yellow, somewhat fragrant globular heads, 2/3 inch across; peduncles lightly pubescent. Flowers February to March.

Fruit Pods rounded, stiff, 1 1/2–3 x 1/2–3/4 inches; deep dark red to black, not constricted between the seeds; seeds tawny brown.

Twigs Glabrous to somewhat pubescent; gray to whitish, straight, sometimes with paired stipular spines 1/4–2 inches long.

Bark Gray brown, with shallow fissures.

Leaves Alternate; bipinnate, containing 2–6 pairs of pinnae and 18–25 pairs of linear to oblong pinnules, 3/16 inch long; petiole and rachis with short soft hairs; a single small raised gland in the middle of the petiole, others between the upper 1–2 pinnae pairs.

Notes This species is one of the few deciduous acacias. It is the source of the essential oil *cassie ancienne,* used for perfumery, and is extensively cultivated in southern France for that industry. Because of its aggressive tendency for invasion, it has been given the name Ellington's Curse in Fiji. The species name *farnesiana* refers to the gardens of the Farnese Palace, Rome from which the original specimen was collected for description.

Locations Small trees in the Santa Barbara Botanic Garden in the Desert Section.

Top: Short, bipinnately compound leaves and large yellow flower heads of Acacia farnesiana.
Bottom: Stout twigs and dark swollen seed pods.

Acacia longifolia
Sallow wattle, Sydney golden wattle

Found among coastal sand dunes of southern and eastern Australia: New South Wales, Victoria, South Australia, and Tasmania.

Habit Large evergreen shrub, sometimes trained as a dense, broad-crowned tree; to 20 feet tall.

Inflorescence Axillary, 1–2 (sometimes 3) simple spikes at each leaf node, $2/3$–$1 2/3$ inches long, containing dense clusters of bright yellow flowers. Flowers January to February.

Fruit Pods 2–4 inches long, $1/4$ inch broad, cylindrical, straight or curved, with an elongate beak, finely ridged, brown; margins constricted between seeds.

Twigs Slightly angled; glabrous or slightly pubescent when young; reddish-green.

Bark Gray, slightly roughened with shallow, vertical, somewhat orange fissures.

Leaves Alternate; reduced to phyllodes; linear-lanceolate to obovate-oblong, $1 1/2$– 6 x $1/4$–$1 1/2$ inches, generally straight, 2–3 obvious longitudinal, parallel nerves with a network of many fine veins; usually with a small, sharp point near the apex; dark green, primary veins and margins yellow-green.

Notes The species name *longifolia* means long-leaved.

Locations A single tree in upper Orpet Park along Lasuen Road; others along Devereaux Road on the west campus of the University of California, Santa Barbara. Several planted along Highway 101 east and west of Santa Barbara.

Top: Dense crown of long linear twigs of Acacia longifolia.
Bottom: Twig of densely placed phyllodes and flowering racemes.

Acacia mearnsii
Acacia decurrens var. *mollis*
Black wattle

Native to the coastal lowlands of New South Wales, Victoria, and South Australia, Australia.

Habit A spreading evergreen tree with branches which may droop to the ground, frequently multi-stemmed and weedy; to 50 feet tall.

Inflorescence Axillary racemes of about 10 pale yellow, fragrant, globular flower heads, 2/3 inch across; peduncles covered with fine golden pubescence. Flowers February to March.

Fruit Pods linear, 2–4 x 1/4 inches, dark brown to blackish, covered with fine whitish hairs; constricted between seeds to give the appearance of a string of beads.

Twigs Angled with ridges extending down from each node; deep green, densely covered with minute hairs.

Bark Smooth, greenish-brown on young branches; rough, blackish on main trunks; frequently exuding a gummy sap.

Leaves Alternate, bipinnate; all parts covered with soft short pubescence; 8–25 pairs of pinnae with 30–70 pairs of crowded minute pinnules, dark to olive-green; petiole 1/2–2 inches long; rachis 1 1/2–6 inches long, with a raised gland just below the junction with each pair of pinnae and additional glands irregularly interspersed between.

Notes *A. dealbata* is very similar and is distinguished by having raised glands on the rachis only at the junctions with pinnae. *A. decurrens* is also similar but has wing-like ridges extending from each leaf down the twigs and has leaves with much sparser pinnae. This species has proven to be highly invasive in South Africa. The species name *mearnsii* honors Dr. Edgar Mearns, who first collected the species in September 1909 on a South African expedition led by then-Colonel Theodore Roosevelt.

Locations Two trees on the campus of the University of California, Santa Barbara on the north side of the Psychology Building. Others on Old Coast Highway adjacent to the east end of the Montecito Country Club. Others along upper Mission Canyon Road and in the 100 block of East Constance.

Top: Dark crown and pale flowers of Acacia mearnsii.
Middle: Dense cluster of pale yellow flower heads.
Bottom: Dark green bipinnately compound leaves and dense cluster of seed pods.

Acacia melanoxylon
Black acacia, blackwood

Native to the tablelands and coastal regions of eastern Australia, from Queensland to eastern South Australia and Tasmania.

Habit A large symmetrical evergreen tree with a dense canopy, usually branching a short distance from the ground; to 50 feet tall.

Inflorescence Axillary racemes, much shorter than the phyllodes, covered with dense minute hairs; racemes containing 2–8 pale yellow globular flower heads, each consisting of 3–50 flowers; peduncles stout, scaly, 1/4–1/2 inch long. Flowers March to April.

Fruit Pods narrow, 1 1/2–5 x 1/4–1/2 inches; flattish, curved, coiled and twisted, fawn-colored to reddish-brown; margins thickened, slightly constricted between seeds; seeds black, encircled by a long coiled salmon-red stalk.

Twigs Pubescent and angled, becoming glabrous and marked with light-colored fissures.

Bark Rough, broken by shallow vertical furrows, light gray, hard.

Leaves Alternate; phyllodes lanceolate or oblanceolate, 2 1/2–5 1/2 x 1/2–1 1/4 inches; frequently one margin straight, the other curved; leathery; 2–5 pairs of prominent, longitudinal nerves, with a dense network of finer veins; small glands along upper margin, near the base; deep, dark, dull green with a whitish glaucous cast.

Notes The species name *melanoxylon* means black wood.

Locations Street trees on Paseo del Refugio, Paseo Tranquillo, and Paseo del Descanso—all east of Alamar Avenue. Others on Nopal Street at Cota Street and on Por la Mar Drive next to Dwight Murphy Field.

Top: Compact symmetrical crown of Acacia melanoxylon. *Bottom: Dark green phyllodes and pale flower heads.*

Acacia pendula
Myall, weeping *myall*, *boree*

Widely distributed in the western regions of New South Wales, Australia and extending into Victoria and Queensland.

Habit Medium-sized evergreen tree with pendulous foliage and branches; to 30 feet tall.

Inflorescence Axillary racemes or clusters of small, globular, dull lemon-colored balls, 1/4 inch across; peduncles 1/3–1/2 inch long. Flowers November to December.

Fruit Very flat, 1 1/4–3 1/4 x 1/3–3/4 inches, sparsely hairy, margins with prominent wings.

Twigs Thin, slightly angled, yellow-green, sometimes initially hairy.

Bark Rough, fibrous, gray-brown, orangish-brown between interlacing ridges.

Leaves Alternate; phyllodes lanceolate, straight or curved, 1 1/2–4 x 1/8–1/2 inches, with several fine, distinct nerves ending in a soft curved apex and tapering at the base into a short curved petiole, 1/16–1/8 inch long, with a gland at or near the base; covered with a silvery gray down over dark green; margins yellow-green.

Notes This species flowers only irregularly in Santa Barbara. The species name *pendula* means pendulous, hanging.

Locations Trees along Cabrillo Boulevard at the Bird Refuge and on the west end of Shoreline Park. Another in the plantings at the Goleta Valley Water District offices on Hollister Avenue.

Top: Weeping crown of Acacia pendula.
Bottom: Silvery gray phyllodes on pendulous twigs.

ANGIOSPERMS / DICOTS / FABACEAE

Acacia podalyriifolia
Queensland silver wattle, pearl acacia

Found on sandy coastal sites of Queensland, Australia.

Habit Tall shrub or small tree, often as broad as tall, evergreen; to 20 feet tall.

Inflorescence Axillary racemes or panicles containing 10–20 globular, bright yellow heads of 20–30 flowers, 1/2–3/4 inch across; rachis thin, gray, minutely hairy. Flowers November to December.

Fruit Pods densely hairy initially; very flat, dark brown, 1 1/2–3 1/2 x 1/2–3/4 inches; margins raised, irregularly and sometimes deeply constricted between seeds.

Twigs Velvety with minute white hairs.

Bark Smooth, purplish-gray.

Leaves Alternate; phyllodes oval to elliptic, 1–2 x 1/2–3/4 inches, with one central nerve and pinnately veined reticulation, sometimes undulating, usually covered with dense soft hairs; apex slightly elongated into a small, blunt, curved point; usually one or two small marginal glands; silvery gray-green.

Notes The species name *podalyriifolia* refers to foliage similar to *Podalyrius,* which is, in turn, named for Podalyrius, son of Aesculapius, celebrated as a famous physician.

Locations Trees in Alice Keck Park Memorial Gardens near Arrellaga and Garden Streets; others in the 900 block of Arbolado Road.

Top: Silvery gray phyllodes and bright yellow flower heads of Acacia podalyriifolia.
Bottom: Flattened, dark brown seed pods.

Acacia pycnantha
Golden wattle

Native to southeastern Australia, including portions of New South Wales, Victoria, and South Australia.

Habit A small evergreen tree with drooping branches; to 30 feet tall.

Inflorescence Axillary racemes of 8–16 globular flower heads, 3–6 inches long, slightly zigzag; heads 1/2–3/4 inch across, densely flowered, heavily scented, lemon-yellow. Flowers February to March.

Fruit Pods straight, flat, 3 1/4–5 x 1/2–3/4 inches; leathery.

Twigs Often pendulous, greenish-yellow or dark red.

Bark Smooth, often covered with green algae.

Leaves Alternate; phyllodes 3–8 x 1/2–2 inches, usually broadest above the middle, frequently sickle-shaped; gray-green; with prominent midvein and lateral veins, usually a single gland prominent near the base, sometimes a second gland along the margin midway to the apex.

Notes *A. pycnantha* provides the National Floral Emblem of Australia. It is also the origin of the country's unofficial colors of green and gold. The bark has an exceptionally high tannin content, and early settlers of Australia believed it was useful in the treatment of diarrhea and dysentery. The species name *pycnantha* means dense, thick.

Locations Trees on Alameda Padre Serra across from Vista Grande Drive. Others on Fairview Avenue near the airport.

Strongly sickle-shaped phyllodes and lemon-yellow flower heads of Acacia pycnantha.

Acacia stenophylla
Shoestring acacia

Widely spread across inland arid regions from Western Australia to Queensland.

Habit A bushy small evergreen tree; to 30 feet tall.

Inflorescence Terminal racemes of 2–6 heads, 1/4–1/2 inch long; heads round, 1/3–1/2 inch across, containing 25–40 creamy white to pale yellow flowers. Flowers in August.

Fruit Pods 4–10 inches long, 1/3–1/2 inch across; strongly constricted and readily breaking between the seeds, glabrous with obscure longitudinal wrinkles.

Twigs Hanging, light green, glaucous, becoming dark red.

Bark Rusty-red, furrowed into longitudinal plates.

Leaves Phyllodes pendulous; 3–15 x 1/3 inch; leathery, glaucous grayish-green, with numerous faint nerves.

Notes This is a very recent introduction to Santa Barbara. It is a drought-tolerant, rapid-growing tree with a pleasant shape; however, it is relatively short-lived. The species was first known to flower and set fruit in Santa Barbara in 2003. The species name *stenophylla* means narrow-leaved.

Locations Trees planted in the median of Hollister Avenue in the 4700 block. Others in a parking lot near La Cumbre Road and State Street.

Top: Compact weeping crown of Acacia stenophylla.
Bottom left: Pale yellow flower heads and long linear phyllodes.
Bottom right: Pendulous pyllodes and strongly constricted seed pods.

Acacia verticillata var. *verticillata*
Prickly Moses

Widely spread in saline and foothill locations of coastal southeastern Australia

Habit   An evergreen shrub or erect tree; to 15 feet tall.

Inflorescence   Axillary racemes of densely packed flowers, 3/4 inch long; peduncles 1/2 inch long. Flowers in February.

Fruit   Pods linear, compressed and hardly constricted between the seeds, 3/4–3 x 1/5 inches.

Twigs   Green, somewhat ridged, becoming reddish-brown.

Bark   Smooth, reddish-gray.

Leaves   Mostly whorled, rarely fascicled or alternate; phyllodes linear, 1/2 inch long, with a sharp apex.

Notes   The species is highly variable and has been divided into four subspecies, each of which is itself quite variable. The needle-like leaves of *A. verticillata* are highly unusual for the genus. The species name *verticillata* means whorled.

Locations   A single spreading tree on multiple stems in Willowglen Park along the northern boundary.

Short, sharply pointed, needle-like phyllodes and bright yellow flower racemes of Acacia verticillata *var.* verticillata.

Acrocarpus

Acrocarpus is a monospecific genus of Southeast Asia. The name combines the Greek *akron* (peak, extremity) and *karpos* (fruit), in reference to the terminal racemes on which the fruit are borne.

Acrocarpus fraxinifolius
Pink cedar, shingle tree

Native to montane rain forests below 4,000 feet along the Himalayas of eastern India and Myanmar (Burma), extending through the Malay Peninsula to Sumatra and Java.

Habit A tall, deciduous tree, often forming buttresses at the base; to 70 feet tall.

Inflorescence Terminal, densely flowered racemes, 3–6 inches long; flowers 1/4–1/2 inch long, petals inconspicuous, green; stamens exserted, to 1 inch long, scarlet. Appearing before the leaves, giving a bright red flame-like appearance to the still deciduous tree. Flowers January to February.

Fruit Pod stalked, flattened, 3–5 x 2/3–3/4 inches, with a strong wing about 1/6 inch wide along one margin.

Twigs Stout, bright yellow, hairy.

Bark Smoothish, light gray.

Leaves Alternate, bipinnately compound; to 24 inches long, with 3–4 pairs of pinnae, each containing 4–9 pairs of leaflets; leaflets ovate to oblong, 2–4 inches long, drooping, dark green, margins entire, pinnate veins curving along the margins towards the apex.

Notes *A. fraxinifolius* is frequently grown in India and Southeast Asia as a shade tree in tea and coffee plantations. It is often considered the largest tree of the rain forests of eastern India and can reach 120 feet tall with a trunk diameter of 10 feet. The species name *fraxinifolius* means ash-leaved.

Locations Two large trees in a parking lot in the 2700 block of De la Vina Street. Two young trees were recently planted in the 600 block of State Street.

Top: *Striking densely flowered raceme of* Acrocarpus fraxinifolius.
Bottom: *Bipinnately compound foliage with dark green leaflets.*

Albizia

Albizia is a genus of about 150 species from tropical regions of the world. It is closely related to Acacia and is distinguished by the many conspicuous white, rose, red, or purple stamens that are fused for more than half their length and by the very reduced inconspicuous petals. Many of the species of *Albizia* are capable of nitrogen fixation and are often used in land reclamation projects in tropical and subtropical regions. However, the same features that make these and many other species effective for land reclamation also contribute to their ability to invade otherwise undisturbed ecosystems. The name honors F. del Albizzi, a Florentine nobleman who brought *A. julibrissin* into cultivation in 1749.

Albizia chinensis
Chinese albizia

Native to tropical southeastern Asia.

Habit A deciduous tree with lower branches held at right angles to the stem; to 30 feet tall.

Inflorescence Terminal panicles; flowers in heads $3/4$–1 inch across, $1/3$–$1/2$ inch long with stamens exserted up to $1\,1/4$ inches, yellow-green. Flowers January to February.

Fruit Pods flat but swollen around the 6–10 seeds, 4–$6\,1/4$ x $2/3$–$1\,3/8$ inches, dark brown.

Twigs Brownish-green, turning red-brown, minutely pubescent, strongly fluted.

Bark Smooth, gray.

Leaves Alternate, bipinnately compound, 8–10 inches long; with 4–14 pairs of pinnae, each with 20–30 pairs of leaflets; leaflets asymmetrical with the midrib very close to the upper margin, $1/4$–$1/2$ x $1/8$ inch, apex acute; the rachis angled, reddish, carrying a gland just below the point of insertion of the lowest pair of pinnae.

Notes *A. chinensis* has become an invasive exotic in Hawaii and Samoa, where it has been introduced. The species name *chinensis* means from China.

Locations A few saplings from a large tree that was recently removed have maintained themselves in Franceschi Park near Franceschi Road.

Top: Lacy dark green foliage and lime green flowers of Albizia chinensis.
Bottom: Tan seed pods swollen around the seeds.

Albizia julibrissin
Silk tree, *mimosa*, silky acacia

Native from Iran to central China.

Habit A fast-growing, deciduous, medium-sized tree, frequently multiple-stemmed forming a vase-shaped tree with a flattish crown; to 40 feet tall.

Inflorescence Slender clusters appearing in the spring and early summer; flowers without petals, containing numerous one-inch-long, thread-like, pink stamens, looking much like a fine-haired brush. Flowers in July.

Fruit Pod paper thin, light gray-brown, 5–7 x 1 inches, frequently persisting until the following spring.

Twigs Greenish-brown, with many lenticels, angled, somewhat zigzag, with prominent leaf scars; buds small, round, brownish, with 2–3 scales.

Bark Smooth, with numerous lenticels, light gray.

Leaves Alternate, bipinnately compound, to 20 inches long; pinnae 10–25 with 40–60 leaflets each; leaflets oblong, curved, $1/4$–$1/2$ inch long, margins ciliate.

Notes The species is very popular in the southeastern United States where it readily reseeds in waste areas. However, it is very susceptible to a wilt in that region and exhibits frequent dieback to its resistant root crown. The origin of the species name *julibrissin* is obscure. It was used invalidly by C. S. Rafinesque as a genus name and may refer to finely dissected leaves.

Locations Several trees in lower Orpet Park west of Lasuen Road. Others in Hidden Valley Park and Alice Keck Park Memorial Gardens. Street trees in the 500–700 blocks of Voluntario Street.

Finely cut bipinnately compound leaves and pink stamens of Albizia julibrissin.

Albizia lophantha
Albizia distachya

Plume albizia, cape wattle, swamp wattle

Native of Western Australia.

Habit A short-lived, fast-growing evergreen tree; to 15 feet tall.

Inflorescence Axillary paired racemes, 1 1/4–2 1/2 inches long; flower calyx and corolla lightly hairy, small, exceeded by longer (1/2 inch long) yellow-green stamens, fragrant. Flowers November to February.

Fruit Pod thin, 3–4 x 2/3 inches, with a sharply pointed apex, margins thickened, brown or glaucous; containing 3–8 black, swollen seeds.

Twigs Golden hairy, becoming dull red-gray, with prominent lengthwise flat ridges.

Bark Smooth, gray-brown.

Leaves Alternate, bipinnately compound, to 5 inches long; pinnae 7–12 pairs, each with 20–40 leaflets; leaflets narrowly oblong, with an obvious asymmetric midrib, lightly hairy beneath; rachis with an elongate gland near the base.

Notes The species name *lophantha* means with crested flowers.

Locations A clump of bushy stems at Coal Oil Point on the campus of the University of California, Santa Barbara.

Top: Coarse foliage and lemon-yellow flowers of Albizia lophantha.
Bottom: Dehiscing seed pods and black seeds.

Bauhinia
Orchid tree, cow hoof, camel hoof

Bauhinia is a genus of about 300 tropical species, many of which are vines. It has an interesting global distribution, occurring at latitudes between 15 to 30°North and 5 to 15°South, but not directly on the equator. Because of the distinctive two lobes of its leaves, the genus was named after two brothers, John and Casper Bauhin, who were 16th-century herbalists in Switzerland.

Bauhinia blakeana
Hong Kong orchid tree

Distributed in the warmer regions of China along the southeastern seaboard (Fukien, Hong Kong, and Kwantung); found only in cultivation.

Habit A small sprawling evergreen tree, more often a shrub; to 15 feet tall.

Inflorescence A raceme; peduncles 2/3 inch long, with 2 inconspicuous bracts; flowers large and strikingly attractive; calyx 1 inch long, pubescent, with reddish and greenish streaks, slit on the lower side and somewhat recurved, apex two-lobed with 2–3 teeth at the tip; petals 5, lanceolate, 2–3 1/3 inches long, rose or reddish-purple, the base of the upper petal deeply colored. Flowers October to March.

Fruit Pods not seen.

Twigs Greenish-brown, with very fine golden-brown pubescence.

Bark Light gray, smooth, somewhat roughened from numerous horizontal lenticels.

Leaves Alternate, simple; round, 3 1/2–5 inches across, with 2 apical lobes, cleft to 1/3 of entire length, sometimes each with a shallow notch at the apex; 11–13 nerves in a palmate arrangement from the base; pale green, somewhat hairy beneath; petiole 1 1/2 inches long, brown pubescent, with a pulvinus at each end.

Top: Short crown of **Bauhinia blakeana.**
Bottom: Reddish-purple flowers and bilobed leaf with palmate venation.

Notes No mature seeds have ever been found on this species, and it is believed to be a sterile hybrid of unknown origin; hence, the lack of fruit. All cultivated specimens have apparently been derived from a single tree found in China. The flower was adopted in 1965 as the emblem of Hong Kong and graces the regional flag. The species name *blakeana* honors Sir Henry Arthur Blake (1840–1914), governor of Hong Kong 1898–1903.

Locations Trees in Alice Keck Park Memorial Gardens near Garden and Micheltorena Streets. Others in the 100–200 blocks of East Padre Street.

Bauhinia forficata
Brazilian orchid tree

Native to Peru, Argentina, and Brazil.

Habit A semi-deciduous shrub or small tree; to 30 feet tall.

Inflorescence Axillary, a reduced raceme of usually 2 flowers; calyx 2–2 3/4 inches long, greenish-white, finely hairy, slit on one side; petals 5, white with a green midrib, linear- to oblanceolate, 2–3 1/4 x 1/4–2 inches. Flowers August to September.

Fruit A stalked pod, oblanceolate, 5–8 x 3/4 inches, leathery, glabrous, dark brown; peduncle 1–1 1/2 inches.

Twigs Yellowish, lightly covered with short pubescence, with short paired or solitary recurved thorns at the nodes, 1/8–3/16 inch long, these sometimes absent.

Bark Smooth light gray, becoming slightly fissured.

Leaves Alternate, simple; ovate, 3 1/4–5 x 2–3 1/8 inches, cleft more or less half the distance to the base, lobes usually acute and divergent, glabrous above, glabrous or pubescent beneath; petiole 1–1 1/2 inches long with a swollen pulvinus at both ends, yellowish, lightly covered with short pubescence.

Notes The species name *forficata* means forked.

Locations A single tree in Alice Keck Park Memorial Gardens near Garden Street. Others in the 600–700 blocks of State Street and on Las Olas Drive on the Mesa.

Top: Open crown of **Bauhinia forficata.**
Middle: Pure white flowers and deeply cleft leaves.
Bottom: Tan seed pod, curling upon dehiscence.

Bauhinia variegata
Orchid tree, mountain ebony

Broadly distributed in India and southern China.

Habit A medium-sized evergreen tree; to 30 feet tall.

Inflorescence Axillary, a flat-topped corymb of 2–5 flowers; calyx slit on 1 side, entire at the tip, very glandular; petals 5, light rose with red and yellow markings, 2 lateral pairs of equal length with curled margins, the uppermost petal broader with a larger channeled claw and deeper color. Flowers in March.

Fruit Pods 8–10 x 2/3–3/4 inches, flattened, glabrous, marked with an oblique wrinkle, with 10–15 seeds.

Twigs Green turning gray after the first year, with scattered individual hairs, not pubescent.

Bark Light gray, smooth, somewhat roughened from numerous horizontal lenticels.

Leaves Alternate, simple; round to oblong, usually broader than long, 3–3½ x 3½–4½ inches, 2 lobes with a rounded, unnotched apex, lobes extending ¼ to halfway to base, with 9–13 palmate nerves; petioles 1–1½ inches, with a swollen pulvinus at both ends.

Notes *B. variegata* has sacred connotations for Buddhists. Its leaves and pods are edible, and the bark is used in tanning and has medical properties. A white-flowered cultivar, *B. variegata* 'Alba' (*B. variegata* 'Candida'), differs only in flower color. The species name *variegata* means of different colors.

Locations Trees in Alice Keck Park Memorial Gardens near Garden and Micheltorena Streets. Others in the 700–800 blocks of Olive Street and the 400 block of East De la Guerra Street.

Top: Short, dense crown of **Bauhinia variegata**.
Middle: Light rose flowers and leaves with unnotched lobes.
Bottom: Straight seed pods with oblique seed placement.

Caesalpinia

Caesalpinia is a genus of about 150 species from the tropical and warm temperate regions of the world. Its species include trees, shrubs, and climbers, several of which are cultivated as ornamentals. The genus is named to honor Andrea Caesalpini(1524/25–1603) who was an Italian botanist, philosopher, and physician to Pope Clement.

Caesalpinia pluviosa var. *peltophoroides*
C. peltophoroides
False Brazilwood

Believed to be native to a small area of coastal forests in the state of Rio de Janeiro, Brazil.

Habit A deciduous shrub or small tree, occasionally with multiple stems from the base; to 35 feet tall.

Inflorescence A densely packed terminal or axillary raceme, with up to 140 flowers; pedicels $1/3$–$3/4$ inch long, with a joint below the calyx; calyx with fringed margins, petals rounded, $1/3$–$1/2$ inch across, yellow with orange spots or veins, inner surfaces frequently hairy; stamens somewhat longer than the petals, pubescent on the basal third.

Fruit Pod woody, opening explosively to disseminate seed, $3 1/4$–$5 1/2$ x $3/4$–$1 1/3$ inches, with 3–6 buff-colored seeds.

Twigs Densely hairy or not.

Bark Gray to grayish-brown or dark brown, smooth or rough, flaking in elongate flakes or chunks to expose a creamy under bark.

Leaves Alternate, bipinnately compound, $2 1/2$–7 inches long; petiole and rachis densely hairy with scattered red glands; pinnae 9–23; leaflets 13–31 per pinna, obovate, $1/5$–$1/2$ x $1/8$–$1/5$ inch, somewhat pubescent on the lower surface, the midvein sometimes ending in a gland at the apex, sometimes with reddish-black epidermal glands scattered on the surface.

Notes A recent revision of *Caesalpinia* has identified this taxon as a variety within a somewhat larger complex; however, it is this variety that is widely cultivated as an ornamental street tree in the cities of Brazil, Bolivia, and Columbia. The flaking bark is very reminiscent of the bark of some Eucalyptus species. This species has not been seen to flower in Santa Barbara. The species name *pluviosa* means pertaining to rain.

Locations One tree in Franceschi Park east of the cottage.

Caesalpinia pluviosa *var.* peltophoroides *has light green foliage that is held in a horizontal plane on the tree.*

Caesalpinia spinosa
Tara

Native to Chile, Brazil, and Peru; widely cultivated today.

Habit Evergreen shrub or small tree with stout spines, frequently with multiple stems and a raggedly branched crown; to 30 feet tall.

Inflorescence Terminal, in clusters of 2–3 densely flowered racemes; flowers with roundish petals, to $1/4$ inch across, yellow and reddish; stamens equal to or somewhat longer than petals; pedicels hairy, $1/4$–$1/2$ inch long. Flowers February to April.

Fruit Pod not opening along a suture before falling; $2^{1}/_{3}$–4 x $^{2}/_{3}$–1 inches, thick, pulpy, becoming fibrous-spongy to leathery and dry, reddish-brown to brown, containing 5–8 dark tan seeds.

Twigs Light green becoming brown, then gray, with small spines scattered along the larger branches; buds covered with tawny hairs.

Bark Gray with shallow fissures and flat-topped ridges.

Leaves Alternate, bipinnately compound, rachis to 6 inches long with a single dark spine at the insertion of each pair of pinnae; pinnae 2–3 pairs, each containing 5–7 pairs of leaflets; leaflets sessile, elliptic, $3/4$–$1^{2}/_{3}$ inches long, base unequal, glabrous, somewhat resinous, glossy green above.

Notes The pods of this species are an important source of tannin in Peru, where it is also used as protective hedging against intrusion by animals and humans. The species name *spinosa* means spiny.

Locations Street trees in the 200–300 blocks of Vista de la Cumbre, in the 300 block of Samarkand Drive, and at the intersection of Samarkand and Stanley Drives. Park trees in Plaza del Mar along the service drive.

Top: Flowering racemes and dark green foliage of Caesalpinia spinosa.
Bottom: Red and green seed pods with bipinnately compound leaves.

Cassia

Once a genus of 500 to 600 species from tropical regions of the world, a taxonomic revision in recent years has distinguished three genera, including *Cassia, Senna,* and *Chamaecrista.* The revised *Cassia* includes about 30 species. Many of the species contain pharmaceutical properties, and others are highly attractive to insects, especially butterflies. *Cassia* is the Greek name for the plants that provide senna leaves and pods for pharmaceutical uses.

Cassia leptophylla
Gold medallion tree

An inhabitant of disturbed forests and woodland margins in southeastern Brazil.

Habit   A small evergreen tree with a leafy rounded crown, branching low; to 20 feet tall.

Inflorescence   Terminal racemes of 30–50 flowers, to 6 inches long; flowers 2–3 inches across, deep yellow, with velvety-pubescent sepals. Flowers July to October.

Fruit   Pods four-angled, to 25 inches long x 1 inch across; the sutures bordered by 2 parallel ribs; partitions occurring between the seeds (although frequently not forming on cultivated material).

Twigs   Stout, green turning red-brown; buds red-brown, small, appressed to the twig above a large leaf scar.

Bark   Reddish-brown, peeling in vertical strips to give a slightly roughened appearance, reddish in the small furrows between peeling strips.

Leaves   Alternate, pinnately compound without a terminal leaflet, 7$^{1}/_{2}$–15 inches long; leaflets 9–20 pairs, linear or elliptic, 1$^{1}/_{2}$–2$^{1}/_{2}$ x $^{1}/_{2}$–$^{3}/_{4}$ inches, shiny green above, pale and dull below.

Notes   The species name *leptophylla* means thin-leaved.

Locations   Planted throughout town; individuals at Spencer Adams Park, MacKenzie Park, and Alice Keck Park Memorial Gardens near the corner of Micheltorena Street and Santa Barbara Street. Others on State Street in the 800 and 1000 blocks and below Gutierrez Street.

Top: Densely flowered tree of Cassia leptophylla.
Middle: Globose flower cluster and pinnately compound leaves without a terminal leaflet.
Bottom: Elongate four-angled seed pods.

Castanospermum

Castanospermum is a genus of 12 species found primarily in the tropical Americas, but extending to Australia. The name combines *Castanea* and *spermum* (seed), in reference to the similarity of its fruit to the chestnut.

Castanospermum australe
Moreton Bay chestnut, black bean

Endemic to tropical and subtropical regions of eastern Australia (Queensland, New South Wales).

Habit A slow-growing evergreen tree with a columnar crown; to 50 feet tall.

Inflorescence Axillary racemes arising from older leafless twigs, 2–6 inches long; flowers pea-shaped, $1^{1}/_{4}$–$1^{3}/_{4}$ inches long, red to reddish-yellow, standard longer than other petals and reflexed, stamens and style exserted. Flowers July to August.

Fruit Pods usually in clusters of 3–5, woody, inflated, 4–10 x $1^{3}/_{4}$–$2^{1}/_{2}$ inches, tan, dehiscing along 2 valves, containing 3–5 large brown seeds, $1^{1}/_{4}$ inches across.

Twigs Stout, green with brown lenticels, becoming gray, roughened by large round leaf scars.

Bark Smooth, gray to brown.

Leaves Alternate, pinnately compound with a terminal leaflet, 12–24 inches long; leaflets 9–17, ovate to oblong, 3–5 x $^{3}/_{4}$–2 inches, dark shiny green with a pale green midrib attached to the rachis by a short, stout pulvinus.

Notes The flowers of this species produce copious amounts of nectar which attract a variety of small pollinating birds in its native habitat. Its dark brown timber is considered to be one the highest quality cabinet woods in the world. Although the roasted seeds are reported to have been eaten by native peoples in times of want, they are considered toxic to cattle and people. They have been screened as a possible vaccine for AIDS. The species name *australe* means southern.

Locations Street trees in the 1400 block of Crestline Drive and the 2100 block of Oak Park Lane; a large tree at Stow House in Goleta was reportedly introduced by Dr. Franceschi and planted in 1895. A younger tree in the parking lot of Goleta Cottage Hospital (200 South Patterson Avenue).

Top: Dense crown and dark green foliage of Castanospermum australe.
Middle: Striking red and yellow flowers.
Bottom: Large seed pods and pinnately compound leaves.

Ceratonia

Ceratonia is a genus of two species from the Arabian peninsula and extending into Somalia. The name derives from the Greek name for the carob tree, *keratonia*.

Ceratonia siliqua
Carob, St. John's bread

Believed to have originated in Oman, although widely distributed along early trade routes.

Habit A medium-sized evergreen tree with a broad, roundish crown; to 40 feet tall.

Inflorescence Monoecious or dioecious; spike-like racemes usually forming on older branches, $1^{1}/_{2}$–6 x $^{1}/_{3}$–1 inches, containing 20–60 flowers; flowers without a corolla, containing 4 tawny anthers on half-inch-long filaments and a stout half-inch-long pistil. Flowers January to February.

Fruit An oblong pod, frequently held in pendulous bunches; 4–12 x $^{2}/_{3}$–$1^{1}/_{2}$ inches, flattened, straight or curved, dark shining brown, base narrowed to a short stalk, apex rounded; seeds $^{1}/_{3}$ inch long, very hard; dark brown; pulp with a heavy sweet smell.

Twigs Stout, reddish, with light brown lenticels.

Bark Rough, dark brown.

Leaves Alternate, pinnately (rarely bipinnately) compound, without a terminal leaflet, 5–12 x $1^{1}/_{4}$–6 inches; leaflets 4–8, oblong, $^{2}/_{3}$–$3^{1}/_{3}$ x $^{1}/_{2}$–$1^{3}/_{4}$ inches, apex indented, leathery, dark shiny green above, pale ashy gray below; petiolule consisting solely of a swollen pulvinus, $^{1}/_{8}$ inch long; petiole and rachis often tinged red.

Notes *C. siliqua* has played an important cultural role for centuries, beginning in the Middle East. Its value for food and forage was recognized by the ancient Greeks, who introduced it to Greece and Italy, and by Arabs, who brought it to the North African coast. The pods contain more sugar than sugar beets or sugarcane. The seeds and the pulp of its pods are reportedly the "locusts and wild honey" eaten by John the Baptist in the wilderness, giving origin to one of its common names which refers to the dried pulp. The high sugar and protein content of the fruit have made it an important livestock forage for centuries. The seeds are particularly uniform in weight and are believed to have been the original jeweler's carat weight. Today, the carob

Top: Dense crown and dark gray bark of Ceratonia siliqua.
Middle: Pinnately compound leaves with glossy curved leaflets.
Bottom left: Spikes of male flowers without corolla on older twigs.
Bottom right: Dark brown seed pods and female flowers without petals or sepals.

is used extensively in reforestation efforts around the world because of its forage value and ability to grow readily in regions receiving as little as 12 inches of precipitation per year. The species name *siliqua* means curved pod.

Locations Common around town. Several trees near the MacDougal Administrative Center at Santa Barbara City College and in upper Orpet Park above the lawn. Street trees on Loma Street and in the 800 and 900 blocks of Spring Street. Others on Calle Rosales at Peabody School.

Cercidium

Cercidium is a genus of four species, all located in the warm desert regions of the southwestern United States and adjacent portions of Mexico. Its name comes from the Greek for weaver's shuttle, in reference to its hard wood.

Cercidium floridum
Blue palo verde

Native to the low-elevation desert of Southern California, southern Arizona, and northwestern Mexico.

Habit   A small densely branched and densely flowered, drought-deciduous tree; to 25 feet tall.

Inflorescence   Axillary, in racemes of 5–8 flowers, usually appearing before the leaves; flowers yellow, 3/4–1 inch across, banner with red splotches at the base; pedicel 1/2 inch long, jointed above the middle. Flowers in April.

Fruit   Pod persistent, tapered to the base, often wavy margined, flattened, 3/4–3 1/2 x 1/2 inches, leathery, tan, containing 1 to a few seeds.

Twigs   Usually zigzag, sometimes sharp-tipped, blue- to gray-green, slender thorns usually present at the nodes.

Bark   Tight, thin, somewhat rough, greenish-gray.

Leaves   Alternate, 1 or 2 from each node, bipinnately compound with a single pinnae pair, 1/2–1 inch long, leaflets 2–3 pairs per pinna, ovate to obovate, 1/8–1/4 inch long, blue-gray.

Notes   *Cercidium* has been included by some authors with *Parkinsonia* as *P. florida.* Many trees, such as *C. floridum,* have a thin, greenish bark or bark that is green underneath. This is most evident in twigs from the current year's growth. The high concentration of chlorophyll in the bark or twig increases the photosynthetic capacity of the plant and often enables it to grow during periods of extreme stress (heat or cold) when leaves would not survive. The species name *floridum* means full of flowers.

Locations   Santa Barbara Botanic Garden in the Desert Section.

Top: Yellow flowers, very small compound leaves, and green photosynthetic twigs of Cercidium floridum. *Bottom: Tan seed pods, green twigs, and sparse foliage.*

Enterolobium

Enterolobium is a genus of five species from tropical North and South America. The genus is very close to *Albizia,* and sometimes the two are difficult to distinguish. However, aside from its obvious fruit characteristics, the genus is distinguished by the absence of a nectariferous gland at the base of the petiole, glands above the base apparently stalked (not flattened), and stamens fused at the base. The name is derived from the Greek words *entero* (intestine) and *lobos* (lobe) and refers to the shape of the fruit which looks like a lobe of a contorted intenstine.

Enterolobium cyclocarpum
Guanacaste, parota

Broadly distributed in tropical deciduous and semi-deciduous forests in the Pacific lowlands and foothills of central and southern Mexico, Central America, and extending to South America.

Habit Potentially a large deciduous tree, with a broad spreading crown; to 20 feet tall.

Inflorescence Axillary, in densely flowered round heads, $1/2$–1 inch across; flowers small, $1/4$ inch long, white, stamens fused at the base. Flowers July to August.

Fruit Pod dark green, becoming lustrous black, $1 1/4$–2 inches wide, curved into an almost complete circle, 3–4 inches across; seeds 10–15, kidney-shaped, $2/3$–1 inch long, surrounded by a sweet pulp.

Twigs Tan, with small lenticels and large raised leaf scars.

Bark Smoothish, grayish-brown, with warty horizontal lenticels.

Leaves Alternate, bipinnately compound, 6–16 inches long; pinnae 5–10 pair; leaflets 15–35 pairs, linear-oblong, sometimes cycle-shaped, $1/3$–$3/4$ inch long, with unequal bases, midrib near the distal margin with 2–3 additional nerves radiating from the base; stalked nectariferous glands present on the rachis below the lowest pinnae and below each successive pinnae pair.

Notes The species name *cyclocarpum* means with fruit structured in a circle.

Locations Upper Orpet Park east of the center steps, adjacent to Alameda Padre Serra.

Puffy appearing flower stamens and compound leaves of **Enterolobium cyclocarpum.** *The leaves tend to close in response to the slightest water stress.*

Erythrina
Coral trees

Erythrina is a tropical genus of 112 species, mostly from the Americas, but also in Asia and Africa. The bright red flowers, long corolla tubes, and production of nectar are adapted to pollination by hummingbirds, although some Malaysian species have long, stout peduncles that serve as perches for sunbirds. Several species in the genus produce curare-like alkaloids which can be highly toxic, inducing paralysis and even death. However, these toxic effects usually require direct introduction into the blood stream and cannot be induced by ingestion. The name comes from the Greek *erythros* (red) in reference to the color of the flowers.

Erythrina abyssinica
Red-hot-poker tree

Broadly distributed in the savannas of central Africa from Sudan and Ethiopia to Angola and Mozambique.

Habit A deciduous tree with a spreading crown or, rarely, a shrub; to 40 feet tall.

Inflorescence Axillary, from older branches and stems of the previous season, erect, to 3–5 inches long, on peduncles to 4 inches; showy red flowers include a banner which is barely distinct from the other petals or stamens, to 1 1/2 inches long; calyx with short or long spreading teeth. Flowers November to December.

Fruit Pods on erect peduncles, heavily woody, 2–4 inches long, densely wooly, light brown, split along one suture, tightly constricted between seeds; seeds bright red with a black spot and no black line at the point of attachment to the pod.

Twigs Stout, light green, covered with fine white hairs, turning corky in the second year, with spiny prickles.

Bark Light brown to gray, corky, often spiny; with vertical light fissures showing layers of cork.

Leaves Alternate, trifoliate; leaflets broadly ovate with a very rounded apex, to 5x7 inches, lateral leaflets somewhat smaller, densely tomentose with gray hairs when young; petiole, petiolules, and major veins on underside of leaflet densely pubescent and often bearing scattered prickles.

Top: Tomentose trifoliate leaves and showy red flowers of Erythrina abyssinica.
Bottom: Furrowed and multi-colored bark.

Notes The species name *abyssinica* means native to Abyssinia (Ethiopia).

Locations Franceschi Park along the entry road near the parking lot.

Erythrina caffra
Coral tree

Native to the coastal regions of South Africa, including the eastern Cape Province and Natal. Never found more than 40 miles from the coast.

Habit A semi-deciduous tree with a broad spreading crown; to 30 feet or more.

Inflorescence Terminal, leafy or flowers in axils of leaves; usually clusters of showy flowers on a short peduncle, less than 2 inches long but to 8 inches across; flowers dark orange to scarlet; banner short and broad, 1 1/2–2 x 3/4–1 1/3 inches, strongly arched to expose floral parts; leafy or deciduous at the time of flowering. Flowers February to March.

Fruit Pod leathery, brownish-black, deeply constricted and frequently angled between the seeds, 6–8 inches long; seeds scarlet with a black spot and a narrow black line at the point of attachment.

Twigs Stout, tannish-brown, with very short prickles.

Bark Very shallowly broken into gray-green ridges and tannish fissures, often with short sharp prickles.

Leaves Alternate, trifoliate; leaflets triangular, broadest at the base, with an elongate apex, as long as wide, 2–5 inches, the lateral leaflets somewhat smaller, without hairs or spines; petiole 6–8 inches long.

Notes In its native land, *E. caffra* is the basis of superstition and frequently will not be used as firewood for fear of attracting lightning. It is one the showiest of the coral trees and has been planted extensively in Southern California. Particularly notable are the plantings along San Vicente Boulevard from Wilshire Boulevard in Los Angeles to the ocean in Santa Monica. It can be confused with *E. lysistemon* but is distinguished by the fact that it has no prickles on the petiole, rachis, or leaflets of the leaf. Its leaves are much smaller than those of *E. latissima* and not hairy. The species name *caffra* refers to South Africa; see notes for *Harpephyllum caffrum*.

Locations One tree in the center of Alice Keck Park Memorial Gardens. Others at the corner of State and Micheltorena Streets and on the north side of State Street west of La Cumbre Road. Others on the campus of the University of California, Santa Barbara.

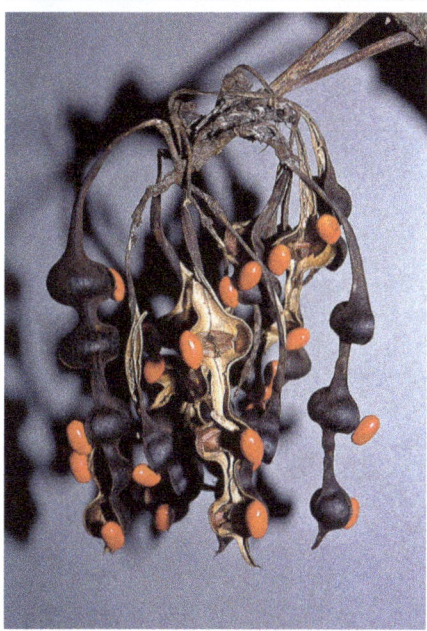

Top: **Erythrina caffra** *flowering before leaves emerge in midwinter.*
Middle: Reddish-orange flowers with broad banner and trifoliate leaves.
Bottom: Deeply constricted seed pods with bright red seeds.

Erythrina coralloides
Naked coral tree, flame coral tree

Native to the mountains of eastern Mexico, at elevations from 2,500 to 8,500 feet.

Habit A deciduous tree with a spreading crown; to 30 feet tall.

Inflorescence Bright red, cone-shaped axillary racemes at the ends of upturned branch tips; flowers somewhat densely clustered on the rachis; banner narrow, long, to 3 x 1/2 inches, recurved only at the tip so that most of the floral parts are hidden, overall the flowers tend to stand away from the rachis giving the inflorescence the appearance of a ballet dancer's tutu; deciduous when flowering. Flowers February to April.

Fruit Pod dull gray brown, to 8 inches long, with an elongated apex, swollen around each seed; seeds red with a black line near the point of attachment, 1/2 x 1/4 inch.

Twigs Stout, smooth, greenish-gray.

Bark Smooth, greenish- to pinkish-gray, with very shallow widely spaced corky furrows and white corky lenticels.

Leaves Alternate, trifoliate; leaflets heart-shaped, 2–5 inches long, usually less broad, dull light green on both sides; petioles 3–5 inches long, quite slender.

Notes *E. coralloides* makes a striking display in late winter when it comes into full flower before the summer leaves have developed. The species has been confused with *E. americana*; the latter, however, has a waxy network on the undersides of the leaflets. It has also been referred to erroneously as *E. poianthes*. The species name *coralloides* means coral red.

Locations One tree in the lawn in upper Orpet Park. Another in Franceschi Park along Mission Ridge Road. Several on the campus of the University of California, Santa Barbara between Kerr Hall and North Hall.

From top to bottom:
1) Flowering Erythrina coralloides *with distinctive greenish-orange bark in midwinter.*
2) Trifoliate leaves with deltoid leaflets.
3) Densely clustered flower racemes with elongate banners.
4) Dull, dark gray seed pods with red seeds.

Erythrina crista-galli
Cockspur coral tree, *ceiba*

Broadly distributed in southern South America east of the Andes, from eastern Brazil to Argentina.

Habit A deciduous tree with a crown that appears to have been strongly pruned, the main branches ending in stumps as the result of yearly dieback of shoots; to 20 feet tall.

Inflorescence Terminal racemes on a long rachis, to 20 inches, or axillary; flowers loosely spread on thin peduncles, bright scarlet or crimson; banner 2 x 1 inches, reflexed to expose a keel at least half its length, the flower twisting on the peduncle at maturity so that the standard is curved down and the keel is on the top of the flower; leafy when flowering. Flowers May to June.

Fruit Pod woody, 5½–15 inches long, somewhat constricted between seeds; seeds dark brown with tan markings.

Twigs Stout, green with a thick white pith, not woody.

Bark Dark brownish-gray, deeply fissured.

Leaves Alternate, trifoliate; leaflets elliptic or ovate, 2–3 x ³⁄₄–1¹⁄₄ inches, papery, sometimes armed with prickles beneath.

Notes The *ceiba,* as it is known there, is the national flower of Argentina. Although originating in South America, this species is the most commonly cultivated representative of the genus and is now found worldwide. Its nectar production is so prodigious that it has acquired the colloquial name "cry baby" in Louisiana. The species name *crista-galli* means cock's comb.

Locations A tree at the south end of the Stow Grove County Park. Another by the #8 tee at the Santa Barbara Golf Club. Several along the south side of the Student Services Building on the campus of the University of California, Santa Barbara.

Top: Short rounded crown of Erythrina crista-galli.
Middle: Scarlet flowers with exposed yellow stamens.
Bottom: Seed pods and trifoliate leaves with long petioles.

Erythrina falcata
Brazilian coral tree

Native to sub-Andean South America from Peru and Bolivia to southern Brazil, Paraguay, and northern Argentina.

Habit A moderate-sized semi-deciduous tree with a very broad spreading crown; to 45 feet tall and 60 feet across.

Inflorescence Axillary, never leafy, pendulous or horizontal racemes 6–12 inches long; flowers orange-red, banners broad, 2 inches long, enclosing other flower parts. Flowers May to July.

Fruit Pod to 5 x 1 inches, flat, black, with an elongated beak.

Twigs Becoming stout, light gray brown, with scattered spines.

Bark Smooth, pinkish-gray, with very shallow vertical breaks.

Leaves Alternate, trifoliate; leaflets oval to triangular, to 5 x 2$^1/_2$ inches; margins entire, slightly wavy; petiole 6–8 inches long, reddish.

Notes The species name *falcata* means sickle-shaped.

Locations Two trees at the center of Alice Keck Park Memorial Gardens. A large tree at the corner of San Pasqual and Pedregosa Street. Others along the northern boundary of La Mesa Park.

Top: Broad, full crown of Erythrina falcata.
Middle: Pendulous inflorescences and glossy trifoliate leaves.
Bottom: Dark gray seed pods.

Erythrina humeana
Dwarf lucky bean tree, dwarf coral tree, *kleinkoraalboom*

Native to the open savanna of southeastern Africa, from Cape Province, South Africa to Zimbabwe.

Habit A semi-deciduous, very thorny shrub or small tree; to 20 feet tall.

Inflorescence Axillary, erect racemes, to 2½ feet long; peduncle dark purple, lenticellate; mature flowers held closely to the peduncle; banners bright orange to deep scarlet, turning crimson, to 2 inches long, hiding other flower parts; calyx paler red, 5 lobes easily distinguished in buds and flowers; flowering throughout the summer months and into the fall.

Fruit Pod leathery, constricted between seeds; seeds red with a grayish-black spot and a black line at the point of attachment.

Twigs Dull green with raised leaf scars, lenticellate, notably covered with small sharp spines.

Bark Thin, dark gray with whitish shallow vertical furrows.

Leaves Alternate, trifoliate; leaflets highly variable, lanceolate to broadly ovate-deltoid, somewhat leathery; minute prickles on the abaxial side of the petiole, and sometimes on the rachis and major veins on the undersides of the leaflets.

Notes The small size of *E. humeana* makes it ideal for the smaller garden. It is easily recognized in the non-flowering periods of the year by the old flower stalks extending beyond the crown of the tree. The species name *humeana* honors Sir Abraham Hume (1748/49–1838), Director of the Honourable East India Company, Fellow of the Royal Society, and owner of a famous garden in Wormelybury, Hertfordshire.

Locations Trees at Leadbetter Beach, Harbor, and Shoreline Parks, and the Cabrillo Pavilion Arts Center.

Top: Erythrina humeana *with several stems and elongate inflorescences extending well beyond the foliage.*
Bottom: Inflorescences and trifoliate leaves.

Erythrina latissima
Broad-leaved lucky bean tree, broad-leaved coral tree

Widely distributed in open savannas of southern Africa from Cape Province, South Africa to Zimbabwe and Zambia.

Habit A small deciduous tree; to 20 feet with a spreading crown.

Inflorescence Densely packed clusters of flowers on a horizontal rachis to 12 inches long, inflorescence itself 6–10 inches long and almost as broad; flowers deep scarlet turning crimson; standard 2 1/2 x 1 1/4 inches, reflexed and spread open to expose a greenish-white keel and stamens; calyx with 5 free lobes, 1/2–2/3 inches long.

Fruit Pod woody, brownish-black, 12 x 1 inches, constricted between seeds; seeds shiny red with a black spot and no black line at the point of attachment.

Twigs Stout, with spiny prickles to 1/3 inch, frequently growing as short spur shoots.

Bark Thick, gray, corky, with vertical ridges containing light-colored lenticels.

Leaves Alternate, trifoliate; leaflets broadly ovate, almost heart-shaped, to 10 inches across, apex slightly elongate; papery, gray-green, with scattered prickles, densely wooly.

Notes The bark of *E. latissima* is used in African medicine in a powdered form to treat open sores. The species is very similar to *E. abyssynica* but can be recognized by its larger flowers and, when not in flower, by its broadly ovate, thick, papery leaflets. The name lucky bean tree comes from the fact that its seeds have been used in necklaces and charms by native peoples to ward off evil. This species has not been seen to flower in Santa Barbara. The species name *latissima* means broad.

Locations A tree in Franceschi Park east of the cottage.

Trifoliate leaves of Erythrina latissima.

Erythrina lysistemon
Coral tree

Native to dry regions of southeastern Africa from Tanzania to Cape Province of South Africa.

Habit A barely deciduous tree with a rounded crown; to 30 feet tall.

Inflorescence Axillary racemes, slightly ascending, peduncle usually more than $2^{1}/_{3}$ inches; flowers declined towards the rachis, dark orange or red, banner long and narrow, $1^{1}/_{2}$–2 x $^{1}/_{2}$–$1^{1}/_{4}$ inches, only slightly arched, enclosing all other flower parts; calyx brownish; leafy at the time of flowering. Flowers February to April.

Fruit Pod slender, leathery, black, constricted between seeds; seeds red with a dark spot and a narrow black line at the point of attachment.

Twigs Stout, light tannish-gray, armed with black prickles.

Bark Rough, gnarled appearing, but not corky, dark gray to gray-brown.

Leaves Alternate, trifoliate; leaflets deltoid with a tapering apex, to 6 x 6 inches; the petiole, rachis, and main veins of the leaflets almost always armed with sharp curved prickles.

Notes *E. lysistemon* has numerous uses in native medicine and culture. It is used to aid in childbirth, for treatment of open sores and earaches, and to gain respect. This species is closely related to *E. caffra* and is distinguished by its shorter, less arched flowers that are declined towards the rachis, its smaller leaves, and the prickles arming the leaves. Where they occur together, these two species readily hybridize. The species name *lysistemon* means with loose stamens, not fused.

Locations Several trees on the campus of the University of California, Santa Barbara between Kerr Hall and North Hall.

From top to bottom:
1) Flowering specimen of Erythrina lysistemon *before leaf emergence.*
2) Trifoliate leaves on stout gray twigs.
3) Orangish-red flowers declined along the rachis of the inflorescence.
4) Black seed pod with curved peduncle and elongate tip.

Erythrina x *sykesii*
Sykes' coral tree

A hybrid of unknown origin.

Habit A deciduous tree; to 30 feet tall.

Inflorescence Axillary racemes, 10–12 inches long; flowers spreading from rachis, scarlet, banner 3/4–1 x 2/3 inch, moderately recurved to expose keel, wings, and stamens; keel and wings less than half the length of the standard, stamens nearly as long as the banner. Flowers February to April.

Fruit Not known to produce fruit.

Twigs Stout, green turning greenish-gray, with large leaf scars and lenticels, unarmed.

Bark Smooth, gray-brown, with creamy lenticellate fissures, sparsely spiny.

Leaves Alternate, trifoliate; overall leaf to 18 inches long; terminal leaflet somewhat diamond-shaped, to 8 inches long and wide; rachis with peduncle to 3–8 inches long, lightly brown hairy.

Notes This hybrid arose in Australia and is of unknown parentage. It shows characteristics similar to *E. lysistemon* but also reflects *E. caffra* and *E. speciosa*. The species name *sykesii* honors Mr. R. A. Sykes, horticultural taxonomist with the New Zealand Department of Scientific Research and expert in the taxonomy of *Erythrina*.

Locations A tree in Franceschi Park along Mission Ridge Road.

Scarlet inflorescences with curved banner and trifoliate leaves of **Erythrina** *x* **sykesii**.

Gleditsia

Gleditsia is a genus of 14 species native to the eastern United States, South America, the Caspian region of western Asia, and Southeast Asia. The genus is named for Johann Gottlieb Gleditsch (1714–1786), Director of the Berlin Botanical Garden.

Gleditsia triacanthos f. *inermis*
Honeylocust, thornless common honeylocust

Broadly distributed in disturbed habitats throughout the deciduous forest region of the eastern United States.

Habit A short to medium-sized deciduous tree with a spreading crown; to 30 feet tall.

Inflorescence Axillary, in racemes to 2 inches long; flowers greenish-yellow, not showy, very fragrant, laden with nectar, appearing with the leaves. Flowers in April.

Fruit A strap-like pod, 7–18 x 1 inches, dark blackish-brown, velvety or not, sometimes twisted or curved; seeds very hard, shiny dark brown.

Twigs Shiny, smooth, reddish to greenish-brown, zigzag, swollen at the nodes.

Bark Grayish-brown, broken into long narrow plates which tend to curl away from the trunk.

Leaves Alternate, pinnately or bipinnately compound, 6–8 inches long; rachis pubescent, grooved; base of petiole swollen and completely enclosing the bud; pinnate leaves with 20–30 oblong-lanceolate leaflets, 1/3–1 1/2 x 3/16–5/8 inches; bipinnate leaves with 8–14 pinnae, leaflets 1/3–1 inch long.

Notes The pods of this species contain a sweet gummy substance which led to the common name. The species, which is broadly spread throughout the eastern United States, is known for its stout, vicious-looking, repeatedly branched thorns to six inches long. However, many cultivars of the unarmed form are widely used in cultivation and serve to replace American elm in the Midwest. The cultivar 'Sunburst' is characterized by golden-colored new leaves which eventually turn green. In Australia the plant is not so favored. It carries the name McConnel's curse because of its invasive behavior. The species name *triacanthos* means three-thorned.

Top: Open lacy crown of Gleditsia triacanthos *f.* inermis. *Bottom: Glossy pinnately compound leaves and long lustrous brown seed pod.*

Locations Parque de los Niños. Others in Chase Palm Park near the Casa de las Palmas and the 1000 block of Milpas Street. The cultivar 'Sunburst' is growing in East Alameda Plaza and in the 1800 block of Chapala Street, and 'Shademaster' is growing in Alice Keck Park Memorial Gardens.

Gymnocladus

Gymnocladus is a genus of only four species. One of these is native to the eastern United States, and the other three are found in central and southeastern China, the Himalayas, and India. It has a number of features in common with *Gleditsia,* including a high concentration of saponins in the fruit, which were used as a soap substitute in China. The name is a combination of the Greek words *gymnos* (naked) and *klados* (branch), in reference to the deciduous nature of the genus.

Gymnocladus dioica
Kentucky coffee-tree

Broadly distributed in the eastern United States from Tennessee to New York.

Habit A round-crowned deciduous tree; to 70 feet tall.

Inflorescence Usually dioecious; panicles 4–12 inches long with hairy branches; flowers small, greenish-white to purple, on stout pedicels, 3/4 inch long. Flowers in spring.

Fruit A large pod, oblong to slightly curved, 6–10 x 1 1/2–2 inches, dark brown with a whitish bloom; peduncle stout, 1–2 inches.

Twigs Stout, brown, with large leaf scars and a salmon-colored pith.

Bark Deeply fissured, tinged with red, peeling away from the trunk in distinctive curls.

Leaves Alternate, bipinnately compound, 24–36 inches long, with 5–7 pairs of pinnae, 6–10 inches long; leaflets in 4–7 pairs, ovate with an acute apex, 2–2 1/2 x 1 inches.

Notes The species is generally associated with rich bottomland soils throughout its natural range; however, it is an uncommon tree and never occurs in local abundance. The large seeds were roasted as a coffee substitute by early settlers. The raw seeds and the pulp that surrounds them contain large amounts of saponins and were used in small amounts as a mild laxative. The species name *dioica* means dioecious.

Locations A young tree in East Alameda Plaza adjacent to Sola Street.

Top: Stout twigs and swollen pulvinus at the base of the petiole of Gymnocladus dioica.
Bottom: Bipinnately compound foliage with purplish rachis.

Inga

Inga is a genus of about 350 species from tropical and warm regions of the New World. Inga is the West Indian name for the group.

Inga pilosula
Inga affinis

Inga, ice cream bean

Scattered throughout northern South America, from Venezuela and the Guianas to Amazonian Peru and Bolivia, usually found in disturbed wet forest lands.

Habit A small to medium-sized evergreen tree; to 30 feet tall.

Inflorescence Axillary, solitary or paired spikes, 1³/₄–4¹/₄ inches; flowers densely congested on terminal ¹/₂–1¹/₄ inches of spike, corolla and perianth tubular, short, ⁴/₅–1 inch long, with 25–35 exserted stamens, bright white. Flowers August to November.

Fruit Pod straight, flattened, 3¹/₃–3¹/₄ x 1¹/₄–1²/₃ inches; glabrous; ends rounded, margins thickened.

Twigs Cinnamon-brown, pubescent, with obvious lenticels.

Bark Smooth, light gray, with faint horizontal lenticels.

Leaves Alternate, pinnately compound with no terminal leaflet; rachis 1¹/₄–2¹/₂ inches long, winged between leaflets and densely rusty pubescent; leaflets 4 pairs, terminal pair elliptic to obovate, 3–5 x 1¹/₄ inches, lateral pairs half as large, apex strongly acuminate, glossy bright green with a pubescent midrib above, entire surface pubescent beneath.

Notes The species name *pilosula* means hairy.

Locations Trees in the 1600 block of Laguna Street. A tree in the Lifescape Memorial Garden at Santa Barbara City College.

Top: Axillary flowers with long-exserted white stamens of Inga pilosula.
Bottom: Pinnately compound foliage with semi-folded leaflets and wings along the rachis, and angular seed pods.

Leucaena

A genus of about 50 species, mostly from warm temperate and tropical zones of North America and extending to Peru. Named from the Greek *leucos* (white) in reference to the flower color.

Leucaena esculenta
Guaje

Native to mountainous areas of central Mexico.

Habit A deciduous tree; to 30 feet tall.

Inflorescence Axillary, long-branched racemes, to 12 inches long; flowers white, to 1/4 inch long, clustered in tight heads (3/4–1 1/2 inches across) on the raceme. Flowers February to March.

Fruit Pod flat, purplish, 6–9 x 3/4–1 1/4 inches, containing 10–25 seeds.

Twigs Strongly angled, almost winged, glabrous, greenish-brown, with numerous vertical lenticels.

Bark Smooth, light gray, becoming cracked into rectangular flakes at the base of larger trees.

Leaves Alternate, bipinnately compound, 6–16 inches long; pinnae 20–60 pairs, each with 40-80 pairs of leaflets; leaflets linear, 1/8–1/4 x 1/20 inch; rachis bearing large red nectariferous glands near the base and between pairs of upper pinnae.

Notes The original specimen from which this species was described was a painting made by artists with the Sesse and Mocino expedition to Mexico (1787 to 1803). During the early period of exploration of Mexico and the southwestern United States, new species were often "collected" by painting them in their native habitat, showing as many features as possible. Unripened seeds of this species are commonly used as spices in Mexico and fill the markets of Guadalajara in the winter months. However, in other species of this genus, the toxic compound mimosine leads to loss of hair and infertility. Until recently, *L. esculenta* was only found in yards in the lower East Side and lower West Side of Santa Barbara and was likely introduced by Latino immigrants. This and other species of the genus have been actively promoted for reforestation in tropical and subtropical regions because of their nitrogen-fixing and "green manure" potential. The species name *esculenta* means good to eat.

Locations One tree in Alice Keck Park.

Top: Open crown of **Leucaena** *esculenta.*
Bottom: Delicate bipinnately compound leaves and flower heads.

Leucaena leucocephala subsp. *glabrata*
Guaje

Originating in Central America, but natural distribution unknown.

Habit An evergreen tree of moderate size; to 45 feet tall.

Inflorescence Axillary clusters of 1–3 heads (capitula), 2/3–3/4 inch across, each containing 120–180 flowers; peduncle 2/3–3/4 inch long; flowers sessile in the head, small, greenish and non-remarkable. Flowers January to February.

Fruit Pods in clusters of 6–20 per capitulum, 5–8 x 1/2–3/4 inches, brown and somewhat grayish pubescent.

Twigs Round, green, turning tannish.

Bark Smooth and light gray-brown on younger branches; becoming darker and rougher on older branches and bole, with rusty vertical fissures.

Leaves Alternate, bipinnately compound, 8–10 x 5–6 inches; pinnae 6–8 pairs, each with 16–19 pairs of leaflets; leaflets 1/2–2/3 x 1/8 inch.

Notes *L. leucocephala* subsp. *glabrata* is widely marketed for food throughout its current range and has been planted in almost every city, town, and village of Mexico and Central America. It appears to have naturalized around Acapulco, and its original distribution is much in doubt. During World War II it was used to camouflage gun emplacements in the South Pacific and has since become a weedy pest of considerable concern. The species name *leucocephala* means white head, in reference to the inflorescence; subspecies name *glabrata* means glabrous.

Locations A single tree on Almond Avenue near Sola Street. Another on San Andres and Valerio Streets.

Top: Bipinnately compound foliage and flower heads of Leucaena leucephalla *subsp.* glabrata.
Bottom: Brown seed pods with grayish pubescence.

Pararchidendron
Pithecellobium

Pararchidendron is a monotypic genus from eastern Australia and Malaysia, and has recently been separated from *Pithecellobium,* which is now entirely a New World genus. The genus name means close to *Archidendron,* an allied genus.

Pararchidendron pruinosum
Pithecellobium pruinosum
Abarema sapindoides

Snowwood, stinkwood

Occurs in disjunct populations in coastal rain forest regions of Queensland, Australia and in Malaysia.

Habit   A finely branched evergreen tree; to 25 feet tall.

Inflorescence   Axillary, in umbel-like heads, 3/4–1 1/2 inches across; flowers to 1/2 inch long, yellow-brown corolla tube with short lobes, calyx very short with minute teeth. Flowers in June.

Fruit   Pods curved in a circle, 3–4 x 1/2–2/3 inches, minutely hairy and yellow outside, rusty-orange inside; seeds shiny black, 1/3 inch long.

Twigs   Dull green with dense hairs, becoming purplish, with ridges running down from the leaf insertions.

Bark   Tight, dark gray, very shallowly furrowed.

Leaves   Alternate or subopposite, bipinnately compound, 10 inches long; pinnae 1–3 pairs; leaflets alternate, 7–10 per pinna; obovate to elliptic, 1 1/2–3 x 1/2–1 1/2 inches, broadest towards the apex, base usually strongly asymmetric, shiny green above, paler below; rachis and pinnae dull green, densely pubescent, with irregularly occurring glands.

Notes   The white wood of this species has a strong unpleasant odor when freshly cut. However, the flowers have a very attractive odor and are alluring to butterflies. The species name *pruinosum* means covered with frost.

Locations   Single trees in the northeast corner of upper Orpet Park and in lower Orpet Park along the upper path.

Top: Long exserted stamens and glossy leaflets of Pararchidendron pruinosum.
Bottom: Curled, open seed pods with glossy black seeds.

Parkinsonia

Parkinsonia includes 29 species, most of which occur in the drier warm portions of the Americas. Four species are found in Africa. The genus is named for John Parkinson (1567–1650), a London apothecary and gardener of considerable reknown, and the author of two important botanical books. His first book (1629) also carried an outrageous pun in its title, *Paradisi in Sole Paradisus Terrestris* (Park in Sun's Earthly Paradise), giving lie to the idea that botanists have little humor. He was Apothecary to King James I, and King Charles I bestowed on him the title of Botanicus Regius Primarius.

Parkinsonia aculeata
Mexican palo verde, Jerusalem thorn

Broadly distributed across the southern United States from Florida to Arizona, extending through the Sonoran Desert of Mexico.

Habit A deciduous shrub or small tree with a lacy appearance; to 30 feet tall.

Inflorescence Axillary or terminal, dense racemes of 2–15 flowers, appearing with the leaves; flowers with a deciduous calyx and yellow corolla, about 3/4 inch across, 4 petals with irregular margins, the standard orange-spotted becoming reddish. Flowers June to October.

Fruit Pod generally round, but flattened between seeds, leathery, light tan, 3/4–4 x 1/4 inches.

Twigs Zigzag, yellow-green, usually armed with spines at the nodes, 1/4–3/4 inch long.

Bark Green becoming gray, somewhat warty.

Leaves Alternate, in clusters of 1–3, bipinnately compound, 4–12 inches long; rachis flattened to a phyllode, leaflets 30–60, elliptic, 1/4 x 1/8 inch, persistent or gradually deciduous leaving the flattened rachis as a persistent phyllode.

Notes The original range of *P. aculeata* is unclear, and it has undoubtedly been introduced throughout much of southwestern North America primarily by cattle in the days of long cattle drives. Today, it is broadly spread throughout the warmer regions of the world and has become an invasive pest in Queensland, Mauritius, Ceylon, and Myanmar (Burma). Although the leaves are technically bipinnately compound, to the inexperienced eye they appear to be simply a pair of distinct pinnately compound leaves. The central rachis by which these two segments of the leaf are connected is almost nonexistent. The species name *aculeata* means spiny.

Locations Trees at Alice Keck Park Memorial Gardens, and the Peterson Plaza at 2900 State Street. Two trees intermixed with *Prosopis glandulosa* var. *torreyana* in the parking lot of Mount Carmel Church on East Valley Road in Montecito.

Top: Thin, open crown and several stems of **Parkinsonia aculeata**.
Bottom: Yellow and orange-spotted flowers and compound leaves with flattened rachis.

Peltophorum

Peltophorum is a genus of eight tropical species and is named from a combination of the Greek words *pelte* (shield) and *phoreo* (to bear), in reference to the shape of the stigma.

Peltophorum africanum
Weeping wattle, African wattle

Broadly distributed in eastern South Africa, north to Zambia and west to Angola.

Habit A small to medium-sized deciduous tree with an open spreading crown, frequently branched from near the ground; to 30 feet tall.

Inflorescence Axillary racemes, densely flowered, to 6 inches long; flowers with 5 showy yellow petals, each about 3/4 inch in diameter and somewhat crinkled. Flowers August to October.

Fruit Pod flat, elliptic, tapering at both ends, to 4 3/4 inches long, with a thin wing-like margin, leathery, dark brown at maturity; sometimes hanging in dense persistent clusters.

Twigs Gray-brown, lightly pubescent in the first year, becoming light gray.

Bark Smooth, gray brown, breaking into rectangular plates on larger stems.

Leaves Alternate, bipinnately compound, to 8 inches long, rachis rusty pubescent; pinnae 5–10 pairs, each with 12–20 pairs of oblong leaflets, 1/2 x 1/8 inch, apex rounded with a fine hair-like tip, dull green above, paler and hairy below.

Notes The bark of this species is used among African peoples to relieve colic and other stomach disorders. The tree is one of several "rain trees" of Africa, so named for the fact that a phloem-sucking insect nymph extracts and ejects water as part of a protective behavior against the sun. The phenomenon, which in some cases is so extreme as to result in puddles of water on the ground, occurs for a week or more, usually at the most intense period of the dry season, just before the beginning of the rainy season. The species name *africanum* means from Africa.

Locations A street tree on Calle Laureles between Foothill and Lucinda Lane. Another in Franceschi Park east of the cottage.

Top: Open spreading crown of **Peltophorum africanum**. *Bottom: Densely flowered racemes, rusty pubescent twigs, and bipinnately compound leaves.*

Prosopis

A genus of 44 species from warm temperate and subtropical regions of North America, southwest Asia and Africa. *Prosopis* is derived from the Greek name for burdock and the origin of its use for this genus is unknown.

Prosopis glandulosa var. *torreyana*
Prosopis julifora var. *torreyana*
Mesquite, western honey mesquite

Found throughout the desert regions of Trans-Pecos (western) Texas to California; however, generally absent in Arizona where *P. velutina,* a competing form, is present.

Habit A small deciduous shrub or tree with a rounded crown; to 20 feet tall.

Inflorescence Axillary, a densely flowered spike-like raceme, 2½–4 inches long; flowers minute, $1/10$–$1/8$ inch, creamy yellow to yellowish-green. Flowers May to June.

Fruit Pod woody, long, somewhat flattened, contracted between seeds, 4–8 x ⅓ inches, tan.

Twigs Green, becoming dark reddish-brown, with paired spines at the nodes, ½–¾ inch.

Bark Fissured, fibrous, brownish-gray.

Leaves Alternate on new growth but mostly clustered on short spur shoots, bipinnately compound, with 1 pair of pinnae; leaflets 10–12 pairs on each pinna, oblong to narrowly oblong, ½–1 x ⅛ inch, loosely spaced, giving a lacy sense to the crown, light green.

Notes A second variety, *P. glandulosa* var. *glandulosa,* occurs in Texas and Oklahoma east of the Pecos River. Mesquite in both of its forms has many times been a savior to drought-stricken ranchers in the Southwest. The mesquite beans provide considerable nutrition for cattle when not a blade of grass is to be found. The species name *glandulosa* means glandular.

Locations A small tree in the Santa Barbara Botanic Garden on the Campbell Trail. Several trees intermixed with *Parkinsonia aculeata* in the parking lot of Mount Carmel Church on East Valley Road in Montecito.

Top: Densely flowered racemes and bipinnately compound leaves of Prosopis glandulosa *var.* torreyana. *Bottom: Tan seed pods and lacy green foliage.*

Robinia

Robinia is a genus of four species from North America (principally in the southeastern United States). The genus is named for Jean Robin (1550–1629), gardener and herbalist to Henry IV and Louis XIII of France, who received and propagated plants from North America and authored several botanical volumes.

Robinia pseudoacacia
Black locust, yellow locust

Broadly distributed throughout the eastern United States from the Connecticut River valley to Georgia and west to Minnesota and Texas.

Habit A fast-growing deciduous tree with a narrow open crown; to 50 feet tall.

Inflorescence Axillary, pendent racemes containing 8–20 flowers, 4–8 inches long; flowers pea-shaped, 2/3–3/4 inch long, white, very sweet fragrance. Flowers March to April.

Fruit Pod flat, dark brown-black, 2–4 inches long, smooth, with 4–10 seeds, persisting for a time following maturity in October.

Twigs Slender, brittle, often zigzag, smoothish but with angled ridges extending down from the leaf scars, sometimes spiny with paired 1/4- to 1/2-inch prickles at the nodes.

Bark Reddish brownish-gray, deeply furrowed into interlacing fibrous and somewhat scaly ridges.

Leaves Alternate, pinnately compound, with a terminal leaflet, 6–14 inches long; leaflets 7–19, elliptic to ovate, 1–1 1/2 x 1/2–3/4 inches, margins entire, light green, turning yellow in the fall.

Notes *R. pseuodacacia* is a tree of disturbed lands in the eastern United States. It occurs in forests following natural or human-caused disturbance and is frequently found on road margins and fallow fields. The tree is of little note when young but matures into a unique specimen with its own grace and beauty. Its wood is highly resistant to decay—fence posts in moist wooded areas of Kentucky have been known to stand solid for over 50 years—and its flowers are an attractive honey source. The species has been widely cultivated in Europe for centuries (a 350 year old specimen was still healthy in the Jardin des Plantes, Paris in the mid-1980s) and is widely used in reclamation projects around the world today. However, the species has been listed as an Exotic Invasive Plant of Greatest Ecological Concern by the California Exotic Pest Plant Council. The species name *pseudoacacia* means false acacia.

Locations Trees planted in a parking lot on Mission Street adjacent to Highway 101. Others at Stow House in Goleta. Several trees have seeded along San Antonio Creek near San Remo Drive and Lincolnwood Drive. Street trees on Anza Drive and Brent Street. The purple-flowered *R.* x *ambigua* 'Purple Robe' cultivar is planted along the railroad frontage greenspace buffer in the 600 and 700 blocks of Wentworth Avenue.

Top: Pendulous flowering racemes and pinnately compound leaves of Robinia pseuodacacia. *Bottom: Dense seed pods and gray-green foliage.*

Schotia

Schotia is a genus of four to five species from open woodlands of South Africa. The genus is named for Richard van der Schot (c. 1730–1819), who was head gardener at the palace of Schönbrunn, near Vienna.

Schotia afra var. *angustifolia*
Karoo boer-bean

Native to coastal regions of Cape Province, South Africa.

Habit A small densely branched semi-deciduous tree with multiple stems and a twisted gnarled trunk; to 15 feet tall.

Inflorescence Axillary, in dense branched heads, 3–3 1/2 inches long; flowers showy red including sepals, corolla 1/2–2/3 inch long; stamens and pistil long exerted, 1 1/4 inches long. Flowers in April.

Fruit Pods woody, 2–5 x 1 1/4–1 1/2 inches, with a long curved beak at the apex and a wing 1/4 inch wide above the suture, light tan; persistent on the tree after seed dispersal; seed oval 1/2–2/3 inch across, light tan.

Twigs Initially light green becoming tannish-gray with numerous minute lenticels.

Bark Dull charcoal-gray throughout; larger stems with vertical cracks and fissures.

Leaves Alternate, pinnately compound without a terminal leaflet, 4 inches long, crowded on short lateral shoots; leaflets 6–18 pairs, small, linear to oblong, to 3/4 x 1/4 inch, dark green, base asymmetrical, margins entire.

Notes The roasted or still-green seeds have been eaten by native peoples and early settlers. The species name *afra* means from Africa. The common name *karoo* refers to semi-desert interior valleys in southern South Africa; Boer means farmer.

Locations A single tree in Franceschi Park above the entrance road.

Top: Red flowers with exserted stamens and pistil of Schotia afra *var.* angustifolia.
Bottom: Tan seed pods, seeds, and compound leaves with linear leaflets.

Schotia brachypetala
Weeping boer-bean, weeping schotia

Found in dry woodlands of eastern South Africa; often associated with termite mounds.

Habit A several-trunked deciduous or semi-deciduous tree, with a rounded crown; to 25 feet tall.

Inflorescence Axillary, dense branched heads on older non-leafy wood, 2–5 inches long; flowers to 2/3 inch long, deep red with slender pink petals which may be reduced or even absent; stamens joined at the base. Flowers April to May.

Fruit Pods dark brown, woody, flattened, with a persistent style, 2–4 inches long, remaining on the tree after seed dispersal; seeds oval, flattened, about 3/4 inch across, pale brown with a large conspicuous yellow fleshy appendage at the point of attachment.

Twigs Smooth, green in first year, becoming brownish, scaly, roughened with raised leaf scars.

Bark Smooth, light gray.

Leaves Alternate, pinnately compound, without a terminal leaflet, 5–6 inches long; leaflets 4–6 pairs, oblong to ovate, 3/4–1 3/4 x 1/2–1 inches, base asymmetric, apex rounded or notched, margins entire and wavy, shiny dark green, when young red or copper-colored; sessile.

Notes The common name stems from the copious amount of nectar produced that tends to drip or "weep," attracting insect and bird pollinators. The roasted seeds are eaten and the bark is used in tanning. An extract of the bark is also used to relieve heartburn and the effects of excessive consumption of alcohol. The species name *brachypetala* means short petals.

Locations A single tree in Manning Park near Area 1.

Crimson flowers and glossy light green compound leaves of Schotia brachypetala.

Schotia latifolia
Bush boer-bean

Found in dry scrublands in southeastern South Africa.

Habit A small evergreen tree with a dense rounded crown; to 25 feet tall.

Inflorescence Terminal, in loose open heads, 3–4 inches long; flowers pink to whitish, to 1 inch long; stamens joined at the base. Flowers October to November.

Fruit Pods flattened, oval to oblong, 3 x 1 2/3 inches, cinnamon-brown, with a persistent hooked 3/8-inch-long style, the persistent rib almost forming a wing about the pod; seeds oval, flattened, to 3/4 inch across, tan, with a large yellow fleshy appendage at the point of attachment.

Twigs Green, becoming warty brown-maroon.

Bark Smooth and finely fissured, grayish- to reddish-brown.

Leaves Alternate, pinnately compound without a terminal leaflet, 5 inches long; leaflets 4 pairs, elliptic-oblong, 1–2 1/2 x 1/2–1 1/4 inches, sessile; base asymmetrical, margins entire, apex rounded or notched; young leaves glistening reddish-bronze, becoming shiny green, thickened, fleshy; rachis flattened, almost winged between the upper pairs of leaflets.

Notes The leaves look strikingly like those of the carob tree *(Ceratonia siliqua)*. The species name *latifolia* means broad-leaved.

Locations A small tree in upper Orpet Park adjacent to Alameda Padre Serra and just east of the center steps.

Top: Terminal raceme with pinkish flowers and dark compound leaves of Schotia latifolia.
Bottom: Tan seed pods with wide marginal wing and leaflets with notched apices.

Sophora

Sophora is a genus of about 45 species which are found mostly in tropical and northern temperate zones, but reaching southern Chile. One species, *S. toromiro,* was the only tree on Easter Island suitable for building the sea worthy canoes of the Polynesians who settled there. However, overpopulation and cultural demands led to the demise of the species and, consequently, the society. The name of the genus is derived from the Arabic name for one of its species.

Sophora japonica
Japanese pagoda tree, Chinese scholar tree

Native to China and Korea, not Japan as implied in the common name.

Habit A deciduous tree with a round spreading crown; to 60 feet tall.

Inflorescence Terminal panicles on current growth, showy, 6–12 inches long and wide; flowers pea-like, creamy white, $1/2$ inch long, fragrant. Flowers in July.

Fruit Pods cylindrical, 2–4 x $1/3$ inches, glabrous, strongly constricted between the 3–10 shiny black seeds.

Twigs Slender, glabrous, green, with grayish lenticels, leaf scars prominently protruding.

Bark Grayish-brown, furrowed into interlacing fibrous and somewhat scaly ridges.

Leaves Alternate, pinnately compound, with a terminal leaflet, 6–10 inches long; leaflets 7–17, ovate to lanceolate-ovate, 1–2 x $1/2$–1 inches, distinctly stalked, apex acute, base rounded, margins entire, shiny green above, glaucous and pubescent beneath.

Notes *S. japonica* has been planted extensively around Buddhist temples in the Orient; hence, perhaps, one of its common names. A yellow dye can be extracted from the flowers. The species name *japonica* means from Japan.

Locations Trees at Spencer Adams Park adjacent to the Davis Center and in Parque de los Niños.

Top: Rounded crown of Sophora japonica.
Middle left: Pendulous creamy flowers.
Middle right: Dense clusters of seed pods and compound leaves.
Bottom: Compound leaves with swollen pulvinus at base of petiole.

Tipuana

Tipuana is a genus of only one species from South America. Its name is derived from the native South American name for the tree.

Tipuana tipu
Tipu

Native to Brazil, Bolivia, and Argentina.

Habit A briefly deciduous tree with a flattened spreading crown and tortuously twisted branches; to 50 feet tall.

Inflorescence Open axillary panicles; flowers showy, pea-shaped, 3/4 inch across, yellow-orange with a reddish center. Flowers June to July.

Fruit A samara-like pod, flat along one margin, broadly curved on the other, reminiscent of an enlarged single wing of a maple samara, 2–2 1/2 inches long, green turning tan.

Twigs Green turning gray-brown, ridged, flattened at the nodes, slightly hairy.

Bark Grayish-brown, fissured into interlacing flakes.

Leaves Alternate, pinnately compound with a terminal leaflet, 6–12 inches long; leaflets 11–21, oblong, 1–1 1/2 x 1/2 inches, light green, apex rounded or slightly notched, margins entire, rachis slightly grooved above, midrib prominent below.

Notes Although rapid-growing and casting a welcome shade, the destructive roots and weak wood of *T. tipuana* limit its use in small yards. The species name *tipu* is a native name.

Locations Increasingly common about town. Trees at Alice Keck Park Memorial Gardens; another on the corner of San Andres and Carrillo Streets. Street trees in the 600–900 blocks of West Valerio Street.

Top: *Broad, rounded crown of* Tipuana tipu.
Middle: *Yellow-orange flowers and pinnately compound leaves.*
Bottom: *Cluster of immature flat seed pods.*

Fagaceae

The Beech Family includes nine genera and 600 to 800 species, almost all of which occur in the Northern Hemisphere. Its greatest diversity is reached in Mexico and southern China. Almost all species produce large fruit that are fed upon and disseminated by animals. They also support a large array of arthropods and their associated predators. Because of these factors members of this family can be considered to be keystones in maintaining the biological diversity of many forested ecosystems.

Lithocarpus

Lithocarpus is a genus of over 100 species primarily found in Indo-Malaysia, and represents the primary extension of the Fagaceae into that region of the world. Numerous fossils of the genus are found in western North America; however, today it is represented on this continent by only one species, described below. The name is a combination of the Greek words *lithos* (stone) and *karpos* (fruit), and refers to the hard acorns.

Lithocarpus densiflorus
Tan oak, tanbark oak

Native to moist forests of western California, extending from southern Oregon to Ventura County.

Habit An evergreen tree with a pyramidal form when young; to 50 feet tall.

Inflorescence Monoecious; densely flowered axillary spikes, stiff, spreading or erect, to 2–4 inches long. Flowers March to April.

Fruit An acorn, solitary or paired, cup 3/4–1 1/4 inches across, saucer-shaped, tan, scales slender, strongly spreading or reflexed; nut ovoid, 3/4–1 1/3 inches long, tan, hairy.

Twigs Covered with thick pale woolly hair which lasts through the second season.

Bark Smooth, brownish-gray.

Leaves Alternate, simple; oblong to ovate, 2–4 x 1–2 1/4 inches, base rounded, apex blunt, with 12–14 pairs of obvious pinnate veins, margins entire to toothed, upper surface dark glossy green, lower surface blue-gray; petiole 1/3–3/4 inch.

Notes The common name reflects the especially high tannin content of the bark of this species. Its large acorn nuts were an important food source for Native Americans throughout its range and were an important item of trade among tribes. The species name *densiflorus* means densely flowered.

Locations Santa Barbara Botanic Garden in the Redwood Section.

Top: Densely flowered spikes of male flowers and foliage of Lithocarpus densiflorus.
Bottom: Mature acorns with bristly cups and prominently veined leaves.

Quercus
Oaks

Quercus is a large genus of about 400 species. The genus is distributed worldwide in the Northern Hemisphere (except for the Arctic and Subarctic regions) and is most diverse in the temperate zone and mountainous regions of the tropics. Because of its strong wood, the larger, better-formed trees are used extensively for timber production; however, the graceful growth forms of the genus, including tall timber trees, spreading shade trees, and smaller shrubs, has attracted considerable horticultural and landscape attention. Individual species can be highly variable, and the genus is well-known for hybridization among species. The genus received its name from the Latin name for *Quercus robur* used in an old European language.

Quercus agrifolia
Coast live oak, live oak

Found in the Coast Ranges, the Transverse Ranges, and the Peninsular Ranges of western California from Sonoma County south into Baja California.

Top: Dark, gnarled crown of Quercus agrifolia.
Bottom left: Pendulous flowering catkins and light green spring foliage.
Bottom right: Acorn clusters and mature cupped leaves.

Habit A broad-crowned evergreen tree, usually branching widely at 10–20 feet in mature trees, horizontal branches on largest trees may naturally extend 45 feet and droop until lying on the ground; to 75 feet tall.

Inflorescence Monoecious; male flowers in axillary catkins 1–2 inches long. Blooms March to April.

Fruit An acorn; nut $3/4$–$1 1/2$ inches long, slender-pointed, chestnut brown at maturity; cup conical, enclosing no more than $1/3$ of the nut; cup scales thin, light brown; peduncle short to non-existent; maturing in first year.

Twigs Slender, gray-brown; heavily pubescent during the first growing season, glabrous thereafter; buds light chestnut brown, ovoid, $1/8$–$1/4$ inch long; bud scales glabrous except for minute hairs along the margins.

Bark Hard, smooth, and light gray in younger stems and branches, with dark, irregular furrows in older stems; 2–3 inches thick on older stems.

Leaves Alternate, simple; oblong to oval, 1–2 inches long; strongly convex from above, dense reticulation visible when backlit; stiff, leathery, dark green above, paler and usually intermittently tomentose along midrib or occasionally glabrous below; with hard, sharp spines at the ends of most veins; petioles short, less than $5/8$ inch long, glabrous, sparsely to densely hairy.

Notes *Q. agrifolia* has played an important role in the human habitation of California. At least 12 tribes of native Californians used its acorns for food. Pioneers made tools and wagon parts from its wood, and it once supported a large charcoal industry. Today, coast live oak, along with valley oak *(Q. lobata)*, has become a symbol of overuse of once-abundant resources. Clearing of landscapes for agriculture, especially vineyards, has resulted in significant losses of once-extensive oak woodlands. The species name *agrifolia* means rough or scabby leaves, also a variant of *aquifolium,* name of holly in medieval times.

Locations Common about town and in the foothills behind Santa Barbara. Trees in the 2000–2500 blocks of State Street, others in East Alameda Plaza, at the Santa Barbara Botanic Garden, and in Rocky Nook and Oak Parks.

Quercus chrysolepis
Canyon live oak, golden cup oak, maul oak, white live oak, hickory oak

Found from southern Oregon through the mountainous regions of California, Nevada, Arizona, and New Mexico to northern Mexico, at elevations ranging from sea level to 8,500 feet.

Habit An evergreen tree with a broad spreading crown, branching widely at 10–20 feet or lower; to 70 feet tall.

Inflorescence Monoecious; male flowers in axillary catkins 2–3 inches long. Blooms April to May.

Fruit A solitary or paired acorn; nut ovoid to ellipsoidal, apex blunt, 1–1 1/2 inches long, light chestnut-brown; cup thick, enclosing only the base of the nut, scales partially covered by a dense felt-like tomentum; maturing in two years.

Twigs Strongly angled, slender, densely golden wooly when young, becoming tan then reddish-gray; buds globose, 1/16–1/8 inch long, scales brown with minute hairs on margins.

Bark Dark gray-brown, scaly in small rectangular plates, not deeply furrowed.

Leaves Alternate, simple; oblong, 1–2 inches long; leathery, gray-green to yellow-green, glabrous above, usually golden wooly beneath when young, becoming glabrous and glaucous with age; margins may be entire or with strong spines, usually spines occur on foliage of younger stems; petiole short, less than 1/3 inch long, with rusty pubescence.

Notes The very strong, close-grained wood was favored by pioneers for tool handles, hence the name "maul oak." It is one of the most variable of the oaks. In California it may grow as a large riparian or forest tree in moist, low-elevation sites or as a low, dense chaparral shrub in dry, high-elevation localities. The species name *chrysolepis* means golden-scaled.

Locations Santa Barbara Botanic Garden at the edge of the parking lot near the entrance. Young trees in the Meadow Section and the Arroyo Section.

Top: Mature foliage with glaucous lower surface and acorns with golden tomentose cups of Quercus chrysolepis.
Bottom: Young leaves with tomentose lower surface.

Quercus douglasii
Blue oak

Occurs in the low mountains and foothills of interior central and northern California, especially surrounding the Central Valley.

Habit A small or medium-sized deciduous tree with a compact rounded crown of many crooked branches; to 50 feet tall.

Inflorescence Monoecious; male flowers in axillary catkins 2–3 inches long.

Fruit An acorn; nut about 1 inch long, chestnut brown when mature, apex acute, sessile; cup thin, shallow, enclosing only the base of the nut; maturing in one season. Flowers in spring.

Twigs Reddish- to yellowish-brown, tomentose when young; buds 1/8–1/4 inch long, with orange-red, pubescent scales.

Bark Thin, 1/2–1 inch thick, scaly, gray.

Leaves Alternate, simple; oblong, 1–3 inches long, shallowly lobed to nearly entire, lobes rounded or with a slight bristle; blue-green, sparsely hairy above, pale and hairy beneath; petiole blue-green, short, 1/8–1/4 inch.

Notes Early settlers of California often called this species iron oak, in reference to the hardness of its wood. Today, it accounts for nearly half of the oak woodlands of California and is the most drought-tolerant of the oak trees. The species name *douglasii* honors David Douglas (1799–1834), Scottish botanical explorer who spent two years collecting along the Columbia River and its tributaries and died in a tragic accident in Hawaii.

Locations Several trees in the Santa Barbara Botanic Garden. Another in Skofield Park near Area A.

Dense shallowly lobed foliage of Quercus douglasii.

Quercus engelmannii
Engelmann oak, mesa oak

Once widely distributed throughout the Los Angeles basin and other areas of Southern California, the species is now limited to scattered trees in the foothills of the San Gabriel Mountains, east of Pasadena in Los Angeles County, and a couple of outliers in southern Orange County. Still locally common in southwestern Riverside County and in much of interior San Diego County, extending into northern Baja California.

Habit An evergreen, drought-deciduous or late-winter-deciduous tree with a broad, round open crown; to 40 feet tall.

Inflorescence Monoecious; male flowers in axillary catkins 2–4 inches long.

Fruit A solitary or paired acorn; nut light brown, ovoid or oblong, apex rounded, $2/3$–1 x $1/2$–$5/8$ inch; cup enclosing $1/3$–$1/2$ of the nut, scales warty, gray pubescent; maturing in one season. Flowers in spring.

Twigs Thin, light brown, initially densely or sparsely pubescent, becoming glabrous and gray.

Bark Thick, not flaky, grayish-white, deeply furrowed.

Leaves Alternate, simple; oblong to elliptic, $1 1/4$–$2 1/2$ x $1/2$–$3/4$ inches; margins entire or slightly toothed near the apex, wavy; thick, leathery, blue-green, lighter beneath, initially densely tomentose, becoming glabrous and glaucous except along the midrib below.

Notes The species name *englemannii* honors Georg Engelmann (1809–1884), German-born St. Louis physician and botanist, who collected plants extensively throughout the western United States and published on several groups of North American plants.

Locations Several trees in the Santa Barbara Botanic Garden in the Meadow Section. A young tree in Oak Park near the tennis courts.

Blue-green leaves with slightly serrate margins of Quercus engelmannii.

Quercus ilex
Holm Oak, holly oak

Broadly distributed around the Mediterranean Sea from Portugal to Turkey and Israel, and from Morocco to Libya (Cyrenaica).

Habit An evergreen tree with a broad domed canopy, often borne on many stems; to 50 feet tall.

Inflorescence Monoecious; male flowers in axillary catkins 1–2 inches long. Flowers in spring.

Fruit An acorn; nut 2/3 inch long, blackish-brown with a small gray wooly tip, cup with gray woolly scales; maturing in one year.

Twigs Slender, dull gray-brown, densely wooly; bud gray wooly, small, less than 1/2 inch, with curled stipules at its base.

Bark Grayish-black or black, broken into small, often rectangular, plates.

Leaves Alternate, simple; variable in shape and size, generally lanceolate to oval, 2–4 x 1 1/2–3 inches; upper surface shiny blackish-green, lower surface densely pubescent and dull tan; margins entire to shallowly toothed with variable bristle tips; petiole 1/2–1 inch, wooly.

Notes The species name *ilex* means holly.

Locations Several trees along Alamar Avenue adjacent to Oak Park; others between Firestone Street and Hollister Avenue near the airport and on Sunset Drive at Woodley Court.

Top: Dense dark crown of Quercus ilex.
Bottom: Leaves with dark upper surface and tomentose lower surface and acorns with wrinkled cup.

Quercus kelloggii
California black oak

In mountainous areas of central Oregon to Southern California, in mixed evergreen and mixed conifer forests, between 1,000 and 5,000 feet in the northern portion of its range and between 4,000 and 8,000 feet in the south.

Habit A tall deciduous tree, with ascending branches and an open crown; to 70 feet tall.

Inflorescence Monoecious; male flowers in axillary catkins 2–3 inches long. Blooms March to April.

Fruit An acorn; nut oblong, 1–1 1/2 x 1/2–1 inches, tan, slightly hairy; cup saucer-shaped to deeply bowl-shaped, covering 1/2–2/3 of the nut, tan, scales more than 1/8 inch long, tips loose, especially near the cup margin; maturing in two years.

Twigs Greenish-brown to red-brown, angled, glabrous; buds chestnut-brown, ovoid, 1/4–1/2 inch; scales glabrous or with minute hairs on the margin.

Bark Tight, not flaky, dark brown to black with broad irregular ridges on mature stems.

Leaves Alternate, simple; ovate to broadly elliptic, 2 1/2–8 x 1 1/2–5 1/2 inches, base usually not rounded; margins with 7–11 lobes, bristle tips at the ends of the primary and secondary veins, sinuses deeper than halfway to the midrib; deep green, shiny, and only slightly hairy above, under sides with tufts of hairs in axils of veins to densely hairy; petiole 1/2–2 1/2 inches long, hairy.

Notes Isolated populations of the species have been identified in northern Baja California. Abundant crops of its acorns were at one time an important food source for Native Americans. In the very early years of the automobile, car axles were produced from choice logs. The species name *kelloggii* honors Albert Kellogg (1813–1887), physician and pioneer California botanist.

Locations Santa Barbara Botanic Garden northeast of the Meadow Section.

Top: Light green crown of **Quercus kelloggii.**
Bottom: Lobed spring foliage and pendulous catkins of male flowers.

Quercus x *kinseliae*
Kinsel oak

An extremely narrow endemic occurring in the canyons above Santa Barbara.

Habit A semi-decidous tree or shrub with a dense rounded crown; to 25 feet tall.

Inflorescence Monoecious; male flowers in axillary catkins 2–3 inches long. Flowers in spring.

Fruit Acorns in pairs or dense clusters; nuts oblong, to 1 1/4 x 2/3 inches; cup hemispheric with thickened scales, covering the base of the nut only.

Twigs Dense in the crown, reddish-brown becoming gray, densely hairy in the first year; buds broadly conical, angled, to 1/3 inch long, hairy.

Bark Thin, scaly, whitish-gray.

Leaves Alternate, simple; oblong to obovate, 1–3 x 3/4–1 3/4 inches, with 6–8 lobes each with 2–3 bristle tips, sinuses narrow and extending halfway to the midrib; dark shining green above, pale and softly hairy below; petiole 3/4–1 3/4 inches, densely hairy.

Notes *Q.* x *kinseliae* has been described as a hybrid between *Q. lobata* and *Q. dumosa* (coastal scrub oak). Although of limited distribution, it is of note for its taxonomic history. This taxon was named by Dr. C. H. Muller for Dr. Katherine Kinsel, who first collected the plant in Rattlesnake Canyon near Skofield Park. Dr. Kinsel, who had become Dr. Katherine K. Muller, served as Director of the Santa Barbara Botanic Garden from 1950 to 1973 and was lead author on the previous version of *Trees of Santa Barbara*.

Locations Two trees in the Santa Barbara Botanic Garden. Individuals in the foothills between San Roque Canyon and Sycamore Canyon.

Top: Full rounded crown of Quercus *x* kinseliae.
Bottom: Lobed blue-green foliage.

Quercus lobata
Valley oak, California white oak, water oak, weeping oak,

Broadly distributed through the interior valleys and foothills of California from Shasta County to Los Angeles County, especially in the hills surrounding the Central Valley and in the Coast Ranges to the west, usually below 2,000 feet.

Habit A large, thick-trunked deciduous tree with a broad, spreading open crown; to 80 feet tall.

Inflorescence Monoecious; male flowers in axillary catkins 2–3 inches long. Flowers in late spring.

Fruit Solitary or paired acorns, on a short stalk; nut slender and pointed, 1–2 inches long; cup hemispherical, covering no more than basal 1/3 of the nut, basal scales notably warty, gray wooly; maturing in the first year.

Twigs Yellowish-gray; hairy at first, then becoming glabrous; buds ovoid, minute, orange-brown.

Bark Light gray to brown-gray, scaly, broken by fissures into thin, vertical plates, on older stems and branches fissures give an alligator bark appearance.

Leaves Alternate, simple; oblong in broad outline, 2–4 x 1–2 inches; deeply cut into 7–11 lobes, sinuses reaching more than halfway to the midrib; upper surface light matte green, lower surface pale green, hairy, veins yellow; petioles stout, 1/4–1/2 inch long, hairy.

Notes Valley oak is the largest and most majestic of the California oaks. It is an indicator of fertile soils with easily-tapped water tables and once covered extensive acreages of prime land. Much of this landscape has been lost to agriculture, residential development, and lowered water tables. The species name *lobata* means lobed.

Locations A surprisingly large tree for a coastal location in a small parking lot behind a storefront in the 5700 block of Hollister Avenue in Goleta. Another on Mulberry Lane. A poor quality tree in the parking lot between City Hall and the News Press Building on Anacapa Street. A street tree on Calle Real near Vista Vallejo and another in the 500 block of East Victoria Street. Trees in the Arroyo and Meadow Sections of the Santa Barbara Botanic Garden, others in Skofield Park.

Elongate acorn and knobby cup of Quercus lobata *with deeply lobed leaves that are dark green above and lighter gray-green below.*

Quercus robur
English oak

Found throughout most of Europe except the extreme northern regions and the drier portions of the Mediterranean Basin.

Habit A widely branched deciduous tree with an irregular appearance to its domed crown, often several-branched from within ten feet of the ground; to 60 feet tall.

Inflorescence Monoecious; male flowers in axillary catkins, $1\frac{1}{2}$–$2\frac{1}{2}$ inches long. Flowers in spring.

Fruit Paired acorns, on $1\frac{1}{2}$- to 3-inch peduncles; nuts ovoid, $\frac{2}{3}$–$1\frac{2}{3}$ inches long, apex blunt, becoming dark brown and often wrinkled when mature; cup shallow, covering less than $\frac{1}{3}$ of the nut, scales ovate-lanceolate, thin, pubescent; maturing in one year.

Twigs Stout, green-brown becoming tan, with pale buff lenticels, roughened by prominent leaf scars; buds conic, pointed, light brown.

Bark Pale to darker gray, broken into short, narrow vertical plates by small fissures, not noticeably flaky.

Leaves Alternate, simple; obovate, with 9–15 lobes; lateral veins making variable angles with the midrib; petiole less than $\frac{1}{4}$ inch long.

Notes Although frequently spoken of as a slow-growing species, English oak is a quite rapid grower and can attain impressive heights. One hundred feet tall and six feet in diameter can be expected when grown on good soil in its native region. The species name *robur* is Latin for strong, oaken.

Locations Several trees in the 100 block of Butterfly Lane off of Coast Village Road in Montecito. Others mixed with *Q. virginiana* in the first–200 blocks of Cooper Road.

Dark green foliage with rounded lobes and large tan buds of Quercus robur.

Quercus rubra
Northern red oak

Broadly distributed on rich soils in moist forests throughout the United States east of the Great Plains, extending marginally into Canada.

Habit A deciduous tree with a straight trunk and a rounded crown; to 70 feet tall.

Inflorescence Monoecious; male flowers in axillary catkins 2–4 inches long. Flowers in spring.

Fruit An acorn on a short pedicel; nut 1/2–1 inch long and as wide; cup shallow, saucer-like, enclosing less than 1/4 of the nut; scales shiny reddish-brown, tightly pressed to the cup; maturing in two seasons.

Twigs Moderately stout, reddish, lustrous; buds ovoid, 1/8–1/4 inch long, dark reddish-brown.

Bark Greenish-brown to gray, smooth when young; becoming brown to black, shallowly fissured, with broad flat ridges; inner bark pinkish.

Leaves Alternate, simple; oval to obovate, 5–9 x 3–5 inches; margins with 7–11 bristle-tipped lobes, sinuses between the lobes extending less than halfway to the midrib; dark green above, somewhat shiny, pale green below, dull; petiole 1–2 inches long, may be tinged red.

Notes *Q. rubra* is an important timber tree in the deciduous forests of the eastern United States, and is used extensively in making furniture and finishing interiors. The species had many medicinal uses among Native Americans and has long been an important food source to forest wildlife. The species name *rubra* means red.

Locations Several trees planted in the first-100 blocks of Alisos Street.

Dark green foliage and angular lobes of **Quercus** *rubra.*

Quercus suber
Cork oak

Endemic to the western Mediterranean region of southern Europe and North Africa.

Habit A low, spreading evergreen tree with twisting branches; to 60 feet tall.

Inflorescence Monoecious; male flowers in axillary catkins 2–4 inches long. Flowers in spring.

Fruit An acorn; nut ovoid-oblong, 3/4–1 1/4 x 3/4 inches; cup covering 1/3 of the nut, scales gray pubescent, tips brownish and loose; maturing in 1 year.

Twigs Gray-green with dense pubescence, becoming winged with dull gray flanges of cork in the fourth year; bud small, round, dark purple.

Bark Corky, thick, up to 4 inches on older trees; pale gray or creamy brown; showing annual growth rings on sides of fissures.

Leaves Alternate, simple; oval, 1 1/2–3 x 1 inches; margins wavy, often revolute, tip somewhat raised and arched, 5–6 pairs of teeth with bristle tips; dark gray-green above, lower surface gray and densely hairy; midrib wavy; petiole 1/2 inch long, densely hairy.

Notes The bark of cork oak was the original source of cork used in the manufacture of gaskets. During World War II, there was considerable interest in developing domestic supplies of cork. To this end, the Santa Barbara Botanic Garden participated in a study to determine the suitability of Southern California climates for growth of *Q. suber*. There are several very old trees in town—one in a yard in the 400 block of West Montecito Street was planted in 1857 by Captain H. G. Trussell from seed obtained from the U.S. Department of Agriculture. The species name *suber* is the Latin word for cork.

Locations Increasingly planted around Santa Barbara. Small trees in the Chase Palm Park and in the Pershing Park parking lot on Castillo Street. Street trees on Orella Street. A large tree at the Sexton House on Hollister Avenue in Goleta, another on Natoma Avenue. A medium-sized tree at the southwest corner of the Davidson Library on the campus of the University of California, Santa Barbara.

Top: Openly branched crown of Quercus suber. *Bottom: Wavy-margined leaves, dark above and gray tomentose below, and green acorns turning walnut brown.*

Quercus tomentella
Island oak

Scattered on open, grassy slopes, and in deep canyons of the Channel Islands of Southern California and Guadalupe Island of Baja California.

Habit An evergreen tree, frequently low-branching and casting a dark shade; to 60 feet tall.

Inflorescence Monoecious; male flowers in axillary catkins 3–4 inches long. Blooms March to April.

Fruit An acorn, usually solitary; nut ovoid, 3/4–1 1/4 x 1/2–3/4 inches, apex rounded; cup shallow, covering only the base of the nut; scales knobby, covered with dense white-brown hairs leaving only the apices visible; maturing in two years.

Twigs Often branching at 45° angles, reddish-brown, densely tomentose into the second year; buds conic, angled, 1/4–1/2 inch, scales brown, gray pubescent towards the apex.

Bark Dark gray, fissured into small rectangular plates, somewhat scaly.

Leaves Alternate, simple; lanceolate or elliptic, 2 3/4–4 1/2 x 1–1 1/2 inches, wavy or distinctly convex from above, not flat, leathery, brittle; secondary veins strongly pinnate, 8–10 pairs; margins often strongly revolute, entire to toothed; lower surface densely tomentose, whitish; upper surface glossy dark green; petiole 1/8–3/8 inch, rusty hairy, flattened.

Notes Although very restricted in its distribution today, *Q. tomentella* was widely spread on the mainland of California during an earlier geologic time, until about three million years ago. The species name *tomentella* means densely hairy.

Locations Trees in the Santa Barbara Botanic Garden. Others in the plantings at the Goleta Valley Water District offices at Hollister Avenue and Puente Drive.

Top: Dense, dark crown of Quercus tomentella.
Middle: Flower catkins and densely tomentose lower leaf surfaces.
Bottom: Coarsely veined foliage and acorns.

Quercus virginiana
Southern live oak

A common tree of the coastal plain of the southeastern United States.

Habit An elm-shaped evergreen tree, branching from 8–15 feet; to 50 feet tall.

Inflorescence Monoecious; male flowers in axillary catkins 2–4 inches long. Flowers in spring.

Fruit Clusters of 1–3 acorns; nut ovoid or cylindrical, about 3/4 x 1/2 inch, dark brown; cup hemispheric to goblet-shaped, 1/3–2/3 inch long and wide; scales whitish or grayish, keeled, tips reddish; peduncle short, 1/2–3/4 inch; maturing in one year.

Twigs Yellowish- to light gray, thin, scaly pubescent in the first year; buds reddish or dark brown, ovate, 1/16 inch.

Bark Dark brown or black, scaly, fissured into small rectangular blocks.

Leaves Alternate, simple; obovate to oblanceolate, 1 1/2–3 1/2 x 3/4–1 1/2 inches, margins slightly revolute or flat, entire or 1–3 toothed on each side, teeth with a slight bristle tip, secondary veins obscure on both sides, leathery, upper surface glossy, undersides densely covered with minute hairs; petiole usually less than 1/3 inch.

Notes Southern live oak played an important role in the early human occupation of the southeastern United States. The hypocotyl of seedlings develops into thick, starchy underground tubers that were cooked for food by Native Americans and early European pioneers. The durability of its wood was important in the framing of ships, and large stands of this species were at one time considered a strategic resource for the country. The species name *virginiana* means from Virginia.

Locations A block of street trees on San Onofre Road. Others in the 2200 block of Santa Barbara Street, in the 1500 and 1600 blocks of Chapala Street, and mixed with *Q. robur* in the first–300 blocks of Cooper Road.

Top: Rounded crown of Quercus virginiana.
Middle: Acorns and gray lower leaf surfaces.
Bottom: Glossy upper surface of leaves.

Flacourtiaceae

The Flacourtia Family includes 81 genera and about 900 species. The family is widely distributed in the tropics, but only a few representatives extend into temperate zones of Japan and Chile. The family has few economic uses; however, some of its species have been used for medicinals, such as for treatment of skin disorders (leprosy). Others have been used as insecticides or to protect crops from the ravages of birds.

Xylosma

Xylosma is a genus of 85 trees and shrubs found throughout the tropical regions of the world. The genus name combines the Greek words *xylos* (wood) and *osma* (smell), in reference to the aromatic smell of the wood.

Xylosma congesta
Shiny xylosma

Native to the warmer regions of China, Japan, and Taiwan.

Habit A small evergreen tree with dense foliage; to 25 feet tall.

Inflorescence Dioecious; short axillary cymes; flowers minute, sepals 4–5, petals absent. Blooms in September.

Fruit A berry with 2–8 seeds.

Twigs Red, minutely hairy, with occasional needle-like axillary spines.

Bark Dark gray, becoming scaly at the base.

Leaves Alternate, simple; lanceolate, 1 1/2–4 1/2 x 3/4–1 3/4 inches, shiny light green, apex elongate, margins red, slightly serrate; petiole 3/16 inch long, red, channeled above.

Notes X. *congesta* flowers infrequently in Santa Barbara. Its shiny leaves can make for a beautiful planting; however, it is susceptible to sooty mold. The species name *congesta* means dense, congested.

Locations Several trees in Willow Glen Park. Small trees in MacKenzie Park along State Street between the Youth Center and the Army Reserve Center.

Top: Shiny leaves and red twigs of Xylosma congesta. *Bottom: Short inflorescence and slight serrations of leaves.*

Hamamelidaceae

This Witch-Hazel Family includes 30 genera and about 100 species. It is an ancient family, and its species occur in relictual populations around the world. Although of limited economic importance, liniments have been extracted from the bark of some species.

Liquidambar

Liquidambar is a genus of five species from North and Central America, Asia Minor, and eastern Asia. Its species are commonly associated with second-growth forests and wetlands. The genus name is derived from the Latin words *liquidus* (liquid) and *ambar* (amber), in reference to the fragrant resin obtained from the following species.

Liquidambar orientalis
Turkish sweetgum

Wild populations are found today in a very limited area (about 3,500 acres) of riparian forest in southwestern Turkey and on the island of Rhodes.

Habit A medium-sized deciduous tree with a pyramidal rounded crown; to 45 feet tall.

Inflorescence Monoecious; inconspicuous; female flowers clustered in a round head, 1/2 inch across; male flowers appearing as terminal racemes, 1 1/4–1 3/4 inches long; both appearing with the leaves. Blooms in March.

Fruit An aggregate of fused pistils, forming a round woody brown ball with protruding pointed or beaked pistils, 1–1 1/2 inches across; on a thin peduncle, 1 1/2–2 2/3 inches long.

Twigs Apple-green becoming reddish-brown in the second year, with small lenticels; buds 3/8–5/8 inch long, scales brown silky pubescent; both twigs and buds emitting a slight sweet-spicy odor when crushed.

Bark Light gray, smooth, becoming deeply fissured and dark gray, older stems appear warty.

Leaves Alternate, simple; palmately five-lobed, the rounded lobes frequently exhibiting secondary lobing; 2–4 x 2 1/2–5 1/4 inches; margins glandular, toothed; shiny dark green above, medium green below with distinct tufts of hairs in the axils of the primary veins; petiole slender, angled, 1 1/3–2 2/3 inches long.

Top: Palmately lobed leaves with sometimes additional secondary lobing of Liquidambar orientalis.
Bottom: Foliage and fused fruit.

Notes The remaining stands of *L. orientalis* have been significantly damaged by the commercial extraction of balsam resins after World War II. This process takes advantage of the fact that resin production is enhanced by wounds to the tree. Thus, trees are intentionally wounded and the bark stripped to be rendered of its resins. Historically, the balm has been used to treat wounds and in embalming the dead. More recently, it has been used in cosmetics and perfumery. The species name *orientalis* means eastern.

Locations Several street trees on Avon Lane west of Grove Lane. Others in the 2300 block of Chapala Street and in Willowglen Park.

Liquidambar styraciflua
Sweetgum

Found in moist bottomlands and disturbed areas of the eastern United States, from Connecticut to Florida, west to southern Illinois and southwest Texas, extending into eastern Mexico and to Guatemala.

Habit An upright deciduous tree with a distinct pyramidal crown when young, becoming oblong or rounded; to 60 feet or more.

Inflorescence Monoecious; inconspicuous; female flowers clustered in a round pendulous head, $1/2$ inch across; male flowers appearing as upright terminal racemes, 3–4 inches long; both appearing with the leaves. Blooms in March.

Fruit An aggregate of fused pistils, forming a round woody brown ball with protruding pointed or beaked pistils, 1–$1\,1/2$ inches across; on a long thin peduncle.

Twigs Light to dark reddish- or yellowish-brown, shiny, often developing corky wings in second year; pith star-shaped, solid, white or brown; terminal buds $1/4$–$1/2$ inch long, with 6–8 exposed imbricate scales, somewhat resinous; lateral buds smaller, divergent from the stem; both buds and twigs aromatic when bruised.

Bark Light gray becoming gray to brown, not hard, with long vertical furrows and narrow flattened ridges.

Leaves Alternate, simple, 3–5 inches across; deeply five- to seven-lobed, lobes and venation palmate; margins finely toothed; aromatic when crushed; shiny dark green above, paler beneath with axillary tufts of hair, turning various shades of yellow, red, or purple in the fall.

Notes *L. styraciflua* is a very attractive tree for shade and fall color. Its hard, pointed fruits, however, are certainly not conducive to walking barefoot beneath it. Several cultivars exist including the *L. styraciflua* 'Rotundiloba,' several trees of which have been planted in front of Roosevelt school. This particular variety was found in the wild in North Carolina, but has been known to revert to its wild-type leaf form. The species name *styraciflua* is the Latin name of a tree producing fragrant gummy resin.

Top: Narrow crown in fall color of **Liquidambar styraciflua**.
Bottom: Palmately lobed leaves and fused fruit.

Locations Trees in Alice Keck Park Memorial Gardens near the map, Willowglen Park and East and West Alameda Plaza. Street trees in 100–200 blocks of West Victoria Street and the 300 block of East Pedgregosa Street.

Parrotia

Parrotia is a monotypic genus. The genus is named for F. W. Parrot (1792–1841), a German naturalist who traveled extensively in the Middle East and climbed Mount Ararat, the tallest mountain in Turkey.

Parrotia persica
Persian ironwood

Native to northern Iran adjacent to the Caspian Sea.

Habit A deciduous tree with an open crown; to 40 feet tall.

Inflorescence Terminal or axillary, clusters of 3–6 flowers, containing 10–15 red stamens surrounded by brown hairy bracts, petals absent. Flowers January to February.

Fruit A woody capsule, splitting in two parts.

Twigs Erect, olive-brown, somewhat zigzag, with long internodes; buds dark brown, hairy.

Bark Smooth, gray brown, flaking off in irregular plates to reveal an orange-brown under bark.

Leaves Alternate, simple; ovate to obovate, 2½–5 x 1–2½ inches, base unequal, margins unevenly coarsely toothed and wavy, dark green above, pale and sparsely hairy below, midrib and secondary veins prominent below, tertiary veins forming ladder steps between the secondaries; petiole very short, ⅛ inch long.

Notes The species name *persica* means from Persia.

Locations Lower Orpet Park west of the center steps, between the path and Alameda Padre Serra.

Top: Flowers without petals appearing before the leaves on Parrotia persica.
Bottom: Ovate leaves with asymmetrical base and wavy margins.

Hippocastanaceae

The Horse-Chestnut Family is small, containing two genera and 15 species that are found in Central America, North America, Europe, and Eastern Asia. Several of the larger trees are used for timber; however, the large attractive seeds contain alkaloids that are toxic.

Aesculus
Buckeyes, horse-chestnuts

Aesculus is a genus of 13 species from southeastern Europe, East Asia, and North America. *Aesculus* is the Latin name for a species of oak, but for unknown reasons was used by Linnaeus to name the genus.

Aesculus californica
California buckeye

Endemic to California, common in the Coast Ranges from San Luis Obispo County north, and in the Sierra Nevada and Cascade Range foothills from Kern County north, with a southern extension into northwestern Los Angeles County (Liebre Mountains).

Habit A large, multi-stemmed deciduous shrub or small tree with a rounded crown; to 40 feet tall.

Inflorescence Terminal densely flowered panicles, 6–8 x 2–3 inches; flowers showy, 1/2–3/4 inch long, white, sometimes with a pink tinge, fragrant, stamens exserted; only one of the uppermost flowers on a spike sets a fruit. Flowers in May.

Fruit A large capsule, 2–3 1/4 inches across, rough-surfaced but not spiny, orange-brown at maturity; usually 1 seed, roundish, to 3 inches across, light mahogany brown with a large scar at the point of attachment.

Twigs Stout, gray-brown to reddish, glabrous, with scattered small brown lenticels; buds large, pointed, dark brown, sticky resinous.

Bark Smooth, silvery gray, peeling in silver-dollar-size flakes on older stems.

Leaves Opposite, palmately compound; leaflets 5, oblong-lanceolate, 2 1/2–6 3/4 x 3/4–1 1/2 inches, finely serrate, shiny dark green above; petiole 3–4 inches long; petiolules 1/2–1 inch long.

Top: Aesculus californica *in full flower and with spring leaves, in Oak Park.*
Middle: Showy terminal flower panicle and palmately compound leaves with five leaflets.
Bottom: Large fruit in fall after leaf drop.

Notes Although a striking tree in the landscape, the species has a number of drawbacks. The seeds contain aesculin, a coumarin-like compound, which was used by Native Americans to poison and collect fish. Also, the nectar and pollen of the flowers are toxic to honey bees. The species name *californica* means from California.

Locations A striking tree in Oak Park; another in the 1700 block of Anacapa Street; others recently planted in Stevens Park near the playground.

Aesculus x *carnea*
Red horsechestnut

This is a hybrid of horticultural origin, and today is one of the most popular trees in England.

Habit A deciduous medium-sized tree with a rounded crown, often branching within 10 feet of the ground; to 40 feet tall.

Inflorescence Terminal showy panicles, 6–8 x 3–4 inches; flowers light pink to red, 3/4 inch long. Flowers in April.

Fruit A round, slightly prickly capsule, 1 1/2 inches across; usually 1 seed, roundish, mahogany brown with a large scar at the point of attachment.

Twigs Stout; buds neither as large nor as sticky as in *A. californica*.

Bark Smooth, light gray.

Leaves Opposite, palmately compound; leaflets 5, oblong, 5–9 x 2–3 1/2 inches, lustrous dark green, margins serrate.

Notes A horticultural product resulting from a cross of *A. hippocastanum* and *A. pavia*, seemingly originating in Germany. The species name *carnea* means deep pink.

Locations A nice tree in Alice Keck Park Memorial Gardens next to the tool shed.

Showy red flowers held on an upright panicle and palmately compound leaves of Aesculus x carnea.

Aesculus hippocastanum
Common horsechestnut, European horsechestnut

Found in the mountainous regions of Greece and Albania; once thought to extend naturally to the Himalayas.

Habit A tall deciduous tree; to 75 feet.

Inflorescence Terminal panicles, 5–12 x 2–5 inches; flowers white with a splash of yellow or red at the base, 3/4 inch long. Flowers in March.

Fruit A round capsule, 2–2 1/2 inches across, surface light brown, spiny; seeds 1, sometimes 2, mahogany brown with a large scar at the point of attachment.

Twigs Stout, reddish-yellow to grayish-brown, with large hemispherical leaf scars; buds large, 1/2–3/4 inch long, dark reddish-brown, covered with a sticky resin.

Bark Dark gray to brown, exfoliating in plates on older stems to expose an orangish-brown inner bark.

Leaves Opposite, palmately compound; leaflets 7, sometimes 5, obovate, 4–10 x 2–5 inches, doubly-serrate, dark green; petiole 3–5 inches long, leaflets sessile.

Notes The species name *hippocastanum* is the classical Latin name for the species.

Locations A single tree in the 1200 block of Punta Gorda Street.

Top: **Aesculus hippocastanum** *with curved terminal flower panicle and leaf with seven leaflets.*
Bottom: Spiny fruit capsule with large mahogany brown seeds.

Hydrophyllaceae

The Waterleaf Family consists of 17 genera and approximately 300 species and is spread through most of the temperate and tropical regions of the world, except Australia. It is especially well-represented in western North America, usually by herbaceous species. A recent taxonomic revision has placed this family in the Boraginaceae; however, this has not been fully accepted.

Wigandia

Wigandia is a genus of three to five species from tropical North and South America. The genus is named for Johannes Wigand (1523–1587), Bishop of Pomerania, who wrote on Prussian plants.

Wigandia caracasana
St. Paul's tree, St. Paul's leaf

Found in brushlands and disturbed areas from southern Mexico to Venezuela and Columbia.

Habit An evergreen erect shrub or small tree with several stems; to 20 feet tall.

Inflorescence Terminal spikes, which unroll to display flowers on one side, to 7 inches long; flowers with 5 petals fused at the base, $1-1^{1}/_{4}$ inches across, blue-purple with a white throat, 5 stamens with hairy filaments, strongly exserted; peduncle very dark hairy. Flowers in March.

Fruit A small capsule, $^{1}/_{4}-^{2}/_{5}$ inch long, densely covered with stinging hairs, containing numerous small winged seeds.

Twigs Greenish-brown, densely hairy, with large round leaf scars and vascular bundles arranged in a near circle.

Bark Dark gray, shallowly fissured.

Leaves Alternate, simple; ovate to elliptic, to 18 x 12 inches, base slightly heart-shaped, margins coarsely doubly-toothed, densely covered underneath with brownish pubescence; petiole $^{1}/_{2}-^{3}/_{4}$ inch long, brown hairy, flat on top.

Notes Although difficult to grow (requiring rich, moist soil, full sun, and protection from cold winter temperatures), the showy floral display of *W. caracasana* warrants its attention. The blue-purple flowers appear, appropriately, at the beginning of the Lenten season and continue into early summer. The plant is used in Central America to treat rheumatism, insomnia, and syphilis. The species name *caracasana* refers to the city of Caracas, Venezuela.

Locations Old Mission parking lot adjacent to Los Olivos Street; another on De la Guerra Lane near De la Guerra Street.

Top: Large leaves, showy inflorescences, and several stems of Wigandia caracasana.
Middle: Inflorescence with large ovate leaves.
Bottom: Purple flowers with whitish throat and yellow stamens.

Juglandaceae

The Walnut Family consists of nine genera and over 60 species, most of which are located in the temperate and subtropical regions of the Northern Hemisphere. Several species are sources of valuable timber and some produce nutritious nuts. The oils of those nuts are also used in the cosmetic and paint industries.

Carya
Hickories

Carya is a genus of 14 species from North and Central America and Eastern Asia. *Carya* is derived from the Greek word *karya* (walnut tree). Legend has it that Bacchus changed Carya, daughter of the King of Laconia, into a walnut tree.

Carya illinoensis
Pecan, sweet pecan

Native to rich, alluvial river bottoms of the central United States, from Indiana and Iowa south to Alabama, Texas, and extending into Mexico.

Habit A tall deciduous tree with a broad oval crown; to 100 feet tall.

Inflorescence Monoecious; inconspicuous, appearing with the leaves; male flowers borne on drooping three-branched catkins, 3–6 inches long; female flowers few, on terminal spikes. Blooms in April.

Fruit A nut enclosed in a thin four-winged husk, in clusters of 3–12; oblong, 1 1/2–2 inches long.

Twigs Stout, olive-brown, pubescent, lenticellate; pith continuous; buds with valvate scales, dull yellowish- to grayish-brown pubescent, 1/4–1/2 inch long.

Bark Light brown to gray, thick, with narrow fissures and scaly ridges.

Leaves Alternate, pinnately compound, with a terminal leaflet, 12–20 inches long; leaflets 9–17, oblong to lanceolate, frequently curved, 4–7 x 1–3 inches, margins serrate, base unequal, with 20–30 pinnate veins, yellowish-green.

Notes Pecans are a major horticultural crop in the southeastern United States, and numerous varieties focusing on nut production have been developed. The species seems to do very well in downtown Santa Barbara, and several individuals have been noted in yards in the vicinity of Chapala and Victoria Streets. The species name *illinoensis* means from Illinois.

Locations Street trees in the 200 and the 900 blocks of West Islay Street. A nice specimen at Franklin School and a smaller tree in a parking lot at Chapala and Victoria. Several trees in the 4000–4100 blocks of Lago Drive.

Top: Pinnately compound leaves and catkins of male flowers of Carya illinoensis.
Bottom: Cluster of angular nuts.

Juglans

Juglans is a genus of 21 species from north temperate regions (the Mediterranean, eastern Asia, and North America) and extending through the tropical Americas to the northern Andes. *Juglans* is the Latin name for a walnut tree.

Juglans californica
California black walnut

Endemic to California, in the Coastal Ranges south of Mendocino County, San Joaquin Valley, and lower slopes of the Sierra Nevada, and south to San Diego.

Habit A deciduous shrub or small tree, frequently with multiple stems; to 50 feet tall.

Inflorescence Monoecious; generally inconspicuous; male flowers in axillary catkins 2–3 inches long, appearing on the previous year's twigs; 1–3 female flowers appearing at the ends of current twigs. Blooms in May.

Fruit A nut enclosed in a leathery husk, 3/4–1 1/2 inches; the shell of the woody nut grooved.

Twigs Stout, with raised flattened leaf scars, becoming purplish-gray, pith cinnamon-brown, chambered.

Bark Gray brown, becoming blackish-brown with a hint of a silvery wash, deeply fissured on older trees into flattened ridges; the ridges deeply chocolate-colored when cut.

Leaves Alternate, pinnately compound with a terminal leaflet, 10–15 inches long; leaflets 11–19, lanceolate to ovate, 1 1/4–4 x 3/4–1 1/4 inches, serrate, sometimes faintly sickle-shaped.

Notes *J. californica* consists of two varieties. *J. californica* var. *hindsii* (the Northern California black walnut) is an upright, single-trunked tree with somewhat larger nuts and was reportedly cultivated near Native American campsites. This may explain the apparent uncertainty about its "native" distribution. The Southern California black walnut (*J. californica* var. *californica*) is a smaller, multi-stemmed specimen with a somewhat smaller nut. The species name *californica* means from California.

Locations *J. californica* var. *californica* can be found along Sycamore Creek, at Carpinteria Street and in other moist locations about town. Two young trees are in the Santa Barbara Botanic Garden along the Woodland Trail. Another at the corner of Puente Drive and More Mesa Drive. A graceful specimen of *J. californica* var. *hindsii* is on the campus of Westmont College below the Student Center. Another on Argonne Circle across from San Roque Church.

Top: Full crown of Juglans californica.
Bottom: Pinnately compound leaves and globose nuts.

Juglans nigra
Black walnut

Widely, though usually not densely, distributed on moist sites with rich soil in the deciduous forests of the eastern United States, from Massachusetts to southern Minnesota, and south to east Texas and northern Florida.

Habit An erect deciduous tree; to 70 feet tall.

Inflorescence Monoecious; generally inconspicuous; male flowers on axillary catkins, 2–3 inches long, appearing on previous year's twigs; female flowers terminal, 2–8 appearing at the ends of current twigs, appearing with the leaves. Blooms in May.

Fruit A nut enclosed in a yellowish-green leathery husk, 1½–2½ inches across; the shell of the round woody nut wrinkled.

Twigs Stout, gray and hairy or reddish-brown and glabrous, with orange lenticels; pith chambered, light tan-brown.

Bark Gray-brown, becoming blackish-brown with a hint of a silvery wash, deeply fissured on older trees into flattened ridges; the ridges deeply chocolate-colored when cut.

Leaves Alternate, pinnately compound, frequently without a terminal leaflet, 12–24 inches long; leaflets 7–12 pairs, ovate-oblong to ovate-lanceolate, apex elongate, 3–3½ inches long; margins finely serrate; dark green above, green and somewhat hairy beneath.

Notes Among gardeners in the eastern United States, *J. nigra* is well-known to be incompatible with many vegetables. Its roots exude a substance, juglone, which is toxic to many herbaceous plants. The wood of well-formed trees commands a very high price for its veneer and furniture quality. This has spawned a small walnut "rustling" industry which relies on midnight operations and horse logging to minimize chances of detection. The species name *nigra* means black.

Locations A single street tree on the southeast corner of De la Vina Street and Alamar Avenue.

Pinnately compound leaves and round nut of Juglans nigra. *The ovate-oblong leaflets are characterized by an elongate apex.*

Juglans regia
English, Persian, or common walnut

Native from southeastern Europe to the Himalayas and China.

Habit A low-branching, broad-crowned deciduous tree; to 40 feet tall.

Inflorescence Monoecious; generally inconspicuous, appearing with the leaves; male flowers on axillary catkins containing many flowers, appearing on previous year's twigs; female flowers terminal, appearing at the ends of current twigs. Blooms April to May.

Fruit A nut in clusters of 2–3, enclosed in a greenish leathery husk, 1 1/2–2 inches across; the shell of the somewhat elongate woody nut wrinkled.

Twigs Stout, green to olive-brown, becoming grayish, lenticellate, pith chambered, tannish.

Bark Silvery gray, with shallow widely spaced fissures; deeply chocolate-colored when cut.

Leaves Alternate, pinnately compound, with a terminal leaflet, 12–18 inches long; leaflets 5–9, elliptic to obovate, apex not elongate, 2–8 x 2 1/2–4 1/2 inches long; margins entire; medium to dark green, with axillary tufts of hairs beneath, rachis lightly hairy.

Notes There are numerous varieties of this edible nut. In California, scions of these are grafted on the root stock of *J. californica* var. *hindsii,* and basal sprouts of the latter are sometimes seen. The species name *regia* means royal.

Locations Scattered trees can be found around upper State Street in the San Roque area, where extensive groves were maintained prior to Santa Barbara's early growth period out of the downtown area.

Pinnately compound leaves and round nuts of **Juglans regia.** *The leaves have fewer leaflets that are more broadly ovate than those of other species.*

Lauraceae

The Avocado or Laurel Family includes 52 genera and about 2,750 species that are located throughout the tropical regions of the world with some extensions into subtropical or temperate zones. High centers of diversity occur in northern South America, Southeast Asia, and Madagascar. Many species have aromatic leaves, others have a a fine-grained wood that is prized by the furniture industry. Unfortunately, overexploitation by the timber industry has led several species to the brink of extinction.

Beilschmiedia

Beilschmiedia is a genus of about 250 species (mostly trees) found throughout the tropics and extending to Chile, Australia, and New Zealand. It is named for Karl Traugott Beilschmied (1793–1848), German botanist and apothecary.

Beilschmiedia miersii
Bellota, **northern acorn**

Found at low elevations in Mediterranean climates of central Chile.

Habit An evergreen tree with a narrow crown; to 50 feet tall.

Inflorescence Axillary panicles of 10–35 flowers, densely pubescent, to $2^{1}/_{2}$ inches long; flowers minute, $1/8$ inch across, hairy pubescent, greenish-white. Flowers April to September.

Fruit An ellipsoid berry, $1^{2}/_{3}$–$1^{1}/_{3}$ inches, purple-black.

Twigs Flattened and channeled on first year's growth, becoming round; densely pubescent.

Bark Gray-brown, thin, flaking to expose a cinnamon-brown inner bark.

Leaves Opposite, simple; ovate, 2–$4^{3}/_{4}$ x $^{2}/_{3}$–$2^{2}/_{3}$ inches; glabrous, very leathery, shiny dark green above, glaucous below; midrib raised below, secondary veins may be raised below; petiole $1/8$–$3/8$ inch long.

Notes The species name *miersii* honors John Miers (1789–1879) British botanist and metallurgist who traveled extensively in South America from 1819 to 1838.

Locations One tree in Lower Orpet Park west of the lawn. Several in the 2800 block of Valencia Drive were planted by Will Beittel. A large tree on Hollister Avenue opposite Kinman Avenue in Goleta.

Beilschmiedia miersii *showing minute flowers and ovate leaves with shiny upper surface and glaucous lower surface.*

Cinnamomum

Cinnamomum is a genus of 350 species extending from eastern Asia to Australia and reaching into the tropical Americas. As with all of the Laurel Family, *Cinnamomum* is a very aromatic genus and its species are widely used as spices, scents, and medications. The name is the classical Greek name for cinnamon.

Cinnamomum camphora
Camphor tree

Native to tropical Asia and Taiwan.

Habit A tall evergreen tree, with stout branches and a spreading crown; to 50 feet tall.

Inflorescence Densely flowered axillary cymes, held within the leaves; flowers small, yellowish- to greenish-white. Flowers April to May.

Fruit A round drupe, to 1/3 inch across, black when mature.

Twigs Dull orange, becoming gray.

Bark Dark gray, deeply furrowed into interlacing flat-topped ridges, reddish-brown underneath with alternating creamy white layers, smells of nutmeg.

Leaves Alternate, simple; ovate-elliptic, 3–5 x 1–2 1/2 inches, apex elongate, with 3 palmate nerves from the base, lateral veins with a characteristic gland at the juncture with the midrib, margins entire; glossy green above, paler and dull below, young leaves reddish; with the smell of camphor when crushed; petiole about 1 inch long, with a red gland at the base.

Notes *C. camphora* has a long ethnobotanical history. One of its earliest mentions in recorded history was by Marco Polo, who observed its uses by the Chinese in the thirteenth century. Distillations of the wood have been used to treat numerous medical conditions, as well as in the manufacture of lacquer and explosives. The wood is also used in cabinetry; its insect-repelling properties provide a preserving environment. The species name *camphora* means resembling camphor.

Locations Common throughout town; street trees in the 1400 block of Laguna Street, 1900 block of Anacapa Street, and 2400 block of Castillo Street.

Top: Rounded high crown and low branching of Cinnamomum camphora.
Middle: Small-flowered inflorescences and ovate leaves with elongate tips (drip tips).
Bottom: Fruit and leaves with three prominent veins from the base.

Cinnamomum japonicum
Yabunikkei

Native to Korea, eastern China, Japan, and Taiwan.

Habit An evergreen tree with a dense crown; to 50 feet tall.

Inflorescence An axillary or terminal cyme, shorter than the leaves; flowers small, to $1/4$ inch wide, densely hairy within the tubular perianth. Flowers in spring.

Fruit A black ellipsoid drupe, to $3/4$ inch long.

Twigs Light green, dull, brittle.

Bark Thin, light gray, very smooth with slight vertical fissures.

Leaves Simple, sub-opposite or alternate; narrowly ovate to oblong, $21/2$–5 x $3/4$–2 inches, leathery, glaucous beneath, the midrib three-parted near the base; petiole $1/3$–$2/3$ inch long.

Notes The species name *japonicum* means from Japan.

Locations A single tree at Franceschi Park east of the cottage.

Cinnamomum japonicum *with leathery dark green leaves showing three strong veins from the base.*

Cryptocarya

Cryptocarya is a genus of about 200 species from tropical and warm regions of the world. The genus name combines the Greek words *krypto* (hidden) and *karos* (nut), in reference to the small size of the fruit.)

Cryptocarya alba
Cryptocarya rubra

Peumo

Native to the wetter mountain slopes and ravines in central Chile.

Habit An evergreen tree with several ascending stems and a rounded crown of dense foliage; to 45 feet tall.

Inflorescence Axillary or terminal racemes, 3/4–2 1/2 inches long; flowers minute, 1/8–1/6 inch long, composed of 6 tepals, united at the base, yellowish-green. Flowers March to April.

Fruit An oval drupe, 2/3 inch long, intense red or sometimes whitish.

Twigs Somewhat flattened, reddish, covered with minute hairs.

Bark Thin, gray-brown, lightly fissured.

Leaves Alternate or opposite, simple; obovate to oblong, 1–3 x 2/3–1 1/2 inches, apex obtuse or slightly notched; stiff leathery, shiny green above, bluish-green below, margins entire, somewhat wavy; emitting an apple-like fragrance when crushed; petiole 1/8 inch long.

Notes The aromatic foliage contains a variety of essential oils that were used by native peoples of Chile for centuries to treat liver diseases and rheumatic pain. The species name *alba* means white.

Locations Franceschi Park, street trees in the 200 block of West Pueblo Street, the 3700 block of Capri Drive, the 600 block of East Micheltorena Street, and the 3300–3500 blocks of Madrona Drive.

Top: Dense, rounded crown of Cryptocarya alba. *Middle: Shiny ovate leaves and axillary inflorescences. Bottom: Glaucous lower surface of leaves and whitish to red fruit.*

Laurus

Laurus is a genus of two species from the Mediterranean region and the Canary Islands. Its name is the Latin name for laurel or bay.

Laurus nobilis
Grecian laurel, sweet bay

Native to Asia Minor, but now naturalized throughout the Mediterranean region and the Balkan peninsula.

Habit A dense, bushy, aromatic evergreen tree, frequently with multiple stems; to 40 feet tall.

Inflorescence Inconspicuous axillary umbels of 5 flowers on short pedicels; flowers small, 1/3 inch across, greenish-yellow. Flowers in March.

Fruit A round to oval, shiny black to purple berry, 1/2 inch long.

Twigs Dull green, brittle.

Bark Smooth, gray.

Leaves Alternate, simple; narrowly oval or ovate, 1 1/2–4 x 1/2–1 1/2 inches, somewhat leathery, dark glossy green with a yellow green midrib, margins often wavy; petiole 1/8–1/3 inch long; strongly aromatic when crushed.

Notes *L. nobilis* is the true laurel of mythology and custom. Its leafy twigs formed the "laurels" with which victors were crowned in ancient Greece, and its fruiting sprays were made into wreaths for worthy poets (hence, the term *poet laureate*). Today, the leaves are the bay of gastronomic importance. The species name *nobilis* means famous, renowned.

Locations A tree in Alice Keck Park Memorial Gardens adjacent to Micheltorena Street near Garden Street.

Top: *Several stems and soft crown of* Laurus nobilis. Bottom: *Dark green leaves turning yellow and small flowers along the twig.*

Persea

Persea is a genus of about 200 species from tropical Asia and America. The name is the Greek name for an Egyptian tree, *Cordia myxa*.

Persea americana
Avocado, alligator pear

Presumed to have originated from southern Mexico, Guatemala, and Honduras.

Habit An evergreen tree with a rounded drooping crown; to 50 feet tall.

Inflorescence Terminal panicles, $1/2$–$2^3/4$ inches long, shorter than the subtending leaves; flowers with 6 perianth segments, $1/4$–$1/3$ inch across, greenish-yellow, hairy. Flowers March to April.

Fruit A pear-shaped berry, 2–6 inches long, green to black when mature.

Twigs Moderately slender, somewhat pubescent, yellowish-green, not aromatic.

Bark Smoothish, gray.

Leaves Alternate, simple; elliptic to roundish, $2^1/2$–12 x $1^1/2$–8 inches, apex usually somewhat elongate, leathery and wavy, upper surface shiny dark green, lower surface pale, almost glaucous, midrib and lateral veins prominent below.

Notes The avocado has been widely cultivated throughout much of tropical America for its highly nutritious fruit since 8,000 BC. The species name *americana* means American.

Locations Common in gardens and in orchards. Street trees on West Arrellaga Street between State Street and Bath Street.

Top: Dark green dense crown of Persea americana.
Middle: Small flowers on long peduncle and glossy ovate leaves.
Bottom: Large black fruit of the Hass variety.

Persea indica
Madeira bay

Native to the Canary Islands, Madeira, and the Azores.

Habit An evergreen tree with a broad rounded crown; to 45 feet tall.

Inflorescence Axillary panicles, $1 2/3$–5 inches long, shorter than the subtending leaves; flowers with 6 perianth segments, densely covered with white pubescence, $1/3$ inch across. Flowers in July.

Fruit An ovoid-ellipsoid berry, $2/3$–$3/4$ inch long, green turning black.

Twigs Green, finely pubescent, with raised leaf scars.

Bark White-gray, breaking into small rectangular blocks and becoming blackish-gray on the lower trunk.

Leaves Alternate, simple; elliptic, 4–8 x $1 1/4$–$3 1/4$ inches, lightly pubescent below, pale green becoming reddish with age, midrib prominent below, with 8–12 pairs of pinnate secondary veins; petiole $1/2$–$1 1/4$ inches long, reddish, pubescent or glabrous, only slightly channeled above.

Notes The species name *indica* means from India.

Locations Street trees in the 1200 block of East Mason Street and in the 1700 block of Hillside Road.

Top: Narrowly ovate leaves with shiny upper surface and small flowers of **Persea indica**.
Bottom: Small fruit and cupped leaves.

Umbellularia

Umbellularia is a monotypic genus from the western United States. The name is from the Latin *umbella,* referring to the structure of the inflorescence.

Umbellularia californica
California bay, California laurel, pepperwood, Oregon myrtlewood

Occurs from San Diego County to southern Oregon, through the Coast Ranges and western Sierra Nevada, mostly below 5,000 feet. Confined to canyon bottoms and shady, moist slopes in the southern portion of its range, but becoming a landscape dominant in the Coast Ranges north of Point Conception.

Habit An evergreen tree with an initially pyramidal, dense, dark crown, becoming rounded at maturity, and a trunk that flares into a burl at ground level; to 70 feet tall.

Inflorescence Axillary umbels with 6–10 flowers; flowers yellow-green with 6 sepals and 9 stamens, 1/3 inch across. Flowers February to March.

Fruit An olive-shaped drupe, 1 inch long, greenish becoming dark purple when mature; peduncle swollen, 1/2 inch long.

Twigs Thin, yellow-green, roughened by raised leaf scars.

Bark Hard, smooth, light gray on smaller branches, turning black-gray with shallow fissures and flat ridges.

Leaves Alternate, simple; oblong to oblong-lanceolate, 1 1/4–4 x 2/3–1 1/4 inches, leathery, shiny dark green, turning yellow-green, with a strong pungent smell when crushed.

Notes The strong odors of the crushed leaves may cause a headache for some people. In spite of this, the leaves are sometimes used in cooking, although gourmets always prefer the smoother flavors of *Laurus nobilis.* The wood is prized by woodworkers for its fine textures. The leaves of this species have recently been determined to be among a number of alternate hosts for *Phytophthora ramorum,* the cause of sudden oak death syndrome. The species name *californica* means from California.

Top: Light crown and several stems from a basal burl of Umbellularia californica.
Bottom left: Inflorescences of six to ten flowers and leaves with entire margin.
Bottom right: Fruit maturing to purple and oblong-lanceolate leaves.

Locations Several trees along Mission Creek in Oak Park. Others in the Santa Barbara Botanic Garden. Street trees intermittently in the 600–1800 blocks of Castillo Street and along Alamar at Oak Park.

Loganiaceae

The Logania or Strychnine Family includes ten genera and about 400 species that are subtropical or tropical in distribution. Many of its species contain poisonous alkaloids, such as strychnine or brucine, that are similar to alkaloids of the Apocynaceae. These have been used by native cultures as fish or arrow poisons and to treat a variety of ailments.

Nuxia

Nuxia is a small genus of 15 species native to the Old World from Arabia to South Africa and Madagascar. *Nuxia* is the vernacular name for these trees in Madagascar.

Nuxia floribunda
Kite tree, white elder

Native to evergreen forests and forest margins extending from tropical eastern Africa to the Natal region of South Africa.

Habit A small evergreen tree; to 40 feet tall.

Inflorescence Densely flowered terminal and axillary panicles, 10–12 inches long; flowers small, 1/8 inch long, creamy white, tubular, with a rich sweet fragrance, not unlike true elder. Blooms January to February.

Fruit A small capsule 1/6 inch long, mostly covered by the persistent calyx, pale creamy brown when mature, splitting into 2 valves.

Twigs Angled, tan, with raised leaf scars and swollen nodes.

Bark Pale gray, becoming dark gray, furrowed into small flakes, with pale orange showing within the furrows.

Leaves Usually in whorls of 3, sometimes opposite, simple; oblong-elliptic, 2–6 x 1/2–2 1/4 inches; light glossy green with a pale green midrib; pinnate veins curving forward along the margin; margins usually entire, often wavy; petiole 2/3–1 1/3 inches long; giving a faint smell of green peppers when crushed.

Notes The yellow wood of this small tree is close grained and strong. For these reasons the Zulus used parts of the tree as a strengthening medicine for their village after the death of one of its members. Settlers used the timber for wagon production, and it is still used today in fencing. The species name *floribunda* means abundant flowers.

Locations A single tree in the first block of East Carillo Street. A large tree in upper Orpet Park, east of the lawn. Others at Franceschi Park near the parking area.

Large terminal inflorescence of creamy white flowers and whorled elliptic leaves of Nuxia floribunda.

Lythraceae

The Loosestrife Family includes 31 genera and about 600 species that are evenly distributed between tropical, subtropical, and even temperate regions of the Eastern and Western Hemispheres. Several species contain a variety of alkaloids that are of pharmaceutical interest. The family also includes the Eurasian purple loosestrife that has become such a noxious pest in North America.

Lagerstroemia

Lagerstroemia is a genus of about 50 species in eastern Asia and extending to Australia. The genus was named by Linnaeus for his good friend, Swedish merchant Magnus von Lagerström of Göteborg.

Lagerstroemia indica
Crape myrtle, crepe flower

Native to China and Korea; first introduced into European culture in 1759.

Habit A deciduous shrub or small tree sometimes with a multi-stemmed trunk; to 30 feet tall.

Inflorescence Showy terminal panicles, 6–8 x 3–5 inches; flowers 1–1 1/2 inches across, with 6 crinkled petals and numerous stamens, pink to deep red or white. Blooms September to October.

Fruit A spherical woody capsule, 1/3 inch across, dehiscing in 3–6 valves, tannish-brown.

Twigs Green, reddish above, hairy with decurrent ridges, becoming tan and fibrous.

Bark Smooth, exfoliating to create a mottled pattern of gray, brown, and pink.

Leaves Opposite, alternate or in whorls of 3, simple; elliptic-oblong, 1–2 1/2 x 3/4–1 1/2 inches, apex rounded or notched, margins entire, hairy along lower midrib above and below; petiole very short.

Notes *L. indica* has been the subject of intense cultivation. It is widely planted in the southeastern United States. The species name *indica* means from India.

Locations A tree in the parking lot of the County Administration Building at Santa Barbara and Victoria Streets. Others planted in a parking lot on the south side of the 3600 block of State Street. Street trees in the 400 block of San Roque Road, the 300 block of West Alamar Avenue, and the 700 and 800 blocks of West Carillo Street.

Top: Rounded crown of Lagerstroemia indica *in full flower in fall.*
Bottom: Terminal inflorescence and dark green elliptic leaves.

Magnoliaceae

The Magnolia family includes about 10 genera and 220 species. The family is especially well-represented in eastern China, southeastern Asia, eastern North America, and the tropical Americas. Its largest center of diversity is Southeast Asia. The showy flowers produce an aroma that attracts pollinating beetles.

Liriodendron

Liriodendron is a genus of only two species and is a classic example of disjunct distributions between eastern North America and eastern Asia. The name combines the Greek words *leirion* (lily) and *dendron* (tree), in reference to the lily-like flowers of this magnificent tree.

Liriodendron tulipifera
Tulip tree, tulip poplar, yellow-poplar

Found in cool, moist, rich sites of the eastern United States from Vermont to Michigan and south to Louisiana and Florida.

Habit A large deciduous tree, initially with a pyramidal crown, becoming rounded or oblong and retaining lower branches when grown in the open; to 100 feet tall.

Inflorescence Terminal, single-flowered; flowers 2–3 inches across, consisting of 6 greenish-yellow tepals with an orange splash at the base of each, numerous stamens and pistils; very showy, however somewhat hidden among the foliage. Blooms in April.

Fruit An upright, cone-like aggregate of tan winged seeds, 2–3 inches long; seeds 1–1 1/2 x 1/4–1/3 inches, disseminating in the fall, leaving the central stalk into the winter months.

Twigs Shiny, brownish to greenish, ringed at each leaf scar by stipule scars; pith diaphragmed; strongly aromatic and refreshing when bruised (reminiscent of a gin and tonic, with lime).

Bark Smooth, gray broken by whitish fissures when young, becoming strongly fissured on older stems with an interlacing pattern of flat-topped ridges.

Leaves Alternate, simple, 3–5 inches long, equally wide or wider, shallowly four-lobed, the apex broadly and shallowly notched so that it appears to have been cut off; shiny green above, pale beneath, turning yellow in the autumn.

Clockwise from top: 1) **Liriodendron tulipifera** *with a typical narrow crown. 2) Flower with six showy tepals and yellow stamens. 3) Leaves turning fall color and fruit aggregate. 4) Flower and four-lobed leaves.*

Notes *L. tulipifera* is an important tree of the deciduous forests of the eastern United States. Although very long-lived (up to 400 years), it is a fast grower and is frequently one of the first species to establish on disturbed sites that are moist and rich. During the late 1800s and early 1900s, subsistence farming in the Appalachians involved a North American version of slash and burn agriculture. Many of these sites were abandoned after three to five years of corn production and have grown up in almost pure stands of *L. tulipifera*. The species name *tulipifera* means tulip-like.

Locations Several young trees were planted on Paseo Tranquillo about 15 years ago. The largest tree in the area is visible on the north side of Highway 101 just east of Casitas Pass Road in Carpinteria.

Magnolia

Magnolia is a genus of about 100 species found from the Himalayas to Japan and western Malaysia to eastern North America and extending to tropical America. The genus is named for Pierre Magnol (1638–1715), director of the botanic garden at Montpellier, France.

Magnolia grandiflora
Southern magnolia, bull bay

Found in moist, rich soils of the coastal plain of the southeastern United States, from North Carolina to Texas.

Habit An evergreen tree with a dense rounded crown; to 60 feet tall.

Inflorescence Terminal, solitary; flowers large, 6–12 inches across, with 6 large thickened white petals, very fragrant (described as "better than the best perfume"). Blooms August to December.

Fruit An upright cone-like head of follicles covered with brown fuzz, 3–5 inches long, each splitting to reveal a red seed.

Twigs Stout, rusty hairy, encircled by obvious stipule scars.

Bark Smooth gray, may develop large scaly plates on older trees.

Leaves Alternate, simple; oblong to elliptic, 5–10 inches long, less than half as wide; margins entire; shiny dark green above, frequently rusty hairy below, very stiff leathery; petioles stout, 1–2 inches long.

Notes *M. grandiflora* has been in cultivation since 1734 and numerous varieties emphasizing floral and foliar differences have been developed. This tree, along with *Quercus virginiana* (Southern live oak) and *Tillandsia usneoides* (Spanish moss), probably symbolize the Old South as much as any other species. The species name *grandiflora* means large or beautifully flowered.

Locations An extensive arcade of street trees in the 800–1900 block of San Andres Street between Carrillo and Mission Streets. A large tree in East Alameda Plaza. Street trees on Cota Street between Olive and Garden Streets and in the 1100 block of Nopal. Others on Vernal and Magnolia (formerly Dixon) Streets.

Top: Dense, dark green crown of **Magnolia grandiflora**.
Middle left: Large, showy white flowers with thickened petals.
Middle right: Flower bud and shiny stiff leathery leaves.
Bottom: Fruit head containing bright red seeds.

Magnolia x *soulangiana*
Saucer magnolia

Of horticultural origin.

Habit A large deciduous shrub or small low-branched tree; to 15 feet tall.

Inflorescence Terminal, solitary; flowers large, upright, bell-shaped, 5–10 inches across, usually with 9 whitish petals with a pinkish tinge on the outside, flowering before or with leaf emergence. Blooms December to February.

Fruit A cone-like head of follicles, infrequently set.

Twigs Brown, glabrous, with gray lenticels and prominent stipule scars, fragrant when crushed; terminal flower buds silky pubescent, $1/2$–$3/4$ inch long; lateral foliar buds with few hairs, smaller than terminals.

Bark Smooth, gray, attractive to sapsuckers.

Leaves Alternate, simple; obovate, apex narrow and short-pointed, 3–6 x $1/2$–4 inches; dark green above, pubescent below.

Notes This hybrid was derived from the intentional cross of *M. denudata* and *M. liliifera* and was first described in 1826. It is the most widely planted of the magnolias. The species name *soulangiana* honors Etienne Soulange-Bodin (1774–1846), French horticulturist who created this hybrid.

Locations Alice Keck Park Memorial Gardens near the Santa Barbara Street side. A shrubby version at the Santa Barbara Natural History Museum at the parking lot exit.

Top: Magnolia *x* soulangiana *in full flower before the leaves emerge.*
Middle: Showy pinkish-white flowers.
Bottom: Light green ovate leaves and fuzzy flower bud.

Michelia

Michelia is a genus of 30 species from China and southern Asia to Malaysia and Japan. The genus is named for Pietro Antonia Mecheli (1670–1737), a Florentine botanist who is noted for his original work on ferns, mosses, and especially fungi.

Michelia doltsopa
Chinese magnolia, sweet michelia

Found in broadleaf forests of the Himalayas at elevations from 5,000 to 8,000 feet, extending from Nepal to Myanmar (Burma).

Habit An evergreen shrub or tree; to 30 feet tall.

Inflorescence Terminal, on short densely rusty or gray haired shoots; flowers solitary, 3–4 inches across, pleasantly fragrant, composed of 12–16 pale creamy tepals with purple margins and numerous stamens ($1/3$–$2/3$ inch long) surrounding a short pistil-bearing stalk. Blooms in January.

Fruit A cone-like head of follicles, $3/4$–1 inch long; seeds $1/3$–$1/2$ inch long, bright red.

Twigs Thin, rusty hairy, becoming glabrous; buds rusty hairy.

Bark Smoothish, tannish-gray.

Leaves Alternate, simple; elliptic to oblong with a somewhat elongate apex, 4–7 x $1 1/2$–$3 1/4$ inches; thin, papery to somewhat leathery, dark green above, paler and somewhat glaucous below, margins entire and rusty hairy, midrib and petiole rusty hairy.

Notes The species name *doltsopa* is the Tibetan name for the species.

Locations Two trees at Westmont College near the Administration Building. Another at the University of California, Santa Barbara on the north side of Noble Hall. Two shrubby individuals at Alice Keck Park Memorial Gardens are the closely related *Michelia figo,* distinguished by the lack of a petiole.

Top: Elliptic leaves of **Michelia doltsopa** *with dark green upper surface and pale lower surface; flower buds with rusty scales.*
Bottom: Showy white flower with 12 to 16 tepals and yellow stamens.

Malvaceae

The Mallow Family includes about 110 genera and 1,800 species, most of which occur in the Western Hemisphere. The family also occurs in Africa, Europe, Asia, Australia, and Oceania. The family is of greatest import for cotton (*Gossypium*), four species of which have been domesticated since before recorded history.

Hibiscus

Hibiscus is a genus of about 300 species from warm temperate and tropical regions of the world. The name is the Greek name for mallow.

Hibiscus elatus
Blue mahoe, mountain mahoe, Cuban bast

Native to Cuba and Jamaica, and now escaped in Puerto Rico.

Habit An evergreen tree with a narrow crown; to 30 feet tall.

Inflorescence Axillary, in clusters of 1 to 3; flowers 3½–4½ inches long, with a nine-lobed involucral bract surrounding the 5 sepals; petals 5, trumpet-shaped, yellow with an orange-red base, fading to deep crimson; the numerous stamens fused around the pistil. Flowers in October.

Fruit A hairy capsule, 1–1½ inches long, brownish-yellow, opening into 5 spreading valves.

Twigs Dull gray, lenticellate, fully encircled by stipule scars.

Bark Smooth, dark gray, becoming broken by longitudinal fissures.

Leaves Alternate, simple; almost round with an elongate apex and heart-shaped base, to 8 x 6 inches, margins slightly round toothed, especially near the apex, with several palmate veins emerging from the base, dark shiny green above, becoming purplish with age; petiole 2–3 inches long, red.

Notes The fibrous bark of this species has been used for making ropes and hats. The species name *elatus* means tall.

Locations A tree at Franceschi Park adjacent to Mission Ridge Road. A sprout in lower Orpet Park east of the center steps.

Top: **Hibiscus elatus** *showing orange-red flower with fused stamens and dark shiny leaf with several palmate veins.*
Bottom: Stout twigs and woody fruit splitting along five valves.

Hibiscus rosa-sinensis
Chinese hibiscus

Unknown in the wild, possibly an ancient hybrid originating in China.

Habit An evergreen shrub or small tree with a dense crown; to 10–20 feet tall.

Inflorescence Axillary, solitary; flowers 4–6 inches across, the five petals broadly outspread, and stamens fused into a strongly exserted column, color highly variable. Flowers August to November.

Fruit A hairy capsule, 1–1 1/2 inches long, brownish-yellow, opening into 5 spreading valves.

Twigs Gray-brown, becoming tan.

Bark Smoothish, with many warty lenticels, light gray-brown.

Leaves Alternate, simple; ovate to elliptic, 2 1/4–4 inches long, margins coarsely toothed towards the apex, base entire, blade thin, glossy green; petiole 3/4–1 2/3 inches.

Notes This species has found particular favor in the horticultural trade, with over 250 cultivars described. However, it is particularly attractive to white flies and their associated problems. The species name *rosa-sinensis* means Chinese rose.

Locations Street trees in the 100 block of South Salinas Street and the first block of East Figueroa Street.

Top: Showy flowers of Hibiscus rosa-sinensis *with fused stamens, five-parted stigmas, and deep pink base of petals.*
Bottom: Thin glossy leaves and flower buds.

Lagunaria

Lagunaria includes only a single species. It has previously been included in the Bombacaceae, which is closely related to the Malvaceae where it is currently placed. It is named for Andrea Laguna (1494–1560), a Spanish botanist.

Lagunaria patersonii
Primrose tree, pyramid tree, Norfolk Island hibiscus, cow-itch tree

Native to Norfolk Island and Lord Howe Island, Australia. Also naturalized in Queensland.

Habit A slender evergreen tree; to 80 feet tall.

Inflorescence Axillary, solitary; flowers showy, 1 1/4–2 1/2 inches across, the 5 petals recurved exposing an exserted style with numerous stamens clustered around it, pale to bright pink with a lighter center; peduncle stout scaly, 1/3–1/2 inch long. Flowers July to August.

Fruit A five-parted capsule, 1 1/2–2 x 1 inches, with a persistent five-lobed calyx; dehiscing to expose papery partitions and dark seeds embedded among sharp, pale tan hairs.

Twigs Pale green becoming gray-brown, covered with whitish scales, with a roughened appearance from raised leaf scars.

Bark Dark gray, rough.

Leaves Alternate, simple; ovate to lanceolate with a blunt apex and rounded base, 2–4 x 2/3–1 inches; margins entire; leathery, dark green above, paler and densely scaly beneath; midvein impressed from above; reticulation dense when backlit.

Notes *L. patersonii* is a very pleasant and showy street tree. However, as one of its common names implies, the sharp hairs inside the fruit can be extremely irritating. The flowers are reported to be extremely attractive to hummingbirds. The species name *patersonii* honors William Patterson (1755–1810), British naturalist who travelled and collected in India, South Africa, and Australia, and who served as Lieutenant Governor of New South Wales from 1800 to 1810.

Locations A large street tree on Santa Barbara Street adjacent to the County Administration Building parking lot. Another at Stow House and at the Sexton House on Hollister Avenue in Goleta. Others on Kimberly Avenue at the railroad depot and on Corona del Mar.

Top: Narrow crown of **Lagunaria patersonii**.
Middle: Flowers with pink petals and yellow stamens, flower buds, and dark green upper surface of leaves.
Bottom: Tan fruit opening along five valves and pale lower surface of leaves.

Robinsonella

Robinsonella is a genus of 14 species from Central America and is named in recognition of Benjamin L. Robinson, Asa Gray Professor of Systematic Botany at the Gray Herbarium (1899–1935).

Robinsonella cordata
Jornate

Found in southern Mexico and Guatemala in wooded or brushy ravines between elevations of 5,000 and 6,500 feet.

Habit A slender deciduous tree; to 40 feet tall.

Inflorescence Open, axillary clusters, flowers 3/4 inch long, purple, with tomentose sepals and stamens fused into a column about the pistil. Flowers May to June.

Fruit A capsule, with 12–13 sections, 2/3 inch long, densely hairy.

Twigs Thin, brittle, initially densely hairy.

Bark Thin, tight, gray, becoming light gray and corky.

Leaves Alternate, simple; ovate to cordate, 1 1/2–4 x 3/4–2 inches, with an elongate apex and 5–7 palmate veins from the base, densely hairy on both surfaces.

Notes The species name *cordata* means heart-shaped.

Locations A single tree in lower Orpet Park, below the lawn and west of the center steps.

Branch of Robinsonella cordata *showing dense purple flowers with fused yellow stamens and ovate leaves with palmate veins.*

Meliaceae

The Mahogany Family includes approximately 50 genera and 550 species found throughout the tropics. The bark of all members produces a spicy aroma when cut. The family is notable, of course, for the lovely cabinet wood, mahogany (*Swietenia mahogoni*). Long-exploited, this once abundant timber tree has been lost to commerce from over-cutting.

Cedrela

A genus of about eight species confined to tropical regions of the New World. Originally this genus included the Old World genus *Toona*. The name is in reference to the Latin *cedrus* (cedar) and reflects the appearance and fragrance of the wood

Cedrela fissilis
Brazilian cedarwood

Native to lowland forests (below 2,000 feet) of tropical America, from Costa Rica to northern Argentina.

Habit A deciduous tree with a straight cylindrical bole; to 50 feet tall.

Inflorescence Axillary or subterminal, a densely flowered panicle, to 10–20 inches long; flowers tubular although the 5 fleshy petals are free, 1/3–1/2 inch long, pale yellow-green; calyx and short pedicel pubescent. Flowers April to May.

Fruit A pendulous five-valved capsule with a woody central column, 2 1/2 inches long; valves woody, dark brown or brownish-black, surface roughened with paler raised lenticels.

Twigs Stout, green becoming gray-brown, lenticellate, with large heart-shaped leaf scars, each containing 5 obvious vascular bundle scars.

Bark Hard, gray to dark brown, strongly furrowed, with interlacing flat-topped ridges.

Leaves Alternate, pinnately compound without a terminal leaflet, 10–26 inches long; rachis densely hairy pubescent; leaflets opposite or subopposite, lanceolate to ovate-lanceolate, 3 1/2–6 x 1 1/4–2 inches, base asymmetrical, glossy dark green above, variably hairy beneath, margins entire.

Notes All parts of the tree smell of garlic when crushed, although the flowers are reported to have an agreeable fragrance. A related species, *C. odorata* (West Indian cedar), is widely used to manufacture cigar boxes. The species name *fissilis* means tending to split.

Locations Several street trees from the first block of West Gutierrez Street to the 100 block of East Gutierrez Street were planted in 1911 by Dr. A. B. Doremus as seedlings from a tree in Dr. Franceschi's nursery. A single tree in the 900 block of West Valerio Street.

Top: Cluster of small yellow-green flowers and pinnately compound leaves of Cedrela fissilis.
Middle: Woody dark brown fruit, opened to expose central column.
Bottom: Foliage with drooping leaflets.

Khaya

Kahya (African mahogany) is a genus of seven species from tropical Africa and Madagascar. It is closely related to and is used as a substitute for the highly prized mahogany of the Americas (Swietenia) which was drastically overexploited during the first half of the 20th century. *Khaya* is the native name for trees of this genus.

Khaya nyasica
Red mahogany

Native to the evergreen tropical forests of Mozambique, Malawi, and Zimbabwe.

Habit A potentially very large evergreen tree with a broad crown and a straight buttressed trunk; over 150 feet tall in its native habitat.

Inflorescence Dioecious; 8- to 12-inch panicles of small white flowers, appearing terminal; flowers to 4/5 inch across, in four and five parts, with a sweet scent. Flowers in July.

Fruit A spherical, woody capsule, 1 1/4–2 inches across, creamy brown, splitting into 4–5 valves; seeds winged.

Twigs Very stout, green turning light gray, with large triangular leaf scars.

Bark Gray to brown, smooth but flaking in silver-dollar-size scales on larger stems.

Leaves Alternate, pinnately compound, with 5–7 pairs of lateral leaflets and no terminal leaflet, to 20 inches long; leaflets, oblong-elliptic, to 6 1/2 x 2 3/4 inches, apex slightly elongate, dark glossy green above, paler beneath.

Notes The bark of this species is quite bitter, resembling quinine, and has been used by native peoples to relieve the symptoms of the common cold. While this is not the species most commonly used to substitute for the American mahogany, it is an extremely important timber tree in its region, and its grainy reddish wood produces fine finished furniture. The species name *nyasica* refers to the N'yasa, indigenous peoples who lived along the shores of Lake Malawi (L. Nyasa), Africa.

Locations Two trees in West Alameda Plaza. Three trees at Lotusland.

Top: Narrow open crown of **Khaya** *nyasica.*
Middle: Terminal panicles of small white flowers.
Bottom: Glossy compound leaves with drooping elliptic leaflets.

Melia

A recent revision of *Melia* simplified the original 15 species into three. They are all confined to the Old World tropics. The name is the Greek word for ash (melia) and refers to the similarity of the leaves to those of that genus.

Melia azedarach
Chinaberry tree, Persian lily, bead tree

Widely spread in Asia, from southern China to northeastern Australia.

Habit   A deciduous tree; to 45 feet tall.

Inflorescence   Loose axillary panicles, 4–8 inches long; flowers $3/4$ inch across, five-parted, the stamens fused into a dark maroon tube around the pistil, petals linear, lilac-colored. Flowers in April.

Fruit   A rounded drupe, $1/2$–$2/3$ inch across, light yellow; seed corrugated.

Twigs   Stout, shiny, greenish- to reddish-brown, with large leaf scars.

Bark   Light gray with underlying orange, composed of long narrow interlacing plates.

Leaves   Alternate, bipinnately compound with terminal leaflets, 10–30 inches long; leaflets ovate to elliptic with an elongate apex, $3/4$–2 x $2/3$–$3/4$ inches, margins with rounded serrations, light green, glabrous.

Notes   *M. azedarach* has been in cultivation on the Indian subcontinent and elsewhere in Asia for centuries. It has been used as a timber tree, a source of medicines, and an insecticide. Today it is widely used in reforestation efforts in China, India, and Central and South America. It has naturalized extensively in northwestern Africa and the Mediterranean where it is a cultivated ornamental, and has shown signs of naturalizing in drier areas of Southern California. It was introduced to North America in the 1600s, and its fruits were used as a source of alcohol during the Civil War. There is some suggestion that its original introduction into California came during the Mission Era and that the missionaries used its corrugated seeds to create rosaries. The species name *azedarach* is from Persian *azaddhirakt* (ash tree).

Top: Loose inflorescence of pale lilac flowers of Melia azedarach.
Bottom: Lacy bipinnately compound leaves and small round fruit containing corrugated seeds.

Locations   Young street trees in the 1300 block of Castillo Street. A large tree at the corner of Grand Avenue and Moreno Road. Another on Fernald Point Lane is visible from Highway 101. One more in the 700 block of West Carrillo Street.

Toona

Toona is a genus of only four to five species of tropical and subtropical regions of the Old World; however, its species are important timber producers and form large emergent trees in their native forests. This genus was formerly included with *Cedrela*. *Toon* is the Indian name for the tree.

Toona sinensis
Cedrela sinensis
Chinese mahogany

Native to forested mountains in south and east Asia (1,000 to 6,500 feet), from India and Nepal to Malaysia and Indonesia.

Habit A deciduous tree; to 100 feet tall in its native habitat.

Inflorescence Monoecious; a much-branched terminal panicle, to 3 feet long; flowers small, 1/6–1/4 inch long; calyx cup-shaped, margins ciliate; petals white or pink-tinged; carrying a strong smell of garlic and pepper. Not known to flower in Santa Barbara.

Fruit A capsule, 3/5–1 1/4 inches long; opening by 5 reddish to dark brown valves extending the full length to expose a central woody column to which the seeds are attached.

Twigs Stout, reddish turning greenish-brown; lenticellate, leaf scars large, heart-shaped, tan, with 5–6 vascular bundle scars.

Bark Gray to dark brown, strongly furrowed, with flat-topped ridges; inner bark pink to red, emitting a strong smell of garlic and pepper when cut.

Leaves Alternate, pinnately compound with a terminal leaflet and a red rachis, 12 to over 36 inches long; leaflets 8–20 pairs, narrowly lanceolate to linear-lanceolate, 4–9 x 1 1/4–2 1/4 inches; margins slightly serrate; initially pinkish-red turning bright green.

Notes The wood of *T. sinensis* is both strong and beautiful and has been used for functions as varied as bridge construction and cabinetry. The species also has many assorted uses in folk medicine. The species name *sinensis* means from China.

Locations Rare. A street tree in the 3700 block of Pescadero Drive. Several small trees in Alice Keck Park Memorial Gardens near the map.

Top: Pinkish-red young leaves and gray bark of *Toona sinensis*.
Bottom: Dark green pinnately compound mature foliage.

Menispermaceae

The Moonseed Family consists of approximately 70 genera and 500 species that are distributed throughout the humid tropics. Several members of the family contain curare-like alkaloids whose use for arrow and fish poisons was discovered independently in Africa, Asia, and the Americas. This family has contributed to many native medicines.

Cocculus

Cocculus is a genus of eight species from warm and tropical regions of the world, but absent in South America and Australia. The genus is named from the Greek word *kokkos* (berry), referring to its small fruit.

Cocculus laurifolius
Cocculus bariensis

Hindu laurel, cocculus, laurel-leaf cocculus, laurel-leaf snailseed

Found in open woodlands and disturbed areas of Southeast Asia, from Java to Nepal and extending into Japan.

Habit A spreading evergreen shrub or tree; to 25 feet tall.

Inflorescence Dioecious; axillary cymes, $1/2$–$1\,2/3$ inches long; flowers minute, yellowish. Blooms February to April.

Fruit A spherical drupe, $1/6$ inch across.

Twigs Stout, light green.

Bark Light gray, smooth but with small corky warts.

Leaves Alternate, simple; elliptic, 3–5 x $1\,1/4$–$2\,1/4$ inches; leathery, dark green, midvein yellow-green, with 2 strong yellow-green nerves extending parallel to the margin for $2/3$–$3/4$ length of leaf.

Notes Alkaloids extracted from the bark have been found to have similar effects to those of curare and are called cocculine or coclaurine. They can be highly poisonous and were used by indigenous peoples of the Malay Peninsula to poison their arrows and darts. The species name *laurifolius* means laurel-leaved.

Locations Small trees in Alice Keck Park Memorial Gardens near Garden Street. Shrubby individuals in upper Orpet Park near the bus stop and in Franceschi Park near Mission Ridge Road.

Elliptic leaves with three prominent veins from the base and axillary cymes of small yellowish flowers of Cocculus laurifolius.

Moraceae

The Mulberry Family includes 37 genera and over 1,000 species that occur primarily in the humid tropics, although some species do occur in warm temperate regions. Most members of the family have milky sap, some of which has been used to concoct arrow poisons. While most other arrow poisons (e.g. Menispermaceae) affect the central nervous system, the sap of a very few species of the Moraceae contains cardiac glycosides which induce cardiac arrest.

Ficus
Fig

Ficus is the largest genus of any represented in Santa Barbara. It includes over 750 species located throughout tropical and warm temperate regions of the world. The genus is well-known for its variability, horticultural uses, and rubber products. The flowers are considerably reduced and are carried inside a fleshy, hollow receptacle—the fig—that is often thought of as the fruit. In addition to containing male and female flowers, the fig has several unique features that attract ovipositing insects (especially wasps) which, in turn, contribute to pollination. The opening to the chamber at the apex of the fig is referred to as the ostiole, and the depression in which it sits is the umbilicus. *Ficus* is the Latin name for the edible fig (*F. carica*).

Ficus auriculata
Ficus roxburghii
Roxburgh fig

Native to the tropical forests of southern China.

Habit A short, spreading evergreen tree, or a shrub; to 20 feet tall.

Fruit Borne on unbranched spurs along the main branches; in bushy plants, they may occur in clusters at the base of the trunk, looking much like brown mushrooms in the soil around the base; large, to 2½ inches in diameter, over 2 inches long; neck prominent, thick, often ribbed; surface marked by somewhat elongated, conspicuous white or rusty spots; peduncles stout, 1 inch or more; prominently pubescent with silky white hairs; green at base, reddish-brown at the apex.

Twigs Hollow; initially green, becoming gray; with white, milky latex; leaf scars conspicuous; lenticels large, chocolate-colored; buds 1–1½ inches long, reddish.

Top: Dense, spreading crown of Ficus auriculata. *Middle: Dense figs growing directly on main branches. Bottom: Large heart-shaped leaves that are red when young.*

Bark Smooth, tannish-gray, often showing residual leaf and bud scars.

Leaves Alternate; ovate, to 16 x 13 inches; base heart-shaped, with sinus open or sometimes narrow; margins wavy to almost entire; hydathodes prominent and scattered between lateral veins; pubescent on the veins beneath; venation conspicuous, midrib flanked by 3 pairs of basal veins; petiole 3–12 inches; new growth copper red.

Notes The leaf surface may exhibit white chalky salts from evaporated water excreted at the hydathodes. The species name *auriculata* means ear-shaped.

Locations Trees in the 900 block of Anacapa Street, and the 1000 and 1100 blocks of State Street.

Ficus benghalensis
Banyan fig

Native to the tropical forests of India, Sri Lanka, and Pakistan.

Habit An evergreen tree capable of developing a massive crown supported by prop roots in the most mild climates; to 100 feet tall.

Fruit Axillary, sessile figs, 2/3 inch across, scarlet with indistinct white flecks and three conspicuous yellow bracts, umbilicus prominent with a depressed center.

Twigs Thick, gray pubescent; buds to 3/4–1 inch long, reddish-brown.

Bark Smooth, light gray.

Leaves Alternate, simple; ovate, 6–10 x 5–7 inches, apex rounded, blunt, venation prominent below, with 2–3 pairs of basal veins and 5–7 pairs of lateral veins, stiff, leathery, velvety-pubescent below, upper surface dull or glossy dark green; petiole to 3 inches long, pubescent.

Notes Because of its extensive canopy, the *Ficus benghalensis* has long held a place in the culture of India. Its common name is derived from the *banyans* (or *banians*), traders who offered their wares underneath its canopy, and it is considered to be sacred by both Hindus and Buddhists. Banyan trees can grow to immense size with canopies covering over ten acres being propped up by aerial roots that come into contact with the ground. Theophrastus wrote an account of one tree sheltering the army of Alexander the Great, and another was reported to have sheltered a city of 2,000 people. The tree is highly susceptible to frost and rarely achieves much size in Southern California. The species name *benghalensis* means from the region of Bengal in eastern India. In his original description Linnaeus misspelled the name, but the misspelling has been maintained.

Locations A single tree on the campus of the University of Califonia, Santa Barbara at the northwest corner of the Biological Sciences II building.

Top: Rounded crown with several stems of Ficus benghalensis.
Middle: Short bud and small scarlet figs.
Bottom: Heart-shaped leaves with prominent midveins, strong basal lateral veins, and shiny green upper surfaces.

Ficus benjamina
Weeping fig, Benjamin tree, Java fig, laurel, tropic laurel, weeping laurel, small-leaved rubber plant

Widely distributed in Southeast Asia from China to Australia and through the southwest Pacific Islands.

Habit An evergreen tree with ascending branches and a broadly spreading crown, providing considerable shade; to 25 feet tall.

Fruit Axillary, sessile, often in pairs; spherical or sometimes oblong, to 1/2 x 1/3 inch; with white flecks on a glabrous surface; initially green, becoming purplish-orange.

Twigs Slender, initially green, becoming grayish-brown, with prominent lenticels; terminal buds green, 1/2 inch, slender, sharp-pointed.

Bark Smooth, light gray, with horizontal white lenticels.

Leaves Alternate, simple; ovate-elliptical, to 4 x 1 1/2 inches; often with a somewhat bent or twisted elongate tip; glossy green; somewhat leathery.

Notes *F. benjamina* has many of the same characteristics as *F. microcarpa* var. *nitida*. However, it is readily distinguished by its twisted leaf apex and never reaches the full size of the latter. *F. benjamina* is probably most commonly seen as the potted fig grown in indoor settings and excels in that environment because of its ability to photosynthesize at low light levels. The species name *benjamina* is derived from the Sanskrit *banij,* meaning banyan.

Locations Several trees planted along Cabrillo Boulevard, just east of the Los Banos Pool. Others on Fig Avenue between Cota and Haley Streets and in the first block of West Islay. A nice park tree in Alice Keck Park Memorial Gardens adjacent to Santa Barbara Street.

Top: Dense crown and several stems of **Ficus benjamina.** *Bottom: Glossy ovate leaves with twisted elongate apex. Numerous small orangish figs are produced among the leaves.*

Ficus capensis
Cape fig

Native to Africa, from the Cape of Good Hope north and east to the Sudan.

Habit A small, repeatedly-branched evergreen tree; to 20 feet tall.

Fruit Borne in dense clusters on repeatedly-branched stalks emerging from older stems; spherical or pear-shaped, to 1 x 3/4 inch, with or without a short neck; surface green, densely hairy with many white flecks; peduncle 1/2 inch long, swollen towards the fruit.

Twigs Gray-brown and softly hairy when young; terminal buds 3/4 inch long, somewhat angular or flattened; brown and pubescent at the base.

Bark Smooth, light gray.

Leaves Alternate, simple; oval, to 9 x 5 inches; base rounded or somewhat heart-shaped; venation prominent, with 1–2 basal vein pairs and 4–5 lateral vein pairs; margins coarsely toothed; glabrous, sometimes sparsely pubescent on lower midrib; somewhat leathery, upper surface dotted with hydathodes; petioles to 4 inches.

Notes *F. capensis* is a major source of food for chimpanzees in central Africa. The species name *capensis* means from the Cape of Good Hope, South Africa.

Locations A good-sized tree in Franceschi Park between the entry road and the nursery. A small tree just below the center steps of Lower Orpet Park.

Top: Broadly ovate leaves of Ficus capensis.
Bottom: Fig clusters borne along older stems.

Ficus carica
Common fig

Naturally distributed from Turkey to Afghanistan.

Habit A deciduous spreading shrub or small tree, often with multiple stems; to 10–30 feet tall.

Fruit Axillary, sessile, often in pairs; oblong to elliptical, to 2 x 1 1/4 inches; with white flecks on a glabrous surface; initially green, becoming dark purplish to black.

Twigs Thick, to 1/2 inch across, reddish-brown, lenticels common, apical bud stipules to 1/2 inch long.

Bark Smooth, light gray.

Leaves Alternate, simple, palmately lobed with 3–5 lobes, to 9 x 7 inches; base rounded or heart-shaped; green with fine, soft pubescence (denser on the underside); margins wavy, almost toothed; 3–5 prominent palmate veins emerging from the base; petiole short and thick, to 2 inches long.

Notes The edible fig was first introduced into California by the Spanish missionaries in 1769. Today, California is third in the world in fig production, behind Turkey and Greece. However, this has not come without a cost. The species has been listed as an Exotic Invasive Plant of Greatest Ecological Concern by the California Exotic Pest Plant Council. It is highly invasive in the Central Valley and on the Channel Islands. Two additional figs, *F. palmata* and *F. pseudo-carica,* are very closely related to *F. carica,* and it is believed that they may all be part of a complex within a single species. Superficial differences suggest that the former two may be distinguished by velvety pubescent twigs and figs that are edible, but very seedy and acidic. The species name *carica* means a kind of dried fig. It is also a reference to Caria, a district of Asia Minor where figs were commonly found.

Locations Common in yards about town. One tree in Alice Keck Park Memorial Gardens. A large bushy individual on Tallant Road at Mission Creek. Another in the inner courtyard of El Paseo.

Ficus carica *with deeply palmately lobed leaves showing strong venation and soft pubescence on lower surfaces. Figs are produced among the leaves on young twigs.*

Ficus gnaphalocarpa
Quicuio, sandpaper fig

Native in central and southwestern Africa from Ethiopia and the Sudan to Angola, Namibia, and the Cape Verde Islands.

Habit An evergreen tree with a narrow crown; to 45 feet tall.

Fruit Axillary; commonly solitary or in small clusters; spherical, with short neck, to 1 inch in diameter; light green to purplish with dense white hairs; bracts variable, on apex of peduncle or on body of fig; umbilicus prominent, star-shaped.

Twigs Green with mostly persistent silky white pubescence; terminal buds 1/2 inch long, stout, light green, densely pubescent; stipules lanceolate, with silky hairs at base and along midvein, persistent for several nodes.

Bark Distinctive, gray-green, smooth with scattered gray scales, light tan then light green where the scales have fallen.

Leaves Alternate, simple; ovate to almost circular, to 6 x 4 inches, with a broadly rounded apex and heart-shaped base; margins coarsely toothed to entire; venation prominent (especially below), with 3–4 basal pairs and 5 lateral pairs, veins with prominent white hairs; leathery and rough to the touch, tending to curl upwards; petioles stout, to 1 1/2 inches long, with silky white hairs.

Notes The species name *gnaphalocarpa* means wooly fruit.

Locations A single tree in Franceschi Park, below the entry drive.

Top: Glossy ovate and curled leaves of Ficus gnaphalocarpa.
Bottom: Round figs with dense pubescence and short terminal bud.

Ficus macrophylla
Moreton Bay fig, Australian banyan

Found in coastal or mountain rain forests of eastern Queensland and New South Wales, Australia.

Habit A large evergreen tree of immense girth and broad spreading crown; to 60 feet tall.

Fruit Axillary; commonly in pairs; oval, 1/2–3/4 inch in diameter, somewhat greater in length; greenish or purple-tinted surface with large, yellowish-green flecks; umbilicus narrow, slightly protruding.

Twigs Stout, new growth green or rusty hairy, becoming green and glabrous, older twigs gray; terminal buds 1 1/2–3 inches long, green or slightly rusty, hairy; 2 stipules to 6 x 3/4 inches, rusty pubescent outside.

Bark Light or dark gray; rough, as though blistered on older stems, lenticellate on young stems.

Leaves Alternate, simple; oblong-ovate, to 4–9 x 3–5 inches; margins entire; extremely leathery; 1–2 basal pairs and 16–20 lateral pairs of veins; dark green above, light green below on younger trees, darker with rusty scales on older trees; midrib very light green, almost white above; petioles stout, 4–6 inches long, light green, slightly flattened above.

Notes Leaves and fruit have been used by Australian ranchers as a supplemental food source for livestock. A subspecies without a central stem, *F. macrophylla* subsp. *columnaris,* has been described from Lord Howe Island. Because of its tendency for surface rooting, the species has been considered less desirable. However, when given sufficient growing room, it can be a magnificent tree, as illustrated by the specimen planted in 1877 by nine-year-old Adeline Crabb at Chapala and Montecito Streets, just west of the railroad station. Long famous as a landmark for the Santa Barbara harbor for seamen, the tree is known today as possibly the largest in California. In its native environment, individuals of this subspecies have been described as covering three to five acres! The species name *macrophylla* means large-leaved.

Locations Trees in East and West Alameda Plaza, and intermixed with *F. rubiginosa* in Plaza del Mar.

Top: Broadly spreading crown of Ficus macrophylla *with enlarged root crown.*
Bottom: Dense foliage with dark green upper surface and gray lower surface that becomes rusty.

Ficus microcarpa var. *nitida*
Laurel fig, Indian laurel

Native from Pakistan and India to southern China.

Habit A large evergreen tree with a distinctive high, repeatedly-branched, rounded crown; to 60 feet tall.

Fruit Axillary, single or paired; spherical, to 1/3 inch in diameter; green, turning light brown, glabrous, with scattered white flecks; umbilicus triangular, brown.

Twigs Terminal bud 1/2 inch long, glabrous, green to light or purplish-brown.

Bark Smooth, light gray throughout.

Leaves Alternate, simple; elliptical, with a wedge-shaped base and a slightly acuminate apex, to 3 x 1 1/2 inches; margins entire, yellowish; leathery, glabrous, deep green, glossy above; petiole 1/3 inch long, slightly channeled above, yellowish.

Notes The age of individuals cannot be determined from annual rings, as the species is prone to develop false rings. A stump in Oaxaca, Mexico with 1,000 rings came from a street tree that was determined to have been planted 80 years earlier. The species name *microcarpa* means small fruit.

Locations Street trees in the first to 800 blocks of Milpas Street, the first block of West Carrillo Street to the 100 block of East Carrillo Street, and the first blocks of West Canon Perdido Street and upper State Street from MacKenzie Park to Ontare Road.

Top: Rounded crown and repeated branching of Ficus microcarpa *var.* nitida.
Bottom: Glossy dark green leaves with slightly elongate apex and small figs, often in pairs.

Ficus mysorensis
Mysore fig

Native from southern India and Sri Lanka (Ceylon) to the base of the Himalayas.

Habit   An evergreen tree; to 40 feet tall.

Fruit   Axillary; commonly in pairs; sessile; oval, without a neck, to 1 2/3 x 1 inches; orange-yellow to scarlet or purplish-black, with conspicuous, raised, whitish or reddish flecks; basal bracts 3, prominent; umbilicus darker orange than the body.

Twigs   Stout, 1/3 inch thick; greenish-brown turning gray; corky lenticels prominent on new growth; terminal buds tapering to an acute apex, to 1 1/4 inches long; densely silky pubescent to puberulent.

Bark   Light gray, roughened by whitish horizontal lenticels.

Leaves   Alternate, simple; oval or broadly elliptical, to 12 x 6 inches; apex tapering to a long (1/2 inch) tip; base rounded to slightly heart-shaped; margins entire; venation prominent as narrow white lines above and raised veins below, with 3–4 basal pairs of veins and 12–14 lateral pairs; leathery; young leaves slightly hairy, especially below; older leaves generally glabrous and glossy; petioles 2 inches long, dull or yellowish-green, pubescent, slightly flattened or channeled above.

Notes   This species includes two varieties, both of which exist in Santa Barbara. *F. mysorensis* var. *pubescens* is shorter, and has smaller leaves with fewer lateral veins and very dense, rusty-brown tomentum, especially on younger parts, than *F. mysorensis* var. *subrepanda*. The species name *mysorensis* refers to the city of Mysore, southern India.

Locations   Two trees in Orpet Park. *F. mysorensis* var. *pubescens* is in lower Orpet Park east of the center steps, and *F. mysorensis* var. *subrepanda* is in upper Orpet Park west of the center steps.

Glossy light green leaves of Ficus mysorensis *var.* subrepanda *and figs that mature orangish-red.*

Ficus rubiginosa
Rusty-leaf fig, Port Jackson fig

Found in a wide range of ecological conditions in eastern Queensland and New South Wales, Australia.

Habit An evergreen tree with a dense, spreading crown; to 50 feet.

Fruit Profuse, axillary, in pairs; spherical to slightly oblong, to $1/2$ inch in diameter; green or rusty to yellowish, rusty pubescent to almost smooth, with prominent greenish or white flecks; bracts 3, deciduous early; umbilicus small; peduncles to $1/3$ inch long, stout, angled, pubescent.

Twigs Scaly pubescent with short internodes, often angular or somewhat flattened; terminal buds 1–2 inches long, densely rusty pubescent.

Bark Dark gray, smooth, but with slight vertical furrows.

Leaves Alternate, simple; oval, to $6 3/4 \times 2 1/2$ inches, apex blunt, base rounded; margins entire; leathery, smooth; venation indistinct in some leaves, prominent in others, 1–2 basal pairs, 10–13 lateral pairs; petiole to $1 1/2$ inches, slightly flattened above, rusty pubescent.

Notes Three varieties occur in Santa Barbara. *Ficus rubiginosa* var. *rubiginosa* has a dense crown of branches with pubescence on the twigs and easily-rubbed-off, but prominent, rusty scales on the lower surfaces of leaves. *F. rubiginosa* var. *pubescens* is conspicuously pubescent on the twigs and leaves, with a very purplish hue when immature. A horticultural variety, *F. rubiginosa* 'Australis,' has slightly smaller leaves and lacks the rusty pubescence of the other two forms. These trees have been marketed at times as *F. microphylla*. The species name *rubiginosa* means rusty.

Locations Scattered about town. Trees in East and West Alameda Plaza, and Orpet Park. Others intermixed with *F. macrophylla* in Plaza del Mar.

Dense, dark green foliage of Ficus rubiginosa *with pale yellow-green petioles and venation. Profuse yellow figs crowd the ends of the branches.*

Ficus rumphii
Rumphius fig

Native to Southeast Asia, from northern and central India to Java and Timor, Indonesia.

Habit   An evergreen or briefly deciduous tree with a thin crown; to 50 feet tall.

Fruit   Axillary; single or in pairs, sessile; spherical or obovate, somewhat asymmetrical, $2/3$ inch in diameter; green, becoming reddish-brown, glabrous, with distinct pale flecks; 3 tightly appressed triangular basal bracts, $1/4$ inch long.

Twigs   Green, glabrous when young, becoming gray with the epidermis breaking longitudinally, leaf scars large, with a distinct longitudinal keel in the middle; lenticels indistinct; terminal buds green, glabrous to 1 inch long ($2^{1}/2$ inches on young trees); stipules to 2 inches long, deciduous.

Bark   Smooth, light gray.

Leaves   Alternate, simple; triangular with an elongate tip, base sometimes extending along the petiole, to $4^{1}/2$ x 3 inches; pale green, glabrous, slightly leathery; margins entire, but undulating; venation thin but prominent, 1–3 pairs of basal veins, 5–7 laterals, lateral veins obviously looping together near the margin; petioles slender, $2/3$ length of leaf, slightly flattened or channeled above, yellowish-white.

Notes   The species name *rumphii* honors Georg Eberhard Rumphi (1628–1702), Dutch naturalist with Dutch West Indies Company and Dutch East Indies Company.

Locations   A single tree in Franceschi Park at the entry gate to the parking lot, planted in 1959.

Top: Glossy triangular leaves of Ficus rumphii. *Bottom: Long terminal bud and reddish-brown mature figs with dense pale flecks. Young figs can be seen in the axils of the leaves on current year's growth.*

Ficus thonningii
Ficus petersii
Common wild fig

Broadly spread throughout northern Africa, south to Angola.

Habit An evergreen tree with a broad crown; to 60 feet tall.

Fruit Axillary, single, in pairs or in dense clusters on twigs, sessile; almost spherical, to $1/3$ inch in diameter; reddish-yellow when mature, with obvious white flecks; ostiole small; basal bracts large and conspicuous.

Twigs Younger twigs light green, with elongated lenticels; older twigs grayish-brown, glabrous; terminal bud to $1 1/4$ inches long.

Bark Smooth, light gray with vertical striping; developing prominent aerial roots.

Leaves Alternate, simple; elliptic to obovate, to $6 1/2$ x $1 1/4$ inches, apex slightly elongate, base rounded, glossy, deep green above, lighter green below, midrib raised below, 1 pair of basal veins, 8–14 pairs of laterals; petiole 1 inch, flattened or channeled above.

Notes *F. thonningii* is one of the most common shade trees of West Africa and is planted commonly in towns and along roadways. It is also noted as an archtypical strangler fig in its native habitat. The species name *thonningii* honors Peter Thonning (1775–1848), Danish botanist, member of botanical expedition to Ghana (then Danish Guinea).

Locations Two trees are located in the northeast corner of lower Orpet Park.

Top: Prominent aerial roots of Ficus thonningii. *Bottom: Elliptic leaves with pale green lower surface and short petiole and small sessile figs.*

Ficus vogelii
Vogel's fig, West African rubber tree

Widely spread throughout northern and central Africa.

Habit An evergreen tree with ascending branches and foliage concentrated towards the ends of branches; to 25 feet tall.

Fruit Axillary, beginning several inches from the tips of twigs, sessile, densely clustered along twig, may occur on branches up to 3 inches in diameter; spherical to oblong, to $2/3$ inch in diameter; densely covered with minute hairs; yellow-orange with brown flecks; ostiole prominent.

Twigs Stout, $1/2$ inch across, warty from leaf and fig scars, light brownish-green; bud stout, short, $1/2$ inch long, light green.

Bark Light gray, smoothish, somewhat roughened by raised lenticels.

Leaves Alternate, simple; oval, to 10 x 5 inches, apex and base rounded; margins entire; venation prominent, with 1 basal pair and 4–6 lateral pairs; petioles stout, to 6 inches long, chocolate-brown changing to green at base of leaf.

Notes *Ficus vogelii* is frequently planted in Africa as a shade tree. It is also commonly used for fence posts, as it can be easily propagated by cuttings. The species name *vogelii* honors Theodor Vogel (1812–1841), a German botanist who died on an expedition to the Niger River.

Locations A tree located in lower Orpet Park above the lawn between the center and west steps. A second in upper Orpet Park below the lawn and west of the center steps.

Twigs of Ficus vogelii *showing large elliptic leaves with long petioles and prominent midveins. The figs are sessile on the twig.*

Ficus watkinsiana
Watkins fig

Endemic to the coastal region of southern Queensland and northern New South Wales, Australia.

Habit A large evergreen fig with multiple stems, a dense crown, and buttressing roots; to 150 feet tall.

Fruit Axillary, single or in pairs, on thick angled peduncles, 2/3 inches long; spherical or oblong, to 1 x 3/4 inch; ostiole obviously protruding; surface green or rusty, finely hairy and rough, spread with white dots; basal bracts early deciduous, leaving a prominent collar.

Twigs Light gray, with conspicuous lenticels; terminal buds slender, to 3 inches long, stipules deciduous, to 3 inches long.

Bark Smooth, light gray.

Leaves Alternate, large; elliptical, 6–12 x 3-4 inches, margins entire; leathery, glossy green, venation densely reticulate, pale, midrib frequently tinged pink or scarlet; 1–2 pairs of basal veins, 15–20 lateral pairs; petioles 2–5 inches, light green to tawny, becoming reddish-brown.

Notes In the wild, large hollow towers often develop from the aerial roots by which this fig "strangles" its host tree. After the support tree has decayed, these structures are often referred to as "Cathedral Trees." In Santa Barbara, this tree is similar in overall appearance to *F. macrophylla* and has been suggested as a possible shade tree. It is distinguished from *F. macrophylla* by the protruding ostiole and lack of rusty scales. The species name *watkinsiana* honors George Watkins (d. 1916), a botanical collector in Queensland.

Locations One tree in Franceschi Park, southeast of the picnic area. A sapling from this tree has been recently planted in Plaza del Mar near the corner of Cabrillo Boulevard and Castillo Street.

Top: Full crown and repeated branching of Ficus watkinsiana.
Bottom: Elliptic leaves and single or paired figs on stout peduncles.

Maclura

Maclura is a genus of 12 species found from Indo-Malaysia to Australia, Africa, and the Americas. The genus is named for American geologist William Maclure (1763–1840).

Maclura pomifera
Osage orange

Native to disturbed areas in northeastern Texas, southern Arkansas, and southern Oklahoma.

Habit A broad-crowned deciduous tree; to 40 feet tall.

Inflorescence Dioecious; axillary; female flowers in dense heads, inconspicuous, male flowers minute, in racemes or spikes. Blooms January to February.

Fruit A large round aggregate of drupes, resembling a grapefruit, 3–5 inches across, yellowish-green, with milky, bitter sap.

Twigs Round to three-sided, orange, frequently with short spur shoots from which several leaves emerge, with stout axillary spines, 1/2 inch long; sap milky.

Bark Brown or dark orange brown, becoming deeply furrowed with interlacing fibrous ridges.

Leaves Alternate, simple; ovate to oblong, apex elongate, 3–5 inches long, glossy green above, initially lightly hairy on both sides, margins entire, veins obvious below; petiole 2/3–3/4 inch long, hairy, with milky sap.

Notes Reputedly, *M. pomifera* provided the Ozarks their name. When French explorers first reached southeastern Arkansas and found native peoples building strong bows from the branches of this species, they named it *bois de arc,* which became bastardized to *beau d'arc* and ultimately became ozark. Although its original distribution was limited, today the species is broadly spread in disturbed places and fence rows throughout the eastern United States. The strong and decay-resistant wood has been used sporadically for fence posts. Reflecting its familial relation with mulberry *(Morus),* the leaves have been used as an alternative food for silk worms. The species name *pomifera* means apple-like.

Locations A male tree at Franceschi Park near Franceschi Road. A female on Riven Rock Road west of Parra Grande, and another on School House Road near Pimiento Lane.

Top: Flower heads and foliage on short spur shoots of Maclura pomifera.
Middle: Large grapefruit-like fruit with very textured surface.
Bottom: Thin ovate leaves with elongate apex.

Morus

Morus is a genus of about 12 species from warm and tropical regions of the world, with some species extending into cooler temperate zones. *Morus* is the Latin name for the mulberry tree.

Morus alba
White mulberry

Native to China, but spread throughout the world with the opening of trade routes to the Far East.

Habit A medium-sized deciduous tree with a dense rounded crown; to 40 feet tall.

Inflorescence Monoecious or dioecious; axillary; short yellowish-green spikes, 1 1/2–2 1/2 inches long, appearing with the leaves. Blooms in March.

Fruit Nearly spherical, an aggregate of drupes similar to a raspberry, 1/2–1 inch long; white, pink, or purple; very attractive to birds and very messy.

Twigs Tan to light gray, roughened by raised leaf scars; buds rounded, to 1/4 inch across, dark brown.

Bark Ash-orange to light brown on smaller stems and branches, becoming light gray-brown with orange-brown showing through.

Leaves Alternate, simple; ovate in broad outline, 2–7 inches long, deeply lobed or undivided; margins coarsely or finely toothed; apex blunt wedge-shaped or somewhat elongate; smooth and shiny dark green above, sometimes hairy on veins beneath; petiole 1/2–1 inch long, channeled above, exuding a white sap when cut.

Notes *M. alba* is the primary food plant for the silk worm. In the early 1600s, King James I set out to make England self-sufficient in the production of silk; however, the plan failed when the many acres planted to support the industry were mistakenly planted with *M. nigra,* some of which can still be found around Buckingham Palace today. The species name *alba* means white.

Locations Trees in Skofield Park near Group Area A, and in a parking lot on the south side of Arlington Avenue. Street trees on Cameta Way and Valdivia Drive.

Top: Clusters of male flower racemes and young leaves of Morus alba.
Bottom: Variably lobed leaves with toothed margins and elongate apex.

Myoporaceae

The Myoporum Family is a small grouping of three genera and about 120 species, all but one of which are found in the Eastern Hemisphere. The greatest diversity of the family is found in Australia and Oceania.

Myoporum

Myoporum is a genus of 28 species mostly from Australia but extending to New Zealand, eastern Asia, and Hawaii. The genus is named from a combination of the Greek words *myo* (to close) and *poros* (opening, pore), which refers to the translucent dots on the leaves that are filled (closed) with a clear liquid.

Myoporum laetum
Ngaio, myoporum

Found in coastal lowland forests throughout New Zealand, except the southern tip of South Island.

Habit A large evergreen shrub or tree with a distinctly rounded crown; to 30 feet tall.

Inflorescence Axillary clusters of 2–6 flowers; flowers bell-shaped, 1/2–3/4 inch across, white with numerous purple spots, 4 stamens and style slightly exserted; peduncles to 2/3 inch long. Blooms December to February.

Fruit Drupe, narrow-ovoid, 1/4–1/3 inch long, pale to dark reddish-purple, wrinkled.

Twigs Green turning tawny brown, roughened by raised leaf scars, frequently with blackened flowers from the previous year.

Bark Gray with orange-brown showing through the shallow-to-deep fissures.

Leaves Alternate, simple; lanceolate to oblong, 1 1/2–4 x 3/4–1 1/4 inches; bright green, somewhat fleshy; dotted with numerous oil glands; margins entire or finely toothed on apical half; midrib and glands translucent.

Notes *Ngaio* has a dense, durable wood that has been used in New Zealand for fence posts and cabinetry. The Maoris used the oil-laden leaves to produce an insecticide against mosquitos and sand fleas. Because of its aggressive growth, *M. laetum* has been listed as an Exotic Invasive Plant of Greatest Ecological Concern by the California Exotic Pest Plant Council. The fruit and leaves are toxic to livestock.

Top: Rounded crown and dark gray bark of **Myoporum laetum**.
Middle: Fleshy glossy green leaves and white flowers with purple spots.
Bottom: Purple fruit clustered along the twig.

One additional species of *Myoporum* occurs on the east side of Franceschi Park, *M. sandwicense* (bastard sandalwood), a highly variable species from Hawaii. The species name *laetum* either means pleasant, or honors Jan de Laet, Belgian patron of botany.

Locations Common as a shrub. Trees on Channel Drive. Others at the Bird Refuge and at the Cabrillo Ball Park.

Myricaceae

The Bayberry Family consists of three genera and about 50 species. Although a small family, it is found in temperate and subtropical regions throughout the world, except Australia and New Zealand. The family is best known for the thick, waxy coating of its fruit, which has been used extensively to make candles.

Myrica

Myrica is a genus of about 48 aromatic shrubs and trees found in all temperate and subtropical regions of the globe, except in the Mediterranean and Australia. The genus is named from the Greek *myrike* (tamarisk).

Myrica californica
Wax myrtle

Found in coastal areas at elevations less than 500 feet, from dunes and scrub to closed-cone pine and coast redwood forests, from the central California coast to Washington.

Habit An evergreen shrub or small tree; to 30 feet tall.

Inflorescence Monoecious; separate male and female catkin-like spikes, to 1/4 inch long, clustered in the leaf axils, individual flowers without a perianth. Flowers April to May.

Fruit A drupe, 1/4–1/3 inch across, covered with large dark resin globules and a white waxy bloom, few set per inflorescence.

Twigs Green becoming gray-brown, appearing roughened from old leaf scars, lightly pubescent.

Bark Dull gray, smooth with obvious lenticels on older branches and stem.

Leaves Alternate, simple; narrowly elliptic-lanceolate, 3–4 1/2 x 3/4–1 inches, glabrous, margins serrate towards the apex, glossy dark green with black glands below, frequently strongly scented when crushed.

Notes Wax myrtle is one of the few non-legume species which form a symbiotic relationship with nitrogen-fixing bacteria. It frequently occurs on poor soils. The species name *californica* means from California.

Locations Santa Barbara Botanic Garden in the Arroyo Section below the library.

Lanceolate leaves with serrate margins and young fruit held closely along the twig of Myrica californica.

Myrtaceae

The Myrtle Family is one of the largest of the world, and includes about 100 genera and 3,000 to 3,500 species. Its species are found in tropical and subtropical regions, primarily in the Southern Hemisphere. The wide diversity of the family contributes to its uses for timber, medicinals, spices, edible fruits, and, of course, ornamentals.

Acca
Feijoa

Acca is a resurrected name that has priority over the former *Feijoa*. The genus, which includes six species from South America, is closely allied with *Myrrhinium*. *Acca* is a Peruvian name.

Acca sellowiana
Feijoa sellowiana
Pineapple guava

Found in the grasslands and *Araucaria* forests of southeastern Brazil and Uruguay.

Habit An evergreen shrub or small tree; to 20 feet tall.

Inflorescence Axillary, single flowers on a densely wooly peduncle; flowers with 4 fleshy petals, white outside, purplish inside, round and 1/2 inch long, reflexing and curling at anthesis; stamens numerous, 1/2–1 inch long, dark red, anthers yellow, style long, pointed, deep red, exserted beyond the stamens. Flowers April to May.

Fruit An ovate berry, 1–3 inches long, yellow green, with numerous small seeds embedded in a fleshy mass; producing a spicy odor when mature.

Twigs Densely wooly, becoming glabrous in second year.

Bark Thin, flaky, brownish-gray with a cinnamon-red undertone.

Leaves Opposite, simple; obovate, 1–3 x 1/2–2 2/3 inches, leathery, densely white wooly beneath, shiny green above; petiole shallowly channeled, densely pubescent initially.

Notes The sweet red petals of *A. sellowiana* are attractive to birds, which contribute to pollination of the flowers. The species was first introduced to California by Dr. Franceschi, whose nursery in Santa Barbara made it available in

Top: Showy red flowers of Acca sellowiana *with long stamens and fleshy petals blooming among obovate leaves with glossy green upper surfaces.*
Bottom: Fleshy fruit and white wooly lower leaf surface.

1906. The species name *sellowiana* honors Friedrich Sellow (1789–1831), German botanist who collected extensively in Brazil and Uruguay.

Locations Frequently found in gardens about town. Two trees in the Lifescape Memorial Garden at Santa Barbara City College. Another in the 600 block of Garden Street. Shrubs in Franceschi Park east of the parking lot.

Acmena

Acmena is a genus of 15 species from Malaysia and eastern Australia. Acmena was one of the names of Venus.

Acmena smithii
Lillipilli, satinash

Found in wet forests of eastern Australia (Queensland, New South Wales, and Victoria); occurring in a variety of habitats from exposed maritime situations to montane rain forests.

Habit A compact evergreen tree, or a shrub in exposed conditions; to 20 feet tall.

Inflorescence A terminal multi-branched head of numerous flowers, sometimes in upper leaf axils; flowers white, small, less than 1/4 inch in diameter.

Fruit In dense clusters; round, somewhat flattened at the ends, with a distinct pit around the persistent style, 1/3–3/4 inch in diameter; white to purple.

Twigs Often four-angled, flattened at the nodes; orange turning gray, rough and fibrous.

Bark Somewhat nondescript; flaky, fibrous.

Leaves Opposite, simple; narrowly lanceolate to ovate, apex bristle-tipped, 1 1/3–6 1/2 x 1–2 1/2 inches; venation pinnate, 7–20 pairs of lateral veins, intramarginal vein somewhat distinct from the margin, margins rolled under; midrib narrowly grooved on the upper surface; oil dots conspicuous, usually numerous; thick leathery, dark shiny green.

Notes The species name *smithii* honors James Edward Smith (1759–1828), British botanist who published prolifically, purchased the Linnean herbarium in 1784, founded the Linnean Society and was its first president (1788–1828), and was knighted in 1814.

Locations Street trees in the 300 block of West Arellaga Street.

Acmena smithii *with glossy green leaves with elongate tips and pinkish fruit. Note the opposite placement of the twigs and leaves.*

Agonis

Agonis is a genus of 12 species, all endemic to Western Australia. The genus is named from the Greek *agon* (a gathering or assembly) and refers to the large number of seeds produced.

Agonis flexuosa
Willow myrtle, willow peppermint, Western Australian peppermint

Found on sandy soils in a variety of habitats ranging from forest to open scrub along the coast of extreme southwestern Western Australia.

Habit An evergreen tree with drooping branches; to 40 feet.

Inflorescence Axillary, globular, sessile heads of 12–14 flowers with short broad bracts, 1/2 inch across, seemingly forming a chain of beads along the twig; flowers white, containing 4–5 spoon-shaped petals. Flowers in March.

Fruit Small round sessile heads of fused fruits, 1/3–1/2 inch across; frequently persistent from previous years.

Twigs Distinctly zigzagged, pendulous, light tan becoming brownish-gray; sometimes with paper-like wings extending down from each leaf node.

Bark Rough, very fibrous, red-brown; fissured and flaky.

Leaves Alternate, simple; lanceolate to linear, narrowed at both ends, 2–6 x 1/4–3/4 inches; the intramarginal veins conspicuous with sometimes another vein 1/3 inch in from the margin, lateral veins pinnate and widely spaced; oil dots numerous and conspicuous; petioles very short.

Notes The species name *flexuosa* means bending.

Locations Park trees in East Alameda Plaza, Franceschi Park, the east end of Shoreline Park, and at Stow House near the caretaker's residence. Several street trees in poor condition in the 900 block of Salsipuedes Street. Another street tree in the 4800 block of Kodak Avenue.

Top: Soft, lacy rounded crown of Agonis flexuosa.
Middle: Sessile flower heads and pendulous leaves.
Bottom: Fruit heads and linear leaves.

Angophora

The seven species of this genus are endemic to eastern Australia. They are closely related to *Eucalyptus,* but the flowers have petals and no operculum and contain bristly glands interspersed with white hairs. *Angophora* is derived from the Greek words *aggeion* (a vessel) and *phoreo* (to carry) and refers to the shape of the fruit.

Angophora costata
Smooth-barked apple, red-barked apple tree, brown apple tree, red gum

Occurs in southeastern Queensland and coastal New South Wales, Australia.

Habit An evergreen tree with an open spreading crown; to 50 feet tall.

Inflorescence Conflorescence consisting of three-flowered umbels; petals creamy white, 1/8 inch long and wide; stamens creamy yellow, 1/4 inch long. Flowers June to July.

Fruit Bell-shaped to ovoid, 1/2 inch in all dimensions; with 5 main longitudinal ribs and 5 or more minor ones; 5 small teeth on the rim; valves 3–4, deeply inserted.

Twigs Initially reddish-yellow, becoming dull green, slightly ridged between the nodes.

Bark Deciduous throughout, leaving a mottled bright orange-brown and pink-brown slightly dimpled surface; becoming gray with age, frequently stained with kino exudates.

Leaves Opposite to subopposite, simple; lanceolate or narrowly oblong, 2 3/4–5 x 1/2–1 1/4 inches; bright green on both sides; midrib distinctly lighter than the leaf blade; submarginal vein distinct from the margin, reticulation dense, secondary veins closely parallel.

Notes The tree has little value as timber, but is considered to be of ornamental value in its native regions and is retained for that purpose. The single specimen in Santa Barbara has not been known to flower. The species name *costata* means ribbed.

Locations Lower Orpet Park, west of the center steps.

Top: Colorful exfoliating bark of **Angophora** *costata. Bottom: Lanceolate leaves and opposite placement on reddish twigs.*

Callistemon
Bottlebrush

Callistemon is a genus of about 30 species from Australia. Like *Melaleuca,* it has the characteristic of continuing twig growth beyond the inflorescence to produce new leaves; however, it differs in that its numerous stamens are free and not fused into bundles. The genus name is derived from the Greek words *kalli* (beautiful) and *stemon* (stamen) and refers to the beautiful flowers of this genus.

Callistemon citrinus
Red bottlebrush

Occurs in moist soils of southeastern Australia (New South Wales, Victoria, and South Australia).

Habit An erect evergreen shrub with a rounded crown, can be trained into a small tree; to 10–20 feet tall.

Inflorescence Dense cylindrical spikes 2–4 inches long; flowers consisting of 5 pubescent green sepals, 1/8 inch long, a cylindrical hypanthium only slightly hairy, and 3/4- to 1-inch-long crimson stamens and pistil. Flowers September to November.

Fruit Woody, cup-shaped, 1/4 inch across; 5 valves enclosed.

Twigs Tan, not turning fully gray until the fourth year.

Bark Gray, very fibrous, furrowed to expose light brown inner bark.

Leaves Alternate, simple; lanceolate with a sharp point, 1 1/4–4 x 1/6–3/4 inches; stiff and leathery, light green, densely dotted with oil glands; midrib prominent below.

Notes A smaller variety (*C. citrinus* 'Jeffersii'—dwarf bottlebrush) has purple to lavender flowers and can be found growing along the south side of the County Courthouse. The species name *citrinus* means relating to citrus.

Locations Increasingly common throughout town. Street trees on Foxen Drive and Island View Drive.

Top: Rounded dense crown and shreddy bark of Callistemon citrinus.
Bottom: "Bottlebrush" of showy flowers with crimson stamens and leathery lanceolate leaves with sharp apices.

Callistemon salignus
Willow bottlebrush, white bottlebrush

Usually found in moist soils of coast and tablelands of Queensland and New South Wales, Australia.

Habit A small evergreen tree with a narrow to broad crown; to 50 feet tall.

Inflorescence A dense spike, 2–5 inches long; flowers yellowish to greenish-white. Flowers April to May.

Fruit Woody, globose capsules, 1/8–1/4 inch across; remaining on the twigs for several years.

Twigs Thin, reddish, becoming grayish-brown.

Bark Paperbark, whitish to light gray, peeling to expose a pinkish-brown color on older stems, much like the paperbark of some melaleucas.

Leaves Alternate, simple; narrow-lanceolate, tapering at each end, 2 1/2–4 x 1/4–3/4 inches, with a prominent midrib; reddish when young, becoming dark green; with scattered oil glands; petiole short, flattened, and twisted.

Notes The species name *salignus* means resembling a willow.

Locations A single tree in Franceschi Park east of the cottage.

Top: Open crown and spreading branches of Callistemon salignus.
Middle left: Spike of yellowish-white flowers and lanceolate leaves.
Middle right: Sessile fruit on older twigs.
Bottom: Reddish young foliage on new twigs.

Callistemon viminalis
Weeping bottlebrush

Native to stream banks in coastal regions and tablelands of Queensland and northeastern New South Wales, Australia.

Habit A small narrow evergreen tree with a short slender twisted trunk in older stems and a dense rounded crown of drooping branches; to 40 feet tall.

Inflorescence Dense to open spikes, to 8 inches long; flowers consisting of 5 short green sepals, a densely pubescent cylindrical hypanthium, and numerous bright red stamens and pistil, 3/4–1 inch long. Flowers February to March.

Fruit Woody, cup-shaped capsules, 1/4 inch across; valves 3, enclosed.

Twigs Light brown, densely covered with silky hairs.

Bark Dark gray, furrowed and rough, appearing to twist around the larger stems.

Leaves Alternate, simple; densely clustered on new growth, most shed after first year; narrow-lanceolate, tapering at each end, 3/4–3 x 1/8–3/8 inches; midrib prominent, soft and lightly pubescent with reddish tips when young, becoming stiff and dark green with hardened tips; oil glands numerous and irregularly spaced, side by side, between the intramarginal vein and the margin; with a strong aroma when crushed.

Notes The species name *viminalis* means willowy.

Locations Street trees on Kentia Avenue, Eucalyptus Avenue, Portosuelo Avenue, Richland Drive, Broadmoor Plaza, and More Mesa Drive.

Top: Tall narrow crown and shreddy bark of **Callistemon viminalis.**
Bottom: Pendulous twigs, narrow-lanceolate leaves, "bottlebrush" flowers, and sessile fruit.

Corymbia
Eucalyptus
Bloodwoods

A recent analysis of the taxonomic relationships of species making up the genus *Eucalyptus* has designated a new genus, *Corymbia,* which is generally distinguished by the combination of compound inflorescences, generally urn-shaped fruit that are often large, and bark that peels in small patches and is generally smooth throughout. *Corymbia* contains 113 species, of which 33 are newly described. The genus name refers to the corymbose structure of the inflorescence in which the pedicels of the lower flowers are longer than those of the upper flowers, thereby lending a flat-topped appearance.

Corymbia calophylla
Eucalyptus calophylla
Marri

Marri occurs widely in the open forests on sandy soils around Perth in southwestern Western Australia.

Habit A tall evergreen tree to a large shrub (mallee) depending on soil conditions; to 50 feet tall.

Inflorescence Terminal, compound, usually seven-flowered; peduncles 1/2–1 3/4 inches, angled; buds pedicillate, pear-shaped to globose, about 1/2 inch long, without a scar; operculum hemispherical with a slight beak; flower clusters large, white to creamy white. Flowers March to June.

Fruit Woody, urn-shaped, 1–2 inches long, dull brown; rim thin, disc descending; valves 4, deeply enclosed, on 1/3- to 1-inch pedicels.

Twigs Angled, red.

Bark Rough, broken into checkered squares; gray-brown flaking to expose a tannish-orange underbark; not fissured into interwoven ridges.

Leaves Juvenile leaves alternate, petiolate, ovate, sometimes peltate, 3–5 x 1 1/2–2 1/2 inches, hairy; adult leaves alternate, petiolate, broad-lanceolate, 3 1/2–6 x 1–2 inches; leathery, pinnately veined, with dense reticulation; 1 minute oil gland in each areole; strongly discolorous, dark green above, midrib yellow-green; petiole flat, twisted, 1 inch long.

Notes *C. calophylla* is very similar to and easily confused with *C. ficifolia*. It is distinguished by its creamy white flower color, strongly urn-shaped fruit, the presence of an oil gland within each areole in the leaves, and the tessellated bark. *Marri* is used principally for wood chips and is an important contributor to honey production in Western Australia. The species name *calophylla* means with beautiful leaves.

Locations Trees in the 200 block of West Pedregosa Street, intermixed with *C. ficifolia*. A single tree at the corner of Modoc Road and Eucalyptus Street.

Top: Dense inflorescence with reddish pedicels of Corymbia calophylla.
Bottom: Large, woody urn-shaped fruit and dark green leathery leaves with whitish midrib.

Corymbia citriodora
Eucalyptus citriodora
Lemon-scented gum

Occurs in several disjunct populations in open forests of Queensland, Australia

Habit A tall, slender, open-crowned evergreen tree; to more than 100 feet tall.

Inflorescence Usually pendulous long terminal corymbs, the ultimate units three- to five-flowered; pedicel round; buds ovoid, 1/2 x 1/3 inch; operculum hemispherical with a slight beak, scar present; flowers white. Flowers December to March.

Fruit Ovoid or urn-shaped, 1/3–2/3 inch long, often warty; disc broad, descending; valves 3–4, inserted.

Twigs Thin, deep red, turning dull red then gray.

Bark Smooth throughout, with scattered dimples, deciduous annually; white powdery, creamy pink, with red or blue-gray mottles, frequently wrinkled at the points where compression wood is formed, such as branch insertions.

Leaves Juvenile leaves opposite for several pairs, petiolate, ovate to broadly lanceolate, 3–6 x 1 1/4–2 1/2 inches, sometimes rough and bristly from long oil glands; adult leaves lanceolate to narrowly lanceolate, 3–6 x 1/3–1 inches, sometimes strongly sickle-shaped; lateral veins just visible, intramarginal vein just distinct from the margin, with a smell of citrus when crushed; petiole flattened.

Notes The large tree on the east side of the 400 block of Santa Barbara Street is locally known as the "Fernald Eucalyptus." It was saved from destruction by Pearl Chase during the development of that block. The species name *citriodora* means lemon-scented.

Locations Common throughout town and on the campus of the University of California, Santa Barbara. Several trees planted in the Five Points shopping center on upper State Street and in other locations along upper State Street above Ontare Road. Others between the Public Library and the city parking lot on Anacapa Street.

Top: The Fernald Eucalyptus with the typically open, airy crown and long smooth branches of Corymbia citriodora.
Bottom left: Dense inflorescences and lanceolate leaves on thin pendulous twigs.
Bottom right: Small urn-shaped fruit.

Corymbia ficifolia
Eucalyptus ficifolia
Red-flowering gum

Endemic to a very restricted region of coastal southwestern Australia.

Habit A broad dense-crowned evergreen tree with pendulous twigs; to 40 feet tall.

Inflorescence Terminal, branched, seven-flowered, to 6 inches across; buds ovoid, 1/2 x 1/4 inch; without a scar, operculum conical, slightly beaked; flower clusters spectacular, bright red to pale pink or orange. Flowers in March.

Fruit Globose, large, 3/4–1 2/3 x 3/4–1 1/4 inches; woody rim thin, disc descending; valves 4 or 5, deeply enclosed; on a short pedicel.

Twigs Red to green; stout, with raised leaf scars, sometimes slightly ribbed.

Bark Rough, persistent, short-fibered, fissured into broad interwoven ridges, red-brown to black-brown or gray.

Leaves Juvenile leaves ovate to broad-lanceolate, to 5 x 2 1/2 inches; light green; adult leaves alternate, broad-lanceolate 2 1/2–5 1/2 x 3/4–2 1/2 inches; strongly discolorous, dull or slightly glossy, dark green above, pale green below; midrib obvious, yellow, sometimes reddish; densely pinnately veined, reticulation dense; petiole 3/4–1 inch long, reddish.

Notes *Corymbia ficifolia* is the only species of the genus that produces winged seeds. See notes for *C. calophylla*. The species name *ficifolia* means with leaves like a fig.

Locations Common throughout town. Trees at Alice Keck Park Memorial Gardens adjacent to Garden Street. Street trees in 100–400 blocks of West Haley Street, the 100–400 blocks of west Pedregosa Street, the 300–400 blocks of West Ortega Street and the 1200–1900 blocks of Chino Street.

Top: Dense crown of Corymbia ficifolia.
Bottom: Spectacular inflorescence, woody globose fruit, and leathery dark green leaves.

Corymbia maculata
Eucalyptus maculata
Spotted gum

Native to coastal ranges from southeastern Queensland to New South Wales and northeastern Victoria, Australia.

Habit A medium to tall, straight-stemmed evergreen tree; to 120 feet tall.

Inflorescence Mostly long terminal corymbs, the ultimate units three- or seven-flowered; buds ovoid, to 1/2 inch long, without a scar; hypanthium hemispherical; operculum usually beaked; flowers white to cream. Blooms December to March.

Fruit Barrel- to urn-shaped, 1/2 x 1/2 inch; woody; disc descending; valves 3 or 4, deeply enclosed.

Twigs Dull maroon, somewhat angled when young.

Bark Smooth throughout, flaking off in small patches; initially cream to pink-colored, weathering to pink-gray or blue-gray, becoming strongly mottled in appearance; often dimpled throughout.

Leaves Juvenile leaves petiolate, opposite for a few pairs then alternate, elliptical to ovate, to 9 x 4 inches, some with petiole attached to underside of leaf; adult leaves alternate, lanceolate to 7 x 1 inches, green and slightly glossy on both sides, lateral veins faint; petiole red, somewhat flattened.

Notes This species is very similar to *C. citriodora*, but is distinguished by its mottled and large-dimpled bark, larger and perhaps darker green leaves, angular (not flattened) petiole, and the lack of lemon-scented leaves. The species name *maculata* means spotted.

Locations Two very nice trees on the south side of the #8 green at the Santa Barbara Golf Club. Two trees on Carpinteria Avenue across from Carpinteria Middle School. Young trees in the 700 and 800 blocks of State Street. Four trees on the south side of Noble Hall on the University of California, Santa Barbara campus.

Top: Open crown and long clear trunks of Corymbia maculata.
Middle: Small flower bud clusters and lanceolate leaves on red petioles and twigs.
Bottom: Small urn-shaped fruit with enclosed valves.

Corymbia torelliana
Eucalyptus torelliana
Cadaga

Limited to a coastal distribution in northeastern Queensland, Australia.

Habit An evergreen tree, with a dense symmetrical crown; to 60 feet tall.

Inflorescence Terminal, three- or seven-flowered; peduncles 1/5–4/5 inch long, pedicels very short; buds oval, 1/3–1/2 inch long, flowers whitish. Flowers in August.

Fruit Round to urn-shaped, 1/3–2/5 inch long and wide, with a broad descending disc and 3 enclosed valves.

Twigs Yellow-green.

Bark Smooth and gray-green above; rough fibrous, gray or black on lower trunk.

Leaves Juvenile leaves alternate, broadly ovate, with the petiole attached near the center, discolorous, hairy; adult leaves alternate, lanceolate, 4–6 x 1/2–1 1/2 inches, discolorous, strongly pinnately veined, highly reticulate, intramarginal vein distinct, midrib yellow-green; petiole yellow-green, flattened and somewhat twisted, 1/5–4/5 inch long.

Notes The species name *torelliana* honors Italian Count Luigi Torelli of Italy (1810–1887), Minister of Agriculture, Industry and Commerce, author of *L'Eucalyptus e l'Agro Romano,* 1878.

Locations A young tree in East Alameda Plaza near the playground.

Top: Open crown and smooth trunk of a young Corymbia torelliana.
Bottom: Dense clusters of oval flower buds and curved lanceolate leaves.

Eucalyptus
Eucalyptus

Eucalyptus is a large and complex genus consisting of more than 600 species, several of which remain undescribed. Only a few species occur naturally outside of Australia and many are endemic to small regions of that continent. Several of the larger species (e.g. *E. globulus*) were originally introduced to California for timber purposes. Many others have been appreciated for their vivid flowers (e.g. *E. sideroxylon*) or unique mallee form. Several species have become invasive in California and are particularly difficult to eradicate once the lignotuber has fully formed (three to five years after germination). The great diversity of species in this genus stems in part from the variety of environments found throughout Australia. Yet, much of the diversity is found naturally in Western Australia where the landscape is reasonably uniform. It is believed that the widely changing climatic history of that region has driven the evolution of new species that are present in the flora today. The genus received its name from the Greek roots *eu* (meaning well) and *calyptos* (covered), referring to the woody operculum cap that covers the flower bud and protects the reproductive structures until it is shed immediately prior to anthesis.

Eucalyptus botryoides
Bangalay, Southern mahogany

Found on coastal sandy flats from southeastern Queensland to northeastern Victoria, Australia.

Habit An evergreen tree with an open crown, but casting a dark shade; to 60 to 100 feet tall.

Inflorescence Axillary, simple, seven- to eleven-flowered; peduncles flattened; buds with a very short pedicel if at all, subcylindrical to ovoid, 1/3 inch long; operculum usually conical; flowers white. Blooms June to August.

Fruit Barrel-shaped, 1/2 x 1/3 inch; rim thin; disc descending; valves usually 4, sometimes 3, inserted.

Twigs Wrinkled, orange.

Bark Persistent, fibrous or flaky-fibrous, rough-textured, thick, with vertical furrows, brown to gray-brown throughout the main stem and larger branches; smooth, brown or gray-white on smaller branches.

Top: Small white flower clusters and lanceolate leaves of Eucalyptus botryoides.
Bottom: Small buds, leaves with flattened petiole, and orange twigs.

Leaves Juvenile leaves on short petioles, opposite for 3–4 pairs, ovate, 6 x 3 1/2 inches, discolorous; adult leaves petiolate, alternate, broad-lanceolate and somewhat curved, to 6 x 1 1/2 inches, strongly discolorous, glossy dark green above, pale green below; pinnately veined, densely reticulate; petioles flattened, 3/4–1 1/4 inches long, orange.

Notes The species name *botryoides* means like a cluster of grapes.

Locations Two trees in East Alameda Plaza near Micheltorena Street.

Eucalyptus bridgesiana
Apple box, apple, apple gum

Apple box is native to the open woodland and forested tablelands immediately inland from the coastal zone of eastern New South Wales, Australia.

Habit A medium- to large-sized evergreen tree with upright branching and an open crown; to 70 feet tall.

Inflorescence Axillary, simple, mostly seven-flowered; peduncles slightly flattened, to $2/3$ inch long; buds on short pedicels, ovoid, $1/3$ x $1/6$ inch, scar of outer operculum present; operculum variable, conical, beaked or hemispherical with a small point; flowers white. Flowers in July.

Fruit On short pedicels, hemispherical, $1/4$ inch in diameter; rim thick; disc ascending; valves usually 3, exserted, triangle-shaped.

Twigs Thin, with decurrent ridges from the nodes; yellow-green.

Bark Rough and persistent on the smaller branches; fibrous, with interlacing ridges; gray or whitish where recently flaked off.

Leaves Juvenile leaves initially sessile and opposite, developing short petioles and becoming sub-opposite for several pairs, clasping the stem, ovate, to 4 x 3 inches, margins wavy, glaucous, tips of saplings pink; adult leaves petiolate, alternate, lanceolate, to 8 x 1 inches; slightly glossy, dark green on both sides, lateral veins distinct, moderately reticulate.

Notes *E. bridgesiana* is considered a useful shade tree and a good honey producer in its native lands. The species name *bridgesiana* honors Thomas Bridges (1807–1865), plant collector in South America and California.

Locations A single tree on the west side of Plaza del Mar.

Dense flower clusters and lanceolate leaves on dull red twigs and dense fruit clusters on older twigs of Eucalyptus bridgesiana.

Eucalyptus camaldulensis
Eucalyptus rostrata

River red gum, red gum, Murray red gum

E. camaldulensis occurs throughout Australia, except in Tasmania. It is the most widespread species of the genus.

Habit A medium-sized to tall evergreen tree, casting a deep shade; to 80 feet tall.

Inflorescence Axillary, simple, seven- to eleven-flowered; peduncles slender, strongly angled; buds globose, on a short pedicel, scar of outer operculum present; operculum strongly beaked; flowers white, 3/4 inch across. Flowers April to May.

Fruit On short pedicels, hemispherical, shorter than broad, rim thick, disc broad, ascending; valves usually 4, strongly exserted.

Twigs Deep red.

Bark Smooth, deciduous, leaving a mottled pattern of white, gray, yellow-green, gray-green, or pinkish red-brown; may accumulate near the base of the trunk.

Leaves Juvenile leaves petiolate, opposite for a few pairs then alternating, ovate to broad-lanceolate, to 10 x 3 inches, discolorous, blue-green above; adult leaves petiolate, alternate, lanceolate to narrow-lanceolate, 3–7 x 1/3–1 inches, dull or slightly glossy, green to blue-green on both sides; reticulation moderate, with numerous oil glands centered in the areoles; emitting a strong odor like Vick's VapoRub when crushed.

Top: Broad, open crown of Eucalyptus camaldulensis. *Bottom left: Strongly beaked flower buds, flower clusters, and blue-green foliage on red twigs. Bottom right: Hemispherical fruit.*

Notes This is a tree that follows river systems and extends to low hills along water courses. It is so broadly spread throughout Australia that it has become a symbol for the great inland regions of the continent and graces the country's $2 stamp. The wood is durable and has a variety of uses from structural components to veneer. The species is prized for "first grade" honey production. The sap of *E. camaldulensis* was frequently used by native peoples as a disinfectant for cuts and sores, and its roots were used as a source of water during extreme drought. Today, it is one of the most widely planted trees in the world and covers an estimated 1.1 million acres of plantation forests.

Most of California's specimens of *E. camaldulensis* have been seriously attacked by the redgum lerp psyllid, a natural pest from Australia that was first found in Los Angeles County in 1998. In the Santa Barbara area, the defoliating effects of this insect are apparent to even the casual observer. *E. camaldulensis* may itself have invasive properties, and it is ironic to consider that an invasive species is controlling population densities of another invasive species. Recent introductions of a parasitic wasp from Australia may be controlling the lerp, adding to the complexities of introduced species. The species name *camaldulensis* means from the garden of the Camalduli religious order near Naples, Italy; the species was first described from a specimen growing in this garden.

Locations Widely distributed throughout town. Trees in Franceschi Park, lower Orpet Park, Mount Calvary, and MacKenzie Park near Las Positas.

Eucalyptus cephalocarpa
Mealy stringybark, silver stringybark, long-leaved Argyle apple

Endemic to south-central Victoria, Australia.

Habit Small to medium-sized tree with a full crown; to 50 feet tall.

Inflorescence Axillary, simple, seven- to eleven-flowered; peduncles slightly angular, short, 1/3 inch long; buds sessile, diamond-shaped, 2/3 inch long, scar present; operculum conical, short; flowers white. Blooms July to August.

Fruit Sessile, obconical, 1/4 inch long; rim thick; disc ascending; valves 3–4, slightly exserted.

Twigs Thin, reddish-tan, turning reddish-gray.

Bark Rough, persistent to the smaller branches, thick, with longitudinal fissures, fibrous, gray or gray-brown.

Leaves Juvenile leaves sessile, bases clasping the stem, opposite for many pairs, orbicular to ovate then becoming broad-lanceolate, to 4 x 2 1/4 inches, gray-green to glaucous, slightly discolorous; adult leaves alternate, petiolate, lanceolate, to 8 x 1 inches, gray-green on both sides, moderately reticulate but veins faint, oil glands sparse; petiole 1/2–2/3 inch long.

Notes This species is closely related to *E. cinerea*. It is distinguished by its larger size, greener and longer leaves, longer petiole, and more numerous flower buds. The species name *cephalocarpa* means head-shaped fruit.

Locations A single tree in Franceschi Park below the drive to the house.

Top: Full crown of Eucalyptus cephalocarpa. *Bottom: Nearly sessile fruit clusters and lanceolate leaves on gray twigs.*

Eucalyptus cinerea
Argyle apple, mealy stringybark

Endemic to the southern tablelands near Canberra, New South Wales, Australia; also found in one small population in northeastern Victoria.

Habit A medium-sized evergreen tree with a dense crown; to 50 feet tall.

Inflorescence Axillary, simple, three-flowered; peduncles 1/3 inch; buds usually sessile, diamond-shaped, glaucous, 1/4 inch long, scar present, operculum conical; flowers white. Flowers April to May.

Fruit Sessile or with short pedicels, obconical, 1/3 inch long, rim thick; disc level or ascending, valves 3 to 5, slightly exserted.

Twigs Extremely glaucous, almost white.

Bark Rough, persistent to the larger branches, thick, fibrous, vertically furrowed, reddish-brown to dull gray-brown.

Leaves Juvenile leaves sessile, the bases clasping stem, opposite for many pairs, orbicular to heart-shaped, to 3 1/2 x 2 1/4 inches, slightly discolorous, glaucous; adult leaves petiolate, alternate, broad-lanceolate, to 4 1/2 x 1 inches, glaucous on both sides; moderately reticulate, venation faint, oil glands indistinct; petiole flattened, 1/8–3/16 inch long.

Notes The species name *cinerea* means ash-colored.

Locations Several trees at the southwest corner of Alston and Summit Roads. Street trees in the 3400 block of Richland Drive, at the corner of West Carrillo and San Pascual Streets, and at the corner of Foothill Road and Cieneguitas Road.

Top: Upright crown of Eucalyptus cinerea.
Bottom: Lanceolate leaves, ashy gray buds and twigs, and nearly sessile flowers.

Eucalyptus cladocalyx
Sugar gum

Although widely planted today in Australia and throughout the world for poles, posts, windbreaks, and shelter belts, this species is known naturally from only four disjunct populations in South Australia.

Habit   An evergreen tree, with an open rounded crown and ascending branches; to 80 feet tall.

Inflorescence   Axillary, unbranched, clustered on leafless twigs inside the crown, seven-flowered or more; buds cylindrical or urn-shaped, sometimes constricted about the middle, often ribbed, 1/3–1/2 inch long, scar present; operculum short, rounded; flowers creamy white. Flowers January to April.

Fruit   Fruit barrel or urn-shaped, ribbed, 1/3–2/3 inch long; rim thin; disc descending, valves 3 or 4, deeply inserted, light tan, on short pedicel.

Twigs   Slender, red.

Bark   Shedding in large flakes throughout to produce a smooth surface, mottled in yellow to orange, gray and blue-gray surfaces, frequently with isolated long vertical cracks.

Leaves   Juvenile leaves petiolate, opposite for a few pairs, then alternating, orbicular, discolorous, dark green above; adult leaves petiolate, alternating, lanceolate, 4–6 x 2/3–1 inches, glossy dark-green above; lateral veins clearly visible; intramarginal vein within 1/8 inch of the margin; reticulation dense, oil glands small, obscure; petiole flattened or four-sided.

Notes   The red twigs and the dull foliage reflect a burnished bronze light from the crown in the late afternoon. The species name *cladocalyx* means flowering twigs.

Locations   One exceptionally nice tree in Mission Park north of the rose garden; others planted along Highway 101 between Patterson Avenue and Las Positas Road; several intermixed in the 1200 block of Coast Village Road, and a wonderful promenade of trees borders Park Lane in Montecito.

Top: Flower clusters and dark green leaves with red petioles of Eucalyptus cladocalyx.
Middle: Distinctive orange-mottled bark.
Bottom: Urn-shaped fruit on short, stout pedicels and pendulous foliage.
(See page ii photo of a specimen tree of E. cladocalyx *in Mission Park.)*

Eucalyptus cornuta
Yate

Occurring in a limited region of coastal southwestern Western Australia, south and east of Perth.

Habit A tall evergreen tree; to 75–100 feet tall.

Inflorescence Axillary, unbranched, more than seven-flowered, usually eleven- to fifteen-flowered; buds sessile or on short pedicels, elongate, 1–1 2/3 inches, mostly from horn-shaped operculum, scar present; flowers yellow. Flowers in July.

Fruit Sessile, cup or bell-shaped, 1/2–3/4 inch long; disc broad, fused to the 3 exserted needle-like valves, which are joined at the center.

Twigs Dull red, with glandular pith.

Bark Persistent on trunk and lower branches, rough, hard, with deep vertical furrows and interlacing ridges, dark gray or black; on upper branches smooth, gray or gray-brown.

Leaves Juvenile leaves petiolate, alternating, round, 2 inches in diameter; light green, thin; adult leaves petiolate, alternating, elliptical, 2 1/3–5 1/2 x 1/2–1 1/2 inches; glossy dark green to gray-green on both sides; intramarginal vein distinct from margin, reticulation dense; oil glands sparse, at the intersections of veinlets.

Notes The wood of yate is among the hardest and strongest in the world. The species name *cornuta* means horned.

Locations Trees in Plaza del Mar and Pershing Park.

Top: Large- and medium-sized trees of Eucalyptus cornuta.
Middle: Bright yellow flower.
Bottom: Dark green leaves and fruit with three fused needle-like valves.

Eucalyptus cosmophylla
Cup gum

Endemic to a small location in southeastern South Australia.

Habit A small evergreen tree; to 30 feet tall.

Inflorescence Axillary, unbranched, three-flowered; peduncles thick, angled to flattened; buds sessile, ovoid, 1/3–1 inch long; scar present; operculum conical to hemispherical; flowers white. Flowers in January.

Fruit Sessile, cup-shaped to cylindrical, 1/3–2/3 x 1/2–3/4 inch, sometimes slightly ribbed; rim thick; disc broad, descending; valves 4 or 5, inserted.

Twigs Yellow green, becoming reddish, roughened from gummy secretions.

Bark Smooth, deciduous, mottled, bluish to blue-gray; partially shed bark may accumulate at the base of the trunk.

Leaves Juvenile petiolate, opposite then alternate; ovate to orbicular, to 2 x 1 1/2 inches; slightly discolorous, gray-green; adult leaves petiolate, alternate; lanceolate to broad-lanceolate, 3–7 x 1/2–1 1/2 inches; light green to gray-green on both sides; lateral veins faint, intramarginal vein conspicuous, numerous oil glands as islands and at the intersections of veins; petiole thick, flattened, channeled.

Notes The species name *cosmophylla* means beautiful leaves.

Locations A single tree in Franceschi Park below the public entrance road.

Top: Flowers with pinkish ovoid buds and blue-green lanceolate leaves of Eucalyptus cosmophylla. *Bottom: Nearly sessile fruit with broad rims and descending discs.*

Eucalyptus crebra
Eucalyptus racemosa

Narrow-leaved ironbark, ironbark, narrow-leaved red ironbark

A tree of open woodlands on plains and low plateaus of southeastern Queensland and northeastern New South Wales, Australia.

Habit A medium-sized evergreen tree; to 80 feet tall.

Inflorescence Terminal, compound, seven- to eleven-flowered; peduncles slender, 1/2 inch; buds barrel- or diamond-shaped, 1/3 inch long, scar present; operculum conical to hemispherical; flowers white. Flowers June to August.

Fruit Hemispherical or ovoid, 1/4 inch long; disc narrow, level or descending; valves 3 or 4, level or included.

Twigs Thin, red.

Bark Ironbark-type, persistent throughout, deeply furrowed, dark gray, tannish on smaller branches.

Leaves Juvenile leaves petiolate, opposite initially, linear to narrow-lanceolate, to 5 x 3/4 inches, green or gray-green, paler beneath; adult leaves petiolate, alternate, narrow-lanceolate to lanceolate, to 6 x 3/4 inches, dull green to gray-green on both sides, reticulation dense, venation faint, submarginal vein barely distinct from the margin; petiole red.

Notes The species name *crebra* means thick, clustered.

Locations Three trees in Plaza del Mar.

Top: *Narrow sparse leaves, slender twigs, and sparse flowers of* Eucalyptus crebra.
Bottom: *Small ovoid fruit with three or four valves.*

Eucalyptus crenulata
Silver gum, Buxton gum

An evergreen tree found only in the swampy bottoms of the Acheron River, Victoria, Australia. Usually occurring in more or less pure stands.

Habit A medium-sized evergreen tree; to 40 feet tall.

Inflorescence Axillary clusters of 7–11 flowers; peduncles round, 1/4 inch; buds glaucous, ovoid, 1/3–1/4 inch long, operculum beaked; flowers creamy to white. Flowers January to February.

Fruit Cylindrical, 1/6 inch long, initially glaucous, becoming dull green; disc narrow, descending; valves 3 or 4, included.

Twigs Thin, glaucous, with raised warty dark spots.

Bark Rough, gray on lower half of trunk, smooth gray above.

Leaves Juvenile leaves clasping the stem, opposite, ovate to cordate, 1 2/3 x 3/4 inches, the base often cordate, margins prominently scalloped (crenulate), glaucous; adult leaves opposite, broadly ovate, 1 1/2–2 2/3 x 1 1/4–1 3/4 inches, the base often cordate and clasping the twig, glaucous, discolorous, petiole (if present) round, to 1/4 inch long.

Notes Because of its narrow distribution and proximity to the population pressures of Melbourne, the species is considered threatened in its native habitat. The species name *crenulata* means with small, shallow, rounded teeth.

Locations A tree on the campus of the University of California, Santa Barbara, in a planter between Broida Hall and the Preston Cloud Building.

Top: Foliage, flowers, and fruit of Eucalyptus crenulata. *Bottom: Nearly sessile leaves with slightly scalloped margins, ashy gray twigs, and flowers.*

Eucalyptus deglupta
Mindanao gum, *kamarere*

Native to the islands of the equatorial western Pacific, from Papua New Guinea to Indonesia and the Philippines.

Habit A tall evergreen tree with a narrow crown; to 200 feet tall in its native habitat.

Inflorescence Large terminal, compound panicles; umbels with 3 to 7 white flowers; buds cylindrical with a steeply conical operculum, less than 1/4 inch across. Flowers in October.

Fruit Almost globular, to 1/5 inch across; disc thin; valves exserted.

Twigs Dull green, with 2 obvious decurrent ridges extending from each node down to the next.

Bark Smooth throughout, deciduous, flaking to reveal a striking pattern of mottled reds, oranges, browns, and purples.

Leaves Juvenile leaves opposite, petiolate, ovate to oblong, apex sharp-pointed, 2 x 1 2/3 inches; adult leaves sub-alternate, ovate-lanceolate, 2–5 1/2 x 3/4–2 3/4 inches, shiny green but noticeably paler beneath, submarginal vein very distinct from the margin, densely reticulate with numerous oil glands of varying size; petiole flattened and twisted, 1/3–1/2 inch long, yellow.

Notes *E. deglupta* has the distinction of the being the only eucalypt which does not occur in Australia and one of only a few that occur outside the continent. It grows in regions of the tropical western Pacific which receive 140 to 200 inches of rainfall per year. The bark of this species is very similar to that of *Angophora costata,* but it develops into a much larger tree. The species name *deglupta* means peeling.

Locations A young tree in East Alameda Plaza. One of moderate size in Montecito at the eastern intersection of Coast Village Road and Coast Village Circle. Others recently planted in the 900 block of State Street.

Top: Dense terminal flower clusters of Eucalyptus deglupta *and leathery leaves with wavy margins and flattened petioles.*
Bottom: Striking bark of various colors.

Eucalyptus diversicolor
Kara

One of the largest trees of Australia, this species originates in a small region of coastal lands in extreme southwestern Western Australia.

Habit A tall evergreen tree, to 100 feet or more; reaches 250 feet in its native habitat.

Inflorescence Axillary, simple, seven-flowered; peduncle flattened or angular; buds pedicillate, club-shaped, $1/3$–$2/3$ x $1/4$ inch; scar apparently missing; operculum rounded; flowers white. Blooms March to August.

Fruit Cylindrical, $1/3$–$1/2$ inch long; rim moderately thick; disc descending; valves 4, enclosed.

Twigs Slender, yellow-green.

Bark Smooth throughout, shedding in long stringy strips, varying from red-gray to pale orange and whitish or yellowish-gray, frequently with long vertical cracks.

Leaves Juvenile leaves petiolate, opposite for 6-8 pairs then alternate, ovate, 3–$4^{1}/2$ x $2^{1}/2$–4 inches; discolorous, green on top; adult leaves petiolate, alternating, lanceolate, $3^{1}/2$–5 x $2/3$–$1^{1}/4$ inches; secondary veins pinnate, intramarginal vein quite distinct from margin, reticulation dense, fine, with numerous oil glands freestanding and at the intersections of veins; discolorous, dull, dark green above.

Notes Because of its interlinking fibers, the wood of *Eucalyptus diversicolor* is one of the strongest in the world. The species name *diversicolor* means different-colored, discolorous.

Locations Several trees along the west side of Sheffield Drive north of the intersection with San Leandro Lane.

Lanceolate leaves and slender twigs of Eucalyptus diversicolor *showing thick-rimmed fruit with enclosed valves.*

Eucalyptus erythrocorys
Red cap gum, *illyarrie*

From a small coastal region north of Perth, Western Australia.

Habit   A medium-sized, ornamental evergreen tree; to 50 feet tall.

Inflorescence   Axillary, unbranched, three-flowered; peduncle stout, flattened, to 1 inch long; petioles short, flat; receptacle cup-shaped in profile, square in cross section, $1\frac{1}{4}$–$1\frac{1}{2}$ x 1–$1\frac{1}{4}$ inches; operculum bright red, creamy inside, four-lobed or squarish, flattened, 1 inch across; stamens in 4 main clusters; flower bright yellow. Flowers in January.

Fruit   On a short pedicel, strongly ribbed, somewhat four-sided; rim thick; disc broad, more or less horizontal with rim; valves 4, enclosed.

Twigs   Red, becoming gray, pith glandular.

Bark   Smooth, white to gray, with gray flakes loosely attached.

Leaves   Juvenile leaves petiolate, opposite for many pairs, ovate, to 4 x $2\frac{1}{2}$ inches; dull gray, densely hairy; adult leaves with square petiole, opposite, falcate, $4\frac{1}{2}$–7 x $\frac{1}{2}$–$1\frac{1}{4}$ inches; sub-marginal vein widely distinct, secondary veins prominent, with numerous irregular island glands; bright green.

Notes   The species name *erythrocorys* means red helmut, cap.

Locations   One tree in the planting in front of a business in the 3700 block of State Street.

Top: Bright red operculum, flowers with bright yellow stamens, and leaves with pale midrib and reddened petiole of Eucalyptus erythrocorys.
Bottom: Flowers with many yellow stamens and enlarged ribbed fruit.

Eucalyptus fibrosa subsp. *fibrosa*
Broad-leaved ironbark

Found on plains and open forests of southwestern Queensland and western New South Wales, Australia.

Habit An evergreen tree with an open crown of ascending main branches and pendulous foliage; to 70 feet tall.

Inflorescence Terminal, compound panicles; seven- to eleven-flowered; buds widest at the middle, tapering to both ends, 1/3–2/3 x 1/4 inch; flowers white; pedicel angled with angles continuing as slight ridges onto the hypanthium. Flowers July to September.

Fruit Somewhat conical or pear-shaped, 1/4–1/2 x 1/4 inch; disc narrow, level to ascending; valves 4 or 5, strongly exserted.

Twigs Thin, angled.

Bark Rough, hard and deeply fissured; gray-black to black, with cream-colored fissures.

Leaves Juvenile leaves roundish, large, to 4 x 3 inches, green, slightly paler underneath; adult leaves lanceolate, 5 1/2–7 x 1 1/4–2 inches; dark green, intramarginal vein distinct from the margin, lateral veins faint, with numerous very fine oil glands.

Notes The species name *fibrosa* means fibrous.

Locations A single tree on the west side of Ashley Avenue next to Lotusland.

Top: Clusters of cigar-shaped buds and lanceolate leaves on slender red twigs of Eucalyptus fibrosa *subsp.* fibrosa. *Bottom: Pear-shaped fruit with strongly exserted valves.*

Eucalyptus globulus
Tasmanian blue gum, blue gum, southern blue gum

Native to the coastal regions of New South Wales, Victoria, and eastern Tasmania, as well as the inner tablelands of southern New South Wales and north central Victoria, Australia.

Habit A medium-sized to very tall evergreen tree, with ascending branches and a narrow crown; to 150 feet tall.

Inflorescence Axillary, unbranched; one-, three-, or seven-flowered; peduncles flattened or round; pedicels present or absent; buds shaped like a top, warty, glaucous, to 1 x 2/3 inch; operculum short, beaked, warty; flowers white. Flowers November to December.

Fruit Obconical, 2/3–1 inch long and across; with 4 more or less strong ribs, frequently very white glaucous; rim thick; disc broad, level or ascending; valves 3 or 4, slightly exserted.

Twigs Square or flattened in cross section; yellow-green on adults, glaucous on juvenile shoots.

Bark Smooth except at base, white to cream, yellow or gray, gray-brown bark accumulating at the base of trunk, with scattered swellings of epicormic buds.

Leaves Juvenile leaves opposite, sessile, clasping the stem; ovate; gray green to glaucous, discolorous; adult leaves petiolate, alternate, falcate, or lanceolate, up to 10 x 1 inches; slightly glossy green on both sides, moderately reticulate.

Notes *Eucalyptus globulus* includes four subspecies of which subsp. *globulus* and subsp. *maidenii* were listed as *E. globulus* and *E. maidenii,* respectively, in the 1974 version of Trees of Santa Barbara. The subspecies are distinguished by the number of flowers in an inflorescence—one (subsp. *globulus*), three (subsp. *pseudoglobulus* and subsp. *bicostata*), or seven (subsp. *maidenii*)—and the occurrence of pedicels on buds and fruit. A dwarf variety of subsp. *globulus* (*E. globulus* 'Compacta') is of horticultural origin and is similar in all respects except that it is a dense bush becoming a medium tree without a central stem, to 50 feet tall. The species has been listed as an Exotic Invasive Plant of Greatest Ecological Concern by the California Exotic Pest Plant Council. The species name *globulus* means round, globular.

Locations Occurring extensively throughout the area. Trees in Mission Park, along Mission Canyon Road, on Highway 101, and on the campus of the University of California, Santa Barbara.

Top: Somewhat cylindrical crown and peeling bark of Eucalyptus globulus.
Bottom left: White flowers and curved leaves with pale midrib.
Bottom right: Yellow-green twigs and enlarged fruit with broad rim.

Eucalyptus grandis
Flooded gum, rose gum

A coastal tree of Queensland and New South Wales, Australia

Habit A tall, upright, narrow-crowned evergreen tree; to 100 feet or more.

Inflorescence Axillary, unbranched, seven-flowered; peduncles angular, to 1/2 inch; buds sessile or with short, stout pedicels, ovoid, 1/3 inch long; scar present; operculum conical, sometimes slightly beaked; flowers white. Flowers August to September.

Fruit Obconical to pear-shaped, often glaucous, narrowed towards top; rim thin; disc obscure, descending; valves 4 or 5, level.

Twigs Smooth, somewhat angled, red.

Bark Rough and persistent at the base (5–15 feet), thin fibrous or flaking, gray to gray brown, newly exposed bark may be bright pink; upper trunk and branches smooth, covered with whitish scales, green underneath.

Leaves Juvenile leaves petiolate, opposite for several pairs, ovate, to 6 x 3 1/2 inches, discolorous, green to dark green above; adult leaves petiolate, alternate, lanceolate to broad-lanceolate, to 6 x 1 inches, base asymmetrical, discolorous, green above, pale green below, with dense reticulation and oil glands, submarginal vein quite distinct from the margin, lateral veins conspicuous.

Notes The species name *grandis* means large, great.

Locations A large tree on Barcelona Drive. Two young ones recently planted in Chase Palm Park by the pond.

Top: Upright crown and flaking bark of Eucalyptus grandis.
Bottom: Angular red twigs, pear-shaped fruit with enclosed valves, and dark green leaves.

Eucalyptus grossa
Coarse-leaved mallee

Native to granitic outcrops in southern Western Australia

Habit A small, straggly evergreen tree or mallee; to 20 feet tall.

Inflorescence Axillary, unbranched, seven-flowered; peduncles very stout, almost swollen, round, rigidly curved down, 2/3-1 inch long; buds sessile, cylindrical, 2/3–1 1/3 inches long, scar present; operculum conical; flowers light yellow-green. Flowers in December.

Fruit Sessile, cylindrical, woody, 2/3 x 1/2 inch long; rim thick; disc descending; valves 4, enclosed.

Twigs Stout, smooth, red above, green below; pith glandular.

Bark Fibrous, gray, with vertical fissures on stems and larger branches; peeling to expose a light brown inner bark.

Leaves Juvenile leaves petiolate, opposite or alternate, elliptical, to 2/3 x 1/3 inch, glossy green on both sides; adult leaves petiolate, alternate, lanceolate, 3–6 x 2/3–2 inches, glossy green to yellow-green on both sides, very thick, leathery; intramarginal vein widely separated from the margin; lateral veins conspicuous with numerous irregularly shaped oil glands; with a slight smell of turpentine when crushed.

Notes The species name *grossa* means very large.

Locations A single tree in lower Orpet Park below the lawn.

Top: Eucalyptus grossa *with short lanceolate leaves, yellow green flowers, and stout cylindrical flower bud clusters on stout recurved peduncles.*
Bottom: Cylindrical fruit with enclosed valves.

Eucalyptus lehmannii
Bushy yate

Found in rocky shrublands of coastal regions of southern South Australia.

Habit Small, spreading evergreen mallee or shrub with multiple stems; to 25 feet tall.

Inflorescence Axillary, simple, with 7–22 fused flowers; peduncles flattened, curved down, 1/2–3 1/2 x 1/3 inches; buds sessile with a fused hypanthium and a distinct narrow curved operculum, 2/3–1 1/3 inches; flowers pale green. Flowers in January.

Fruit Sessile, fused into a tight dark brown ball, to 1 3/4–2 inches across; rim thick; disc broad, lobed, ascending, radially ribbed; 3–4 valves, strongly exserted and tapering to a persistent pistil.

Twigs Yellow-green, zigzag at leaf nodes, roughened by gum secretions.

Bark Tannish-gray or gray-brown, strongly exfoliating in long strings which accumulate along the trunk and base of the tree.

Leaves Juvenile leaves petiolate, alternating, elliptical to ovate, to 3 x 2 inches; dull green, rough; adult leaves alternate, with flattened or angled petiole, narrow-lanceolate, to 3 1/2 x 3/4 inches, glossy green to gray-green on both sides; reticulation moderate with irregular, isolated oil glands.

Notes The species name *lehmannii* honors Johann Georg Christian Lehmann (1792–1860), German botanist and professor of natural history, Director of the Hamburg Botanical Garden.

Locations Several specimens at MacKenzie Park along Las Positas Road. Others at Stow Grove County Park along La Patera Lane. A number have been planted along Highway 101 east and west of Santa Barbara.

Top: Several trunks and broad crown of Eucalyptus lehmannii.
Middle: Fused yellow-green flowers on flattened recurved peduncle.
Bottom: Fused fruit cluster and sessile flower buds on flattened peduncle.

Eucalyptus leucoxylon
Yellow gum, white ironbark

Native to coastal regions of southeastern South Australia and western Victoria, Australia.

Habit A small to medium-sized evergreen tree, with ascending branches and pendulous foliage; to 50 feet tall.

Inflorescence Axillary, unbranched, three-flowered; peduncles slender, to $1/2$ inch long, held perpendicular to the twig; buds ovoid, to $2/3 \times 1/3$ inch, scar absent; operculum conical to beaked; flowers white, pink, or red; pedicel to $1/2$ inch. Flowers January to February.

Fruit On long pedicels, barrel-shaped, to $1/2 \times 1/2$ inch; dark reddish-brown, warty; rim thick, sometimes split; disc descending; valves 4–6 enclosed.

Twigs Reddish to light green, somewhat rough.

Bark Rough, flaky, fibrous below 6 feet; smooth, white-, gray-, yellow- and/or blue-mottled above.

Leaves Juvenile leaves sessile, opposite for many pairs, ovate to broad-lanceolate, to $3^{2}/3 \times 1^{1}/3$ inches, dull green above; adult leaves on flat or round petioles, alternating, lanceolate to broad-lanceolate, to $4 \times 2/3$ inches; dull to slightly glossy green to blue-green on both sides; reticulation moderate with numerous isolated oil glands of differing size, intramarginal vein quite distinct, margins wavy.

Notes The species includes two varieties: *Eucalyptus leucoxylon* 'Rosea' (white ironbark) is noted for its crimson flowers, and *Eucalyptus leucoxylon* subsp. *megalocarpa* 'Rosea' is a smaller willowy tree to 20 feet tall with crimson flowers. The species name leucoxylon means white wood.

Locations Several trees of the species along with a single specimen of *Eucalyptus leucoxylon* 'Rosea' in the median of Coast Village Road near Hermosillo Drive. Two trees at La Mesa Park. Others at the University of California, Santa Barbara at the west end of the lagoon near the stairs from San Rafael Hall.

Top: Open crown and twisted trunk of Eucalyptus leucoxylon *'Rosea'.*
Middle left: White flowers, beaked operculum, and dark green lanceolate leaves.
Middle right: Pink flowered variety.
Bottom: Single and paired fruit with broad rim and enclosed valves and dull gray and brown twigs.

Eucalyptus macrandra
River yate, long-flowered marlock

Occurs along rivers and wet areas in a restricted region of extreme southwestern Western Australia.

Habit An evergreen mallee; to 35 feet tall.

Inflorescence Axillary, simple, seven- to fifteen-flowered; peduncles flattened, 3/4–1 1/4 inches long; buds on short pedicels, scar present; hypanthium cylindrical, 1/4 x 1/4 inch; operculum long and narrow, to 1 1/4 x 1/4 inches; flowers lemon-yellow. Flowers in July.

Fruit Cup-shaped, flat-topped, 1/3 x 1/3 inch; rim thick, disc broad, level; valves 3 or 4, level or slightly exserted above the rim, often fused at the tips.

Twigs Red to orange-red, pith glandular.

Bark Grayish-brown, rough below, peeling in long vertical strings above to leave a smooth coppery bark.

Leaves Juvenile leaves, petiolate, alternating, lanceolate, to 3 1/2 x 1 1/2 inches, glossy green on both sides; adult leaves petiolate, alternate, lanceolate with a long tapering point, to 4 x 1 1/4 inches, glossy green to olive-green on both sides; venation faint; oil glands present.

Notes The species name *macrandra* means long stamens.

Locations One tree in upper Orpet Park, east of the upper center steps. Others in the lawn to the south of Santa Rosa Hall at the University of California, Santa Barbara.

Top: Lemon-yellow flowers, orange twigs, and olive green leaves of Eucalyptus macrandra.
Middle: Elongate flower buds.
Bottom: Fruit clusters and dull twigs.

Eucalyptus megacornuta
Warted yate, warty yate

Known from only a very few restricted sites in southwestern Western Australia.

Habit A small evergreen tree, with a dense tufted crown and multiple low branches; to 30 feet tall.

Inflorescence Axillary, simple, five- to seven-flowered; peduncles broad-flattened, curved down; buds sessile, elongated to $2^{2/3}$ x 1 inches, scar present; operculum long, very warty; hypanthium with coarse, rounded ribs; flowers yellow-green. Flowers in December.

Fruit Bell-shaped, to $1^{1/2}$ x $1^{1/4}$ inches; woody and lightly ribbed, rim thick, disc broad, lobed, ascending, radially ribbed, and extending over the 3 exserted valves.

Twigs Thin, reddish, turning yellow-green, roughened by gum secretions.

Bark Smooth throughout, reddish-brown to reddish-gray.

Leaves Juvenile leaves petiolate, alternate, triangular to ovate, to 3 x $2^{1/3}$ inches, green, sandpapery rough; adult leaves alternate, lanceolate, to $4^{1/2}$ x $3/4$ inches, dull to glossy green on both sides, surfaces roughened by gum secretions; submarginal vein distinct, reticulation dense, faint, with scattered isolated oil glands; petioles rounded or channeled.

Notes The species name *megacornuta* means large-horned.

Locations Several trees along the northern boundary of Earl Warren Showgrounds at the Las Positas Entrance. A poor individual in Franceschi Park east of the cottage.

Top: Yellow-green flowers and lanceolate leaves of Eucalyptus megacornuta.
Middle: Long warty flower buds on flattened peduncles.
Bottom: Smooth, peeling bark.

Eucalyptus nicholii
Narrow-leaved black peppermint, willow-leaved peppermint

Limited distribution in northeastern New South Wales, Australia.

Habit A small to medium-sized evergreen tree with a dense leafy crown; to 60 feet tall.

Inflorescence Axillary, unbranched, seven-flowered; peduncles short, slender; buds ovoid, small, less than 1/4 inch long, scar present; operculum hemispherical with a slight beak; flowers white. Flowers in June.

Fruit Hemispherical, to 1/4 inch, disc level; valves 3, slightly exserted.

Twigs Thin, red; young branches rusty-red.

Bark Rough, fibrous throughout, coarsely furrowed to give a slight diamond pattern, reddish-gray.

Leaves Juvenile leaves with a short petiole, alternate, crowded on the stem, narrow, to 2 x 1/4 inches, gray-green on both sides; adult leaves petiolate, alternate, narrow-lanceolate, to 5 x 1/2 inches, dull blue-green on both sides; submarginal vein distinct, lateral veins and reticulation faint.

Notes The species name *nicholii* honors William Henry Nichols (1885–1951), Australian bookbinder, orchidologist, propagator, and gardener at Footscray (Melbourne) Municipal Gardens.

Locations Three trees at the west end of the Public Library were planted in 1980. A street tree in the 2500 block of Castillo Street. Others in the parking lot of the Santa Barbara Airport and in the 2100 block of Gillespie Street.

Top: Rounded crown and roughened bark of Eucalyptus nicholii.
Bottom left: Small white flowers, curved blue-green leaves, and slender twigs.
Bottom right: Small hemispherical fruit.

Eucalyptus odorata
Eucalyptus fruticetorum
Peppermint box

Found in southeastern South Australia and western Victoria, Australia.

Habit A small evergreen tree or mallee; to 45 feet tall.

Inflorescence Axillary, simple, seven- to eleven-flowered; peduncles angled, short, 1/2 inch; buds cigar-shaped, 1/3 inch long, without scar; operculum conical; flowers white, rarely pink, small, 1/2–2/3 inch across at anthesis. Flowers in July.

Fruit Cylindrical or urn-shaped, to 1/3 inch long; often with slight ridges extending from the angles of the peduncle; rim thin; disc descending; valves 4 or 5, below the rim.

Twigs Thin, angled, dull green turning reddish.

Bark Rough and persistent on the lower trunk, fibrous, dull gray; upper trunk and branches smooth, gray-brown, peeling in long stringy strips.

Leaves Juvenile leaves petiolate, opposite for a few pairs then alternate, narrow-elliptic then ovoid, to 3 x 1 inches; slightly discolorous, green above; adult leaves petiolate, alternate, lanceolate, to 4 3/4 x 2/3 inches; dull, green or gray-green on both sides; densely reticulate, veins faint, submarginal veins distinct, oil dots present; with a smell of menthol when crushed.

Notes The species consists of two varieties—var. *odorata* and var. *angustifolia,* of which the latter is the former *E. fruticetorum* (blue mallee). The species name *odorata* means odorous.

Locations One tree at Franceschi Park along the upper path adjacent to Franceschi Road. Another in Mackenzie Park between the baseball fields and near the corner of the John C. Fremont Army Reserve Center.

Top: Small white flowers, cigar-shaped buds, and dull gray-green leaves of Eucalyptus odorata.
Bottom: Dull twigs and urn-shaped fruit with inserted valves.

Eucalyptus polyanthemos
Red box, Australian beech

Native to tablelands of southeastern New South Wales and eastern Victoria, Australia.

Habit A medium-sized evergreen woodland tree with a dense crown; to 70 feet tall.

Inflorescence Terminal, branched, seven-flowered; peduncles slender to 1/3 inch long; buds on short pedicels, diamond-shaped, glaucous, to 1/4 x 1/8 inch, scar present; operculum conical; flowers creamy, 1/2 inch across. Flowers December to February.

Fruit Barrel-shaped, to 1/4 x 1/8 inch; rim thin, often split; disc steeply descending; valves 3 or 4, enclosed.

Twigs Pendulous in clumps, thin, roughened by surface oil blisters; red above, green below, turning dull red or green.

Bark Quite variable, may be fibrous-flaky and brown to gray, or smooth and gray-yellow to white-gray.

Leaves Juvenile leaves petiolate, opposite initially, circular and notched at the apex, to 1 1/2 x 3 1/8 inches, dull gray-green on both surfaces; adult leaves petiolate, alternate, ovate to broad-lanceolate, to 3 1/2 x 1 1/4 inches, slate gray or glaucous on both surfaces, densely reticulate-veined, intramarginal vein widely distinct from the margin, with oil blisters scattered on the surface and smaller oil glands at the ends of the reticulation; petiole, margins, and midrib red.

Notes The mature tree is frequently dominated by an intermediate (alternate and ovate) leaf phase. The species name *polyanthemos* means many-flowered.

Locations Several trees along Cabrillo Boulevard west of Garden Street. Others on San Rafael Street and in the Santa Barbara Harbor parking lot.

Top: The upright compact crown of Eucalyptus polyanthemos.
Bottom: Slate-gray ovate leaves, red twigs, creamy flowers, and barrel-shaped fruit.

Eucalyptus punctata
Gray gum

Native to coastal and inland mountain ranges of New South Wales, Australia.

Habit A medium-sized evergreen tree with a thin crown of ascending branches; to 100 feet tall.

Inflorescence Mostly axillary and simple, some terminal and compound, seven-flowered; peduncles somewhat flattened, to 3/4 inch; buds pedicillate, ovoid, short, to 3/8 inch long, scar present; operculum variable; flowers white. Flowers June to July.

Fruit Pedicillate; hemispherical, to 1/2 inch long; disc broad, level or ascending; valves 3 or 4, level or exserted.

Twigs Slender, red.

Bark Shedding in large thick patches to ground level; creamy to orange on newly exposed areas, weathering to dull gray.

Leaves Juvenile leaves petiolate, opposite initially, narrow-lanceolate to lanceolate, to 6 x 2 inches; adult leaves alternate, lanceolate to slightly falcate, to 6 x 1 1/4 inches, thick, shiny dark green above, pale below, densely reticulate, venation faint, intramarginal vein quite distinct; petiole flattened or channeled.

Notes The species name *punctata* means marked with translucent dots.

Locations Several trees above the road on the west side of Sheffield Drive between San Leandro Lane and Valley Club Road.

Top: White flowers and curved lanceolate leaves of Eucalyptus punctata.
Middle: Beaked flower buds and slender red twigs.
Bottom: Hemispherical fruit with broad rim.

Eucalyptus robusta
Swamp mahogany, swamp messmate

As is clear from its name, swamp mahogany is naturally found in wetlands of coastal New South Wales and coastal southeastern Queensland, Australia.

Habit A small to medium-sized evergreen tree, with an open crown; to 50 feet tall.

Inflorescence Axillary, simple, nine- to fifteen-flowered; peduncles flattened, 1 1/4 inches long; buds with obvious pedicels, 1/2–2/3 inch long, scar from outer operculum present; operculum long, beaked; flowers white. Flowers February to March.

Fruit Cylindrical, sometimes constricted, 2/3 x 1/2 inch, on a prominent pedicel; rim thick; disc descending; valves 3 or 4, usually connected across the orifice, deeply inserted.

Twigs Angled, shiny green turning reddish-gray.

Bark Rough and persistent through the trunk and larger branches, thick, in long vertical ridges separated by deep furrows, soft, fibrous, gray or reddish gray-brown.

Leaves Juvenile leaves petiolate, ovate, to 8 x 3 inches, strongly discolorous; adult leaves petiolate, alternate, broad-lanceolate, to 6 x 2 inches, lateral veins fine, intramarginal vein within 1/16 inch of the margin, oil glands dense, strongly discolorous, glossy dark green above, pale green below; moderately thick; petiole 3/4 inch long, flattened and twisted.

Notes The species can be highly variable in fruit shape and structure. The species name *robusta* means strong, robust.

Locations A tree in Franceschi Park below the entrance drive. Street trees on Emerson Street at Orena and at the corner of De la Vina and De la Guerra Streets. Another at the corner of Mission Ridge Road and Mountain Drive. Two young trees in Chase Palm Park east of the carousel.

Top: Open upright crown and fibrous bark of Eucalyptus robusta.
Bottom left: White flowers, beaked buds, and leathery leaves.
Bottom right: Cylindrical fruit with deeply inserted valves on stout twigs.

Eucalyptus saligna
Sydney blue gum, blue gum

Native to coastal regions of New South Wales and southeastern Queensland, Australia

Habit A medium-sized evergreen tree; to 80 feet tall.

Inflorescence Axillary, simple, seven- to eleven-flowered; peduncles flattened, 3/4 inch; buds sessile or with short stout flattened pedicels, buds with a conical operculum and a long-conical hypanthium, to 1/3 inch long, scar present; flowers white. Flowers April to May.

Fruit Cup-shaped, to 1/3 inch; rim thin; disc obscure; valves 3 or 4, exserted, erect or strongly turned outwards.

Twigs Yellow-green, very angled.

Bark Rough, gray, and flaky at the base; peeling above in long strings to expose a smooth green or grayish-green underbark.

Leaves Juvenile leaves petiolate, initially opposite, ovate to broadly lanceolate, to 5 x 2 inches, green to dark green above, pale beneath; adult leaves on a one-inch-long flattened petiole, alternate, lanceolate to broad-lanceolate, to 6 x 1 inches, green above, pale green beneath, densely reticulate with numerous oil glands, intramarginal vein distinct.

Notes The species name *saligna* means willow-like.

Locations Three trees on the western boundary of the University of California, Santa Barbara campus at the east end of Cordoba Road, planted about 1955.

Top: Clusters of small flowers, flower buds, and narrow lanceolate leaves of Eucalyptus saligna.
Bottom: Cup-shaped fruit with exserted valves.

Eucalyptus sideroxylon
Red ironbark, *mugga*

Native to eastern Australia from southeastern Queensland to Victoria.

Habit A medium-sized, erect evergreen tree with a full cylindrical crown and pendulous branches; to 80 feet tall.

Inflorescence Axillary, simple, three- or seven-flowered; peduncles and pedicels long, slender; buds ovoid, to $1/2 \times 1/4$ inch, without a scar; operculum conical or beaked; flowers white, pink, red, or pale yellow. Flowers December to February.

Fruit Hemispherical or urn-shaped, to $1/2 \times 1/2$ inch; glossy red-brown; rim thick; disc descending; valves 5 or 6, enclosed.

Twigs Dark purple red, glaucous.

Bark Hard, dark reddish- or orangish-black, deeply and coarsely furrowed, showing orange in the furrows, persistent throughout; smooth, light rusty-red on smaller branches.

Leaves Juvenile leaves petiolate, opposite initially, linear to narrow-lanceolate, to 6×1 inches, glaucous or dull green on both sides; adult leaves on a red petiole, alternate, lanceolate, to $6 \times 3/4$ inches, dull green, gray-green, or blue-gray on both sides, margins reddish; lateral veins faint, reticulation dense; submarginal vein separate from the margin; oil glands present; petiole and midrib reddish.

Notes Two subspecies are distinguished. *E. sideroxylon* subsp. *sideroxylon* includes those individuals with seven-flowered umbels. *E. sideroxylon* subsp. *tricarpa* includes individuals with three-flowered umbels and slightly larger fruit. The species name *sideroxylon* means ironwood.

Locations Common throughout town. Several plantings along Highway 101. Individuals at La Mesa Park and in Rocky Nook Park. Street trees on Las Positas in front of Adams School and on Vista del Mar.

Top: Crooked trunk and upright crown of Eucalyptus sideroxylon.
Middle left: Red flowers, beaked flower buds, gray-green leaves, and red twigs.
Middle right: Dense, glossy red-brown fruit clusters.
Bottom: Hard dark red-black bark with light orange furrows.

Eucalyptus spathulata
Swamp mallet

Found in southwestern Western Australia.

Habit A small evergreen tree or mallee; to 30 feet tall.

Inflorescence Axillary, simple, three- to seven-flowered; peduncles flattened, to 1/2 inch long; buds cigar-shaped to 2/3 x 1/4 inch, scar present; operculum cylindrical to conical, narrower than hypanthium, usually warty; flowers white. Flowers in March.

Fruit Shaped like a top, 1/2 x 3/8 inch; rim thick; disc level; valves 3 or 4, slightly exserted.

Twigs Thin, reddish, pith glandular.

Bark Smooth, gray, reddish-gray or coppery.

Leaves Juvenile leaves petiolate, alternate, narrow-lanceolate to linear, to 3 x 1/3 inches, dull blue-green; adult leaves petiolate, alternate, linear to narrow-elliptic, to 3 x 5/8 inches, sometimes with a hooked end, held somewhat erect in the crown, glossy olive-green on both sides, venation obscure, reticulation sparse with numerous round oil glands.

Notes Two subspecies are distinguished on the basis of leaf shape. Adult leaves of *E. spathulata* subsp. *spathulata* are linear-lanceolate, less than 1/4 inch wide. In *E. spathulata* subsp. *grandiflora* adult leaves are more than 1/4 inch wide. The species name *spathulata* means spoon-shaped.

Locations Trees in the island on Emerson Drive at Oreno Avenues. Another in the island on Paseo Ferrelo.

Eucalyptus spathulata *with small white flowers, fruit clusters, and olive-green leaves with elongate apices.*

Eucalyptus steedmanii
Steedman's mallet

Native distribution restricted to one isolated locale in southwestern Western Australia.

Habit A moderate-sized evergreen tree; to 50 feet tall.

Inflorescence Axillary, simple, three-flowered; peduncles angular or flattened, curved down, 1 1/4 inches long; buds pendulous, square in cross section with obvious wings at the corners, 1 1/2 x 1/2 inches, scar present, often with vestiges of 4 sepals remaining from split outer operculum; persistent inner operculum often narrower than the hypanthium; flowers white. Flowers June to July.

Fruit Pedicillate, top-shaped, square in cross section with obvious wings at the corners, 7/8 x 2/3 inch; rim thick; disc level or descending.

Twigs Pith glandular.

Bark Smooth, bluish-gray or gray-white over red-brown or copper; accumulating peeling strips at the base and in the forks of branches.

Leaves Juvenile leaves petiolate, alternate, ovate to broad-lanceolate, to 3 1/2 x 1 1/4 inches, dull light green; adult leaves alternate, elliptical to lanceolate, to 3 x 2/3 inches, glossy olive-green to green on both sides; reticulation sparse with numerous round oil glands; petiole flattened.

Notes This species comes from an isolated area of Western Australia and was considered to be extinct in its native habitat following its initial discovery in 1928. However, it was rediscovered in 1978. It was introduced to Santa Barbara by E. O. Orpet, who propagated it from seed sent to him by its discoverer, Mr. H. Steedman. The species name *steedmanii* honors Henry Steedman (1866–1953), Australian plant enthusiast and collector.

Locations A single tree in lower Orpet Park, west of the center steps and above the upper walk.

Top: Flowers, twigs, and elliptical leaves of Eucalyptus steedmanii.
Bottom: Flowers with four-angled hypanthium and red operculum, and glandular twigs.

Eucalyptus stellulata
Black Sally (Sallee)

Native to open woodlands in the tablelands of eastern new South Wales and Victoria, Australia.

Habit A small to medium-sized evergreen tree, with a dense rounded crown; to 25 feet tall.

Inflorescence Axillary, simple, 7- to 23-flowered, in radiating clusters; peduncles less than 1/4 inch; buds cigar-shaped, to 1/4 inch long, without a scar; operculum long, pointed; flowers white. Flowers June to August.

Fruit Sessile, crowded, cup-shaped, to 1/4 x 1/4 inch, dark reddish-brown, rim thick, disc level; valves 3, enclosed.

Twigs Thin, yellowish-brown, turning reddish-gray.

Bark Rough on the lower half, hard, dense, with narrow fissures, dark gray to gray-black, peeling in a strongly spiraling manner; upper trunk and limbs smooth, oily yellow-green to olive green, with numerous warty bumps from epicormic buds.

Leaves Juvenile leaves sessile, opposite initially, round to ovate, to 3 1/2 x 2 1/2 inches, dull green above; adult leaves petiolate, alternate, elliptical to broad-lanceolate, with a hooked tip, to 3 1/4 x 1 inches, glossy green on both sides, 3 primary veins parallel to the margin, with little reticulation and numerous oil glands; petiole to 1/2 inch long, flattened.

Notes The species name *stellulata* means with small star-like markings.

Locations A single tree at the south end of the County Administration Building parking lot, near Santa Barbara Street.

Top: Elliptical leaves and clusters of flower buds on older twigs of Eucalyptus stellulata.
Bottom: Small white flowers, yellow buds, and cup-shaped fruit.

Eucalyptus tereticornis
Forest red gum, red irongum

Widely distributed in eastern Queensland, New South Wales, and Victoria, Australia.

Habit A tall, vase-shaped evergreen tree, with an open, steeply-branched crown; to 150 feet tall.

Inflorescence Axillary, simple, seven- to eleven-flowered; peduncles to 1 inch long; buds on pedicels as long as themselves, elongated to $3/4$ inch long, scar present; operculum conical, several times longer than the hypanthium; flowers white. Flowers June to July.

Fruit Ovoid, to $1/4$ inch long and wide; rim thick; disc broad, steeply ascending; valves 4 or 5, strongly exserted.

Twigs Dull green.

Bark Flaking off in large plates to leave a smooth surface throughout with vertical stripes of cream, brown, gray, dark gray, and bluish-gray.

Leaves Juvenile leaves petiolate, opposite initially, broad-lanceolate to ovate, to $8 1/4$ x 4 inches, bluish-green above, somewhat paler beneath; adult leaves petiolate, alternate, narrow-lanceolate to lanceolate, to 8 x 1 inches, thick, shiny green on both sides, moderately reticulate.

Notes *E. tereticornis* is a major producer of honey that has a caramel or toffee flavor. The species name *tereticornis* means round-horned.

Locations A single tree in East Alameda Plaza, between the play area and Micheltorena Street.

Large lanceolate leaves, flower buds with large conical opercula, and white flowers of Eucalyptus tereticornis.

Eucalyptus torquata
Coral Gum

Native to southwestern Western Australia.

Habit Small evergreen tree or mallee; to 30 feet tall.

Inflorescence Axillary, simple, seven-flowered; peduncles hanging, to $1^{1}/_{2}$ inches; buds on hanging pedicels, scar present; hypanthium cylindrical, but with a broad, ribbed ring at the base, operculum consisting of broad, ribbed ring and strong narrow beak; flowers turning coral-red at anthesis. Flowers December to January.

Fruit On hanging pedicels, cylindrical to urn-shaped, ribbed at the base, to $^{2}/_{3}$ x $^{1}/_{2}$ inch; rim somewhat thick; disc broad, steeply descending; valves 4, level with the rim or inserted, shiny green-brown.

Twigs Pith glandular, red.

Bark Roughened throughout, hard, dark gray-brown to gray-black, broken into diamond pattern; tending to shed in large plates.

Leaves Juvenile leaves petiolate, alternate, elliptical to lanceolate, to $2^{1}/_{2}$ x $1^{1}/_{4}$ inches; adult leaves petiolate, alternate, lanceolate, sometimes curved, to 6 x 1 inches, dull light green to gray-green on both sides, reticulation dense with numerous oil glands, submarginal rib distinct from the reddish margin.

Notes A good honey plant. The species name *torquata* means adorned with a necklace.

Locations Trees along Las Positas Road adjacent to the Municipal Golf Course and Adams School. Others on Cathedral Oaks west of Fairview Avenue.

Top: Eucalyptus torquata *with rounded silvery gray crown and reddish twigs.*
Middle: Deep pink flowers with red hypanthium, red twigs, and gray-green lanceolate leaves.
Bottom: Ribbed and strongly beaked flower buds and light pink flowers.
Left: Ribbed fruit with descending valves.

Eucalyptus viminalis
Manna gum, ribbon gum, white gum

Found in extreme southeastern Queensland through New South Wales and Victoria to extreme southeastern South Australia; also throughout the eastern half of Tasmania.

Habit A tall evergreen tree with an open crown and knobby projections on the stem from epicormic buds; to 80 feet tall.

Inflorescence Axillary, unbranched, three- or occasionally seven-flowered; peduncles slightly flattened, to $1/3$ inch; buds usually sessile, ovoid, to $1/2$ inch long, scar present; operculum conical or pointed, hemispherical; flowers white. Flowers in August.

Fruit Usually sessile, cup-shaped or hemispherical, to $1/3$ inch long and wide; rim thick; disc ascending; valves 3 or 4, exserted.

Twigs Thin, yellowish-green, turning dull red.

Bark Flaking off to ground level, leaving a light tan surface, weathering to gray or reddish-gray, crown frequently with long ribbons of flaking bark, flakes seeming to spiral around the stem.

Leaves Juvenile leaves sessile, opposite, the bases of a pair clasping the stem and overlapping, lanceolate, often curved down, to 6 x $1 1/4$ inches, bright green and slightly glossy above; adult leaves petiolate, alternate, lanceolate to narrow-lanceolate, often wavy, to 8 x $3/4$ inches, green on both sides, lateral veins distinct.

Notes *E. viminalis* is the most widespread eucalypt of southeastern Australia. This wide distribution and the adaptation to many habitats have led to considerable variation in species characteristics. The species name *viminalis* means willowy.

Locations A single tree in Franceschi Park between the parking area and the main house. One very nice specimen adjacent to the #10 tee at the Santa Barbara Golf Club. Another at the Santa Barbara Museum of Natural History next to the McVey House. Others on the campus of the University of California, Santa Barbara northwest of Engineering III Building and between the Chemistry and Physical Sciences South Buildings.

Top: Broad rounded crown of **Eucalyptus** viminalis. *Middle: Small white flowers and narrow curved leaves. Bottom: Foliage, fruit clusters, and thin yellowish twigs.*

Eucalyptus woodwardii
Lemon-flowered gum, lemon-flowered mallee

Endemic to a few isolated sites in southern Western Australia.

Habit A small evergreen tree or mallee; to 40 feet tall.

Inflorescence Axillary, simple, seven-flowered; peduncles stout, flat, to 3/4 inch long; buds on short pedicels, urn-shaped, hypanthium slightly ribbed, warty, with a prominently beaked operculum, to 3/4 x 2/3 inch, scar present; flowers bright lemon-yellow. Flowers in January.

Fruit Bell-shaped, lightly ridged, to 2/3 inch long and wide; rim thick; disc descending; valves 4 or 5, at rim level or slightly inserted.

Twigs Yellow-green turning reddish-brown, pith glandular.

Bark Smooth throughout, dull white, pink, greenish, or light coppery; often hanging in ribbons.

Leaves Juvenile leaves petiolate, alternate, ovate to broad-lanceolate, to 7 x 3 1/2 inches, gray-green; adult leaves, petiolate, alternate, broad-lanceolate, to 7 x 2 inches, very thick, leathery, with an irregular margin, dull yellow- to gray-green; reticulation dense with irregular, axillary oil glands, intramarginal vein distinct.

Notes This species has been successfully crossed with *E. torquata*. The species name *woodwardii* honors Thomas Jenkinson Woodward (1745–1820), British country gentleman of leisure and botanist whose contributions seemingly were of enough significance to warrant memorializing his name in three genera: *Woodwardia, Woodwardides,* and *Woodwardites.*

Locations A single tree along Franceschi Road below the entrance to Franceschi Park.

Top: Lemon-yellow flowers, beaked opercula, and thick leaves of Eucalyptus woodwardii.
Bottom: Ridged, bell-shaped fruit with thickened rims and enclosed valves.

Leptospermum

Leptospermum is a genus of 79 species, all but four of which are endemic to Australia. *Leptospermum* is formed from the combination of the Greek words *leptos* (slender) and *sperma* (seed), referring to the shape of the seeds.

Leptospermum laevigatum
Coast tea-tree, Australian tea-tree

Found in dry coastal forests of Victoria, South Australia, and Tasmania.

Habit An evergreen shrub to small tree with a twisted trunk; to 30 feet tall.

Inflorescence Axillary or terminal on short shoots, two flowers clustered together; flowers 1/2–3/4 inch across, containing 5 free oval white petals and 25 stamens inserted on the margin of a green 1/4-inch disc. Flowers March to April.

Fruit A short capsule, 1/4 inch long, valves exserted, but nearly flat-topped.

Twigs Initially silky, becoming glabrous.

Bark Shaggy gray-brown, shredding in strips.

Leaves Alternate, simple; narrow-obovate 1/3–1 1/4 x 1/4–1/3 inches, stiff leathery, dull gray-green; apex broad, obtuse, with a sharp point, base tapering; glaucous, three-nerved, the 2 side nerves faintly visible on the lower surface when backlit, with numerous transparent dots; petiole flattened.

Notes Several species of the genus were used by indigenous peoples to brew tea, which is reported to have been served by Captain Cook to his crew to prevent scurvy. The species name *laevigatum* means smooth.

Locations A lovely tree at the corner of Garden and Micheltorena Streets in Alice Keck Park Memorial Gardens. Others at the Cabrillo Ball Field and in the parking lots on both sides of Cabrillo Pavillon Arts Center.

Top: Broad, rounded crown of Leptospermum laevigatum.
Middle: Flowers with five white petals and gray-green obovate leaves with pointed apex.
Bottom: Twisted trunk with fibrous shredding bark.

Lophostemon
Tristania

Lophostemon is a genus of four species of northern and eastern Australia and southern New Guinea, and was formerly part of the larger genus, *Tristania*. Its name is derived from the Greek words *lophos* (crest) and *stemon* (stamen) and refers to the crested stamens of the flower.

Lophostemon confertus
Tristania conferta

Brush box, pink box, Queensland box, Brisbane box

Native to coastal regions of southeastern Queensland to northeastern New South Wales, Australia.

Habit An evergreen tree with a dense crown consisting of tiered clumps of glossy green foliage; to 60 feet tall.

Inflorescence Seven-flowered axillary cymes; flowers 1 inch across, petals white with wavy margins, stamens united into 5 bundles. Flowers June to July.

Fruit Capsules, similar to those of *Eucalyptus*; hemispherical to bell-shaped, 1/4–1/2 inch in all dimensions, woody, valves 3, level with the rim.

Twigs Hairy, dormant vegetative buds with broadly overlapping scales, terminal buds large, conical, 1/2–3/4 inch long, waxy resinous.

Bark Persistent on the lower trunk, furrowed into flat ridges, light gray or pinkish-brown; deciduous above, leaving a pinkish-cinnamon to orange- or red-brown smooth surface, with whitish vertical threads.

Leaves Mostly opposite, grouped in false whorls of 4–5 at the tips of twigs; ovate to elliptical, 4–6 x 1 1/2–1 3/4 inches; dark glossy green above with a pale green midrib, pale beneath.

Notes The species name *confertus* means crowded together, dense.

Locations Several street trees along upper State Street between Ontare Road and La Cumbre Road. Others in the 1300–1600 blocks of Anacapa Street and the 200–400 and 3000 blocks of Samarkand Drive.

Top: Narrow crown and flaking bark of Lophostemon confertus.
Middle: White flowers with five bundles of fused stamens. Leathery leaves, dark green above and pale green below.
Bottom: Branch bearing ovate leaves with pale midrib and clusters of fruit capsules with broad rims.

Melaleuca

Melaleuca is a genus of 220 species, all but ten of which are endemic to Australia. The other ten are distributed about Indo-Malaysia. Its species are superficially very similar to those of *Callistemon;* however, they are distinguished by the clustering of the many stamens into five distinct bundles. The genus name combines the Greek *mela* (black) and *leukos* (white) because frequently the trees have black trunks with white branches.

Melaleuca armillaris
Giant honey-myrtle, bracelet honey-myrtle

Native to river banks and sandy, rocky soils of coastal areas of eastern Australia (Queensland, New South Wales, Victoria, and Tasmania).

Habit A large evergreen shrub or small tree, with a dense, bushy crown and a repeatedly-branched and crooked trunk; to 30 feet tall.

Inflorescence Dense spikes, 1 1/4–4 inches long; flowers white to creamy. Flowers March to April.

Fruit Woody, tawny becoming gray-brown; round, less than 1/4 inch in diameter, with a persistent style, 5 inserted valves and 5 points.

Twigs Thin, initially yellow-green, turning somewhat shiny gray-brown.

Bark Gray-brown, with tan underneath, peeling in vertical strips.

Leaves Alternate, simple; densely placed on twigs; narrow-lanceolate to linear with sharp downwardly curved tips, 1/2–1 1/4 inches long, very narrow, needle-like; dark green; dotted with oil glands, aromatic when crushed; veins indistinct.

Notes The species name *armillaris* means with a bracelet or collar.

Locations A large repeatedly-branched tree in the western section of Upper Orpet Park along Lasuen Road.

Top: Dense creamy white bottlebrush flowers of Melalecua armillaris.
Bottom: Cluster of sessile fruit and sharp-tipped linear leaves.

Melaleuca decora
Melaleuca genistifolia
Snowy fleece tree

Found on sandy soils of northwestern Australia, Northern Territory, and Queensland.

Habit An evergreen tree with several stems and ascending branches; to 60 feet tall.

Inflorescence Terminal cylindrical spikes containing many flowers, $3/4$–$2 1/4$ x $3/4$–1 inches; flowers in clusters of 1–3, creamy white, sweetly fragrant. Flowers in November.

Fruit A cup-shaped woody capsule, about $1/8$ x $1/8$ inch, densely crowded on the axis.

Twigs Bright green, becoming reddish-cream, hairy.

Bark Pale brown, fibrous, layered, fissured into interlacing ridges.

Leaves Alternate, simple; linear, oblong, or elliptic, $1/4$–$2/3$ x $1/12$ inches, somewhat channeled, with an acute apex, dark green; petiole very short or absent, slightly twisted.

Notes When in flower, the whole tree is densely covered with white, sweetly smelling blossoms. The species name *decora* means elegant, decorous.

Locations A single tree in East Alameda Plaza near the corner of Santa Barbara and Sola Streets. Others in Franceschi Park above the cottage. Street trees in the first block of East Junipero Street to the 100 block of West Junipero Street and intermixed with *M. styphelioides* in the 200–300 blocks of East Canon Perdido Street.

Top: Upright crown and fibrous bark of Melaleuca decora.
Bottom left: Terminal flower clusters and short dark green leaves.
Bottom right: Fruit clusters and dense foliage.

Melaleuca ericifolia
Pineleaf paperbark, swamp paperbark

Native to lagoons and swamps of southeastern Australia (southern Queensland, New South Wales, Victoria, and Tasmania).

Habit A large shrub or small tree with a dense crown; to 20 feet.

Inflorescence Short spikes, 3/4–2 3/4 inches; flowers dense, creamy white to yellow. Flowers in January.

Fruit Globular capsules, 1/8 inch in diameter; tightly and densely clustered on the stem.

Twigs Thin, grayish-brown.

Bark Pale brown to gray, peeling in long thin flakes.

Leaves Alternate, simple; narrow-lanceolate to linear, the apex curved downwards, 1/4–2/3 inch long, very narrow; dark green, veins obscure.

Notes *M. ericifolia* is very similar to *M. armillaris,* but can be distinguished by its shorter flower spikes, short stamens, stouter and darker twigs, and more strongly curved leaves. Also, the somewhat denser foliage of *M. ericifolia* appears much more dense on a dried twig. The species name *ericifolia* means with leaves like those of the genus *Erica* (heather).

Locations A single specimen at Santa Barbara City College north of the Administration Building.

Top: Broad, bushy crown of Melaleuca ericifolia.
Middle: Dense linear leaves with curved apices and bottlebrush flower cluster.
Bottom: Sessile fruit borne on grayish-brown twigs.

Melaleuca linariifolia
Flaxleaf paperbark

Found in swampy soils along the coast of New South Wales and southern Queensland, Australia.

Habit A rounded small tree with ascending branches; to 30 feet tall.

Inflorescence Many flowered spikes to 1 1/2 inches long; flowers solitary, opposite, white, the staminal bundle multi-branched, to 1/2 inch long, giving the appearance of a tree covered with cotton balls. Flowers May to June.

Fruit Scattered on the stem; globose to cylindrical, 1/10–1/8 inch in diameter, with 5 inserted valves, light tannish-gray.

Twigs Thin, tan.

Bark Paperbark, but shreddy, peeling in small plates, dull white.

Leaves Mostly opposite, simple; linear, apex acute with a bristle-tip, 1/2–1 1/4 x 1/8 inches; initially pubescent, becoming glabrous; with 2 nerves faintly visible beside the prominent midrib below, densely covered with transparent oil glands; sessile.

Notes The species name *linariifolia* means linear leaves.

Locations Three trees along the fairway and three near the green of the 12th hole of the Santa Barbara Golf Club. Young street trees intermixed with *M. styphelioides* in the 1000–1300 blocks of East Carpinteria Street.

Top: Dense, rounded crown of Melaleuca linariifolia.
Middle: Pendulous flower clusters with many-branched stamen bundles and linear leaves.
Bottom: Sessile fruit and linear leaves.

Melaleuca nesophila
Pink bottlebrush, showy honey-myrtle

Native distribution limited to very restricted locations on the southern coast of Australia near Eyre and on adjacent islands; rare in nature.

Habit A tall evergreen shrub or small tree with a dense crown; to 20 feet tall.

Inflorescence Conspicuous terminal round heads, 1–1 1/4 inches across; flowers small, densely packed, deep violet or purple, fading rapidly. Flowers June to September.

Fruit Woody capsules, about 1/5 inch across, in a fused round cluster, 1–1 1/4 x 3/4–1 inches, with shoot growth continuing through the end of the cluster.

Twigs Thin, green-brown, becoming somewhat shiny light gray.

Bark Grayish-cream to pale brown, fissured to expose many papery-thin fibrous layers.

Leaves Alternate, simple; elliptical to oblong, 1/2–1 2/3 x 1/4–1/2 inches, frequently curved like a spoon, leathery, glabrous, dull to bright green, densely covered with oil glands, ascending to erect.

Notes The species name *nesophila* means island-loving.

Locations Common as a shrub. A single-stemmed specimen near the east end of the lawn in Lower Orpet Park. Others along Cabrillo Boulevard at the western end of the Bird Refuge and east of the pool. Also found in the plantings around the Municipal Tennis Courts on Old Coast Highway.

Top: Dense flower heads and oblong leaves of Melaleuca nesophila.
Bottom: Sessile fruit clusters on graying twigs.

Melaleuca quinquinervia
Five-veined paperbark, broad-leaved paperbark, teatree

Native to moist soils adjacent to streams and estuaries in the coastal regions of eastern Australia from Sydney, New South Wales to Cape York, Queensland.

Habit An erect evergreen tree with an oval, rounded crown, sometimes with several ascending stems; to 50 feet tall.

Inflorescence 1–3 densely flowered, terminal spikes, 1½–3½ inches long; flowers creamy white, rarely greenish- or reddish-white. Flowers October to November.

Fruit Woody, globose to somewhat cylindrical, 1/6 inch in diameter; valves 5, level with the rim; crowded on the stem, usually persisting for 1 year.

Twigs Orange, densely pubescent, turning light gray.

Bark Creamy white to light brown layers of thin paper-like cork separated by thin fibrous layers, tending to unroll, appearing loose and ragged on lower trunks, to 1 inch thick.

Leaves Alternate, simple; lanceolate to oblanceolate, 1½–3½ x ½–1¼ inches; leathery, dull green, lightly silvery pubescent especially on the lower surface, with 5 (sometimes 3 or 7) obvious longitudinal veins; glandular dots minute, numerous; petiole red, flattened and twisted, 3/16 inch long.

Notes *M. quinquinervia* is one of several species which have a high essential oil content of medicinal importance. The extract has germicidal properties and has had application in treatment of wounds, surgery, and dentistry. The extract has also been used in production of pesticides and perfumes. Commercial extraction of the oils ceased, however, in 1955 when a Swiss firm was able to synthesize an adequate substitute for the perfume industry. Because of the similarity of their bark, this species has been confused with *Callistemon salignus*. However, the latter has only one central vein, its new foliage is bright pinkish-red, and its many stamens are not fused into five bundles. It has also been misidentified as *Melaleuca leucadendra,* which has longer glabrous leaves and longer, more open, inflorescence spikes. *M. quinquinervia* has

Top: Tall, compact crown and creamy bark of Melaleuca quinquinervia.
Bottom: Terminal inflorescences of creamy flowers, sessile fruit, and dull dark green leaves.

become an aggressive invader in southern Florida. The species name quinquinervia means five-nerved, veined.

Locations Street trees scattered in the 400–800 blocks of East Gutierrez Street. Others in the 100 block of East Cota Street, in the 1700 block of Vernon Drive, and on Loyola Drive. A single tree in Lower Orpet Park along the lower border near Moreno Street.

Melaleuca styphelioides
Prickly leaved paperbark, rigidleaf melaleuca

Native distribution restricted to moist heavy soils of the coast and lower tablelands of New South Wales and Queensland, Australia.

Habit A small to medium-sized evergreen tree with a rounded, densely branched crown and slightly drooping branches; to 45 feet tall.

Inflorescence Few- to many-flowered dense spikes, about 3/4 inch long; flowers in threes, white. Flowers in March.

Fruit Woody, roundish, 1/10–1/4 inch in diameter; sepals persistent about the orifice; densely clustered on the twig.

Twigs Slender, tan, densely covered with silky white pubescence.

Bark Creamy white, peeling like layers of paper.

Leaves Alternate, simple; dense on the stem; ovate to narrow-ovate, the blade twisted with a sharp prickly point, 1/4–1 x 1/10–1/4 inch; slightly hairy becoming glabrous and dark green, with many fine parallel veins; sessile.

Notes The species name *styphelioides* means hard, tough.

Locations A single tree along the northern border of La Mesa Park. Others in the 1000–1100 blocks of Carpinteria Street and intermixed with *M. decora* in the 200–400 blocks of East Canon Perdido Street.

Top: Melaleuca styphelioides *with narrow crown, somewhat drooping foliage, and creamy bark.*
Middle: Dense flower spikes and leaves with sharp, twisted blades.
Bottom: Sessile fruit and sharp leaves.

Metrosideros

Metrosideros consists of about 50 species spread from Malaysia to New Zealand, with one disjunct population occurring in South Africa and another in the Hawaiian Islands. Many characteristics of the genus appear to merge with *Callistemon* in New Caledonia. The genus combines the Greek words *metra* (heartwood) and *sideros* (iron) in reference the hardness of the heartwood.

Metrosideros excelsa
New Zealand Christmas tree, *pohutukawa*

Native to coastal rocky outcrops of the North Island, New Zealand, extending south to 39° South latitude.

Habit An evergreen spreading tree with a twisted trunk; to 60 feet tall.

Inflorescence Terminal in paired compact racemes; flowers to 3 inches across, densely tomentose, with small red petals and abundant long exserted red stamens, each tipped with a yellow anther; prolific nectar production. Flowers July to September.

Fruit A densely white hairy three-valved capsule with a persistent style, about 1/2 inch long, enclosed to the middle by the persistent calyx; seeds very small, numerous, golden brown.

Twigs Densely white hairy, turning dark gray.

Bark Light gray, thick, fibrous, deeply fissured, flaking in narrow chunks.

Leaves Opposite, simple; elliptic oblong, apex usually acute, to 4 x 2 inches; leathery, glossy light green above, densely white hairy below (hairless on young plants), margins revolute and somewhat wavy, submarginal vein distinct, with scattered oil glands.

Notes On larger trees, twining aerial roots are suspended from lower branches. The strong, curved branches were used by the native peoples of New Zealand as stays in boat building. The species name *excelsa* means tall, elevated.

Locations Several large trees along the west side of the north wing of Davidson Library at the University of California, Santa Barbara. Others in the first–200 blocks of State Street, the first–300 blocks of Bath Street, the first blocks of East and West Figueroa Street, on Santa Rita Circle. Others at Leadbetter Beach and in Plaza del Mar across from Mason Street. The yellow-flowered cultivar *M. excelsa* 'Aurea' is in Franceschi Park.

Top: Compact crown and several stems of Metrosideros excelsa.
Bottom left: Crimson stamens, gray pubescent flower buds, and bicolored leaves.
Bottom right: Young fruit and dark green upper surface of leaves.

Myrrhinium

Myrrhinium is a unique genus that is a close relative to *Acca*. It has had a varied taxonomic history and has included as many as seven species. Taxonomists today believe that these are all variations within a single species. The name of the genus derives from myrrh and references the pleasant perfume exuded by the flowers.

Myrrhinium atropurpureum var. *octandrum*
Myrrhinium salicinum

Myrrhinium

Native to wet areas along streams and in forests in a narrow band extending from southeastern Brazil through Uruguay, northern Argentina, and along the Andes to Columbia.

Habit A large evergreen shrub or small tree with a bushy rounded crown; to 20 feet tall.

Inflorescence Clusters of 10–50 flowers on mature twigs or branches; flowers $1/3$–$1/2$ inch across with 4 glandular, fleshy, red or purplish petals and 4–8 red stamens $2/3$–1 inch long; the petals somewhat resembling swollen ticks. Flowers February to March.

Fruit A small dark purple-black berry, somewhat spherical, $1/8$ inch long, containing 1–4 sickle-shaped seeds.

Twigs Thin, moderately pubescent, gray to dark reddish-brown.

Bark Dull gray, very finely fissured.

Leaves Opposite, simple; narrowly elliptic to lanceolate, $3/4$–$2 1/2$ x $1/3$–$3/4$ inches, somewhat leathery, apex pointed, glossy green above, paler beneath, the margin somewhat rolled under; petiole very short, perpendicular to the leaf blade, yellow-green, grooved on top.

Notes Little is known about the natural history of this species; however, it has been hypothesized that pollination is by birds. The red stamens and fleshy purple petals of the flowers purportedly serve as an attractant to avian pollinators. This species is also capable of vigorous reproduction from root sprouts. The species name *atropurpureum* means dark purple.

Locations A tree in lower Orpet Park at the west end of the lawn.

Flowers of Myrrhinium atropurpureum *with crimson stamens and fleshy swollen petals; elliptic leaves with angled petioles.*

Myrtus

Myrtus is a genus of two species from the Mediterranean region. *Myrtus* is the Greek name for the plant.

Myrtus communis
Common myrtle

Origin unclear, today abundant in southern and eastern Europe, believed to have originated in Iran or Afghanistan.

Habit   An evergreen bushy shrub developing, with age, into a small tree; to 25 feet tall.

Inflorescence   Axillary, solitary flowers, white, 3/4 inch across, with 5 rounded petals and numerous crowded stamens, fragrant. Flowers June to July.

Fruit   A purplish-black berry, 1/2 inch long.

Twigs   Finely hairy, tannish, ridged.

Bark   Smooth, warty from epicormic bud sprouts, light gray, peeling to expose a cinnamon-brown under layer.

Leaves   Opposite, simple; oval to lanceolate, 1–2 x 1/3–3/4 inches, dark glossy green above, pale green beneath, margins entire, somewhat revolute, covered with translucent oil dots, fragrant when crushed; petioles very short, reddish.

Notes   *M. communis* has long held a place in folklore. It was a sacred tribute to the Goddess of Love, and sprigs of the foliage are an important component of wedding bouquets today. The essential oil of the foliage is the source of the scent *Eau d'Ange*. Tannins derived from the bark and roots are used to produce the finest leathers of Russia and Turkey. It is the sole representative of the Myrtaceae growing naturally in Europe. The species name *communis* means common, general.

Locations   A small tree in Alice Keck Park Memorial Gardens on the island. Another in the Santa Barbara Cemetery. Two others in West Alameda Plaza near the bandstand.

Top: Thin, open crown of **Myrtus communis**. *Bottom: White flowers with numerous stamens, round flower buds, and glossy oval leaves.*

Plinia
Myrciaria

Plinia is a genus of 30 species from the tropical Americas. It was named for Pliny the Elder.

Plinia edulis
Myrciaria edulis
Cambuca, willow-leaved eugenia

Native to forest margins and disturbed plant communities from southern Brazil to Argentina.

Habit An evergreen tree or shrub with strongly pendulant branches; to 35 feet tall.

Inflorescence Axillary racemes with 2–4 flowers; flowers 1/2–3/4 inch across, whitish. Blooms in December.

Fruit An enlarged round berry, to 3 1/2 inches long, yellow when ripe.

Twigs Thin, pendulous, light green, becoming tan then gray, minutely hairy in the first year.

Bark Dull gray, with reddish-brown showing through shallow fissures.

Leaves Opposite, occasionally alternate on fast-growing twigs, simple; ovate to elliptic-oblong, 2–3 1/2 x 1/3–3/4 inches, margins entire, apex acute or slightly acuminate, venation finely reticulate, midvein prominent beneath, both surfaces slightly hairy; petiole pubescent, 1/4–1/2 inch long.

Notes This species is frequently cultivated in Brazil for its edible fruit. The species name *edulis* means edible.

Locations A tree in upper Orpet Park along Moreno Road.

Top: Narrow, drooping crown of Plinia edulis.
Bottom: Narrowly elliptic leaves and large yellow fruit.

Psidium

Psidium is a genus of 100 species from the tropical Americas. *Psidium* is the Greek word for pomegranate.

Psidium cattleyanum
Strawberry guava

Native to openings in the tropical rain forests of Brazil.

Habit   An evergreen shrub or small tree; to 15 feet tall.

Inflorescence   Axillary, solitary; flowers white, 1 inch across, with 4–5 outspread petals and numerous stamens. Flowers in July.

Fruit   A globose purple-red berry with persistent sepals, 1–1 1/2 inches across, flesh white, with the taste of strawberries.

Twigs   Green in the first year, becoming dull gray.

Bark   Smooth, gray-brown, exfoliating to expose tan-brown splotches.

Leaves   Opposite, simple; elliptic to obovate, 2–4 x 1 1/4–2 1/2 inches, shiny light green, turning reddish before dropping, leathery, venation indistinct, margins entire, slightly revolute.

Notes   The fruit of *P. cattleyanum* is edible and the species has been planted around the world. In Hawaii it has become a serious invasive pest whose influence is exacerbated by the fact that it is extremely toxic to the growth of other plants. The species name *cattleyanum* honors William Cattley (d. 1832), English patron of botany and collector of rare plants.

Locations   A small tree in Franceschi Park between the main house and the cottage.

Top: Glossy leathery leaves, white flowers, and round flower buds of Psidium cattleyanum.
Bottom: Purple-red fruit and dull gray twigs.

Syncarpia

Syncarpia is a genus of five species distributed from Malaysia to northeastern Australia. Its name combines the Greek words *syn* (together) and *karpos* (fruit) and refers to its fused fruit.

Syncarpia glomulifera
Syncarpia laurifolia
Turpentine tree, red turpentine tree

Native to the mixed rain forest/eucalyptus forest transition in eastern Queensland and New South Wales, Australia.

Habit A narrow evergreen tree, with pendulous branches; to 30 feet tall.

Inflorescence Axillary, usually 4–8 heads on one- to 2-inch white wooly peduncles, whorled or in 2 opposite pairs, each head 1–1 1/2 inches across, containing 7 flowers whose bases are united. Flowers in March.

Fruit A round head composed of 7 fused fruits, hard, woody, 1/2–3/4 inch across, white wooly becoming somewhat glabrous.

Twigs Exuding a clear orange or reddish sap when cut; vegetative buds black, to 1 inch long.

Bark Thick, fibrous, stringy, with deep longitudinal furrows, gray-brown or reddish.

Leaves Opposite, pairs grouped to appear whorled in fours, simple; ovate to broadly elliptical, 3–4 x 1–2 inches; margins slightly recurved and wavy; thick, stiff, dark dull green above with a light-colored midvein and numerous oil dots, densely white or pale brown pubescent below; petiole 3/4–1 inch long, wooly pubescent.

Notes The species derives its common name from the resinous exudate which flows between the bark and the wood and exudes from cut twigs. It has, however, no similarity to the turpentine of commercial use. The wood is highly resistant to decay. The species name *glomulifera* means flowers clustered in rounded heads.

Locations Two street trees on the east side of the 1900 block of Anacapa Street. A very nice small grove of trees at the Santa Barbara Golf Club.

Top: Narrow crown and fibrous bark of Syncarpia glomulifera.
Bottom: White flowers, clusters of white wooly fruit, and elliptic leaves.

Syzygium

Syzygium is a large genus of about 1,000 species from the Old World tropics. It is very closely related to *Eugenia* and differs in microscopic characteristics of ovule development. The genus includes the commercial clove *(S. aromaticum)* used in spices and the production of the Indonesian *kretec* cigarettes. *Syzygium* is the Greek word for joined, referring to the opposite branching of the Jamaican species *(Calyptranthes syzygium)* for which the name was originally used.

Syzygium australe
Brush cherry

Natural stands restricted to moist forests in eastern Queensland and New South Wales, Australia.

Habit A narrow evergreen tree with dense foliage; to 90 feet but more commonly 30 to 50 feet and sometimes shaped as a hedge.

Inflorescence A terminal cyme or in upper axils, frequently three- to seven-flowered; flower buds club-shaped; flowers four-parted, creamy white, about 1/2 inch in diameter. Flowers in July.

Fruit Round to oval, 1/2–1 x 1/3–2/3 inch, pink, red, or purplish-red.

Twigs Four-angled or even four-winged; with a pocket, hump or spur above each node, these formed from the merging of wings extending from the node above.

Bark Flaky, shallowly furrowed into intersecting ridges; light to dark gray over chocolate-brown.

Leaves Opposite, simple; lanceolate, obovate, apex sometimes bristle-tipped, 1 1/4–3 3/4 x 1/2–1 1/4 inches; pinnately veined with 9–23 pairs of indistinct veins, intramarginal vein separate from the margin; shiny green above, paler below, lower surface pitted, oil dots sparsely scattered; midrib grooved above.

Notes This species has been noted as *S. paniculatum* in previous versions; however, the merged wings forming a pocket, hump, or spur above each node clearly identify it as *S. australe*. The species name *australe* means southern.

Locations Common about town. Street trees in the 100 to 500 blocks of East Arrellaga Street and the 600 to 800 blocks of West Arrellaga Street.

Top: Tall constrained crown and flaking bark of Syzygium australe.
Bottom left: White flowers and glossy leathery leaves.
Bottom right: Dense purple fruit and opposite branching.

Syzygium cumini
Eugenia jambolana

Jambolan plum, Javan plum

Common in moist regions of India and Malaysia.

Habit An evergreen tree of medium to large size, with a straight trunk and a narrow to rounded crown; to 60 feet tall.

Inflorescence Emerging from the previous year's twigs in compound cymes, 1–2½ inches long; flowers white, ½ inch across, the petals fused. Flowers in August.

Fruit Oblong, ¾–1 inch long, pink becoming deep purple to black, with a single seed surrounded by a juicy pulp.

Twigs Reddish or green in the first year, becoming tan-gray.

Bark Smooth, very light gray, tending to wrinkle and crack.

Leaves Opposite, simple; elliptic to lanceolate, 2–6 x 1–3½ inches, with an elongate apex, leathery, glossy dark green above, paler beneath, turning yellow before being shed, with scattered transparent dots, midrib yellow-green, prominent below, with very fine parallel secondary nerves; petiole channeled above, yellow-green, ½–1 inch long.

Notes The fruit of this species is much used for juice throughout the world. Unfortunately, it does not readily develop in Santa Barbara. The species name *cumini* means similar to cumin.

Locations Several trees in the 1400 and 1500 blocks of Santa Rosa Avenue. Two trees in the 500 block of West Valerio Street.

Top: Dense, constrained crown and light gray bark of Syzygium cumini.
Bottom: Small flowers and glossy leathery foliage.

Syzygium jambos
Rose apple

Widely spread throughout southeastern Asia.

Habit An evergreen, multi-stemmed, shrubby tree; to 30 feet tall.

Inflorescence Terminal once-branched cymes, to 1 inch long; buds globular, $2/3$ inch across; flowers whitish to yellowish with long showy stamens $1/2$–4 inches long; peduncle $1/3$–$2/3$ inch long. Flowers in January.

Fruit A berry, $3/4$–2 inches long, with a persistent calyx; whitish to yellowish, becoming maroon, with a rose-scented fragrance.

Twigs Reddish-brown, smooth, somewhat flattened.

Bark Grayish-brown, smooth, not exfoliating.

Leaves Opposite, simple; narrowly lanceolate, $3 1/2$–8 x $2/3$–2 inches, base wedge-shaped, apex elongate, with 14–20 pairs of slender nerves, distinctly elevated underneath; petiole to $1/2$ inch long, drying black.

Notes The species has been long known for its edible fruit and has been planted throughout much of the southern Pacific. It has, however, become an invasive species in many of these habitats. The species name *jambos* is the native name for the tree.

Locations Upper Orpet Park above the lawn on the east side.

Top: Flowers and flower buds of Syzygium jambos *on red peduncles.*
Bottom: Reddish fruit and opposite placement of lanceolate leaves.

Tristaniopsis

A genus of 40 species from Southeast Asia to Australia and New Caledonia. *Tristaniopsis* combines the genus name *Tristania* (named for Jules Tristan, 1776–1861, a French botanist) with the Greek *opsis* (likeness), referring to the similarity to *Tristania*.

Tristaniopsis laurina
Tristania laurina

Water gum, *kanooka*

Native distribution along waterways and creek banks of the coastal region of Queensland to Victoria, Australia.

Habit A small evergreen tree; to 30 feet tall.

Inflorescence Axillary cyme; flowers 1/4 inch across; petals yellow. Flowers in August.

Fruit Hemispherical to bell-shaped capsules, 1/4 inch in all dimensions, woody; valves 3, exserted and divergent.

Twigs Dark purple with short gray pubescence, becoming tannish-gray and glabrous.

Bark Light gray and scaly in older trees, smooth in younger trees; often blotched with gray, white, or brown.

Leaves Alternate, simple, well-distributed along the twig; lanceolate to narrow-obovate, to 5 1/2 inches long; dark green above, pale yellow-green and hairy along the midrib beneath, margins very slightly revolute; petiole 1/4–1/3 inch long, densely white pubescent.

Notes The species name *laurina* means resembling *Laurus*.

Locations Street trees planted in the 1700–1900 blocks of Anacapa Street and along upper State Street above Ontare Road.

Top: Open crown of Tristaniopsis laurina.
Middle: Clusters of yellow flowers and dark green lanceolate leaves.
Bottom: Dull brown fruit opening along three valves.

Waterhousea

Waterhousea includes only four species, all endemic to Australia. The genus is named for John T. Waterhouse, an Australian taxonomist with great interest in the genus *Syzygium* from which this genus was separated.

Waterhousea floribunda
Syzygium floribundum
Weeping satinash

Native to riparian forests from central Queensland to northern New South Wales, Australia.

Habit An evergreen tree with somewhat pendulous branches; to 50 feet tall.

Inflorescence Terminal or in the upper leaf axils, a much-branched panicle with many flowers; flower buds club-shaped; flowers four-parted, creamy white, about 1/2 inch in diameter. Flowers June to July.

Fruit Globose, flattened at the ends, 1/2–3/4 inch across; the calyx tube and style persistent at the apex; initially purple, turning yellow-orange at maturity; hanging in large weighty clusters.

Twigs Flattened, light green, becoming brown and flaky.

Bark Conspicuously but shallowly fissured into very small flakes; light gray with a cream brown or pinkish inner bark.

Leaves Opposite, simple; lanceolate, apex elongate, 2–6 x 1/2–2 inches; thick, waxy, shiny dark green above; indistinctly pinnately veined with 17–40 pairs, intramarginal vein faintly distinct from the margin, midrib obscurely grooved on upper surface; oil dots numerous and obvious.

Notes *W. floribunda* looks superficially like *Syzygium australe,* but is distinguished by its longer, less recurved leaves, with more obvious venation, yellow-orange fruit, and lack of a hump or spur above the nodes of newly grown twigs. The species name *floribunda* means many flowers.

Locations One tree in the lower planting of upper Orpet Park, immediately west of the center steps.

White flowers, flower buds in a sparse inflorescence, and glossy lanceolate leaves with elongate apex of Waterhousea floribunda.

Oleaceae

The Olive Family consists of about 23 genera and over 400 species and occurs worldwide. However, its greatest diversity is to be found in Southeast Asia. Some of its dioecious species (especially *Fraxinus*) have the unique characteristic of producing male flowers in one year and female flowers in another.

Chionanthus

Chionanthus is a genus of approximately 100 species native to tropical Africa, temperate eastern Asia, and eastern North America. The name is derived from the Greek *chion* (snow) and *anthos* (flower).

Chionanthus retusus
Chinese fringe tree

Native to moist mixed forests below 6,000 feet in central China, Japan, and Korea.

Habit Evergreen shrubs or trees; to 30 feet tall.

Inflorescence Showy, terminal or axillary panicles, 1 1/2–5 inches long; flowers white, 2/3–1 inch long. Blooms in March.

Fruit An ovoid drupe, 1/3–2/3 inch long; blue-black or black, with a waxy coating.

Twigs Smooth, light gray.

Bark Light gray and finely flaky, with scattered horizontal lenticels.

Leaves Simple, opposite; oblong to round, 1–5 x 3/4–2 1/2 inches, somewhat leathery, margins entire, midrib and larger veins densely hairy below; petiole 1/4–3/4 inch, densely hairy, channeled above.

Notes The species name *retusus* means terminating with a shallow notch in a rounded apex.

Locations A single tree on the campus of the University of California, Santa Barbara, east of San Miguel Hall.

Top: A young **Chionanthus retusus** *in full spring flower. Bottom: Flowers with linear white petals; simple leaves with opposite placement.*

Fraxinus
Ash

Fraxinus is a genus of 65 species from temperate regions of the Northern Hemisphere. Its members consist of large, medium, and small trees and are characterized by opposite branching, usually pinnately compound leaves, and fruit consisting of a single samara. Twigs and young branches are frequently of a long, sweeping character with swollen nodes, and the genus displays a characteristic purple coloration on the nodes of twigs and at the points of attachment of the leaflets to the rachis. Distinguishing characteristics of the species include the number of leaflets, degree of pubescence on twigs and leaves, timing of appearance of flowers relative to leaf break, and size and shape of the samara, including the degree to which the wing extends down the seed capsule. *Fraxinus* is the classical Latin name for ash.

Fraxinus dipetala
California ash, foothill ash, flowering ash

Distributed through the California Coast Ranges and the foothills of the Sierra Nevada.

Habit A slender deciduous tree or tall shrub; to 20 feet tall.

Inflorescence Showy axillary panicles of white flowers, 3–6 inches long, appearing at leaf break; flowers 3/8 inch across, consisting of only 2 petals. Blooms March to April.

Fruit A somewhat twisted oblong to elliptic samara, 3/4–1 1/4 inches long, less than 1/2 inch across; wing notched at the tip; seed not conspicuously thickened in the wing.

Twigs Strongly four-sided, the angles almost winged, greenish-brown, turning gray.

Bark Dark gray, finely fissured.

Leaves Opposite, pinnately compound with 5–9 leaflets, 3–6 inches long; leaflets ovate, 1/2–1 1/2 inches long, serrate, dark green above, paler beneath; petiolules 1/2 inch long, appearing winged from the decurrent leaf blade.

Notes In a genus that is usually dioecious, *F. dipetala* and *F. malacophylla* are among the few exhibiting perfect or bisexual flowers. The species name *dipetala* means two petals.

Fraxinus dipetala *with showy inflorescences of white flowers and pinnately compound leaves.*

Locations A tree in the Santa Barbara Botanic Garden on the bank between the parking lot and Mission Canyon Road. Others along the Campbell Trail and in the Ceanothus Section.

Fraxinus malacophylla
Chinese ash, Japanese ash

Native to the mountains of Thailand and southern China at elevations of 1,500 to 6,000 feet.

Habit A deciduous tree with a rounded crown; to 30 feet tall.

Inflorescence Terminal or axillary panicles of many minute bisexual flowers, to 6 inches long, appearing after the leaves. Blooms in August.

Fruit Narrow samara, broadest at the top, 1 1/4–1 1/2 x 1/4 inches; wing extending about halfway down the seed; held in dense clusters.

Twigs Ridged, four-angled, brown hairy; buds without scales, leaf scars large and round, with vascular bundle scars forming a horseshoe.

Bark Thin, gray to reddish-gray, peeling off in irregular plates.

Leaves Opposite, pinnately compound with a terminal leaflet, to 10 inches long; leaflets 9–15, elliptic, 1–3 x 1/2–1 1/4 inches, thin leathery, hairy beneath and sometimes above, margins entire; rachis densely brown hairy and channeled above.

Notes The species name *malacophylla* means soft-leaved.

Locations Trees in the 2100 block of Castillo Street. A young tree in MacKenzie Park near the Youth Center and adjacent to State Street.

Top: Rounded crown of Fraxinus malacophylla.
Middle: Inflorescence of small flowers; pinnately compound leaves with elliptic leaflets.
Bottom: Dense cluster of winged fruit; leaves with depressed venation.

Fraxinus uhdei
Shamel ash

Native to central Mexico

Habit A deciduous or semi-evergreen tree; to 75 feet tall.

Inflorescence Dense, six-inch-long panicles; flowers minute, with a very reduced calyx and no petals.

Fruit An elliptic samara, 1 1/4–1 1/2 x 1/3 inches, the wing extending more than half the length of the cylindrical seed cavity, wing apex flattened, notched or not. Blooms January to February.

Twigs Swollen and flattened at the nodes, green; buds flattened, red-brown.

Bark Smooth, gray turning brownish on older stems, becoming cracked with narrow fissures and flat ridges.

Leaves Opposite, pinnately compound, 5–8 inches long; leaflets 5–7, oblong-lanceolate, 2–3 x 3/4–1 1/4 inches, deep green, venation below may be white tomentose, margins coarsely serrate; rachis may be densely white tomentose, becoming glabrous towards the end of the season.

Notes *F. uhdei* and *F. velutina* are closely related species that are quite variable and difficult to differentiate. The larger overall tree size and larger samaras with a notched or flattened wing are the most reliable features to distinguish *F. uhdei*. The species name *uhdei* honors Carl Uhde, German plant collector who explored and collected in eastern Mexico from 1844 to 1848.

Locations Common about town. Only one of two large specimens planted in Franceschi Park in 1948 remains. Others at University of California, Santa Barbara southeast of Ortega Commons. Street trees on Alan Road.

Top: Open, multi-branched crown of Fraxinus uhdei *in spring flower.*
Bottom: Compound leaves with serrate leaflets and winged fruit.

Fraxinus velutina
Velvet ash, Arizona ash

Found in scattered populations along waterways in the coastal mountains of Southern California (Santa Barbara County to western Riverside County), and in desert mountains from Southern California to Texas, extending into Baja California and Sonora, Mexico.

Habit A slender, deciduous tree with a round spreading crown; to 30 feet tall.

Inflorescence Dioecious; in hairy panicles; flowers minute, without petals. Blooms March to April.

Fruit Oblong to elliptic samaras, seed cavity sharp-pointed, 3/4–1 inch long; wing not extending to below middle of cylindrical seed cavity, apex rounded or slightly apiculate.

Twigs Round, slender, green turning gray, velvety the first year, with scattered lenticels, tending to flatten at the nodes.

Bark Dull gray, with tight interlacing ridges.

Leaves Opposite, pinnately compound, with 3–5 leaflets, 3–6 inches long; leaflets elliptic to lanceolate, 1–2 inches long, shallowly round-toothed above the middle, thick, pale green and glabrous above, tomentose below, especially along the veins; rachis hairy, distinctly channeled above.

Notes This species is highly variable with regard to the degree of pubescence and the extent to which the samara wings extend down the seed cavity. Several varieties and cultivars exist. In addition, the species is known to hybridize with *F. latifolia* in the wild. *F. velutina* var. *coriacea* is characterized by very thick, leathery leaves, an example of which is growing in the Santa Barbara Botanic Garden. The horticultural product, *F. velutina* 'Glauca' (Modesto ash) is a glabrous form which has been planted extensively throughout Goleta. The species name *velutina* means velvety.

Locations Common in the El Encanto subdivision of Goleta.

Compound leaves and dense clusters of winged fruit of Fraxinus velutina.

Ligustrum

Ligustrum is a genus of about 40 Old World species found from Europe and North Africa to eastern Asia and Australia. *Ligustrum* is the classical Latin name for privet.

Ligustrum lucidum
Glossy privet

Native to China and Korea.

Habit An evergreen shrub or tree; to 40 feet tall.

Inflorescence Large terminal panicles, 4–7 inches long and wide; flowers small with a tubular corolla, $1/8$ inch long, white. Blooms in March.

Fruit A fleshy drupe, $1/4$–$1/3$ inch across, purple-black.

Twigs Purple on new growth, becoming tan with scattered lenticels.

Bark Dark gray with vertical fissures.

Leaves Opposite, simple; ovate, $2 1/3$–4 x $1 1/4$–2 inches, apex somewhat elongate, leathery, dull to shiny dark green above, lighter beneath, margins entire; petiole purplish, $1/3$–$2/3$ inch.

Notes The species name *lucidum* means bright, shining.

Locations Street trees on Brenner Avenue.

Top: Dense, dark crown and multiple branches of Ligustrum lucidum.
Bottom left: Terminal inflorescence and dark green leathery leaves with opposite placement.
Bottom right: Purple-black fruit and glossy leaves.

Olea

Olea includes about 30 species from tropical and warm temperate regions of the Old World. *Olea* is the classical Latin name for olive.

Olea europaea
Olive

Native habitat unclear.

Habit A medium-sized evergreen tree with an open crown; to 30 feet tall.

Inflorescence Axillary or terminal heads, 2–2½ inches long; flowers ¼–½ inch long, greenish-white to cream, sweet scented. Blooms March to April.

Fruit An ovoid drupe, fleshy around a hard, stony pit, ½–¾ inch long, dark brown to purplish-black when ripe.

Twigs Thin, brittle, light gray, with faint ridges extending from the leaf scar down the twig, these sometimes resulting in an angular appearance.

Bark Smooth, becoming cracked and roughened into small plates when older, light gray to blackish.

Leaves Opposite, simple; narrowly oblong-elliptic, 1–4 x ⅓–⅔ inches; apex sharp-tipped; margins entire, tending to roll under; gray-green to shiny dark green above, with a dense covering of silvery or yellow-brown scales underneath, midrib translucent yellow when held up to the light; tending to droop on slender petioles.

Notes *O. europaea* has a long history in human cultures; olive stones have been found in archeological excavations dating to 3700 BC near the Dead Sea. The origins of the species have been lost, and there is some disagreement over whether the "wild olive" to be found in the Middle East is in truth indigenous to the area or has naturalized from the domesticated plant. The species exhibits wide variation, and numerous species and varieties have been described. Recent analysis, however, has combined all of these variants into four subspecies. *O. europaea* subsp. *europaea* is the domesticated olive, and the other three "wild types" are distinguished by, among other things, geographical location. *O. europaea* subsp. *europaea* was first introduced to Santa Barbara County by Fr. Junipero Serra's Franciscan missionaries. The original orchard was located on the Bixby Ranch along the

Top: Tall, constrained crown and multiple branches of Olea europaea.
Bottom left: Creamy flowers with yellow stamens; dark green leaves with silvery gray lower surfaces.
Bottom right: Fruit maturing to dark purple-black.

Jalama drainage. Molecular analyses of these trees indicate that they represent a cultivar previously lost to the contemporary world of olive culture. In addition to its fruit, olive bark and leaves have been used to treat colic, eye infections, and as a gargle for sore throats. The species name *europaea* means from Europe.

Locations Common throughout town. Extensive street tree plantings along Olive Street, on South Ontare Road, and in the 200–600 blocks of De la Guerra Street. The trees in Mission Park between Alameda Padre Serra and Los Olivos Street have special signifance. A plaque in the park indicates that they were "planted by the Garden Club of Santa Barbara and Montecito as a memorial peace offering to victory in the World War—1914 to 1918."

Phillyrea

Phillyrea is a genus of four species distributed from Madeira Island in the North Atlantic to northern Iran. The genus uses the classical Greek name for one of its species. The name is derived from the name given by Theophrastus to the linden tree and refers to the similarity of their leaves.

Phillyrea latifolia
Mock privet

Widespread in the Mediterranean region.

Habit An evergreen shrub or small tree with multiple stems and somewhat pendulous branches; to 25 feet tall.

Inflorescence Axillary, short racemes, to $3/4$ inch long; flower small, less than $1/8$ inch long, white or tinged purple, consisting of a four-lobed calyx and four-lobed corolla with 2 exserted yellow stamens. Blooms in February.

Fruit A small fleshy drupe, $1/4$ inch across; blue-black, waxy, with a pointed apex from the persistent style.

Twigs Thin, greenish-brown and pubescent, turning light brown and lenticellate.

Bark Pale to dark gray, finely fissured into small squarish blocks.

Leaves Opposite, simple; ovate, $2/3$–$1 1/4$ x $1/4$–$2/3$ inches; leathery, shiny dark green above, paler beneath; margins serrate; petioles less than $1/5$ inch, slightly pubescent.

Notes The species name *latifolia* means broad-leaved.

Locations Two trees in lower Orpet Park near the west steps.

Top: Small flowers and dark green leaves of **Phillyrea latifolia**.
Bottom: Glossy leaves and blue-black fruit.

Phytolaccaceae

The Pokeweed Family includes 17 genera and 72 species and is found in tropical and subtropical regions of the world. Its greatest diversity is found in the New World tropics where the family is believed to have originated. Although several species contain toxic principles, the young foliage of some is eaten as greens.

Phytolacca

A genus of 25 species from tropical and warm regions of the world. Several of its species are highly poisonous. *Phytolacca* combines the Greek *phyton* (plant) with the modern Latin *lacca,* which in turn is derived from the Hindi *lakh* (the dye obtained from insects in the family Lacciniferae). This refers to the staining juice of the berries, which has been used to enhance the color of red wine.

Phytolacca dioica
Umbu, ombu

Grows as prominent isolated individuals in grasslands of Argentina, Uruguay, and Brazil, where it is frequently the only tree species present.

Habit A fast-growing, large, semi-deciduous to deciduous tree with a thick trunk and a massive base; to 50 feet tall.

Inflorescence Dioecious; a raceme, 4–8 inches long; flowers without petals, creamy white. Blooms March to May.

Fruit A yellow-green berry, 1/4–1/3 inch across, held in long pendulous clusters, becoming purple at maturity.

Twigs Stout, dull green becoming light brown, somewhat chaotically curved, appearing warty from raised leaf scars.

Bark Smooth, light brownish-gray.

Leaves Alternate, simple; oval-elliptic, 4–6 inches long, margins entire, secondary veins strongly pinnate; petiole stout, purple-red 1 1/2–3 inches.

Notes Although not native to that land, Hawaiian culture holds that anyone who walks under the ombu must watch out for evil magic. The wood of the tree is particularly brittle, and all parts of the plant are toxic. Over most of its range *P. dioica* holds its leaves throughout the year; however, in colder regions and in our area

Top: Simple leaves with reddish petioles and elongate floral racemes characterize **Phytolacca dioica.** *Bottom: Long fruit clusters maturing to yellow.*

it tends to lose its leaves during the winter months. The species name *dioica* means dioecious.

Locations A large tree at the Santa Barbara Zoological Gardens. Another on the grounds of Lotusland along with a specimen of the hybrid *P. dioica* x *weberbaueri*.

Pittosporaceae

The Pittosporum Family consists of ten genera and about 200 species that are native to the warmer regions of the Old World. The greatest diversity of the family is found in Australia and Oceania.

Hymenosporum

Hymenosporum is a genus with only a single species and is distinguished from *Pittosporum* by the presence of winged seeds. The genus name reflects this by combining the Greek *hymen* (membrane) and *spora* (seed).

Hymenosporum flavum
Sweetshade, *frangipani*

Native to New Guinea, and Queensland and New South Wales, Australia.

Habit An erect, slender, evergreen tree; to 40 feet tall.

Inflorescence Terminal clusters of usually 16 flowers, to 8 inches across; peduncles and pedicels slightly hairy; flowers yellow or cream tinged with yellow, becoming reddish with age; $1 1/4$–$1 3/4$ inches long, basal portions of petals erect, falsely appearing to be fused into a tube, terminal portions reflexed; petals silky hairy on the outside. Blooms March to May.

Fruit A round capsule, 1–$1 1/2$ inches long, on a short stalk; smooth-walled and two-valved; silky hairy, becoming less so with age; pedicels frequently persistent into the following year; seeds flat round, surrounded by a $1/8$-inch wing, $1/2 \times 3/8$ inch.

Twigs Orangish-gray, becoming dull gray.

Bark Light gray, flaking in very small plates to reveal a cinnamon-brown inner bark.

Leaves Alternate, simple, crowded towards the ends of twigs; obovate, 3–$6 \times 2/3$–$1 3/4$ inches; often hairy beneath, primarily along the raised midrib; leathery; dark glossy green, becoming curled and wrinkled.

Notes The species name *flavum* means yellow.

Locations Three trees at MacKenzie Park near the Youth Center. Others in Alice Keck Park Memorial Gardens and Willowglen Park. Street trees in the 1500–1600 blocks of Garden Street, 1900 block of De la Vina Street, and on Diblee Avenue.

Top: Open crown of Hymenosporum flavum *in full flower.*
Bottom left: *Yellow and cream flowers together with glossy dark green leaves.*
Bottom right: *Fruit capsules displaying winged seeds.*

Pittosporum
Cheesewood

This genus includes some 150 species distributed throughout the tropical and subtropical regions of the Southern Hemisphere, except South America. Its species contain a rich variety of chemicals which have many uses in native cultures, ranging from childbirth aids to fish poison and witchcraft. The intense fragrance of its flowers is attributable to the essential oils it produces. *Pittosporum* combines the Greek *pitta* (pitch) and *spora* (seed), in reference to the sticky, resinous coating of the seed.

Pittosporum crassifolium
Karo

Found in forest margins and streamsides of the North Island, New Zealand.

Habit An evergreen shrub or small tree with a narrow compact crown of ascending or erect branches; to 25 feet tall.

Inflorescence Monoecious; in terminal umbels of 5–10 male or 1–2 female flowers; flowers heavily scented; petals 5, narrow, dark red, 1/2 inch long, strongly recurved. Blooms in January.

Fruit A woody capsule with a persistent style; roundish, 3/4–1 1/4 inches long, densely hairy; valves usually 3; peduncle to 2/3 inch long, lying close to the stem; seeds shiny black, embedded in a dark honey-colored glutinous gel.

Twigs Dull, light gray to gray-brown, densely hairy.

Bark Pale to dark gray or brownish; usually smooth.

Leaves Alternate, simple, clustered at the ends of twigs; obovate to elliptic, 2–3 x 3/4–1 inches, shiny green above, whitish pubescent below, margins slightly rolled under, very leathery; petioles stout, light green, to 3/4 inch long, covered with dense white hairs.

Notes This species hybridizes readily with *P. tenuifolium* in the wild. Variegated forms also occur. The species name *crassifolium* means thick-leaved.

Locations Single trees at the east end of lower Orpet Park, in the east section of Franceschi Park, and in the Santa Barbara Cemetery near the offices.

Top: Dark green obovate leaves and dark red flowers of Pittosporum crassifolium.
Bottom: Fruit capsules displaying black gelatinous seeds; whitish pubescent lower surfaces of leaves.

Pittosporum floribundum
Himalayan pittosporum

Widely distributed in southern India and Madagascar.

Habit A small evergreen tree with a narrow crown; to 40 feet tall.

Inflorescence Usually terminal and much-branched clusters containing numerous small yellowish flowers. Blooms March to May.

Fruit Capsules round, 1/4 inch in diameter, dark brown; valves 2; containing no more than 4 dark- to orange-red seeds.

Twigs Light gray with obvious lenticels.

Bark Thin, greenish-gray, with obvious lenticels.

Leaves Alternate, simple, crowded at the ends of the twigs; lanceolate to oblong, margins sometimes undulating, apex usually acute, 2 1/2–5 x 3/4–1 1/2 inches; thin and leathery, shiny dark green above, pale green beneath.

Notes The species name *floribundum* means many-flowered.

Locations A single specimen in upper Orpet Park east of the center steps above the lawn. Smaller individuals in Franceschi Park along Franceschi Road above the entry and along the #8 fairway at the Santa Barbara Golf Club. A street tree on the west side of the 2100 block of Garden Street.

Top: A young tree of **Pittosporum floribundum.**
Middle: Inflorescences with small yellowish flowers; dark green obovate leaves.
Bottom: Orange fruit maturing dark brown accompanied by revolute-margined leaves.

Pittosporum phylliraeoides
Weeping pittosporum, narrow-leaved pittosporum, willow pittosporum, desert willow

Native to eastern Australia and areas away from the coast of Queensland, New South Wales, and Victoria.

Habit A graceful evergreen tree with a narrow open crown of pendulous twigs, to 30 feet tall.

Inflorescence Axillary or terminal, usually simple; flowers five-parted, 1/4 inch long, light yellow or cream tinged with yellow, basal portions of petals erect and falsely appearing to be fused into a tube, terminal portions reflexed; pedicel 1/8 inch long. Blooms February to March.

Fruit A round and laterally compressed capsule, 1/2–3/4 inch across, light orange at maturity, opening by two valves to expose rusty-red sticky seeds; pedicel 3/8–1/2 inch long.

Twigs Thin, yellow-green turning reddish-brown.

Bark Brownish-gray with horizontal lenticels, becoming checkered with cracks near the base.

Leaves Alternate, simple; linear-lanceolate, 3–4 1/2 x 1/4 inches, apex elongate and frequently curved into a slight hook, midvein prominent below, thick and leathery, dull yellowish- to dark green; petiole 3/8–1/2 inch long, yellow-green.

Notes In the absence of flowers and fruit, *P. phylliraeoides* looks quite similar to *Geijera parviflora*. While all of the pittosporums are drought-tolerant, this species is well-known for its xerophytic qualities. The species name *phylliraeoides* means similar to *Phillyrea*, in reference to the leaves of *P. angustifolia*.

Locations Four trees as foundation plantings against a commercial building in the 400 block of Santa Barbara Street.

Top: Narrow, thin crown of Pittosporum phylliraeoides.
Bottom left: Pendulous twigs with yellow flowers and orange fruit.
Bottom right: Fruit with rusty-red seeds; stem with linear leaves.

Pittosporum rhombifolium
Queensland pittosporum, diamond leaf pittosporum

Native to New South Wales and Queensland, Australia

Habit A small evergreen tree with a rounded crown; to 40 feet tall.

Inflorescence In dense terminal clusters; petals white, 1/4 inch long, spreading from below the middle. Blooms in August.

Fruit A round capsule, 1/4 inch in diameter, yellowish-orange; seeds black.

Twigs Tan with orange lenticels, becoming gray.

Bark Smooth, gray.

Leaves Alternate, simple, clustered in groups at the ends of twigs; diamond-shaped, usually 1 1/2–4 x 3/4–2 inches; margins irregularly toothed along upper part, lower portion entire.

Notes This is an extremely variable species and hybridizes extensively with *P. colensoi*. It is a very pleasant mid-sized tree; however, it is also susceptible to the unsightly sooty mold that grows on the honeydew produced by aphids feeding on the tender leaves and twigs of new growth. The species name *rhombifolium* means diamond-shaped leaves.

Locations Occasional. Trees on Constance Avenue between Anacapa and Santa Barbara Streets. Another in West Alameda Plaza. An exceptionally large tree at the entrance to the old Sexton House on Hollister Avenue in Goleta.

Top: Open, rounded crown of Pittosporum rhombifolium.
Bottom left: Inflorescence and diamond-shaped leaves with serrations along upper margins.
Bottom right: Dense cluster of yellowish-orange fruit.

Pittosporum tobira
Tobira, Japanese pittosporum

Native to coastal forests below 600 feet elevation in Japan, China, and southern Korea.

Habit An evergreen spreading shrub or small tree with a dense rounded crown; to 20 feet tall.

Inflorescence In terminal clusters, downy with soft whitish or brownish hairs, with a whorl of leaves or bracts at the base; flowers fragrant, white, about 1/2 inch long. Blooms March to April.

Fruit A roundish capsule, swollen at each joint, covered with sparse light hairs, valves 3, not woody, containing several small red seeds.

Twigs Usually several in a cluster from the end of the previous year's growth, dully light gray-brown, lightly hairy.

Bark Light gray or brownish, speckled with lenticels.

Leaves Alternate, simple, on long shoots or crowded at the ends of twigs; obovate, 2–4 x 1/2–1 2/3 inches, tapering towards the base, rounded at the apex, dark green above with sparse white hairs, paler beneath, midrib prominent beneath.

Notes This species was the first introduction of the genus to European botanists. It was collected by Engelbert Kaempfer in 1690 to 1692; he initially described it under the genus *Tobira.* Kaempfer was a German physician who traveled extensively throughout the Middle East and Asia from 1683 to 1693. The species name *tobira* is derived from the Japanese *tobera,* meaning "door tree."

Locations A tree in Franceschi Park east of the cottage. Trees in Alice Keck Park Memorial Gardens.

Top: Dense, rounded and broad crown of Pittosporum tobira.
Middle: Inflorescence of white flowers.
Bottom: Green fruit with red seeds and leathery dark green obovate leaves.

Pittosporum undulatum
Victorian box, mock orange, orange pittosporum, sweet pittosporum

Native in lowland forests and scrub lands of the eastern side of the North Island, New Zealand.

Habit A medium-sized evergreen tree with a dense rounded crown; to 60 feet tall.

Inflorescence In terminal clusters; petals 5, pale white, 1/2 inch long; flowers with a strong fragrance of orange blossoms. Blooms February to March.

Fruit A round capsule with a persistent style; 1/2 inch in diameter, bright orange when mature, valves 2; seeds rusty-red, sticky.

Twigs Maroon, turning green then gray, with obvious longitudinal lenticels.

Bark Gray brown, smooth, slightly roughened by corky lenticels.

Leaves Alternate, simple, sometimes clustered at the ends of the twigs, frequently in groups of 3 to 6; ovate-oblong, usually 2 1/2–6 x 2 3/4–1 2/3 inches, leathery; margins wavy; dark green above, lighter below, midrib prominent below; petiole initially maroon and hairy, turning pale green and glabrous.

Notes *P. undulatum* is commonly used in barrier plantings in Santa Barbara. In some parts of the world it has become an aggressive invader, a characteristic that is only somewhat muted here. The species name *undulatum* means wavy-leaved.

Locations Several trees in West Alameda Plaza. Others in Orpet Park. Street trees on Micheltorena Street from Chapala Street to Highway 101, in the first–600 blocks of East Sola Street, and in the 100–300 blocks of West Micheltorena Street.

Top: Dense, upright crown of Pittosporum undulatum.
Middle: White flowers and pale green under surface of leaves.
Bottom: Orange fruit and dark green leaves with wavy margins.

Pittosporum viridiflorum
Cape pittosporum, *kasuur*

Native to southern Africa from the Cape of Good Hope to northern Zimbabwe.

Habit An evergreen open-crowned tree; to 40 feet tall.

Inflorescence In terminal, branched heads with supplementary inflorescences in the axils of the upper leaves; flowers small, greenish-white to cream, somewhat fragrant. Blooms in March.

Fruit A round capsule with a persistent style, 1/3–1/2 inch across; yellowish- to creamy brown; valves 2; seeds 2–4, bright red-orange, in a sticky resin.

Twigs Somewhat stout and coarse, dull gray.

Bark Roughened by horizontal lenticels, brownish-gray.

Leaves Alternate, simple, crowded at the ends of twigs; variable in size and shape; usually obovate to broadly oblanceolate, 1–4 x 3/4–2 inches, apex rounded or indented; dark green to bluish-green, dull or rather glossy; midrib inset from above, prominent below, reticulation dense in small polygons, lighter than the blade, best observed with the leaf backlit by the sun; margins slightly rolled under, especially along the sides.

Notes The species is highly variable and has previously been divided into several intergrading species. The bark of this species is said to have medicinal properties and has been used by native peoples for stomach complaints. The species name *viridiflorum* means green-flowered.

Locations A tree in La Mesa Park, another in Upper Orpet Park east of the center steps.

Top: Cream-colored flowers and glossy dark green leaves of Pittosporum viridiflorum.
Bottom: Revolute leaves surrounding dark brown fruit with red seeds.

Platanaceae

The Plane Tree Family includes only one genus consisting of six species. It is restricted to the temperate and subtropical regions of the Northern Hemisphere. Although the seeds of this family are light and can be wind-dispersed, the main mode of dissemination is by floating in the water of the streams along which the species grow. The multitude of hairs arising from the base of the seed resemble a fisherman's dry fly and aid in keeping the seed afloat.

Platanus

Platanus is a genus of about eight species from the Northern Hemisphere. The classical Greek name for *P. orientalis* was *platanos*.

Platanus racemosa
Western sycamore

Found along watercourses in the Sacramento Valley, the foothills of the southern Sierra Nevada, the South Coast Ranges and Southern California, and southward into northern Baja California.

Habit A large open deciduous tree with massive branches; to 100 feet tall.

Inflorescence Monoecious; inconspicuous, developing with the leaves. Flowers in late spring.

Fruit A globose fruit containing small dry seeds, to 1 inch across, usually 3–5 per peduncle; ultimately breaking apart to release the light brown, hairy seeds.

Twigs Zigzag, somewhat dull greenish-brown; buds conical, to 3/8 inch long, covered with 1 visible scale, dull reddish-brown, resinous, covered entirely by the base of the petiole of the subtending leaf, hence entirely surrounded by the leaf scar when deciduous.

Bark Olive-green to creamy, exfoliating in large, puzzle-like patches, becoming gray at the base.

Leaves Alternate, simple; 4–10 inches long; three- or five-lobed, sinuses extending 1/2–2/3 of the length of the blade, margins with many small teeth; medium to dark green; may be very hairy becoming progressively glabrous at maturity; petiole 1–3 inches, very hairy; stipules frequently surrounding the twig and remaining as a free-turning wheel after the leaves have dried and abscissed.

Notes The London plane tree (*P.* x *acerifolia*)

Top: Open crown and flaking smooth bark of **Platanus racemosa**.
Bottom left: Stipules surround twigs at base of each leaf.
Bottom right: Palmately lobed leaf and raceme of seed aggregates.

is a hybrid of special concern. Believed to be a hybrid between the eastern North American *P. occidentalis* and the Old World *P. orientalis*, it has been planted extensively in Santa Barbara, giving rise to concerns that gene flow is strongly influencing native populations of *P. racemosa*. *P.* x *acerifolia* is distinguished by its shallow sinuses extending only half the length of the blade, its glabrous leaves lacking persistent stipules surrounding the twig, and the veins ending in obvious bristle-tips at the margin of the leaf. The species name *racemosa* means raceme.

Locations Common. Several large trees at the east end of the Bird Refuge. Others at the west end of MacKenzie Park and along Mission Creek at the Santa Barbara Botanic Garden and the Santa Barbara Museum of Natural History. A special tree is in the courtyard of a restaurant in the 5500 block of Hollister Avenue in Goleta. It has plaques commemorating it as a witness tree at the time of the land grant of Rancho de la Goleta to Daniel A. Hill in 1846 by Gov. Pio Pico, the last Governor of Mexican California, and as having been alive at the time of the signing of the American Constitution.

Proteaceae

The Protea Family includes about 80 genera and 1,700 species that are almost entirely restricted to the Southern Hemisphere. Its greatest diversity is found in Australia and southern Africa. Like the Ericaceae, members of this family are noted for their strong preference for acidic soils. Although many efforts have been made, the more showy members of the Proteaceae have failed to grow vigorously in the basic (non-acidic) soils of Santa Barbara.

Banksia

Banksia is a genus of 73 species all but one of which are endemic to Australia. The genus is named for Sir Joseph Banks (1743–1820), President of the Royal Society and Director of the Royal Botanic Gardens, Kew.

Banksia integrifolia
Coast banksia, white honeysuckle, honeysuckle oak

Native to coastal zones of eastern Australia from Victoria to northern Queensland. Frequently occurring close to the ocean in exposed locations.

Habit An evergreen tree with a somewhat narrow, open crown; to 40 feet tall.

Inflorescence An erect terminal spike, 2–5 x 2–3 inches; flowers pale yellow, becoming bronzed with age, pistils exserted curving down and then out, 1–1 1/2 inches; flowers attracting some nectar-seeking birds. Flowers March to April.

Fruit Woody spikes, 3–6 x 3–3 1/2 inches; often only a few follicles maturing to carry seed.

Twigs Rusty-brown and lightly pubescent in the first year, becoming gray-brown.

Bark Roughly fissured; light gray, with orange showing in the fissures.

Leaves In apparent whorls of 3–5, although older leaves sometimes appearing alternate due to internodal extensions; narrowly oblong, to 6 x 3/4 inches; margins entire or sometimes with scattered teeth; dark green above, silvery white tomentose below; midvein rusty-tan on both sides.

Notes This is the largest-growing and one of the most variable of the banksias. A prostrate cultivar has been developed in Australia. The species name *integrifolia* means with entire or uncut leaves.

Locations Two trees on the campus of the University of California, Santa Barbara, east of the Biological Sciences greenhouses. Another at the southeast corner of the Geological Sciences Building.

Top: Silvery green crown and yellow inflorescences of Banksia integrifolia.
Bottom left: Flower spikes and leathery dark green leaves with silvery lower surface.
Bottom right: Fruit spikes with scattered seed follicles.

Banksia verticillata
Granite banksia

Isolated populations found on granitic outcrops on the southern coast of Western Australia.

Habit A dense evergreen shrub or small tree; to 15 feet tall.

Inflorescence Terminal, subtended by a whorl of branches and somewhat hidden in the foliage; cylindrical, 3–8 x 2–2½ inches; flowers golden yellow, 1–1¼ inches long with a protruding curved style. Flowers November to December.

Fruit A gray cone of smooth tomentose follicles, most of which do not mature, 3–8 x ½ inches.

Twigs Tannish, minutely pubescent; becoming reddish-gray and smooth.

Bark Gray, roughened by shallow fissures.

Leaves Whorled, usually in fours, sometimes scattered; simple, narrowly elliptic to oblong, apex obtuse, 4–8 x ¼–½ inches; margins with small recurved teeth on the apical end; shiny dark green above (bright green on new growth), white wooly tomentose below.

Notes The species name *verticillata* means whorled.

Locations A single specimen in upper Orpet Park, just west of the lower center steps.

Banksia verticillata *showing narrow leaves with silvery lower surfaces and spikes of golden yellow flowers.*

Grevillea

Grevillea is a large genus consisting of 261 species, 254 of which are endemic to Australia. The remaining few are to be found in Sulawesi, New Guinea, and New Caledonia. Seeds of some species are ant-dispersed and have wings rich in lipids and protein; however, the seeds themselves are protected by cyanide. The genus is named for Charles Francis Greville (1749–1809), a founder of the Horticultural Society of London and a Vice-President of the Royal Society.

Grevillea robusta
Silky oak, silk oak tree

Grevillea robusta originates in a limited area of coastal rain forest in southern Queensland and northern New South Wales, Australia.

Habit A pyramid-shaped evergreen tree with an open crown; to 50 feet tall.

Inflorescence Two-several terminal racemes on short leafless branches; racemes 4 inches long, appearing one-sided with the flowers facing up; flowers in pairs, on pedicels 1/2 inch long; perianth orange-yellow, consisting of 4 tepals less than 1/2 inch long, anthers inserted in the tips of each tepal, stigma cone-shaped, on a one-inch style. Flowers March to May.

Fruit Boat-shaped, two-seeded follicle, less than 1/2 inch long, with a persistent one-inch-long style, dull brown; seeds brown, flat, with shiny center surrounded by papery wing.

Twigs Silky pubescent with rust-colored hairs; vegetative buds without protective scales, covered with rusty-brown hairs; leaf scars flattened, with three prominent clusters of vascular bundles.

Bark Hard, furrowed to give a lace-like pattern, gray with a reddish-brown undertone, inner bark pink.

Leaves Alternate, pinnately compound, 6–10 inches long; leaflets 11–23, lanceolate, entire or lobed on apical margin, margins recurved, apices with a small abrupt tip; leaflets sometimes deeply bobed, especially towards the base of leaf; upper surface light green with obvious, coarse reticulation, lower surface densely silky pubescent; rachis slightly winged between the leaflets.

Notes The timber was once used extensively for cabinets and furniture. Unfortunately, its attractiveness has led to excessive cutting in the rain forests of its origin. In its native forest it does not occur in pure or nearly pure stands; instead, individuals are widely scattered among other species. Today, *G. robusta* is used throughout the world in forest plantations and agroforestry. The species name *robusta* means strong, robust.

Location Common, several trees along the Garden Street side of East Alameda Park and in the 1200 block of Anacapa Street. The Arlington Silk Oak is on the west side of State Street in the 1300 block. Several trees have been planted at interchanges of Highway 101.

Top: Narrow, dense crown of **Grevillea robusta**. *Bottom: Cluster of yellow-orange flowers, dark brown fruit, and pinnately compound leaves.*

Hakea sauveolens
Needle bush, sweet-scented hakea

Native to granitic outcrops in southern Western Australia.

Habit An evergreen shrub or small tree with ascending branches and a needle-leaved "piney" appearance; to 20 feet tall.

Inflorescence Axillary cylindrical to globular racemes, 1/2–1 inch long, near the tips of branches; flowers dense on the rachis, small, 1/8 inch long, white, sweetly scented. Flowers December to January.

Fruit An oval woody capsule, 1 inch long, grooved on one side with two small horns near the apex, pale brown to grayish with darkish spots.

Twigs Ascending to spreading, shiny reddish-brown.

Bark Dark green.

Leaves Alternate, pinnately compound, 3–5 x 2–3 1/4 inches; segments round to flat, apices sharply pointed; rachis grooved on top, with scattered white hairs.

Notes *H. sauveolens* has been widely planted throughout the world. Unfortunately, it is an effective invader and has become a noxious weed in South Africa. The species name *sauveolens* means sweet-smelling, sweet-scented.

Locations A small street tree in the 800 block of La Cumbre Road, another in the 3400 block of Madrona Drive, and others on Shoreline Drive opposite Leadbetter Beach.

Clusters of white flowers, spotted woody fruit, and compound leaves with round to narrowly linear segments of Hakea sauveolens.

Macadamia

Macadamia is a genus of twelve species—ten endemic to Australia and two from New Caledonia. The genus is named to honor John Macadam (1827–1865), a chemist and medical lecturer in Melbourne, Australia.

Macadamia integrifolia
Macadamia ternifolia

Macadamia nut, Queensland nut

Native to the rain forests of southeastern Queensland, Australia.

Habit A moderate-sized evergreen tree with an uneven, dense crown; to 40 feet tall.

Inflorescence Axillary, raceme, 4–12 x $3/4$–$1 1/4$ inches; flowers creamy white or pinkish, small, $1/3$–$1/2$ inch long, style protruding well beyond the perianth. Flowers December to January.

Fruit Globular, 1–$1 1/2$ inches; rind thick, green, becoming brown to dark brown, containing 1 hard-shelled seed; seed smooth, shiny, light brown, $3/4$–1 inch in diameter.

Twigs Creamy gray, lenticellate.

Bark Light gray; smooth, slightly roughened by dense pale corky horizontal lenticels.

Leaves Mostly in whorls of 3; oblong with a rounded apex, 2–6 x 1–2 inches; margins usually entire, slightly undulating, juveniles slightly serrate; thick, leathery, glossy dark-green, reticulation dense.

Notes The species name *integrifolia* means with entire or uncut leaves.

Locations Frequent in private gardens. A tree in West Alameda Plaza. Street trees in the 900 block of West Islay Street.

Top: Unkempt crown of **Macadamia integrifolia**. *Bottom: Leathery leaves, raceme of white flowers, and globular fruit.*

Stenocarpus

Stenocarpus is a genus of 25 species from the western Pacific Ocean region. Eight species are endemic to Australia. The genus name combines the Greek *stenos* (narrow) and *karpos* (fruit), in reference to the flat, narrow fruit.

Stenocarpus sinuatus
Queensland fire-wheel tree, wheel of fire

Native to the rain forests of eastern Australia from northern New South Wales to northern Queensland, extending to Papua New Guinea.

Habit An evergreen tree with an irregular narrow crown; to 30 feet tall.

Inflorescence Terminal or in upper leaf axils, umbels of 6–20 flowers in a wheel-like arrangement; flowers elongate, 1–1 1/2 inches long, bright red with a globular yellow apex; producing a wonderfully sweet tasting nectar. Flowers November to January.

Fruit A cylindrical follicle, 2–4 inches long; grayish-brown, with short rusty hairs.

Twigs Brown, pubescent, lenticellate.

Bark Gray to grayish-brown; with shallow vertical furrows.

Leaves Alternate, simple; variable, entire to deeply pinnately lobed, frequently with lobes towards apex, 6–15 inches long with lobed leaves longer than entire ones; margins wavy; thick, leathery, dark glossy green above, paler with a raised midrib beneath; petiole 1/2 inch long.

Notes *S. sinuatus* produces a wonderfully sweet nectar, the amount of which suggests that its natural pollinators are birds. The species name *sinuatus* means with wavy margins.

Locations Increasingly common throughout town. Street trees on West Arrellaga Street between State Street and Bath Street. Others on Padre Street between Garden Street and Laguna Street, Casiano Drive, and Grand Avenue.

Top: Dense cylindrical crown of Stenocarpus sinuatus. *Middle: Wheel-like inflorescences of red flowers; wavy-margined leathery leaves in background. Bottom: Fruit cluster with persistent style.*

Rhizophoraceae

The Mangrove Family includes about 15 genera and 130 species. It is found worldwide in warm temperate and tropical regions and is noted for the ability of many of its species to grow in brackish or saline waters along coastlines, often as the dominant components in "mangrove" vegetation. The roots of those species have specialized morphology that enables them to store oxygen for use during high tide. They are also capable of excluding uptake of salt.

Cassipourea

Cassipourea is a genus of about 40 species from tropical America and tropical and South Africa. The genus name is derived from the native name for trees of this group.

Cassipourea gummiflua var. *verticillata*
Cassipourea verticillata

Gummy onionwood

Found in the coastal zones of eastern South Africa.

Habit A small to medium-sized evergreen tree with a dense crown of upright stems and pendulous branches; to 30 feet tall.

Inflorescence Axillary clusters along the twigs; flowers about 1/4 inch across, with 5–7 white-fringed petals and up to 14 conspicuous stamens, on short pedicels. Flowers in November.

Fruit A roundish capsule, 1/4–1/3 inch long, yellowish-green when mature; with a lobed calyx and a conspicuous persistent style; seeds with a yellow aril.

Twigs Reddish, slightly angled, especially near the nodes.

Bark Gray- to reddish-brown; smooth with lenticels, becoming fissured.

Leaves Usually in whorls of 3 (sometimes whorls of 4 or in pairs), simple; oval or oblong, 2 1/2–6 x 1 1/2–3 1/2 inches; leathery, yellowish-green to dark green above; margins usually entire, sometimes with shallow rounded teeth, slightly revolute on the basal half; midrib prominent below, yellow, lateral veins about 9 pairs which branch and loop near the margin; petiole and young leaves reddish.

Cassipourea gummiflua *var.* verticillata *showing slender reddish twigs bearing young fruit with persistent styles; simple leaves with opposite placement.*

Notes This species is very attractive to bees and ants due to gummy secretions from the axils of the stipules. Its wood has a distinct onion smell when cut. The species name *gummiflua* means gummy sap.

Locations A single tree at Franceschi Park behind the house.

Rosaceae

The Rose Family includes approximately 100 genera and over 3,000 species. Its greatest diversity is in the temperate and subtropical regions of the Northern Hemisphere.

Eriobotrya

Eriobotrya is a genus of 26 species extending from the Himalayas to eastern Asia and western Malaysia. The name is derived from the combination of the Greek words *erion* (wool) and *botrys* (cluster of grapes) and refers to the dense wooly, clustered panicles.

Eriobotrya deflexa
Bronze loquat

Native to low elevation forests of Taiwan and southeastern China.

Habit An evergreen small tree with a densely branched crown; to 20 feet tall.

Inflorescence Terminal panicles, rusty tomentose; flowers $2/3$ inch across, the 5 sepals rusty tomentose and the 5 petals white, with numerous stamens and 3 styles. Flowers January to February.

Fruit A fleshy pome, $2/3-1$ inch long, skin velvety yellow-green, turning brown, crowned with a persistent calyx.

Twigs Stout, dull red, turning light gray.

Bark Slightly roughened, brownish- to blackish-gray.

Leaves Alternate, simple, crowded at the ends of the twigs; ovate to elliptic, $5-10 \times 1^{3}/4-2^{1}/4$ inches, leathery, bronze-red when young, becoming dark green above, paler beneath, glabrous on both surfaces when mature, margins coarsely serrate; 13–15 pairs of lateral veins, raised on both surfaces; petiole $1-1^{3}/4$ inches long, blade extending as wings halfway along the petiole.

Notes Although related to the following species, the fruit of *E. deflexa* is not edible. The species name *deflexa* means bent abruptly downwards.

Locations Common. Trees in the first blocks of West and East Ortega Street, in the 1400-1600 blocks of Mountain Avenue, on Terni Lane in Hidden Hills, and on Calle Real west of Patterson Avenue.

Top: Wide crown with bronze young foliage of Eriobotrya deflexa.
Middle: Terminal inflorescence and leathery dark green leaves with coarse serrations.
Bottom: Small fleshy fruit and bronze young foliage.

Eriobotrya japonica
Loquat

Native to China and Japan.

Habit A rounded bushy evergreen tree; to 30 feet tall.

Inflorescence Terminal panicles, 3-6 inches long; flowers 3/4 inch across, with 5 yellowish-white petals, the pedicel and calyx densely covered with brown velvety pubescence. Flowers in November.

Fruit An oblong fleshy pome with a persistent calyx at the apex, 1 1/2 inches long, apricot-colored when ripe, borne on a stout pubescent peduncle.

Twigs Stout, wooly.

Bark Smooth, light gray.

Leaves Alternate, simple, crowded at the ends of the twigs; ovate to elliptic, usually 6–9 x 3–4 inches, but may be larger on vigorous shoots, leathery, dark glossy green above, covered with dense brown wool beneath, margins coarsely serrate; with several pairs of parallel pinnate veins 1/4–1/2 inch apart, inset from above; petiole very short and wooly.

Notes The species name *japonica* means from Japan.

Locations Frequent in yards about town. A small tree in East Alameda Plaza adjacent to the playground. Two trees in Franceschi Park between the main house and the cottage. A street tree in the 1700 block of Santa Barbara Street.

Top: Broad, rounded crown of Eriobotrya japonica. *Middle: Terminal inflorescence covered with dense brown velvety pubescence; leathery dark green leaves. Bottom: Apricot-colored fleshy fruit.*

Lyonothamnus

Lyonothamnus is composed of a single species from the Channel Islands of Southern California. The name is derived from that of W. S. Lyon (1851–1916), an American collector who sent specimens to Asa Gray (renowned American taxonomist) and refers to the perceived shrubby character of the plant (*thamnos*—shrub).

Lyonothamnus floribundus subsp. *aspleniifolius*
Santa Cruz Island ironwood

Found only on Santa Cruz, Santa Rosa, and San Clemente Islands of Southern California.

Habit A narrow upright evergreen tree with an open crown; to 45 feet tall.

Inflorescence Terminal flat-topped panicles, 3-6 inches across; flowers white, 1/4 inch across. Flowers May to June.

Fruit Composed of 2 brown woody follicles, 1/8 inch across, with a persistent calyx.

Twigs Angular, green, becoming deep red-brown.

Bark Gray- to reddish-brown, peeling in strips and flakes.

Leaves Opposite, palmately to pinnately compound, 4–8 inches long; leaflets 3–9, linear, 2–4 1/2 x 1/2–5/8 inches, cut into segments resembling those on a spleenwort fern.

Notes The species (*L. floribundus* subsp. *floribundus*), found on Santa Catalina Island, is similar in all regards except for its simple, entire leaves. However, in their native localities there is considerable gradation among the two extremes. Dr. Francisco Franceschi was quite taken with the Santa Cruz Island ironwood and tried without success to propagate it from seed. He finally resorted to digging a mature tree in order to propagate it from sprouts. His trip to the island was a success, but on the return voyage his boat was set upon by the Coast Guard, who suspected him of running rum. In the ensuing chase, the boat was fired upon, and Dr. Franceschi's sons found themselves bailing in order to stay afloat. Upon reaching the safety of the Santa Barbara harbor, our horticultural forbearer was able to identify himself and his purpose, which was far from smuggling. In 1935 the Board of Supervisors adopted *Lyonothamnus floribundus* as the official tree of Santa Barbara

Top: Open crown and several stems of **Lyonothamnus floribundus** *subsp.* **aspleniifolius**.
Bottom: Pendulous inflorescence of white flowers; compound leaves with deep lobing of leaflets.

County. The species name *floribundus* means abundant flowers; *aspleniifolius* means with spleenwort-like leaves.

Locations Increasingly common about town. Trees at the Santa Barbara Botanic Garden near the entrance and at the library. Others adjacent to the entrance of Rocky Nook Park on Mission Canyon Road. Others in lower Orpet Park below the lawn and on the south side of La Cumbre Middle School.

Prunus
Cherries, peaches, plums, apricots, almonds

Prunus is a genus of over 200 species of deciduous and evergreen shrubs and trees from temperate regions, especially northern Europe and extending into high-elevations in the tropics. The name is the classical Latin name.

Prunus armeniaca
Armeniaca vulgaris
Apricot

Native to northern China.

Habit A rounded deciduous tree with an open crown and multiple stems; to 30 feet tall.

Inflorescence Axillary, solitary, on previous year's growth, often crowded on short spur twigs; flowers 1 inch across, white or pinkish, calyx red-brown. Flowers in March.

Fruit A round drupe, to 2 inches across, skin maturing to orange with a reddish tint, velvety pubescent; stone smooth with a thickened furrowed margin.

Twigs Glossy, red-brown.

Bark Brown-gray, with broad flat lenticellate plates and shallow rough fissures.

Leaves Alternate, simple; broadly ovate, apex elongate, $2^{1}/_{2}$–$3^{1}/_{2}$ x $1^{1}/_{2}$–2 inches long; margins finely serrate; deep lustrous green; petiole reddish, to 1 inch long, often with 2 or more glands near the leaf base.

Notes *P. armeniaca* is believed to have been cultivated in China for over 2,500 years, gradually spreading west over trade routes. The species name *armeniaca* means from Armenia.

Locations A single tree in Franceschi Park above the entrance road.

Branch of Prunus armeniaca *with finely serrate, broadly ovate leaves with red petiole.*

Prunus campanulata
Bell-flowered cherry, Taiwan cherry

Native to southern China, Taiwan, and Japan's Ryukyu Islands.

Habit A small deciduous tree; to 30 feet tall.

Inflorescence Axillary clusters of 2–6 flowers on 1- to 1½-inch peduncles; petals deep rose, ¾ inch across, on ½- to ¾-inch pedicels. Flowers January to February.

Fruit A flesh-coated drupe with a large stone, ½ x ⅜ inch, glabrous, red when mature.

Twigs Dull reddish-brown to gray, with numerous lenticels; buds frequently in pairs, divergent, dark reddish-brown, to ⅓ inch long.

Bark Dark gray with horizontal grain and lenticels, cracking vertically.

Leaves Alternate, simple; ovate to oval, apex elongate, 2½–4 x 1–1¾ inches; margins with fine forward-pointing teeth; shiny dark green, glabrous; veins 6-8 pairs; petiole ½–¾ inch long, with 2 prominent glands at the base of the blade.

Notes The species name *campanulata* means bell-shaped flowers.

Locations Street trees in the 2900 block of Calle Noguera and the 800 block of East Yanonali Street. Trees in Alice Keck Park Memorial Gardens near the corner of Arrellaga and Santa Barbara Streets.

Top: A multiple-stemmed Prunus campanulata *in full flower before leaf-out.*
Bottom: Bell-shaped flowers and finely serrate leaves.

Prunus caroliniana
Carolina cherry-laurel

Native to the coastal plain of the southeastern United States, from Virginia to Texas.

Habit A small evergreen tree with an oval crown; to 30 feet tall.

Inflorescence Axillary racemes, 1 1/2–3 x 3/4–1 inches; flowers five-petaled, white, with a heavy sweet fragrance. Flowers February to March.

Fruit A fleshy drupe, 3/8–1/2 inch across; turning lustrous dark black, frequently masked by the foliage.

Twigs Reddish, becoming brownish, with a distinct odor of Maraschino cherries when bruised.

Bark Smooth, dark gray to almost black.

Leaves Alternate, simple; oblong to lanceolate, 2–3 x 3/4–1 inches, apex sharp, margins entire or toothed towards the apex; lustrous dark green; petiole slender, sometimes with 2 very small glands at base of the blade, red in sun, green in shade.

Notes The species name *caroliniana* means from the Carolinas.

Locations Street trees on La Marina north of Cliff Drive and Eileen Way. Others in 400 and 500 blocks of Consuelo Drive and the 600–800 blocks of West Valerio Street. A single tree near the front entrance to Santa Barbara Junior High School on Cota Street.

Top: Dense, rounded crown of **Prunus caroliniana.**
Middle: Racemes of small white flowers together with dark green leaves.
Bottom: Dark black fruit and lustrous leaves with entire margins.

Prunus cerasifera 'Atropurpurea'
Prunus cerasifera subsp. *pissardi*

Cherry plum, myrobalan plum, Pissard plum

Originating in Iran, probably as a mutant. First introduced to western culture in 1880 by Mr. Pissard, gardener to the Shah.

Habit An upright, densely branched deciduous tree with a rounded crown; to 30 feet tall.

Inflorescence Axillary, usually solitary flowers; flowers light pink, $1/3$ inch across, with a heavy sweet fragrance. Flowers February to March.

Fruit A fleshy drupe, 1 inch across, reddish.

Twigs Thin, deep red in the first year, turning gray, with 1–3 lateral buds sitting on raised leaf scars.

Bark Thin, reddish-gray with small horizontal lenticels.

Leaves Alternate, simple; ovate, to obovate, $1 1/2 – 2 1/2 \times 1 – 1 1/4$ inches, apex somewhat pointed; margins finely round-toothed, veins to 6 pairs; ruby-red initially, turning dark reddish-purple, glabrous above, pubescent along the midrib and veins beneath; petioles $1/2$ inch long, glands present or not at the base of the blade.

Notes Three additional varieties of *Prunus cerasifera* exist in the nursery trade—'Krauter Vesuvius,' 'Newport,' and 'Thundercloud.' 'Krauter Vesuvius' is named for Carl Krauter, who introduced the variety to Bakersfield in 1950. The species name *cerasifera* means bearing cherries or cherry-like fruit; *atropupurea* means deep purple.

Locations Street trees on Calle Noguera and Vista de la Cumbre adjacent to Peabody School. Others in the 3600 and 3700 blocks of San Remo Drive. A plantation of trees in the northeast clover leaf of the Fairview Avenue/Highway 101 interchange.

Top: Springtime flowering branches of **Prunus** *cerasifera 'Atropurpurea'.*
Bottom left: Flowers with pinkish centers.
Bottom right: Dark reddish-purple, finely toothed leaves.

Prunus dulcis
Prunus amygdalus
Almond

Ancestral stock thought to be native to southwestern Asia, the Balkans, and perhaps North Africa.

Habit A deciduous tree with erect branches becoming bushy; to 30 feet tall.

Inflorescence Axillary, solitary or in pairs on the previous year's growth; flowers 1–2 inches across, nearly sessile, petals pale rosy pink or white, calyx bell-shaped with 5 rounded lobes and pubescent to margins, appearing before the leaves. Flowers March to April.

Fruit A non-fleshy drupe; ovate, 1½–2½ inches long; shell velvety pubescent; stone lightly pitted.

Twigs Upper half reddish, lower half greenish, smooth, shiny but with a somewhat grainy appearance, with raised leaf scars.

Bark Gray-brown, with horizontal grain and lenticels, broken with vertical cracks, becoming rough.

Leaves Alternate, simple; lanceolate with a somewhat elongate apex, 3–5 x ¾–1½ inches; margins finely toothed; light green, glabrous; petiole with 2–4 glands, to 1 inch long.

Notes Several ornamental varieties of *P. dulcis* exist, none of which bears edible nuts. Species *dulcis* means sweet.

Locations Small trees in Alice Keck Park Memorial Gardens adjacent to Arrellaga Street.

Top: Springtime flowering branches of **Prunus dulcis.** *Bottom: Lanceolate leaves and velvety pubescent young fruit.*

Prunus ilicifolia
Holly-leaved cherry, *islay*

Native to the Coast Ranges of California from Mendocino County south to Baja California, also found on the islands of Southern California and Baja California.

Habit An evergreen shrub or small bushy tree; to 20 feet tall.

Inflorescence Axillary, racemes 1 1/2–3 inches long; flowers 1/3 inch across, white, very short-stalked. Flowers June to July.

Fruit A fleshy drupe; roundish but slightly pointed at the end, 1/2–2/3 inch across; green changing to red, then black-purple.

Twigs Angled, green becoming red-brown.

Bark Smooth, light to dark gray.

Leaves Alternate, simple; ovate, 1–2 x 3/4–1 1/2 inches; margins rounded between widely spaced spines, wavy; blade stiff leathery, shiny dark green; petiole 1/6–1/2 inch long.

Notes A closely related subspecies, *Prunus ilicifolia* subsp. *lyonii* (formerly *P. lyonii*) is found naturally on the Channel Islands and is characterized by greater overall height (to 35 feet), larger leaves to 5 inches long, with nearly entire and flat leaf margins and thinner and lighter green blades, longer petioles (1/2–1 inch), and longer inflorescences (to 5 inches). The lack of spines on the leaves of the island populations may be an interesting example of plant adaptation. Spines and thorns are generally viewed as having evolved as a mechanism of protection against plant herbivory. However, *Prunus ilicifolia* subsp. *lyonii* has long grown in a habitat where native herbivores do not forage on its foliage. This has led to speculation that in the absence of herbivory, the selective pressure for maintaining spiny leaves was lost. The species name *ilicifolia* means holly-like leaves.

Locations Santa Barbara Botanic Garden; also growing wild throughout the foothills and mountains above Santa Barbara.

Top: Dense, shrubby crown of Prunus ilicifolia *subsp.* lyonii.
Middle: Long raceme of small flowers and glossy smooth-margined leaves.
Bottom: Dark red fruit and discolorous leaves.

Prunus laurocerasus
Common cherry-laurel, English laurel

Native to southeastern Europe and Asia Minor.

Habit A large evergreen shrub or small tree with a dense crown; to 20 feet tall.

Inflorescence Axillary racemes, 2–5 x 3/4 inches; flowers five-petalled, white, 1/4–1/3 inch across, with a heavy sweet fragrance. Flowers in March.

Fruit A small fleshy drupe, 1/3–1/2 inch long, purple to black.

Twigs Stout, green becoming grayish-brown.

Bark Smooth, gray-brown.

Leaves Alternate, simple; oblong, 2–6 x 1/3–1/2 inches, margins obscurely serrate or almost entire, leathery, lustrous medium to dark green; petiole 1/2 inch long, channeled above, with 2 glands at the base of the blade.

Notes The species name *laurocerasus* means laurel-cherry.

Locations Tall shrubs on the northeast side of Stow House, Goleta.

Top: Upright inflorescence and slightly serrate, leathery leaves of Prunus laurocerasus.
Bottom: Black fruit and leathery leaves.

Prunus persica
Peach

Native to China, but cultivated for so long that its exact origins remain unknown.

Habit A small deciduous tree with a low, broad rounded crown; to 25 feet tall.

Inflorescence Axillary, solitary or in pairs, on growth of previous year; flowers 1–1 1/2 inches across, petals pink or red, sepals pubescent on the exterior side. Flowers in February.

Fruit A fleshy drupe; roundish, 2–3 inches across, skin velvety hairy, yellowish-tinged with red on the sunny side; stone with furrows and pits.

Twigs Upper part reddish, lower part greenish, smooth shiny but with a somewhat grainy appearance, with very raised leaf scars.

Bark Gray-brown, with horizontal grain and lenticels, broken with vertical cracks, becoming rough.

Leaves Alternate, simple; elliptic-lanceolate, broadest in the middle, apex elongate, 3–6 x 3/4–1 1/2 inches; margins finely toothed; glabrous, dark green; petioles grooved, 1/2 inch long, with 2 prominent glands at the base of the leaf blade or on the lower margin.

Notes The species name *persica* means Persian or peach.

Locations Three trees in Alice Keck Park Memorial Gardens adjacent to Arrellaga Street. A tree in the roundabout on Weldon Road.

Top: Prunus persica *in full springtime flower with dark gray-brown bark.*
Middle: Twig densely covered with pink flowers.
Bottom: Young, light green lanceolate leaves.

Pyrus
Pears

Pyrus is a genus of about 25 species centered in Eurasia, especially Armenia. The genus at one time included many more species, which are now placed in *Malus* and *Sorbus*. It now includes only those species which contain extrafloral nectaries and sclerenchyma cells in the flesh of the fruit, lending its characteristic gritty texture. There are now over 1,000 cultivars of edible pears, some of which date back to the Neolithic and Bronze Ages. The name is the classical Latin name for pear.

Pyrus calleryana
Callery pear

Native to Korea and China.

Habit A fast-growing deciduous, pyramidal tree; to 25 feet

Inflorescence Dense axillary corymbs, 3 inches across; flowers 3/8–3/4 inch across, white, appearing in spring with or before the leaves, with a strong odor; when in full flower, the tree is a striking mass of white.

Fruit A small rounded pome, no more than 1/2 inch across, russet-colored; although numerous, usually lost in the foliage.

Twigs Stout, brownish, sometimes with ridges from the base of the leaf scar; usually white wooly pubescent becoming glossy brown at maturity; buds ovoid, terminals and laterals of approximately the same size, to 1/2 inch long, very wooly, gray to gray-brown.

Bark Lustrous gray-brown on young growth; somewhat ridged, furrowed, and dull grayish-brown later.

Leaves Alternate, simple; broad-ovate, 1 1/2–3 inches long and across; apex elongate, base flat, margins irregularly round-toothed; glabrous, leathery, dark green with a light green midrib; petiole 1 1/2 inches long, light green.

Notes *P. calleryana* was originally introduced to bring fireblight resistance to *P. communis,* the edible pear. While this was never successful, the species produced numerous cultivars of horticultural interest. In the last 20 years the 'Bradford' cultivar of *P. calleryana* has taken urban landscapes (especially sidewalk plantings) of much of the eastern United States by storm.

Top: Flowering twig and young leaves of **Pyrus** calleryana.
Bottom: Dark green mature leaves with long petioles.

Its fast growth and prolific flowers heralding the beginning of spring have tempted numerous less discriminating homeowners and developers. Unfortunately, its tendency to branch prolifically at eye-level along sidewalks and break apart in moderate winds, as well as its short life, has left many neighborhoods in the East with a monoculture of not particularly desirable trees. The species name *calleryana* honors Joseph Callery (1810–1862), French missionary and botanical collector who discovered the species in 1858.

Locations Trees in the first block of East Anapamu Street, the 500 block of La Marina, and the 100 block of San Antonio Road.

Pyrus kawakamii
Evergreen pear

Native to China and Taiwan.

Habit An evergreen or only briefly deciduous tree, with twisted branches and an open crown; to 30 feet tall.

Inflorescence Few-flowered clusters on short spur shoots; flowers white with a glabrous calyx. Flowers January to February.

Fruit A fleshy pome; round, 1/2 inch across; glabrous with tan lenticels; peduncle 1–1 1/4 inches, red.

Twigs Reddish-gray, with tan lenticels.

Bark Dark brown-black, frequently with a grayish tint, becoming broken into small squares or rectangles with age.

Leaves Alternate, simple; often clustered in groups of 3–4 on the ends of short spur shoots; ovate to obovate, 2 1/2–4 x 1 3/8–2 1/8 inches long, margins serrate; leathery, glabrous, lustrous dark green, developing red splotches in the fall, midrib red; petiole 1–1 3/4 inches long, red.

Notes In addition to the above species, *Pyrus communis* (the common pear) is found in some gardens. It is distinguished, of course, by its much larger edible fruit, but also by more ovate or elliptical leaves with rounded base and apex and more obvious serrations. The young leaves can be quite downy underneath. The species name *kawakamii* is named for a city in central Japan.

Locations Several trees in the parking lot adjacent to City Hall on Anacapa Street. Others on the west side of Ferrara Way and Palermo Drive in Hidden Valley.

Top: **Pyrus kawakamii** *in full springtime flower.*
Bottom: Flower clusters and finely serrate ovate leaves.

Quillaja

Quillaja is a genus of three species from the temperate zone of South America. *Quillaja* is the Chilean name for the tree.

Quillaja saponaria
Soapbark tree, *quillaja*

Endemic to a restricted foothill region of Chile south of Santiago, characterized by a moist Mediterranean climate, and extending from sea level to 5,000 feet.

Habit A slender evergreen tree; to 45 feet tall.

Inflorescence Terminal corymbs; flowers creamy white, 1/2 inch across, with 5 petals and 5 leathery pubescent sepals. Flowers May to June.

Fruit A rosette of 5 leathery follicles, 3/4 inch across, with a persistent calyx, each follicle dehiscing into 2 valves.

Twigs Light brown with minute gray lenticels, becoming light gray, somewhat zigzag; buds small, yellow-green.

Bark Dark gray, with longitudinal furrows appearing to spiral around the stem.

Leaves Alternate, simple; broadly elliptic, 3/4–1 2/3 x 1/2–1 inches, leathery, shiny yellowish-green, margins entire or sparingly toothed along the apical half, apex notched, sessile.

Notes Soapbark tree is favored in Chile by bees, which produce a dark honey from its pollen. The bark is very rich in saponins and is exported to Europe and Asia for medicinal and cosmetic uses. The species name *saponaria* means with a soapy characteristic.

Locations A tree in West Alameda Plaza near Santa Barbara Street. Street trees in the first and 100 blocks of Castillo Street, the 1500–1700 blocks of La Coronilla Drive, and the 800 block of Dolores Drive.

Top: Loose, somewhat narrow crown of Quillaja saponaria.
Middle: Creamy flowers with narrow petals and yellow stamens.
Bottom: Dehiscent leathery fruit and leathery dull green leaves.

Rutaceae

The Rue Family includes approximately 160 genera and 1,600 species. It is found in tropical and subtropical regions around the world, but is also conspicuously abundant and diverse in the warm-temperate and Mediterranean-climate portions of Australia and South Africa. The family is well-known for its numerous fruits. The leaves of almost all members are dotted with translucent oil-bearing glands, and are used to produce pharmaceuticals. One species produces an alkaloid that is used to treat glaucoma.

Calodendrum

Calodendrum is a genus of two species from East Africa and extending to the Cape of South Africa. Its name combines the Greek words *kalos* (beautiful) and *dendron* (tree), which it certainly is.

Calodendrum capense
Cape chestnut

Broadly spread in tropical and southern Africa, from sea level to the mountainous interior.

Habit A briefly deciduous tree with a pyramidal crown that becomes spreading at maturity; to 40 feet tall.

Inflorescence Terminal, panicle; flowers large and showy, to 1 3/4 inches across; sepals 5, appearing as petals, linear, curved down, hairy, rich rose-pink; stamens 5, petal-like, held upright, marked with crimson or purple glandular dots. Blooms in March.

Fruit A woody capsule with a knobby surface, opening by 5 valves; seeds small, jet black, angled, oily.

Twigs Gray-green, initially minutely hairy, with numerous lenticels.

Bark Gray, smooth.

Leaves Opposite, simple; oval or oblong, apex bluntly pointed or round, 2–9 x 1 1/4–4 inches; dark green with scattered translucent glandular dots, initially hairy beneath; margins entire, wavy; midrib and many pinnate veins very conspicuous on the under side of the leaf.

Notes The seeds of this tree were believed by native hunters to have magical properties and bring them skill and luck. However, the species is known primarily for its spectacular show of flowers in early to midsummer. The species name *capense* means from the Cape of Good Hope, South Africa.

Locations Street trees in the 3700 block of Portofino Way. A young tree was planted in lower Orpet Park on October 13, 2000 in memory of Santa Barbara public safety officers who have lost their lives in the line of duty. Another young tree in Alice Keck Park Memorial Gardens.

Top: Rounded crown of Calodendrum capense *in full flower.*
Bottom left: Lacy flowers with narrow petal-like sepals and long stamens.
Bottom right: Fruit with knobby surface and dark green simple leaves.

Casimiroa

Casimiroa is a genus of five species from the Central American highlands. The genus is named for Cardinal Casimiro Gomez de Ortega, a Spanish botanist of the late 18th century.

Casimiroa edulis
White sapote, Mexican apple

Native to the tropical highlands of Mexico and Central America, above 3,500 feet.

Habit An evergreen tree; to 40 feet tall

Inflorescence Terminal or axillary clusters; flowers small, five-parted, yellow-green, inconspicuous. Blooms January to February.

Fruit Roundish, 2½–5 inches across, somewhat five-lobed; skin thin, light green; whitish flesh containing many yellow oil glands that lend a gritty characteristic to the flesh.

Twigs Angled, purplish-gray, with short white hairs, becoming gray and lenticellate in the second year.

Bark Light gray, smoothish, but with warty lenticels.

Leaves Alternate, palmately compound with usually 5 leaflets; leaflets lanceolate, 3–4½ x ¾–1¼ inches, margins faintly serrate, light green, densely dotted with translucent glands, midrib yellow-green, prominent below; petiole to 2½ inches long, faintly hairy.

Notes *C. edulis* was introduced into Southern California by the Franciscans in 1810. The fruit is sweet with a slightly bitter after-taste resulting from several alkaloids. These alkaloids have numerous useful qualities, including insecticidal and effective soporific properties. Although the fruit is edible, the seeds are fatally toxic if ingested by humans or animals. The sap of the tree has been used in the manufacture of chewing gum. The species name *edulis* means edible.

Locations Planted in numerous yards through town; a large tree in a yard at Modoc and Mission; a street tree in the 600 block of West Cota Street.

Top: Rounded crown of Casimiroa edulis.
Middle: Minute yellow-green flowers.
Bottom: Large, light green fruit and palmately compound leaves with lanceolate leaflets.

Citrus

Citrus is a genus of about 16 species from Southeastern Asia, extending down the Malay Peninsula. The origins of many taxa remain obscure, but it is generally believed that most of the varieties now cultivated came from ancient hybrids, possibly involving only three recognizable species—*C. maxima, C. medica,* and *C. reticulata. Citrus* is the Latin name for *C. medica.*

Citrus sinensis
Orange, sweet orange

Native to China and Indochina.

Habit An evergreen tree with a rounded crown and somewhat drooping lower branches; to 20 feet tall.

Inflorescence Axillary, in small racemes or solitary; flowers with 5 calyx lobes, 5 white waxy petals, and 20–25 stamens. Blooms year-round.

Fruit Roundish, to $3^1/2$ inches across; with a thin, tight rind surrounding 10–13 locules; familiar orange color.

Twigs Somewhat angled and flexible when young, becoming brittle with age; sometimes with a few short blunt spines in the axils of the leaves; green becoming tannish-gray.

Bark Thin, smoothish; gray-brown.

Leaves Alternate, simple; oblong to lanceolate, $3-4^1/2$ x $1-1^1/2$ inches; somewhat leathery, margins entire or very faintly serrate, usually shiny dark green unless in need of supplemental nitrogen, densely dotted with translucent oil glands on lower surface; petioles jointed at the twig and at the base of the leaf, $1/2$ inch long.

Notes Numerous cultivar selections of *C. sinensis* have been made. While the species is believed to have originated in Southeast Asia, it has been in cultivation for so long that it is no longer known from its wild condition. Several other citrus are grown in the Santa Barbara area, including *C. aurantifolia* (lime), *C. aurantium* (Seville orange, sour orange), *C. limon* (lemon), *C.* x *paradisi* (grapefruit), and *C. reticulata* (Mandarin orange). The jointed and variously winged petioles are believed to be a throwback to the compound-leaf form generally found in the Rutaceae. The species name *sinensis* means Chinese.

Locations Alice Keck Park Memorial Gardens and many gardens throughout town.

Top: Dense, rounded crown of Citrus sinensis.
Middle: White flowers and leathery dark green leaves.
Bottom: Orange fruit, leaves, and flowers.

Fortunella

Fortunella is a small genus of four to five species found in eastern Asia and extending to the Malay Peninsula. It is known primarily for its citrus-like fruit, the kumquat. The genus is named for Robert Fortune (1812–1880), Scottish horticulturist and botanical collector in China.

Fortunella margarita
Nagami kumquat

Believed to be native to southeastern China, but today only known from cultivated material.

Habit A short rounded evergreen tree; to 15 feet tall.

Inflorescence Axillary, solitary or in small racemes; flowers small, five-parted with 16–20 stamens, white, fragrant. Blooms year-round.

Fruit Oblong, to 1 3/4 x 1 1/4 inches, usually composed of 5 sections, rind smooth and spicy aromatic, bright orange.

Twigs Green, becoming streaked with gray lenticels, with decurrent ridges from the leaf nodes.

Bark Smooth, gray-brown, appearing somewhat striped.

Leaves Alternate, simple; lanceolate, 1 1/4–3 1/2 x 3/8–1 1/4 inches; shiny dark green above, lighter beneath, densely dotted with oil glands, aromatic when crushed; petiole stout, slightly winged, 1/4–5/8 inch.

Notes *Fortunella* is closely related to *Citrus* and was at one time included in that genus. The species name *margarita* means pearl-like.

Locations County Courthouse, near the corner of Anapamu and Anacapa Streets. Young trees at the east end of MacKenzie Park.

Top: Somewhat narrow crown of **Fortunella margarita**. *Bottom: Narrow lanceolate leaves and fruit with smooth orange rind.*

Geijera

Geijera is a genus of eight species from New Guinea, eastern Australia, and New Caledonia. It is named for J. D. Geijer (1687).

Geijera parviflora
Australian willow, sheep bush, *wilga*

Native to the dry interior of eastern Australia.

Habit A small evergreen tree, with upright branches and drooping twigs; to 30 feet tall.

Inflorescence Terminal or in upper leaf axils, many-flowered green panicle; flowers small, less than 1/4 inch across, flower parts 5, petals small, white. Blooms December to January.

Fruit Spherical, less than 1/4 inch across.

Twigs Dull grayish-purple, pendulous.

Bark Smooth gray, wrinkled around branch insertions, becoming shallowly furrowed.

Leaves Alternate, simple; linear, 3–6 x 1/4–3/8 inches; margins entire; thick, waxy; yellow-green; margins and midvein light yellow; midvein raised on lower surface, not so above; densely dotted with minute glands on the upper surface; lateral veins and reticulation obscure; petiole 1/8 inch, or sessile.

Notes The species name *parviflora* means with small leaves.

Locations Increasingly common throughout town. Three trees in front of the Youth Center at MacKenzie Park. Others on Loma Street, in the first blocks of East and West Micheltorena Street, and in the 1800–2000 blocks of Mountain Avenue.

Top: Geijera parviflora, *with lacy crown and pendulous foliage.*
Bottom: Numerous greenish flowers and narrowly linear leaves with distinct midveins.

Sarcomelicope
Bauerella
Acronychia

Sarcomelicope is a genus of six species from eastern Australia and Fiji. Its name combines three Greek roots (*sarco*—fleshy, *meli*—honey, *kope*—division) and refers to the four nectaries at the base of the fleshy fruit.

Sarcomelicope simplicifolia
Bauerella simplicifolia
Acronychia baueri
Scrub yellow-wood, yellow aspen

Widespread in the rain forests of eastern Australia, from northern Queensland to southeastern New South Wales.

Habit A small to medium-sized evergreen tree; to 20 feet tall.

Inflorescence Monoecious; axillary, few-flowered clusters, $3/4$–$1 1/2$ inches long; flowers small, $1/2$ inch across, yellow-green, fragrant. Blooms June to July.

Fruit A round drupe, $1/2$ inch across.

Twigs Light tan-gray.

Bark Smooth with minute cracks, tannish-gray.

Leaves Opposite, simple; elliptic or ovate, $2 1/3$–5 x $3/4$–$1 1/2$ inches; thin, dark green; strongly pinnately veined with interconnections near the margin, densely dotted with fine oil glands in the areoles of the venation; aromatic when crushed; petiole flattened on top, light tan-gray.

Notes The species name *simplicifolia* means with simple leaves.

Locations A single tree in upper Orpet Park east of the lower center steps.

Thick, leathery dark green leaves and small yellow-green flowers of Sarcomelicope simplicifolia.

Tetradium
Euodia

The genus *Tetradium* consists of nine species that have recently been separated from an all-inclusive genus, *Euodia*. The genus occurs from the Himalayas to Japan and south to eastern Indonesia. Its name comes from the Greek *tetradion,* meaning quarter and alluding to the four-parted floral characteristic of the type species.

Tetradium daniellii
Euodia daniellii
Euodia hupehensis
Evodia hupehensis

Bebe tree, bee bee tree

Broadly spread in the central regions of China and Korea.

Habit A moderately sized deciduous tree with a broad crown; to 35 feet tall.

Inflorescence A large terminal panicle, to 7 x 12 inches; flowers five-parted, small, white. Blooms June to July.

Fruit A cluster of 2–5 follicles, tapering into a narrow beak, $1/4$–$1/2$ inch long, dull purplish-red, each follicle containing 2 black seeds.

Twigs Dull gray, with scattered lenticels and large leaf scars; buds brownish pubescent.

Bark Smooth, dull gray.

Leaves Alternate, pinnately compound, with 4 lateral leaflets and a terminal leaflet, 6–17 inches long; leaflets broadly ovate to lanceolate, 2–$7 1/2$ x 1–4 inches, margins entire to somewhat scalloped, deep green above, somewhat silvery beneath.

Notes *Tetradium danielli* is well-known for attracting honey bees. The species name *daniellii* honors William Freeman Daniell (1818–1865), British pharmacist and botanist, Assistant Surgeon for the British Army in Africa, India, and China, and plant collector in these locations for the Royal Botanic Gardens at Kew.

Locations A single tree in Franceschi Park immediately east of the cottage.

Top: Tetradium daniellii, *with compound leaves and large terminal inflorescence of small white flowers.* Bottom: *Small pinkish-red fruit and dark green leaflets with pale green midribs.*

Vepris

Vepris is a genus of 15 species of the Old World tropics and subtropics, from South Africa to the Mascarene Islands. The name is derived from *vepres* (briar).

Vepris undulata
White ironwood

Found along the eastern margin of southern Africa facing the Indian Ocean from near Cape Town, South Africa to Mozambique.

Habit   An evergreen shrub or small tree; to 45 feet tall.

Inflorescence   Terminal panicles, 1–5 inches long; flowers small, yellowish-green, inconspicuous in the foliage. Blooms July to August.

Fruit   Small, roundish, leathery, four-lobed, to 1/4 inch across; black when mature.

Twigs   Thin, green, turning brownish-gray.

Bark   Smoothish, brownish-gray to dark gray.

Leaves   Alternate, palmately trifoliate; leaflets lanceolate, sessile, 2–4 x 1/2–1 2/3 inches, densely gland-dotted, pinnate veins looping and connected near the margin, margins entire, wavy, light green; strongly lemon-scented when crushed; petiole thin, 1 1/2 inches long.

Notes   The powdered roots of this species were used in some folk herbals to treat influenza. Ignoring the compound leaves and long, thin petiole, the undulating leaflet margins and bark of this tree are strongly reminiscent of *Pittosporum undulatum*. The species name *undulata* means wavy-leaved.

Locations   A single tree in West Alameda Plaza.

Top: Light crown and gray trunk of Vepris undulata. *Bottom: Trifoliate leaves with wavy margins of leaflets and inflorescence of small yellow-green flowers.*

Salicaceae

The Willow Family contains just four genera that include about 300 species. It is primarily found in the temperate and boreal zones of the Northern Hemisphere. Salicin, the principle ingredient of aspirin, is found in the bark of almost all species of the family.

Populus
Poplars, cottonwoods, aspens

Populus is a genus of about 35 species from northern temperate regions. Its name is the classical Latin name for poplar.

Populus balsamifera subsp. *trichocarpa*
Populus trichocarpa
Black cottonwood

Broadly distributed in western North America from Alaska to northern Baja California, in alluvial bottoms and streamsides below 9,000 feet.

Habit A deciduous tree with a broad crown; to 90 feet tall.

Inflorescence Dioecious; male catkins 3 inches long, female catkins 4–5 inches long. Blooms March to April.

Fruit Several closely spaced round capsules on the catkin, 1/4 inch across, covered with short hairs, splitting into 3 parts at dissemination; seeds small with a tuft of white silky hair.

Twigs Tan becoming gray, initially covered with short pubescence, then becoming glabrous, with vertical lenticels; winter buds with fine hairs along scale margins, very resinous and fragrant when opening.

Bark Smooth, dull gray on branches, turning black-gray on stems, with deep furrows and interlacing flat-topped ridges, hard, not flaky.

Leaves Alternate, simple; ovate, 1 1/4–2 3/4 inches long, base round to heart-shaped, apex acute to elongate; margins finely scalloped or toothed, especially towards the base; green above, glaucous stained with brown resin beneath; petiole 1/3–1/2 length of blade, lower side round, upper side channeled, sometimes with a pair of glands at base of blade.

Notes The species name *balsamifera* means containing balsam; *trichocarpa* means with hairy fruit.

Top: Leaves and "puff ball" masses of tiny long-haired seed of Populus balsamifera *subsp.* trichocarpa.
Bottom left: Catkins of maroon male flowers.
Bottom right: Finely scalloped ovate leaves in fall.

Locations Naturally occurring trees in the Santa Barbara Botanic Garden, Tuckers Grove on Cathedral Oaks Road, Stevens Park, and along Hot Springs Creek at Mountain Drive, as well as most of the perennial streams flowing from the Santa Ynez Mountains.

Populus fremontii
Fremont cottonwood, alamo cottonwood, alamo

Native to the southwestern United States, throughout California, but usually below 5,000 feet, and extending to the central Rocky Mountains and into northern Mexico. May grow at some distance from streamsides, suggesting a greater tolerance for dry soils than black cottonwood.

Habit A deciduous tree with a broad crown; to 50 feet tall.

Inflorescence Dioecious; catkins 2–4 inches long. Blooms April to May.

Fruit A small capsule containing numerous minute seeds, each with long white cottony hairs.

Twigs Green, turning tannish-gray, with vertical lenticels; winter buds resinous.

Bark Dull to dark gray, with vertical flat-topped ridges.

Leaves Alternate, simple; broadly triangular with a flat base, apex only slightly elongate, 1 1/4–3 inches long, somewhat broader, margins coarsely round-toothed, without glands at the base, light gray-green on both sides; petiole half the length of the blade or more, laterally flattened.

Notes The natural ranges of *Populus fremontii* and *P. balsamifera* subsp. *trichocarpa* overlap in many places, where hybrids are commonly produced. The species name *fremontii* honors John C. Fremont (1813–1890), explorer of the western United States and discoverer of many trees and shrubs new to science.

Locations A street tree on the corner of Pesetas Lane and La Colina Road. A small grove of trees at the Santa Barbara Golf Club between the #1 and #18 fairways. Others at a business in the 100 block of Gray Avenue. Two others in the Desert Section of the Santa Barbara Botanic Garden were removed in 2003.

Top: *Catkins of red male flowers, twig, and resinous winter buds of* **Populus fremontii**.
Bottom: *Deltoid leaves attached by flattened petioles and edged by coarse round teeth; catkin of female flowers.*

Populus nigra 'Italica'
Lombardy poplar, Italian poplar

Widely planted throughout the world.

Habit A fast-growing, upright, deciduous tree with a somewhat cylindrical crown of tightly ascending branches; to 90 feet tall.

Inflorescence Dioecious; male catkins 2–3 inches long; female trees are not known to exist.

Fruit Not known to produce fruit.

Twigs Slender, round, lustrous brown, frequently turning upright at the ends of pendulous branchlets.

Bark Light gray, hard, with strong interlacing ridges.

Leaves Alternate, simple; triangular-ovate with an elongate apex, 2–4 inches long and wide; margins finely round-toothed, base wedge-shaped, almost entire; dark green above, light green and glabrous beneath; petioles slender, bright red, 3/4–2 1/4 inches long.

Notes *P. nigra* 'Italica' arose as a cultivar in the 17th century in Lombardy, Italy. It rarely reaches its potential height because of a canker disease which starts in the upper branches. Because no female trees are known, propagation is entirely by cuttings. The species name *nigra* means black.

Locations Trees on the corner of Calle Noguera and Calle Alamo Streets. A volunteer tree between Arroyo Burro Creek and Las Positas Road.

Top: Tall, columnar form of Populus nigra *'Italica'. Bottom: Deltoid leaves with elongate apex, dark green above and pale green beneath.*

Salix
Willow

Salix is a genus of about 400 species primarily from the northern temperate zones of North America, Europe, Siberia, and China. It includes the most northerly occurring vascular plant, *S. arctica,* which occurs at 83ºNorth latitude, is well-known as the origin of aspirin (acetylsalicylic acid), and has long been considered a symbol of chastity due to its spontaneous generation from cuttings. Its name is the classical Latin name for willow.

Salix babylonica
Weeping willow

Originally from central and northern China, introduced to Europe in the 17th or early 18th centuries probably through the silk trade, and now somewhat naturalized throughout many regions of the world.

Habit A deciduous tree with a broad rounded crown and long pendulous branches frequently sweeping the ground; to 60 feet tall.

Inflorescence Dioecious; dense catkins 3/4–1 1/2 inches long, terminating short lateral branches; floral bracts tawny. Flowers in spring with emerging leaves.

Fruit A one-inch-long cluster of valve-like capsules, light brown, containing many fine, cottony seeds.

Twigs Yellowish to yellowish-brown, becoming glabrous but with persistent hairs at the nodes, brittle at the base; buds yellowish or brownish, with lateral ribs, somewhat flattened, covered by a single cap-like scale.

Bark Smooth, greenish-gray, splitting in very shallow but wide brownish fissures.

Leaves Alternate, simple; narrowly lanceolate, 3–5 1/2 x 1/3–3/4 inches, apex elongate, margins finely serrate, glabrous; light green above, grayish-green beneath; stipules rarely present; petiole yellow, densely hairy beneath, flattened, and twisted, grooved above.

Notes *S. babylonica* has been popularly believed to be the Babylonian willow of the Bible (Ps. 137, ver. 1–2) and was one of the *arbor tristes* (mourning trees) planted at tombs as a sign of loss. A cultivar, *S. babylonica* 'Crispa,' with curled leaves is grown in Santa Barbara; however, many other cultivars and hybrids exist. The species name *babylonica* means from Babylon.

Locations A tree in Chase Palm Park near the pond.

Top: *Willowy form of* Salix babylonica. Bottom: *Narrowly lanceolate leaves with dark green upper surface and gray-green lower surface on pendulous twigs.*

Salix lasiolepis
Arroyo willow

Widely distributed from Washington and Idaho to Texas and extending into Mexico.

Habit A deciduous shrub or small tree; to 20 feet tall.

Inflorescence Dioecious; dense catkins, 2/3–3 inches long, sessile or on short leaf shoots to 1/2 inch; floral bracts dark brown; appearing before the foliage. Blooms in February.

Fruit A one- to three-inch-long cluster of valve-like capsules, containing many fine, cottony seeds.

Twigs Yellowish to brownish, hairy becoming glabrous, generally brittle at the base; buds with scale margins fused.

Bark Light gray, with irregular long cracks on larger branches and stems.

Leaves Alternate, simple; lanceolate to oblanceolate, 1 1/2–5 inches long; margins entire to somewhat toothed, slightly rolled under; with white or rusty hairs becoming glabrous and shiny above, glaucous beneath.

Notes The species name *lasiolepis* means with wooly scales.

Locations Common along creeks in the Santa Barbara area. Trees in the Santa Barbara Botanic Garden at the dam and in Arroyo Burro Creek at Cliff Drive.

Fruiting twigs of Salix lasiolepis *with dark green lanceolate leaves that are wooly-white beneath.*

Salix matsudana 'Tortuosa'
Corkscrew willow, dragon's claw willow, Hankow willow

Commonly planted throughout much of central China.

Habit A deciduous tree with a rounded crown of contorted twigs and branches, giving a very gnarly appearance in winter; to 50 feet tall.

Inflorescence Dioecious; dense catkins 1/2–3/4 inch long, terminating short lateral branches. Flowers in spring with emerging leaves.

Fruit A one-inch-long cluster of valve-like capsules, containing many fine, cottony seeds.

Twigs Greenish, turning tan, strongly contorted.

Bark Greenish-brown, bleaching grayish-brown, with very shallow fissures.

Leaves Alternate, simple; linear-lanceolate, 2–4 x 1/3–2/3 inches, wavy and twisted; base rounded, margins toothed, glandular; shiny bright green above, pale green below; petiole 1/4–1/2 inch long, twisted.

Notes Although not unattractive, inspection of each of the parts of the plant inspires nothing less than a "bad hair day." The corkscrew twigs are often used in flower arrangements. The natural distribution of this species is unclear and at least one authority believes that it is synonymous with *S. babylonica*. The species name *matsudana* refers to the city of Ma-tsu, Taiwan.

Locations One tree in Alice Keck Park Memorial Gardens, on the west side of the pond. Several trees planted adjacent to the bike path along Atascadero Creek between Patterson Avenue and Gwyne Avenue.

Top: Lacy and weeping crown of Salix matsudana 'Tortuosa'.
Bottom: Pendent and corkscrew-shaped twigs with discolorous lanceolate leaves.

Sapindaceae

The Soapwort Family consists of 147 genera and over 2,200 species that are found in tropical and subtropical regions of the world. Centers of diversity are found in the Americas and tropical Asia. The family is named for generally high saponin (soap) content of many of its species.

Alectryon

Alectryon is a genus of about 35 species from eastern Malaysia extending to New Zealand and Hawaii. Although not present in Santa Barbara, the genus includes *A. oleifolius,* the rosewood used in finer furniture. *Alectryon* means rooster, and the genus received its name because of the scarlet fleshy covering of the seed and its resemblance to a rooster's comb.

Alectryon excelsus
Titoki, New Zealand oak

Native to lower mountain slopes of New Zealand.

Habit An evergreen tree with stout branches; to 40 feet tall.

Inflorescence Terminal panicles, to 12 inches long; calyx cup-shaped, deeply divided into 5 lobes; corolla lacking; stamens 6–8, carrying large, dark red anthers; rachis, pedicels, calyx, and ovary all densely rusty pubescent. Blooms in January.

Fruit A somewhat woody capsule, 1/3–1/2 inch long; usually winged on one side; densely pubescent; seeds round, lustrous black, partially encased in a scarlet fleshy aril.

Twigs Thin with scattered lenticels, covered with dense rusty down.

Bark Smooth, dark gray.

Leaves Alternate, pinnately compound, with a terminal leaflet, 4–16 inches long; leaflets 4–6 pairs, ovate-lanceolate to ovate-oblong, apex slightly elongate, convex from above, wavy margined, entire or strongly toothed; with 10–12 pairs of pinnate veins, somewhat glossy green with light green pubescent midrib and veins above, densely pubescent with distended midrib and veins beneath; rachis densely rusty pubescent.

Notes The species name *excelsus* means tall, elevated.

Top: Alectryon excelsus, *showing small flowers with dark red anthers and pinnately compound leaves with revolute leaflets.*
Bottom: Pubescent fruit with shiny black seeds in a scarlet aril.

Locations A single tree at Stow House in Goleta. A young tree in front of the Carrillo Recreation Center on Carillo Street. Another in lower Orpet Park above the Survivor Tree and one more on the west side of the 2000 block of Castillo Street.

Cupaniopsis

Cupaniopsis includes about 60 species and is distributed from central Malaysia to eastern Australia. It is named for the genus *Cupani*, honoring Francesco Cupani (1657–1711), a Sicilian monk and botanical author.

Cupaniopsis anacardioides
Tuckeroo, cashew-leaf cupania, carrot wood

Broadly distributed in coastal regions of northern Australia from northern Western Australia to Queensland and extending into northeastern New South Wales.

Habit An evergreen tree with several ascending branches and a rounded crown; to 35 feet tall.

Inflorescence Terminal or axillary panicles, 3–14 inches long, peduncles hairy; flowers inconspicuous, 1/8 inch across, light green, somewhat fragrant. Blooms December to February.

Fruit Roundish, 3/4–1 1/2 inches across, somewhat ridged at the sutures, red-tinged golden-yellow at maturity; valves thick, leathery, pale orange when mature, covered with pale orange hairs inside; seeds 3/8–1/2 inch long, brown to black, covered by a thin orange skin, turning black.

Twigs Stout, light tan-brown, densely covered with white lenticels.

Bark Smooth, light brownish-gray.

Leaves Alternate, pinnately compound without a terminal leaflet, to 12 inches long; leaflets 2–6 pairs, frequently not opposite, obovate to elliptic, 1 3/4–7 1/2 x 3/4–3 inches, acute at the base, apex indented, margins entire, strongly rolled under, leathery, dark green, midvein yellow-green, prominent below.

Notes *C. anacardioides* has been used for street and park plantings around the world. However, although attractive, it has become an unwelcome pest in some regions. In Florida it has been listed on the State List of Noxious Weeds because of its ability to crowd out native species in settings ranging from mangrove and cypress swamps to pine flatwoods. The species name *anacardiodes* means like the Anacardiaceae.

Locations Street trees in the 700 block of Meigs Road, the 1800 block of La Coronilla, and the 200–400 blocks of Laguna Street. Others in the parking lot on the south side of 2900 State Street.

Top: Rounded crown of **Cupaniopsis anacardioides.**
Middle: Dark green foliage and inflorescence of small green flowers.
Bottom: Yellow-green fruit and pinnately compound leaves with notched and revolute leaflets.

Dodonaea

A genus of 68 species, most of which are endemic to tropical Australia. However, representatives exist in tropical America, temperate Africa, and the Pacific. The genus was named to honor Rembert Dodoens (1517–1585), noted Flemish royal physician and herbalist.

Dodonaea viscosa 'Purpurea'
Purple hop-bush, *akeake*

Of horticultural origin. The parent species is extremely broadly spread and is found in Australia but extending to southern Africa, South America, tropical Asia, and New Zealand.

Habit An evergreen shrub or tree with ascending branches; to 30 feet tall.

Inflorescence Mostly dioecious; inflorescence a terminal panicle of inconspicuous flowers. Blooms February to March.

Fruit A two- to four-winged capsule, $1/3$–$1 1/8$ inches across; wings around the seed capsule $1/8$–$1/2$ inch wide, membranous or leathery; often remaining on the tree until the following year.

Twigs Thin, purple in the first year turning light gray, with a faint single ridge extending down from each leaf base.

Bark Creamy gray, fibrous, splitting on older stems to show an orange inner bark.

Leaves Alternate, simple; linear to obovate, $2/3$–6 x $1/2$–$1 2/3$ inches, with the very edge of the margin turned under; shiny green and rough above, turning dark purple-red in winter.

Notes *D. viscosa* 'Purpurea' is one of the most variable species in Australia and contains seven subspecies within that continent alone. Its winged fruit was purportedly used as a substitute for hops in efforts by early settlers in Australia to brew beer. The wood is very hard, and in New Zealand the Maoris used it to make war clubs. The species name *viscosa* means sticky; *purpurea* means purple.

Locations Trees in the El Mercado Shopping Center in the 4100 block of Hollister Avenue. Others on the north side of the Counseling and Testing Center on the campus of the University of California, Santa Barbara.

Bronzed obovate leaves and winged fruit of **Dodonea viscosa** *'Purpurea'.*

Harpullia

Harpullia is a genus of 37 species from Indo-Malaysia to tropical Australia and New Caledonia. The genus name is derived from the Indian name for trees of this group.

Harpullia arborea
Harpullia, *puas*

Broadly distributed in the rain forests of India, Southeast Asia, Australia, and the island archipelagoes of the South Pacific.

Habit An evergreen tree with a dense rounded crown; to 35 feet tall.

Inflorescence Axillary or coming from branches or twigs, panicles 1 1/2–9 inches long; flowers 1 1/3 inches across, whitish-green. Blooms in January.

Fruit On a small stalk; bi-lobed producing a heart-shape with the broadest end at the apex, 2/3–1 x 2/3–2 inches, orange-yellow to red, woody, hairy; seeds shiny black.

Twigs Tannish-brown, hairy, buds small, 1/16–1/8 inch, hairy.

Bark Smooth, light gray with a pinkish undertone, eventually breaking into rectangular plates.

Leaves Alternate, pinnately compound without a terminal leaflet, 1 2/3–9 inches long, rachis lightly hairy; leaflets 3–5 pairs, elliptic to obovate, 4–8 x 1 2/3–3 inches, margins entire, somewhat leathery.

Notes The bark of *H. arborea* is used as a fish poison, a soap substitute, and a pain killer. The species name *arborea* means like a small tree.

Locations A tree in Franceschi Park just below the entrance gate. Another at the University of California, Santa Barbara in the lawn on the south side of Noble Hall.

Top: Rounded crown with many low branches of Harpullia arborea.
Bottom: Greenish-white flowers and pinnately compound leaves.

Koelreuteria

Koelreuteria is a genus of three species from China and Taiwan. The genus is named for Joseph Gottlieb Koelreuter (1733–1806), Professor of Natural History at Karlsruhe, Germany and innovative student of plant hybridization.

Koelreuteria bipinnata
Bougainvillea goldenrain tree, Chinese lantern tree

Broadly distributed in the lowlands of southern and eastern China.

Habit   An upright deciduous tree; to 60 feet tall.

Inflorescence   Terminal upright panicles, 12–24 x 8–18 inches, densely covered with short hairs; flowers small, yellow. Blooms in September.

Fruit   Puffy, papery, three-valved capsules in dense clusters, 1–2 inches long, nearly round, pink to rose when young becoming brownish at maturity, seeds spherical, dark brown, 1/4 inch across.

Twigs   Stout, green turning reddish-brown, densely covered with cinnamon-brown lenticels, leaf scars large.

Bark   Smooth, light gray, broken into small rectangular plates on larger stems.

Leaves   Alternate, bipinnately compound, to 11–12 x 9–16 inches, 8–11 pinnae; leaflets oval to oblong, to 3 x 1 1/2 inches, apex elongate, base symmetrical, margins entire to finely serrate, dull dark green with deeply impressed veins, midvein with short hairs above, hairs longer beneath and frequently in tufts.

Notes   *K. bipinnata* was first introduced to Santa Barbara (and the United States) by Dr. Franceschi. The species name *bipinnata* means bipinnate.

Locations   Several trees in Franceschi Park between the main house and the cottage. Others on Gillespie Street between Anapamu and Mission Streets, on Kimberly Avenue, and in the lower parking lot in the 3800 block of State Street. Young trees at the entrance to Franklin School on Mason Street can be readily compared with four older trees of *K. elegans* in the turf area at the corner of Mason and Soledad Streets.

Top: Rounded crown of Koelreuteria bipinnata.
Middle left: Upright inflorescence and compound leaves with drooping leaflets.
Middle right: Yellow flowers with red centers.
Bottom: Clusters of puffy fruit.

Koelreuteria elegans
Koelreuteria formosana
Koelreuteria henryi

Flamegold

Native to Taiwan and Fiji.

Habit A medium-sized deciduous tree; to 50 feet tall.

Inflorescence A densely flowered terminal panicle, 12–20 x 8–10 inches, densely glandular hairy at flowering; flowers 1/4 x 1/8 inch, yellow, with a slight sweet fragrance, at anthesis petals recurved to reveal a bright orange base. Blooms in September.

Fruit A puffy, papery, three-valved capsule, 1 1/3–2 x 1 1/4–1 3/4 inches, nearly round, deep rose-purple when young, becoming brown at maturity; seeds nearly globose, 1/4 inch across, black.

Twigs Dark green, with numerous small raised corky cinnamon-brown lenticels.

Bark Peeling in small square plates, furrowed vertically; light gray.

Leaves Alternate, bipinnately compound, terminal pinna and leaflets absent or very small, 10–25 x 6–18 inches; leaflets 8–17 on the pinna, strongly asymmetric at the base, lanceolate to elliptic, 2–4 x 1/2–1 1/4 inches, margins entire to irregularly round-toothed, lustrous green above with veins barely noticeable, midvein below may be sparsely hairy.

Notes *Koelreuteria elegans* and *K. bipinnata* can be easily confused but are distinguished when in flower by the five petals of the former and four petals of the latter. The leaflets of *K. bipinnata* are somewhat larger, more coarsely toothed, and less asymmetric than those of *K. elegans*. Although the two native locations of *K. elegans* are separated by almost 4,500 miles, their geography and climates are exceedingly similar and barely distinct. Two subspecies have been described, *K. elegans* subsp. *elegans* (Fiji) and *K. elegans* subsp. *formosana* (Taiwan). The flowers have a pleasant orange blossom fragrance and are attractive to honey bees. The species name *elegans* means neat, elegant.

Locations A lovely tree in upper Orpet Park at the east end of the lawn. Five large trees at Franklin School in the turf area on the corner of Mason and Soledad Streets.

Top: Dense crown and showy inflorescences of Koelreuteria elegans.
Bottom: Inflorescence and bipinnately compound leaves with nearly entire margins and asymmetric bases of leaflets.

Koelreuteria paniculata
Goldenrain tree, bride of India

Found on well-drained soils of mountain slopes, streamsides, and open forests in China, Japan, and Korea.

Habit A medium-sized, deciduous tree with a dense, round crown composed of ascending branches; to 35 feet tall.

Inflorescence Terminal panicles, 12–18 inches long; flowers 1/2 inch across, yellow. Flowers June to July.

Fruit A puffy, papery, 3-valved capsule, 1 1/2–3 inches long, tapering like a cone towards the apex, dark lustrous brown at maturity, containing hard black seeds about 1/4 inch across.

Twigs Stout, buff to light brown; leaf scars large, shield-shaped, raised; lenticels raised, orange-brown; pith solid, white; buds with 2 gray-brown valvate scales, 1/8 inch long.

Bark Very light gray-brown, showing orange within the deeper fissures.

Leaves Alternate; pinnately or bipinnately compound, sometimes with a terminal leaflet, 10–20 inches long; leaflets 11–18, ovate to ovate-oblong with a symmetrical base, 1–4 inches long, coarsely and irregularly serrate with rounded teeth, sometimes deeply lobed at the base; rich green above, pubescent on the veins beneath; leaves and leaflets with an obvious swollen pulvinus at the base of the petiole and petiolules.

Notes *K. paniculata* is often planted around temples and gardens in its native land and holds a sacred connotation because its seeds are used in religious rites. The flowers of this species are used for their medicinal properties and are a source of yellow dye in China. The seeds are often used as beads. The species name *paniculata* refers to the structure of the inflorescence.

Locations Two young trees in Hope Ranch at the corner of Las Palmas Drive and Via Laguna Drive. A single tree in the 700 block of West Victoria Street among several *Koelreuteria bipinnata*. Another single tree in the 500 block of East Cota Street. Several trees in a parking lot in the 900 block of East Haley Street.

Top: Koelreuteria paniculata, *with large showy inflorescences and rounded crown.*
Middle: Terminal inflorescence of many small flowers and compound leaves.
Bottom: Individual flowers and leaflets with coarse serrations.

Sapindus

Sapindus is a genus of 13 species from tropical and warm regions. Its name combines the Latin *sapo* (soap) and *indicus* (Indian), referring to the use of the fruit as a soap by native peoples. It derives ultimately from the Akkadian word meaning "to bathe."

Sapindus rarak
Soapberry

A native of Java.

Habit A deciduous tree with a narrow thin crown of leaves clustered at the ends of long twigs; to 40 feet tall.

Inflorescence Monoecious; terminal panicles, 6–14 inches long; flowers small, 1/4 inch long, pubescent; peduncle yellowish pubescent. Not seen flowering in Santa Barbara

Fruit A leathery berry, 3/4–1 inch long, wrinkled, brown.

Twigs Dull gray; roughened by raised round leaf scars.

Bark Smoothish, light gray.

Leaves Alternate, pinnately compound, with a terminal leaflet and a thin red rachis, to 12 inches long; leaflets 7–15 pairs, oblong to lanceolate, 1 3/4–6 x 2/3–1 2/3 inches, margins entire, midrib red.

Notes The leaves and bark of this species are reputed to have fungicidal properties and have been used as insect repellents in its native land. It has also been used quite successfully in the replanting of degraded forests in Thailand. The species name *rarak* is a botanical name of unknown origin.

Locations A single tree in the upper planting of lower Orpet Park east of the center steps.

Compound leaves of Sapindus rarak *clustered towards the ends of the twigs.*

Sapindus saponaria
Soapberry

Widely distributed from South Florida through the West Indies.

Habit A semi-deciduous evergreen, rounded tree; to 30 feet tall.

Inflorescence Monoecious; terminal panicles of inconspicuous greenish flowers. Blooms December to February.

Fruit One- or two-lobed, giving the sense of separate berries which have been fused together at the base; each lobe round, 3/4 inch across, yellow-brown turning black, leathery, containing a single large black seed.

Twigs Velvety hairy, with large heart-shaped leaf scars; buds velvety, small, 1/8 inch across.

Bark Smooth, light gray.

Leaves Alternate, pinnately compound, without a terminal leaflet, to 15 inches long; leaflets, 3–6 pairs, oblanceolate, 2–6 x 3/4–2 inches, base strongly unequal, bright green above, lightly hairy beneath, margins entire, somewhat wavy, on a short swollen pulvinus-like petiole; rachis minutely winged or appearing ridged, velvety hairy above.

Notes The common name derives from the very soapy characteristic of the leaves and fruit, which have been used as a soap alternative. However, these compounds can cause a severe dermatitis in sensitive individuals. The species name *saponaria* means containing saponins, soapy.

Locations Trees in the 300–700 blocks of Alisos Street. Others in the 600 block of West Ortega Street and the 1200 block of Del Sol Avenue.

Top: Dense terminal inflorescence and compound leaves of Sapindus saponaria.
Bottom: Fruit consisting of one or two bulb-like lobes.

Scrophulariaceae

The Foxglove Family includes about 250 genera and 4,000 species that are most common in temperate regions and tropical mountains throughout the world. However, they extend from tropical coastlines to alpine tundra. The family is the source of digitalin and lanoxin, drugs that are used to treat congestive heart failure, but can be fatal in high doses.

Paulownia

Paulownia is a genus of six species from eastern Asia. It is named for Anna Paulowna (1795–1865), daughter of Czar Paul I of Russia.

Paulownia tomentosa
Princess tree

Native to lowlands, mountain valleys, and foothills of central China below 6,000 feet elevation.

Habit A deciduous tree with a broad crown; to 40 feet tall.

Inflorescence Terminal and axillary; a pyramidal or narrowly conical panicle, to 20 inches long; flowers bell-shaped, 2–3 inches long, purple. Blooms February to March.

Fruit An ovoid glandular capsule, 1–2 inches across, with a persistent style, densely sticky hairy; seeds small winged.

Twigs Densely pubescent, becoming glabrous; green with vertical brown lenticels, becoming light brown; pith punky or diaphragmed.

Bark Smooth, light brownish-gray.

Leaves Opposite, simple; oval, to 10 x 12 inches; margins entire, base cordate, apex slightly elongate, with 5–7 palmate basal veins; abaxial surface densely to sparsely hairy; petiole hairy, 6–8 inches long.

Notes *P. tomentosa* is highly invasive in parts of the eastern United States. The species name *tomentosa* means densely wooly or pubescent.

Locations Trees at Lotusland, in a business planting in the 1100 block of Coast Village Road, on the grounds of the Sexton House on Hollister Avenue in Goleta, and in the 800 block of Roberto Avenue.

Top: Showy inflorescence of tubular flowers of Paulownia tomentosa.
Bottom left: Tan seed capsules after seeds have been shed.
Bottom right: Large oval leaves with palmate venation; terminal inflorescence of flower buds.

Simaroubaceae

The Quassia Family includes 13 genera and about 130 species and is primarily found in the humid lowland tropics around the world. The primary center of diversity is in the tropical Americas. A secondary center is found in West Africa. Members of the family produce a unique bitter compound, quassinoids, that have been shown to be effective in the treatment of amoeboid infections, malaria, and some cancers.

Ailanthus

Ailanthus is a genus of five species found from China to Australia. The name is derived from the native Moluccan name *ailanto* (sky tree), referring to its rapid growth.

Ailanthus altissima
Tree-of-heaven, Chinese sumac

Native to mountainous regions of China between 5,500 and 8,000 feet.

Habit A fast-growing deciduous tree with a spreading crown and often a forked trunk with upright branching; to 50 feet tall.

Inflorescence Dioecious; erect terminal clusters of small, light green flowers. Blooms in June.

Fruit Dense clusters of samaras, each consisting of a long twisted wing surrounding a central seedcase, 1–1½ inches long; turning reddish in the fall and frequently remaining on the tree as a light tan cluster through the deciduous season.

Twigs Stout, reddish-brown, with obvious lenticels; without a terminal bud; lateral buds round, brownish, hairy, sitting on large heart-shaped leaf scars.

Bark Smooth, grayish-red on young stems; becoming dark gray, rough, with lighter brown between the furrows.

Leaves Alternate, pinnately compound with 11–41 leaflets on a stout rachis, 10–30 inches long; leaflets lanceolate, 2–6 inches long, with a basal lobe on one side bearing a warty gland; having a strong, unpleasant odor when bruised.

Notes Tree-of-heaven is well-known for the noxious odor of its foliage and its aggressive colonization of disturbed sites in the eastern United States. It is often seen in urban settings growing from cracks between sidewalks and the foundations of buildings and is becoming a significant invasive exotic in rural areas throughout North America. In California, it is a common occurrence throughout the "gold country" in the foothills of the Sierra Nevada, where it was introduced by Chinese laborers as a reminder of home. The California Exotic Pest Plant Council has listed it as an Exotic Invasive Plant of Greatest Ecological Concern. However, the species does appear to have a number of less malevolent characteristics. A cultivar (*A.* 'Vilmoriniana') has been used as an alternate host to the Chinese silk moth. While initially strong smelling, honey produced from this species is reputed to be delicious upon standing. The species name *altissima* means very tall, tallest.

Locations Several trees along Mission Creek at Valerio Street have naturalized, probably from a nearby yard tree.

Top: Large pinnately compound leaves on a stout rachis and short terminal inflorescences of Ailanthus altissima. *Bottom: Red winged fruit with swollen seed cavity.*

Sterculiaceae

The Chocolate Family includes 67 genera and almost 1,800 species that are widely distributed in temperate and tropical regions of the Southern Hemisphere. It is most noted for the production of chocolate from the fermented seeds of *Theobroma*. Some recent analyses have suggested that the family should be included in the Malvaceae.

Brachychiton
Bottle-trees

Brachychiton is a genus of 31 species, all but two of which are endemic to Australia. The remaining two are found in Papua New Guinea. These monoecious shrubs and trees are dry-season deciduous or evergreen and are typically found on rocky soils in relatively open forests, savannas, and shrublands. The flowers lack petals and consist of a lobed tubular perianth formed from the calyx. The fruit are stout boat-shaped follicles. The leaves are simple and palmately lobed. The name combines the Greek words *brachys* (short) and *chiton* (tunic) and refer to the short overlapping hairs and scales.

Brachychiton acerifolius
Flame tree, flame *kurrajong*

Native to the coastal mountain rain forests of eastern Australia, from northern Queensland to southern New South Wales.

Habit An erect, deciduous tree with an oval crown; to 50 feet tall.

Inflorescence Monoecious; open axillary panicles, to 16 inches long; flowers 3/4–1 1/4 inches long, consisting of a waxy scarlet to crimson calyx tube with 5–6 triangular lobes; petals absent; stamens and stigmas yellow; pedicel 1/4–3/4 inch long, scarlet to crimson; deciduous when flowering. Flowers August to September.

Fruit Follicles boat-shaped, rounded at the base, pointed at the apex, 4–8 inches long; glabrous, leathery, dull dark green-brown outside, tawny hairy inside; seeds 10–20, shaped like kernels of corn, dark brown but covered with tawny yellow hairs.

Twigs Stout, appearing warty from large leaf scars.

Bark Grayish-brown, with very shallow fissures or wrinkles on larger stems; with a very fibrous inner bark.

Top: Erect crown with thickened trunk of **Brachychiton acerifolius**.
Middle left: Large cluster of waxy scarlet flowers.
Middle right: Woody boat-shaped fruit on pink peduncles.
Bottom: Glossy green leaves with deep palmate lobing.

Leaves Alternate, simple; of two forms; with 5–7 deep palmate lobes on younger trees, 4–10 inches long; few-lobed or entire on older larger trees, ovate or diamond-shaped, frequently with palmate venation still present; in either case leathery, glossy dark green on both sides.

Notes The fibrous inner bark of this species was used by native peoples of Australia for making ropes and fishing nets. The species name *acerifolius* means with maple-like leaves.

Locations Street trees in the 1800 block of Mountain Avenue, the 700 and 800 blocks of East Yanonali Street, the 1000 block of Quinientos Street, and intermixed with *B. discolor* in the 400 and 500 blocks of Garden Street.

Brachychiton discolor
Lacebark tree, scrub bottle-tree, pink flame tree

Found in dry subtropical forests of southeastern Queensland and northeastern New South Wales, Australia.

Habit   A rounded semi-deciduous tree with a very stout trunk; to 50 feet tall.

Inflorescence   Monoecious; emerging from the branches, five- to eight-flowered, $2^{1}/_{2}$–$3^{1}/_{4}$ inches long, peduncles brown hairy; flowers $1^{1}/_{2}$–$2^{1}/_{4}$ x 2–$2^{1}/_{2}$ inches, consisting of a tubular calyx with 5 or more reflexed lobes, petals absent, calyx lobes rose-pink, tube darker orange-red. Flowers May to September.

Fruit   Follicles ellipsoid, on a short stalk and with a short beak at the apex, 4–5 x $1^{1}/_{2}$–$1^{3}/_{4}$ inches; densely light brown hairy, containing 30–50 tightly packed yellow seeds.

Twigs   Stout, minutely hairy, gray-green.

Bark   Creamy pale- or green-gray to dark gray, fissured in a lace-like pattern.

Leaves   Alternate, simple, but lobed almost to the middle, 4–8 x 4–8 inches; lobes and veins 5–7, palmate, base heart-shaped; dark green, shiny and glabrous above, pale gray-green and somewhat hairy beneath.

Notes   The adult leaves of *B. discolor* are very reminiscent of *Liquidambar styraciflua* or even *Acer saccharum* in outline. The species name *discolor* means of two different, and usually distinct, colors.

Locations   Street trees in the 3600 block of Foothill Road, intermixed with *B. acerifolius* in the 400 and 500 blocks of Garden Street, and intermixed with *Koelreuteria bipinnata* in the 1200–1900 blocks of Gillespie Street. Trees in the 100–400 blocks of West Cota Street were planted by former Parks Superintendent Finley MacKenzie.

Top: Brachychiton discolor, *with pink flowers and woody fruit covered with light brown hairs. Bottom: Dehisced fruit showing white seeds; dark green palmately lobed leaves with gray-green lower surface.*

Brachychiton gregorii
Brachychiton populneus x *occidentalis*
Desert *kurrajong*

Found in open shrublands and woodlands on sandy soils in arid Australia—Western Australia, South Australia, and Northern Territory.

Habit An evergreen tree with a cylindrical or slightly bulbous trunk; to 35 feet tall.

Inflorescence Axillary, 20–50 flowered panicles, the final branches with 3 flowers each; flowers maroon-red outside, stippled red on a cream background inside, 1/2–1/3 inch across, perianth five-lobed to 1/3–1/2 of length, with golden-brown pubescence on the outside. Flowers February to March.

Fruit An ellipsoid follicle, 2/3–1 1/4 x 1/2–3/4 inches, golden-brown pubescent, on a twisted stalk.

Twigs Yellow-green, turning brown and gray.

Bark Light gray, may be finely fissured into small squarish blocks.

Leaves Alternate, simple; ovate, entire or usually two- to three-lobed, central lobe 2 1/2–7 1/2 x 1/4–2 1/4 inches, lateral lobes about half as large; shiny above, dull below, margins slightly wavy, primary veins raised below; petiole 1 1/4– 4 1/3 inches.

Notes *B. gregorii* is very similar to *B. populneus* subsp. *triloba* and is distinguished by the hairy perianth, smaller fruit, and more deeply lobed leaves. The species name *gregorii* honors Augustus Charles Gregory (1819–1905), explorer of the northern parts of Western Australia and original collector of the species.

Locations A single tree is located in lower Orpet Park near the corner of Alameda Padre Serra and Pedregosa Street.

Top: Dense cluster of waxy maroon-red flowers of Brachychiton gregorii.
Bottom: Deeply palmately lobed leaves with prominent pale veins.

Brachychiton populneus
Kurrajong bottle-tree

Occurs in dry woodlands of eastern Australia, from central Queensland to southern New South Wales.

Habit An erect semi-deciduous tree with an enlarged trunk; to 50 feet tall.

Inflorescence Monoecious; axillary panicles; flowers bell-shaped, about $1/2$ inch long, consisting of a cream to greenish calyx tube with red flecks and 5 lobes; petals absent; frequently scarcely visible within the crown. Flowers May to June.

Fruit Boat-shaped follicles, $3/4–2\,3/4$ x $1/2–1\,1/4$ inches, apex strongly beaked; leathery, dark brown, not hairy; dehiscing along 1 suture, tawny hairy inside, with 8–12 orange-brown seeds covered on the lower part by a hairy sheath; on a basal stalk $1/2–2$ inches long.

Twigs Yellow-green, roughened from raised leaf scars; mid-branches sometimes swollen at the nodes.

Bark Thin, hard, light gray becoming dark, with shallow vertical fissures, very tight.

Leaves Alternate, simple; mostly entire, oval with an elongated apex, $2\,1/2–3$ x $3/4–1\,1/4$ inches; sometimes with 3 or even 5 lobes; glossy green, paler beneath, midveins yellow-green; petiole thin, yellow-green, $2/3–3$ inches long.

Notes *B. populneus* is very drought-tolerant and is used in its native range by stockmen as a supply of fodder during drought. Native peoples used the roots of young trees for food and the fibrous innerbark for making nets. The species name *populneus* means poplar-like.

Locations Street trees in the 100–600 blocks of Alamar Avenue, the 300–400 blocks of Quarantina Street, the 1500–1600 blocks of Castillo Street, and the 500 block of West Pueblo Street.

Top: Brachychiton populneus, *with erect conical crown and swollen trunk.*
Middle: Pale green flowers with pinkish lobes and usually unlobed oval leaves.
Bottom: Dark woody fruit with orange-brown seeds.

Brachychiton x *roseus*
Brachychiton populneo-acerifolius

Sexton flame tree

This hybrid is known only from cultivation and is the result of cross-pollination between cultivated trees of *B. acerifolius* and *B. populneus*.

Habit An evergreen tree with a rounded crown; to 70 feet tall.

Inflorescence Monoecious; dense axillary panicles, 4-10 inches long; flowers $1/2$–$3/4$ x $1/2$–$2/3$ inch, composed of a fused bell-shaped calyx with 5 recurved lobes to $1/3$–$1/2$ its length, petals absent, pink to red. Flowers April to May.

Fruit Follicles ellipsoid, on a stalk, apex beaked, $2 3/4$–$4 1/2$ x 1–$1 1/4$ inches; glabrous outside, hairy inside; containing 3–13 seeds.

Twigs Becoming stout, dull green, roughened by gray-brown leaf scars.

Bark Gray or brown-gray, shallowly fissured, broken into an alligator pattern on older stems.

Leaves Alternate, simple; ovate to lanceolate, $3 1/2$–6 x $1 2/3$–$2 3/4$ inches, margins entire or very shallowly three-lobed; shiny glabrous green above, paler beneath, midrib and lateral veins yellow-green, prominent below; petiole thick, 1–$1 3/4$ inches long.

Notes The species name *roseus* means rose-colored.

Locations A large tree on the grounds of the Sexton House on Hollister Avenue in Goleta. A tree on the southwest side of State Street at Gutierrez is on the site of the original Franceschi nursery. Another tree in the 200 block of Palisades Drive is the last of several planted on that street.

Top: Tall, upright crown of Brachychiton *x* roseus.
Middle: Red waxy flowers with five lobes on the calyx tube.
Bottom: Densely clustered lanceolate leaves and inflorescences.

Chiranthodendron

Chiranthodendron is a monospecific genus, reflecting its floral structure which is vastly different from its nearest relatives. Its name combines the Greek words *cheir* (hand) and *dendros* (tree) and refers to the hand-shaped nature of the flower.

Chiranthodendron pentadactylon
Handflower tree, monkey's hand tree, devil's hand tree

Native to the high mountains of southern Mexico and Guatemala, between 7,000 and 10,000 feet.

Habit A fast-growing slender evergreen tree with a dense crown; to 60 feet tall.

Inflorescence Axillary, single-flowered; flowers 2–3 inches long, contain a five-parted leathery maroon calyx with 3 basal bracts and 5 red finger-like stamens united at the base, thereby forming the "hand." Flowers in May.

Fruit A woody capsule, 5 inches long, elliptic, deeply fluted and covered with velvety light brown hair, splitting into 5 lobes when mature.

Twigs Yellow-green, covered with brown fuzz, becoming gray-brown.

Bark Smooth, dull gray.

Leaves Alternate, simple, somewhat drooping; palmately lobed or entire, 6–12 inches long, with 3–7 rounded lobes and 9 palmate veins emerging from the strongly heart-shaped base, veins prominent below, smooth above, covered with a dense light brown velvet beneath, margins sinuate; petiole 5–12 inches long.

Notes *Chiranthodendron pentadactylon* was first seen by European explorers in the 1750s when Spanish naturalists observed it in the extensive gardens maintained by the Aztec emperors. The tree was celebrated not only for the shape of its flowers, but also for its medicinal properties as a heart tonic and for relief of inflammation of the eyes. The species was first introduced to Santa Barbara (and California) by Dr. Franceschi in 1908. The species name *pentadactylon* means having five fingers.

Locations Five large trees are near the northeast corner of Stow Grove Park. Another large tree in the green space between Lassen Drive and Maria Ygnacio Creek north of Hollister Avenue. A young tree in East Alameda Plaza.

Top: Tall, open crown of Chiranthodendron pentadactylon.
Middle: Flowers with deep red calyx and five red stamens.
Bottom: Five-parted woody fruit with velvety surface.

Dombeya

Dombeya is a genus of about 225 species that occurs in central Africa and extends to the Mascarene Islands. The center of its development is on Madagascar, which contains over 180 species. The Sterculiaceae is a large and variable family, and *Dombeya* is sometimes put in a separate family, the Byttneriaceae. The genus is named for Joseph Dombey, an 18th-century French botanist.

Dombeya cacuminum
Strawberry snowball tree

Endemic to the tropical forests of Madagascar.

Habit An upright evergreen tree with irregular and pendulous branches; to 50 feet tall.

Inflorescence Multiple-flowered axillary clusters at the ends of the branches, 5–6 inches across; flowers 1 1/2–2 inches across, consisting of 5 obovate pinkish petals and 5 narrow-lanceolate creamy sepals, with 10–15 stamens and a single long exserted style. Flowers January to March.

Fruit A small capsule developing inside the papery persistent petals, 1/3 inch long, covered with soft tan hairs.

Twigs Slender to stout, bearing round to semi-circular leaf scars and pale raised lenticels.

Bark Light tannish-gray, smooth.

Leaves Alternate, simple; almost round to three- to five-lobed, strongly heart-shaped at the base, 5–7 inches across, lightly hairy on both sides, apical lobe not noticeably more elongate than the lateral lobes, with 5–7 nerves extending in a palmate fashion from the base, nerves densely hairy underneath, dark green above, lighter beneath; petiole round, to 10 inches long, densely hairly at the apex, often holding the blade at an angle.

Notes The densely flowered tree drops its still-colorful flowers in a dense carpet under the tree, adding another dimension to the floral display. The species name *cacuminum* means at the apex or tip, in reference to the floral clusters at the ends of the twigs.

Locations A single tree in Alice Keck Park Memorial Gardens, another at the southwest corner of Noble Hall on the campus of the University of California, Santa Barbara.

Top: Upright crown of **Dombeya cacuminum.**
Bottom: Cluster of pink flowers and heart-shaped leaves with palmate veins.

Firmiana

Firmiana is a small genus of 12 species of the Old World tropics. Its species are found from East Africa to Japan. The genus is named for Karl Joseph von Firmian (1716–1782), who was Governor of Lombardy and a patron of the Padua Botanic Garden, considered to be the oldest botanic garden in the world.

Firmiana simplex
Firmiana platanifolia

Chinese parasol tree

Native to the warm regions of southern China and low elevations on Taiwan.

Habit A deciduous tree with upright branching; to 35 feet tall.

Inflorescence Monoecious; axillary or terminal panicles, hairy, 8–12 inches long; flowers inconspicuous, yellowish-green, without petals, in male flowers the 10–15 stamens fused into a column bearing the individual anthers. Flowers May to June.

Fruit A follicle, 2–3 1/4 inches long, reticulately veined, dehiscing into 5 spreading leaf-like carpels, each with seeds (2–3 1/4 inches) borne along the margin.

Twigs Stout, bright green, sometimes maroon becoming bright green, with obvious circular leaf scars.

Bark Smooth, gray-green.

Leaves Alternate, simple; palmately three- to seven-lobed, the sinuses extending halfway or more to the base, each lobe with a stout reddish midrib and a strongly elongate apex, 12–16 inches across, the base strongly heart-shaped, margins entire, finely hairy below, glabrous above; petiole stout, maroon, to 24 inches long.

Notes *F. simplex* is a commonly used street tree in Asia, especially in Japan. Its common name stems from the fruit, the shape of which is reminiscent of a parasol. The species name *simplex* means simple.

Locations Street trees in the 700 block of San Pascual Street and the 400–500 blocks of Laguna Street. Two young trees were planted in West Alameda Plaza in recognition of the contributions of Bruce Van Dyke and Dan Condon, former City Arborists.

Top: **Firmiana simplex**, *with velvet covered flower buds; heart-shaped leaves with palmate veins. Bottom: Fruit of five leaf-like carpels.*

Tamaricaceae

The Tamarix Family consists of four genera and 120 species from temperate and subtropical regions of the Old World. Its greatest diversity is in Eurasia and Africa, and it is absent from the Americas, Malesia, and Australasia.

Tamarix

Tamarix is a genus of 54 species from Eurasia and Africa. Its name is the classical Latin name for the tree.

Tamarix aphylla
Athel tree

Found in sandy soils and disturbed areas from Morocco to Pakistan.

Habit An evergreen tree with a wispy crown and multiple stems; to 30 feet tall.

Inflorescence Terminal panicles, 1 1/4–2 1/2 inches long; flowers minute, 1/5 inch across, pink, subtended by a bract on the raceme. Blooms late spring and summer.

Fruit A minute capsule, 1/16 inch long.

Twigs Seemingly jointed, the joints enclosed in minute leaf bases.

Bark Dull reddish-brown to gray, slightly furrowed.

Leaves Alternate, scale-like with a short reddish point, 1/12 inch long, forming a sheath about the twig.

Notes This deep-rooted species of dry regions develops adventitious roots when its branches are buried by shifting sands. The salt-secreting glands on its twigs and foliage are an adaptation which allows the species to deal with the highly salty soils of its arid environment. *T. aphylla* is highly invasive in the deserts of California and has had significant effect on water-bearing aquifers of this already arid region. Because of their particularly high tannin content, insect galls from this species have been used in the tanning of Moroccan leather. The species name *aphylla* means without leaves.

Locations Several trees planted as a wind break along El Collegio Road near the west gate of the University of California, Santa Barbara campus. Others on the cliffs at Coal Oil Point to the west of the UCSB campus.

Top: Soft crown of Tamarix aphylla.
Bottom: "Foliage" consisting of jointed twigs with minute leaf bases.

Thymelaeaceae

The Daphne Family includes 45 genera and 450 species and occurs in tropical, subtropical, and temperate regions throughout the world. Its greatest diversity is in Australia and central Africa. Several species are used as fish poisons, and the fibrous bark has been used for a variety of purposes.

Dais

Dais is a small genus containing only two species, one in Madagascar and the other in South Africa. *Dais* is the Greek word for torch and refers to the form of the inflorescence.

Dais cotinifolia
Pompon tree

Native to southeastern South Africa, from Cape Province to Natal.

Habit   A deciduous shrub or small tree; to 20 feet tall.

Inflorescence   Densely flowered terminal heads, to $1^{1}/_{2}$ inches across, with 4 large green bracts drying reddish-brown; flowers consisting of a lilac-pink cylindrical calyx tube with five lobes, 10 stamens with bright yellow anthers. Flowers in February.

Fruit   A small reddish-brown nutlet enclosed in the base of the persistent calyx tube.

Twigs   Dull cinnamon-red with a glaucous bloom.

Bark   Smooth, gray-brown.

Leaves   Opposite, simple; oblong-elliptic to obovate, $2^{3}/_{4}$–$3^{1}/_{2}$ x $1^{1}/_{2}$–2 inches; margins entire, sometimes rolled under; dark olive-green; midrib and veins yellow-green, raised below, translucent; petiole to $^{1}/_{4}$ inch long.

Notes   Native peoples of South Africa used the bark of this species to make thread or rope. It is said to have the strongest fiber of any species in the region. It has been in cultivation since the 1790s when it was introduced to the Netherlands. The species name *cotinifolia* means with leaves like *Cotinus*.

Locations   Two trees in lower Orpet Park at the west end of the lawn.

Dense inflorescences of Dais cotinifolia *with tubular lilac-pink flowers; dark olive-green elliptic leaves.*

Tiliaceae

The Linden Family includes 50 genera and over 700 species. Although the genus *Tilia* is found in northern temperate zones, the family is characteristically tropical and subtropical with distributions in the Americas, Africa, Asia, Australia, and Oceania. Several species are of timber quality, and the versatile fiber jute is obtained from this family. Some recent analyses have suggested that the family should be included in the Malvaceae.

Luehea

Luehea is a genus of about 15 species from the tropical Americas. It was named for F. Karl van der Lühe, an Austrian student of botany.

Luehea divaricata
Whip-horse, *ka'a oveti*

Frequently found in floodplain forests of Brazil.

Habit   An evergreen tree with a somewhat narrow crown; to 50 feet tall.

Inflorescence   Terminal or axillary panicles; flowers showy, 3/4–1 1/4 inches across, with 5 rose-pink petals and 5 pale green sepals, subtended by 6–8 narrow pubescent bracts, the many stamens clustered in fascicles around the single pistil; pedicel 1/2 inch long, pubescent. Flowers August to September.

Fruit   A capsule, oblong, 1 inch long, brown pubescent, dehiscing about halfway to the base.

Twigs   Dull green, pubescent, showing stipule scars at the base of each leaf.

Bark   Smooth, gray.

Leaves   Alternate, simple; ovate, 2 1/2–4 x 1 1/2–2 1/2 inches, with 3 palmate veins from the base, dark green above, gray-green pubescent below, the margin densely but irregularly toothed; petiole 1/2 inch long, pubescent.

Notes   *Luehea divaricata* is a timber tree from the lowlands of Brazil. Because of its rapid growth, it has been used in reforestation efforts after logging. The species name *divaricata* means widely divergent.

Locations   A single tree in lower Orpet Park above the lawn and east of the center steps.

Leuhea divaricata *showing pink flower with many yellow stamens, brown pubescent fruit, and curled leaves with gray-green lower surface.*

Ulmaceae

The Elm Family includes 15 genera and approximately 150 species. It occurs throughout tropical and temperate regions of the Northern Hemisphere. Although some species have timber value, overall the family has little economic value.

Ulmus
Elms

Ulmus is a genus of about 30 species restricted to the temperate zone of the Northern Hemisphere. The genus is usually distinguished by alternate simple leaves with unequal leaf bases and pinnate veins, and fruit in the form of a roundish samara with the wing extending around the seed. Although only six species occur in Europe, their abundance and multitude of uses extends far back through the ages and considerable myth has grown up around them. The wood has a wavy grain that makes it very difficult to split. Although this feature makes it less desirable for firewood, it enhanced its use in the early development of wooden water pipes. *Ulmus* is the classical Latin name for the tree.

Ulmus americana
American elm

Very broadly distributed in moist forest conditions throughout eastern North America, from Newfoundland to Florida and west to Sakatchewan and Texas.

Habit A large, deciduous tree with a vase-like crown created by several ascending branches emerging from the single trunk; to 80 feet tall.

Inflorescence Axillary, much reduced, appearing before the leaves. Blooms February to March.

Fruit An oval samara, the wing extending around the fruit, 1/2 inch across; the margin hairy and notched at the apex.

Twigs Dark red-brown, with lenticels; leaf scars elevated; buds dark brown.

Bark Gray to gray brown; fissured leaving interlacing flat-topped ridges; cross sections exposing alternating creamy white and reddish-brown layers.

Leaves Alternate, simple; ovate to oblong with an elongate apex and asymmetrical base, 3–6 inches long; dark green and shiny above, paler and dull beneath, sometimes initially hairy becoming smooth; margins doubly serrate; petiole 3/16 inch long.

Notes Because of its graceful shape and shade qualities, *Ulmus americana* was planted extensively in cities throughout the United States. However, Dutch elm disease has decimated plantings throughout much of the country. In spite of its common name, the disease originates from Asia. The species name *americana* means from America.

Locations Street trees on Micheltorena Street between Anacapa and Garden Streets. An exceptionally large tree in the 1200 block of East Carpinteria Street was protected as a specimen tree in 1990. A young tree germinated from seed of the Survivor's Tree was planted in lower Orpet Park in memory of the 168 people who lost their lives in the bombing of the Alfred E. Murrah Federal Building in Oklahoma City on April 19, 1995.

Top: Vase-like shape of Ulmus americana *with several large ascending branches.*
Bottom left: Spring-time winged fruit.
Bottom right: Ovate leaves with asymmetrical bases (characteristic of the Elm Family) and elongate apices.

Ulmus parvifolia
Chinese elm, lacebark elm

Native to northern and central China, Korea, and Japan.

Habit A medium-sized nearly evergreen tree with a broad rounded crown, somewhat pendulous branches, and a sinuous trunk; to 50 feet tall.

Inflorescence Axillary, much reduced, obscured in the foliage. Blooms July to August.

Fruit A round samara; elliptic to ovate, 1/3 inch long; wing glabrous, notched at the apex; appearing in dense clusters in late summer and fall.

Twigs Pubescent; buds small, pointed, without distinctive purple color.

Bark Smooth and exfoliating in small plates to leave a mottled combination of gray, green, orange, and cinnamon-brown.

Leaves Alternate, simple; elliptic to ovate, 3/4–2 1/2 x 1/3–1 1/3 inches; veins 10–12 pairs, obscure; margins asymmetrical at the base, with many regular, rounded, forward-pointing teeth; shiny dark green above, pale beneath; petiole 1/4–1/2 inch long, slightly pubescent.

Notes The species name *parvifolia* means with little or small leaves.

Locations Increasingly common about town. Trees at Dwight Murphy Field and in the 5500 block of Cathedral Oaks Road. A smaller, more weeping form (*U. parvifolia* 'Sempervirens') is found in the 100–200 block of Las Ondas.

Top: Open crown of **Ulmus parvifolia**.
Bottom: Small serrate leaves with asymmetric bases; winged fruit.

Ulmus pumila
Siberian elm

Broadly distributed in Siberia, northern China, Manchuria, and Korea

Habit A deciduous tree with ascending, then spreading, branches and pendulous twigs; to 70 feet tall

Inflorescence Axillary, red, appearing in spring.

Fruit A samara; elliptic, notch nearly closed at the apex.

Twigs Light gray, with raised leaf scars and small offset buds; densely set at the ends of branches, giving a brushy appearance.

Bark Gray-brown; with deep, long vertical fissures and long flat-topped ridges.

Leaves Alternate, simple; elliptic, apex elongate, 2 1/2–3 1/4 inches long; margins very asymmetrical at the base, doubly serrate or with single rounded teeth; veins 12 pairs; bright shiny green above, with white hairs in the axils of veins beneath; petioles hairy, 1/4–1/2 inch long.

Notes The species name *pumila* means dwarf.

Locations Street trees at the corner of Carpinteria and Soledad Streets and in the 1100 block of West Valerio Street. A tree at the University of California, Santa Barbara south of the swimming pool.

Top: Vase-like shape and dense crown of Ulmus pumila. *Bottom: Elliptic leaves with slightly elongate apices and asymmetric bases.*

Zelkova

Zelkova is a genus of four species from the Mediterranean (Crete) and Asia. Its name is derived from the local name in the Caucasus for *Z. carpinifolia*.

Zelkova serrulata
Japanese zelkova

Found in rich soils on lower mountain slopes and along stream and river banks in Japan, Korea, Taiwan, and Manchuria (northeastern China).

Habit A deciduous low-branched and vase-shaped tree; to 80 feet tall.

Inflorescence Monoecious; axillary; flowers small, inconspicuous; male flowers in the axils of the lower leaves, female flowers in the axils of the upper leaves. Blooms March to April.

Fruit A small dark brown drupe, $1/6$ inch across, ripening in fall.

Twigs Zigzag, initially brown or bright red, turning dull greenish-gray, lenticellate.

Bark Smooth, with horizontal lenticels, gray, exfoliating to expose orange patches.

Leaves Alternate, simple; ovate-lanceolate, usually $3 3/4$–$5 3/4$ x $1/3$–$2/3$ inches, apex elongate; margins with sharp coarse teeth, base rounded to somewhat heart-shaped, asymmetrical, veins 8–14 pairs, sometimes branching near midrib, prominent underneath; dark lustrous green and sandpapery above, pale and smooth beneath; petiole stout, $1/4$ inch.

Notes The species name *serrulata* means with small saw-like teeth.

Locations Street trees in the 6000–6200 blocks of Stow Canyon Road in Goleta.

Top: **Zelkova serrulata,** *showing dark green upper surface of leaves with coarse serrations, elongate apices, and slightly asymmetric bases.*
Bottom: Pale green under surface of leaves with prominent veins.

Verbenaceae

The Verbena Family includes approximately 70 genera and 2,000 species from all parts of the world except the driest and coldest extremes. The largest number of species occur in tropical forests. The family includes the important timber tree teak, and numerous species have medicinal properties.

Duranta

Duranta is a genus of 35 species from tropical and subtropical America. It was named by Linnaeus for Castor Durante, a botanist and physician of Rome who died about 1500.

Duranta repens
Duranta erecta
Pigeonberry

Occurs in disturbed areas and open rocky woodlands from Florida to Brazil.

Habit An evergreen shrub or small tree with slender branches that may arch or trail; to 20 feet tall.

Inflorescence Terminal or axillary racemes, 2–6 inches long; flower corolla tubular with 5 spreading lobes, deep blue to purple, usually pubescent in the throat, $1/2$–$3/4$ inch across, stamens and pistil contained within the throat; calyx tubular, composed of 5 fused sepals. Blooms September to October.

Fruit A round drupe, each $1/3$–$1/2$ inch across, completely enclosed by the mature calyx which extends into a slight curved beak, yellowish, turning dark brown-black when mature; sometimes held in grape-like clusters.

Twigs Thin, dull brownish-gray.

Bark Light gray, slightly fissured.

Leaves Opposite, simple; ovate to obovate, to 1–3 x $3/4$–$1 1/2$ inches, entire or serrate on the distal half, glabrous on both surfaces, petiole $1/2$–$3/4$ inch long.

Notes Its smooth shiny leaves seem to never collect dust. The species name *repens* means creeping.

Locations Trees in Alice Keck Park Memorial Gardens.

Top: Unkempt crown of Duranta repens *with numerous orange fruit clusters.*
Bottom: Purple flowers, round orange fruit, and opposite ovate leaves.

Vitex

Vitex is a genus of 250 mostly tropical species. Its name is the classical Latin name for *V. agnus-castus*.

Vitex agnus-castus
Chaste tree, monk's protector

Native to the eastern Mediterranean region and extending eastward to the western Caucasus Mountains.

Habit A deciduous shrub or small tree; to 25 feet tall.

Inflorescence A dense terminal or axillary cyme; flowers pale lilac to blue, about 1/3 inch wide, composed of a distinct tube and a strongly asymmetric five-parted corolla, calyx and flower tube short hairy, stamens and pistil exserted. Blooms June to July.

Fruit A black or reddish round drupe.

Twigs Brittle, greenish, becoming gray-brown, short hairy.

Bark Gray-brown, fissured into an alligator pattern.

Leaves Opposite, palmately compound; leaflets 5–7, lanceolate to ovate, 1 1/2–6 x 1/2–1 1/4 inches, dull green above, white tomentose below; petioles to 1 2/3 inches long.

Notes The medicinal uses of *V. agnus-castus* fruits have been known since before the ancient Greeks. Theophrastus, Pliny the Elder, and Dioscorides wrote about its uses in the treatment of wounds, complaints of the spleen, and childbirth. More importantly, it was used to promote lactation and to ensure chastity of young women. Although there is no evidence that it suppresses the libido, the Catholic Church used it with young monks to help maintain their vow of chastity, hence one of its common names. The species name *agnus-castus* is a combination of the Greek name for the tree (*agnus*) and a confusingly similar word meaning chaste (in Latin, *castus*).

Locations Two trees in lower Orpet Park below the lawn.

Top: Rounded crown of Vitex agnus-castus *in full summer flower.*
Bottom: Terminal inflorescence of deep blue flowers; palmately compound leaves with five to seven lanceolate leaflets.

Vitex lucens
New Zealand chaste tree, *puriri*

Found in coastal and lowland forests of New Zealand from North Cape south to 39°30'.

Habit An evergreen tree with stout spreading branches; to 60 feet tall.

Inflorescence Axillary heads of 5–10 flowers, usually lost within the foliage; flower tube pink to dull red, pubescent, strongly two-lipped, 1–1 1/2 inches long, with exserted stamens and pistil strongly exserted. Blooms April to May.

Fruit Round, fleshy coated hard seed, 3/4 inch across, bright red.

Twigs Stout, four-angled, green becoming dull gray, with obvious lenticels in the first year.

Bark Tannish-gray, smooth, but with thin vertical furrows.

Leaves Opposite, palmately compound, to 7 inches long; leaflets 3–5, the basal pair much smaller than the terminal 1–3; elliptic to obovate, 2–4 x 1 1/4–2 inches; glabrous, leathery, glossy dark green, margins entire, the lateral veins obviously connected near the margin by a series of arching loops; petioles to 4 inches long, grooved above.

Notes *Vitex lucens* is sacred to the Maori people who used the deep hollows among the roots as a final resting place for important tribal members. The wood is highly valued for its deep reddish-brown color and great strength. The species does well in Santa Barbara but is subject to attack by white flies. The species name *lucens* means shining, bright.

Locations Several trees in the 400–700 blocks of Grove Lane were planted in 1961.

Top: Vitex lucens, *with pink flower tubes and exserted stamens; palmately compound leaves with notched leaflets.*
Bottom: Under surface of leaves and pink fruit.

Agavaceae

The Agave Family includes eight genera and about 300 species that are found in warm, arid regions throughout the world, with a high proportion in the Americas. The strong fibers found in many of its species have been used for many purposes by native peoples. In some taxonomic treatments the Agavaceae are included in the Liliaceae.

Cordyline

Cordyline is a genus of about 15 species and is closely related to Dracaena, which is also found in Santa Barbara. It differs in having two or more ovules per locule and in not having secondary thickening of the roots. Cordyline is derived from the Greek word for club and refers to the tufts of foliage at the head of a long branch.

Cordyline australis
New Zealand cabbage tree, green dracaena, *ti kouka*

Native to open areas from coastal lowlands to the lower mountains of New Zealand, on both the North and South Islands.

Habit A single-stemmed, or branched, evergreen tree, with the foliage clustered in a head at the end of each branch; to 25 feet tall.

Inflorescence Terminal, much-branched panicles emerging from the leaf clusters, 2–4 feet long, the individual racemes 4–8 x 1 inches; flowers 1/4–1/3 inch across, creamy white, sweet-scented. Blooms April to May.

Fruit A round berry, 1/6 inch across, white or bluish-white; seeds in the shape of a comma, black.

Twigs Stout, somewhat swollen, 1 1/2–2 inches across; gray brown, ridged with leaf scars.

Bark Thinly fissured into small plates, gray-brown on older stems, lighter brown and showing horizontal leaf scars on younger stems.

Leaves Clustered at the ends of branches, sword-shaped, 12–40 x 1 1/2–2 1/3 inches, pointed but only slightly narrowed, newer leaves more or less erect, older leaves drooping from the base only, green with a pale yellow-green margin.

Notes This tree is a common and characteristic element of New Zealand landscapes. The fibers of the leaves were used by native peoples

Top: Wide base and open branching of Cordyline australis.
Bottom: Large terminal inflorescence amidst narrow sword-shaped leaves.

for weaving, and decoctions of the leaves were used to treat dysentery and diarrhea. While the dried leaves make a very hot fire, the stem does not burn, and early settlers used hollowed stems as chimneys. Settlers also cooked and ate the tender inner leaves and stem as a vegetable, hence the common name. The species name *australis* means southern.

Locations East Alameda Plaza. County Courthouse along Figueroa Street.

Yucca

Yucca is a genus of about 30 species from the warm regions of North America. *Yucca* is a misnomer for this genus. The word is derived from the Caribbean name for manihot or cassava, which is in the Euphorbiaceae.

Yucca elephantipes
Giant yucca

A tropical species, native to the Gulf Coast of Mexico near Veracruz to Guatemala.

Habit A multi-branched evergreen tree-yucca with an enlarged fluted base; to 30 feet tall.

Inflorescence Densely flowered panicles to 24 inches long; flowers creamy white, bell-shaped, 2 inches long. Blooms August to October.

Fruit Not developing here.

Twigs Stout, dull green, becoming gray-corky as the leaves are lost.

Bark Dark gray, with shallow plates.

Leaves Clustered at the ends of branches, simple; sword-shaped, to 48 x 2–3 inches, dark green, slightly glossy, without a terminal spine, midrib prominent and yellow-green below on the basal half; younger leaves stiff and radiating from the tip of the stem, older leaves lax, pendulous.

Notes The species name *elephantipes* means like an elephant's foot.

Locations A tree in East Alameda Plaza; another in front of the Old Mission. Others on the County Courthouse grounds adjacent to Figueroa Street.

Top: Yucca elephantipes, *with flattened trunks, dense crown of coarse foliage, and terminal inflorescences.* Bottom: *Inflorescence of large white flowers and large sword-shaped leaves.*

Arecaceae

The Palm Family includes 189 genera and over 2,000 species and occurs throughout the tropical regions of the world, with some extensions into subtropical areas. The family is well-known for its preference for non-acidic soils. Palms have been important to the cultures of many societies, contributing food, fiber, and shelter.

Archontophoenix

Archontophoenix is a genus of three species from eastern Australia. The name combines the Greek words *archontos* (chieftain) and *phoenix* (the date palm) and refers to the regal look of these palms.

Archontophoenix cunninghamiana
King palm, piccabeen palm, piccabeen bangalow palm

Native to the coastal rain forests of Queensland and New South Wales, Australia.

Habit A single-stemmed feather palm; to 40 feet tall.

Inflorescence Emerging from below the crown shaft; peduncle short, stout, with two papery bracts; repeatedly branched; flowers lilac to purplish, slightly fragrant. Blooms November to February.

Fruit Globose, 1/2 inch long, red, on a creamy white branched peduncle.

Stem Light gray, smooth, with shallow but obvious leaf scars.

Leaves Pinnate, unarmed, 8–10 feet long; petiole less than 12 inches long; crown shaft 2–2 1/2 feet long, slightly swollen at the base, green to purplish; leaflets 1 1/2 feet long, 3–4 inches wide, acute, dark green, secondary veins not prominent.

Notes This species has been sold in the nursery trade as *Seaforthia elegans,* which is a different, but related genus. It is rare but not threatened in its native habitat in Australia. The species name *cunninghamiana* honors James Cunningham (d. c. 1709), East India Company surgeon who made large collections of plants from the Far East between 1698 and 1702.

Locations Common about town. Trees intermixed with *Syagrus romanzoffiana* in the 800–2100 blocks of Anacapa Street and the 1000–2100 blocks of Santa Barbara Street. The trees in the 400–1100 blocks of Chapala Street were planted by Santa Barbara Beautiful in recognition of the contributions of past presidents and board members.

Top: Archontophoenix cunninghamiana *showing ringed stem, long crown shaft, and pinnate leaves.* Phoenix roebelenii *is below.*
Bottom: Multiple inflorescences emerging from below the crown shaft.

Brahea
Erythea

Brahea is a genus of 12 species restricted to limestone soils of Mexico and Central America. The genus is named for Tycho Brahe (1546–1601), a noted Danish astronomer.

Brahea armata
Erythea armata

Blue hesper palm, gray goddess blue palm, blue fan palm, Mexican blue palm

Found on rocky soils of cliffs and canyons in Baja California.

Habit   A single-stemmed fan palm with 25–30 leaves compacted into a tight, round crown and a persistent sheath of dead leaves; to 45 feet tall and 15 inches in diameter (massive for the genus).

Inflorescence   Spectacular plumes 12–15 feet long, emerging from within the leaves and extending well beyond the crown; flowers gray-white to cream-colored, profuse. Blooms in August.

Fruit   Globose, 3/4 inch in diameter, fleshy, tan to brownish-black.

Stem   Covered with persistent leaf bases and fibrous mats.

Leaves   Costa-palmate; blade silvery gray to blue-green, 3–4 feet across, divided about halfway to the petiole into 40–60 stiff segments; petiole 3–5 feet long, with yellow hooked, sometimes bifid, spines.

Notes   Because of its size, this species can be mistaken for a young *Washingtonia;* however, the green leaves and pendulous leaf tips of the latter are distinguishing. The species name *armata* means armed.

Locations   A single individual in the palm planting at the center of East Alameda Plaza. Young trees in Alice Keck Park Memorial Gardens near Micheltorena Street and Chase Palm Park in the Great Meadow section. Others at Natoma Avenue and Burton Circle, near the entrance to the Cabrillo Pavilion Arts Center, and adjacent to the Sunken Gardens of the County Courthouse.

Top: Full gray-green crown and emergent inflorescences of Brahea armata.
Bottom: Profuse inflorescence of small cream-colored flowers.

Brahea brandegeei
Erythea brandegeei
San José hesper palm, *palma negra*

Native to northwestern Mexico in dry canyons and mountains.

Habit A somewhat open crown on top of a stout stem, covered by a shag of persistent leaves if not pruned; to 40 feet or more tall.

Inflorescence As long or longer than the leaves, much-branched; flowers in clusters of 3 on soft hairy peduncles. Blooms in June.

Fruit Globose, 3/4 inch in diameter, shiny yellow-brown with stripes, flattened on one side.

Stem Tannish-gray, with shallow vertical fissures; annular rings from leaf scars evident but not deep, sometimes described as having the overall look of an elephant's trunk.

Leaves Palmate; blade 3–5 feet across, green above, glaucous below, split about midway to the petiole into 50–60 segments which themselves are deeply split, not as stiff as other species of Brahea; petiole 3 feet long, slender, armed with hooked, spine-like teeth, yellow along the margins, bases strongly appressed to the stem; fibrous mat among petiole bases lacking.

Notes *B. brandegeei* can be mistaken for *Washingtonia,* which has green leaves and pendulous leaf tips. Where the persistent leaves have been pruned, the remaining bases have neither the striking cross-hatched pattern of *W. robusta* nor the irregular appearance of *W. filicifolia*. An apparently dwarf variety, formerly *Erythea elegans* (known locally as Franceschi palm), is now included with *B. brandegeei*. The species name *brandegii* honors Townsend Seth Brandegee (1843–1925), American civil engineer and noted student of plants of California and Mexico.

Locations Individuals in East Alameda Plaza. A single palm on the Figueroa Street side of the County Courthouse. Individuals of the dwarf variety can be seen in the Sunken Garden of the County Court House and in Lotusland. Others mixed with *Brahea edulis* in the west parking lot of Goleta Beach County Park.

Full crown of **Brahea brandegeei** *with stout stem and persistent leaf bases.*

Brahea edulis
Erythea edulis
Guadalupe palm

Endemic to Guadalupe Island off the west coast of Baja California.

Habit A stocky fan palm with a solitary stem and a broad, open crown of about 20 leaves; to 30 feet tall.

Inflorescence Many-branched flower stalks are visible from within the leaves, 3–4 feet long; flowers creamy yellow, in clusters of three on soft hairy peduncles. Blooms February to April.

Fruit Globose, 1–1 1/2 inches in diameter, black, pulpy; in large hanging clusters on a stout stalk.

Stem Tannish-gray, with shallow vertical fissures; annular rings from leaf scars evident but not deep.

Leaves Palmate; blade 3–5 feet across, green on both sides, divided halfway to the petiole into 70–80 stiff segments which are then briefly divided at the apex, segments generally stiff; petiole 3–5 feet, stout, hairy at base, with short knobby teeth or none.

Notes The introduction of goats to Guadalupe Island in the early 1800s has severely impacted native vegetation and has severely restricted regeneration of the Guadalupe palm, threatening its future. However, recent action by the Mexican government to remove goats from Guadalupe Island is expected to restore this and other endemic species to their former abundance. The species name *edulis* means edible.

Locations Franceschi Park east of the cottage; several individuals in East Alameda Plaza; another on the Figueroa Street side of the County Courthouse.

Open crown of large, fan-shaped leaves of **Brahea edulis**. *The stout, ringed stem and profuse fruit held within the leaves are distinctive.*

Butia
Syagrus

This genus includes eight to twelve species from southern South America, many of which are highly variable. It is commonly found in open lands and is in danger from continuous expansion of agricultural activities. *Butia* is the local Brazilian name for *B. capitata*.

Butia capitata
Syagrus capitata

Jelly palm, South American jelly palm, pindo palm

The jelly palm is found in two disjunct populations on sandy soils of Uruguay and southern Brazil.

Habit A short and stout solitary feather palm, with an open crown; to 20 feet tall.

Inflorescence Up to 2–4 feet, emerging from among the lower leaves, with 50–100 flowering branches; flowers about $3/8$ inch long, yellow to red. Blooms in July.

Fruit Ovoid, $1/2$–$1 1/2$ inches long, yellowish- or orange-brown.

Stem Solitary, to 18 inches in diameter, dull gray, with leaf scars apparent.

Leaves Pinnate, several feet long, strongly arched, in shorter trees reaching almost to the ground; leaflets 40–80 on each side, gray-green, $2 1/2$ feet x $3/4$ inch, rising from the rachis to give a V-shaped appearance in cross section; petiole with coarse black spines.

Notes The species is quite variable and several varieties have been described. To add to the confusion, it has been sold in nurseries as *Cocos australis* and *C. campestris*. If unpruned, the dead leaves remain just below the crown for several years before falling. When pruned, the upright nature of the lower rachis often results in upward-pointing gray stobs 6–10 inches long. The species name *capitata* means growing in a dense head.

Locations Several trees planted in the median of State Street between Mission Street and Constance Avenue. Others in East Alameda Plaza, at the County Courthouse on the Anacapa Street side, along the Micheltorena Street side of Alice Keck Park Memorial Gardens, and near the entrance to the Cabrillo Pavillion Arts Center.

Top: Rounded crown of **Butia capitata**.
Bottom: Inflorescence included within the pinnately compound gray-green foliage.

Caryota
Fishtail palms

Caryota is a small genus of about 12 species occurring in China, India, Southeast Asia, and northern Australia. It has several unique features among the feather palms. It is the only genus whose leaves are bipinnate. The leaflets are folded such that the outer folds are pointed skyward. (With the exception of Arenga and Phoenix, the outer folds of all other feather palms point towards the ground.) Its species do not flower until the plant is mature, at which point the initial flower stalk appears from within the uppermost leaves. Subsequent inflorescences continue to emerge from progressively lower leaves until the lowest branches are reached, at which point the plant dies. The name originates from the Greek *karyon* (nut), which was first applied to the date palm.

Caryota gigas
Giant Thai mountain palm

Native to a remote mountainous region in northern Thailand near the border with Laos.

Habit A solitary, massive fishtail palm, with 6–15 leaves clustered in a compact crown; to 130 feet tall in its native habitat.

Inflorescence Monocarpic (flowering only once, after which the plant dies); inflorescences emerge from within the leaves at the top of the stem and continue progressively towards the base, branched and massive, to 18 feet long; peduncle to 3 feet long by 6 inches in diameter.

Fruit Globose, somewhat flattened, to 1 1/2 x 1 1/4 inches, red.

Stem Constricted at the base and top, strongly elliptical in cross section, 10–36 inches in diameter, 8–12 inches between leaf scars.

Leaves Massive, bipinnately compound, broadly ovate in outline, strongly drooping in all directions, to 20+ feet long, with 19–22 pinnae on each side, pinnae to 12 feet long; leaflets to 27 on each side of the pinnae, wedge-shaped with the apex broad and jagged, resembling the dorsal fin or tail fin of a fish, 8–14 x 3–6 inches; leaf sheath to 12 feet long, strongly split on side opposite the petiole and held to the stem by a black fribrous mat.

Notes Although not botanically described

Top: Broad crown of extensive leaves and spire-like new leaf of Caryota gigas.
Bottom: Bases of large leaves clasping the elliptic stem.

until 1998, *Caryota gigas* has been available in the nursery trade in Southern California since the early 1990s. The species name *gigas* means giant; in botanical use the term refers to a genetic variation that is larger and more vigorous than normal.

Locations A large individual in front of the fire station on East Valley Road in Montecito. Others in a parking lot on the 6700 block of Hollister Avenue in Goleta, and on the southeast side of the Francisco Torres dormitory in the 6800 block of El Colegio Road.

Caryota urens
Wine palm, jaggery palm, sago palm, toddy palm, kittul tree

Native to the rain forests of India, Sri Lanka (Ceylon), and Myanmar (Burma).

Habit A solitary fishtail palm; to 25 feet tall.

Inflorescence Monocarpic (flowering only once, after which the plant dies); inflorescences emerge from within the leaves at the top of the stem and continue progressively towards the base, consisting of multiple chain-like strings of flowers, to 24 inches long, each borne on a short pedicel.

Fruit Red to black, 2/3–3/4 inch across.

Stem Solitary, to 15 inches in diameter, 7–10 inches between leaf scars, stem initially covered by white fuzzy scales grown under the leaf sheath, green becoming brown.

Leaves Bipinnately compound, 10–12 x 6–8 feet, ascending or arching; leaf sheath green becoming creamy gray, 4–6 feet long; leaflets wedge-shaped with the apex broad and jagged, resembling the dorsal fin or tail fin of a fish.

Notes The inedible fruit of this and other fishtail palms contains a large quantity of oxalic acid crystals which burn the mouth and tongue. However, the trunks are tapped for their sugary sap, which is used to produce wine or sago. The species name *urens* means stinging.

Locations Several individuals planted in a commercial parking lot in the 6700 block of Hollister Avenue, Goleta, near Storke Road. Another individual in the palm planting of East Alameda Plaza.

Full crown of Caryota urens *with "fishtail" leaflets.*

Chamaerops

A genus of one species, this was the first palm described by Linnaeus in 1753. The name is the combination of the Greek words *chamai* (dwarf) and *rhops* (bush).

Chamaerops humilis

European fan palm, Mediterranean fan palm

Native to the western Mediterranean, from southern Portugal to Malta and Monaco to Libya.

Habit A short clump of dark stems each topped by a rounded, bristly-appearing crown; to 20 feet tall.

Inflorescence Usually dioecious; emerging from among the leaves, very short; flowers usually contained within the leaves, bright yellow. Blooms December to January.

Fruit Oval, somewhat three-sided near the base, 1/2–1 1/2 inches long, shiny olive-green, maturing reddish-purple.

Stem Dark brown to black, covered with a dense mat of dark fibers between persistent leaf bases, sometimes becoming bare on the lower trunk.

Leaves Palmate, to 2 1/2 feet across, deeply cut almost to the petiole; segments stiff (not drooping), split deeply again at the ends, green, gray-green or bluish-gray; petiole to 2 feet x 1–1 1/2 inches, armed with stout spines along margins to 1 inch long pointing towards the leaf blade.

Notes This is the only palm native to Europe and is usually found in coastal areas, although it occurs at elevations up to 6,000 feet in the Great Atlas Mountains of northern Africa. It holds the distinction of being the most northerly occurring of the palms. A specimen of this species planted in 1585 is the oldest tree at the Padua Botanic Garden and is referred to as the "Goethe palm." The German writer's study of this plant in 1786 led to his perceptions of evolution, which he published in his essay *Metamorphosis of Plants*. The species name *humilis* means small, dwarfed.

Locations Plants in East and West Alameda Plaza, others at Leadbetter Beach and on the campus of the University of California, Santa Barbara.

Top: Several stems of Chamaerops humilis *with persistent leaf bases and stiff crown of palmate leaves.*
Middle left: Dense inflorescence of yellow flowers contained within the leaves.
Middle right: Mature shiny red to purple fruit.
Bottom: Leaf petioles with needle-like spines that point upward.

Dypsis

The subtribe of palms that includes *Dypsis* is quite variable, and a recent revision has combined some 13 genera into a large complex group of about 140 species, all but three of which are endemic to Madagascar. It includes the smallest palms, including one that is less than 24 inches tall. The origin of the name was not noted by either author and has been lost to history.

Dypsis decaryi
Neodypsis decaryi

Triangle palm, Madagascar three-sided palm

Found only in a very restricted geographic zone between the humid rain forest and the seasonally dry forests of extreme southwestern Madagascar.

Habit A solitary feather palm; to 25 feet tall.

Inflorescence Branched, emerging from within the lower leaves, to 5 feet long; flowers yellow to green. Not seen flowering in Santa Barbara.

Fruit Round, to 1 inch across, glaucous green turning black.

Stem Circular, to 16 inches in diameter, marked by closely spaced leaf scars; crown with a distinctly three-sided shape due to the triangular arrangement of the leaves.

Leaves Pinnate, 15–20 in the crown; 8–10 feet long, emerging vertically from the stem then arching within 2 feet of the apex, leaflets gray-green, the lower ones developing long hanging threads; petiole tannish, covered with a white bloom, sheath with rust-colored wooly hairs.

Notes The fruits of *Dypsis decaryi* are an important food source to several animals during the dry season. The plant is harvested for thatching and food; however, overharvesting places this species near to extinction in its native habitat. The species name *decaryi* honors Raymond Decary (1891–1973), French botanical collector who collected the type specimen.

Locations Individual trees in the Alice Keck Park Memorial Gardens, East Alameda Plaza, and in front of a business in the 3500 block of State Street. Others planted north of Broida Hall on the campus of the University of California, Santa Barbara.

Top: Open crown of pinnately compound leaves with short stem of **Dypsis decaryi**.
Bottom: Clasping leaf bases that form a distinctive triangle cross section of the stem.

Howeia
Sentry palms, kentia palms

Howeia is a genus of two species found only on Lord Howe Island, Australia. Both the genus and the island are named for Lord Howe (1726–1799).

Howeia belmoreana
Sentry palm, Belmore sentry palm, curly palm

Restricted to sandy soils on Lord Howe Island, Australia.

Habit A solitary feather palm; to 35 feet tall.

Inflorescence Monoecious; emerging from the lower leaves, a single downward curving, unbranched spike, to 5 feet long. Blooms February to July.

Fruit Shaped like a lemon with a beak at the apex; to 1 1/4 inches long, brownish-red.

Stem Solitary, to 25 feet, ringed with old scars of deciduous leaves, swollen at the base.

Leaves Pinnately compound; to 7 feet long, strongly arching; leaflets 1 1/2–2 feet x 1 inch, strongly upright lending a V-shape to the overall leaf, green on both sides; petiole 1–1 1/2 feet, unarmed.

Notes If left unpruned, the lower leaves of this species arch into a semi-circle. The species name *belmoreana* honors M. De Belmore, former Governor of New South Wales.

Locations A single specimen in the Santa Barbara Cemetery. Another next to the east entrance to the Davidson Library on the campus of the University of California, Santa Barbara.

Stiff crown of arching leaves and long unbranched inflorescence spikes of Howeia belmoreana.

Howeia forsteriana
Paradise palm, kentia palm, thatch-leaf palm, sentry palm

Often found in pure stands below 1,000 feet on Lord Howe Island.

Habit A solitary feather palm; to 40 feet or more tall.

Inflorescence Emerging from the lower leaves, 3–4 in a leaf axil, 2½ feet long, branched, hanging. Blooms February to September.

Fruit Narrowly ovoid, gradually narrowed to the apex, 2 inches long, orange, closely packed.

Stem Slender, to 15 inches in diameter; somewhat swollen at the base; strongly marked by leaf scars, usually green above, light gray below.

Leaves Pinnate, 6–9 feet overall, ascending or horizontal, arching slightly from the weight of the leaf; leaflets to 20 x 2½ inches, held on a horizontal plane or drooping, green on both sides, spotted and scaly along the midrib beneath; petiole 3–5 feet long.

Notes *Howeia forsteriana* has been used horticulturally for over a century. As an interior planting, it has "graced every imaginable chamber from saloons and cheap hotel lobbies to spacious presidential ballrooms." The species name *forsteriana* honors William Forster (1818–1882), Senator and Premier of New South Wales, Australia.

Locations Individuals in East Alameda Plaza and in front of the Carriage Museum at Pershing Park. Several in the Sunken Gardens at the County Courthouse; others on the campus of the University of California, Santa Barbara.

Open crown of pinnate leaves with drooping leaflets and short inflorescence spikes of Howeia forsteriana.

Jubaea

This genus consists of the single species described below. It is named for Juba, King of Numidia (present-day Algeria), who took his own life in 46 BC when the ever-expanding Roman Empire annexed his North African kingdom.

Jubaea chilensis
Chilean wine palm

Native to central Chile, in the Coastal Range where an unusually mild Mediterranean climate prevails.

Habit A solitary, bulky feather palm with a dense crown; to 50 feet tall.

Inflorescence Emerging from within the leaves, 2–3 feet long, shielded by a persistent woody bract that is orange on the inner side; flowers maroon with a yellow center. Flowers April to May.

Fruit Globose, 1 1/2 inches long, in a yellow-orange fibrous skin.

Stem To 3–5 feet thick, appearing too massive for the crown it supports, but in most mature trees narrowing halfway toward the crown to about half its lower diameter; dark gray, smooth but with scars from deciduous leaves remaining faintly apparent.

Leaves Pinnate, 6–12 feet long; leaflets 2 feet x 1 inch, split at the apex, bluish gray-green; on a 1 1/2- to 3-foot petiole with stiff hairs but not spines.

Notes Once common throughout its native range, *J. chilensis* is now restricted to a few preserves, notably La Campana National Park. Its common name refers to the cause of its demise. Trees were cut to collect sap which has been sold as palm honey and is still used to make palm wine. An active research program in Chile today seeks to find sustainable ways to continue the extraction of sap. As a final note, Charles Darwin considered these to be "ugly trees;" however, many of those who have seen the extensive natural stands at La Campana consider these to be a marvelous sight. The species name *chilensis* means from Chile.

Locations Trees in East and West Alameda Plaza and in Mission Park. Another at Stow House in Goleta.

Swollen gray trunk that narrows towards the top and bluish gray-green foliage of Jubaea chilensis.

Livistona

Livistona is a genus of 28 species from tropical and subtropical regions of the Southern Hemisphere. Ecological preferences of its species range from fresh water and peat swamp forest to tropical forest understory to canyon bottoms in desert areas. The genus is named for Patrick Murray, Baron of Livingston whose expansive garden, created prior to 1680, was the basis of the Edinburgh Botanic Garden.

Livistona australis
Australian fan palm, cabbage tree palm

Widely distributed in rain forests and sheltered moist forests of eastern Australia from the south coast of New South Wales to northern Queensland.

Habit A solitary fan palm with a clean trunk; to 50 feet or more tall.

Inflorescence Emerging from within the leaves, 1½–3 feet long, branched to 5 times; flowers yellow, in clusters of 2 or 3. Blooms February to June.

Fruit Spherical; ½–¾ inch across, reddish-brown to purple-black.

Stem Brownish-gray to dark brown, with short vertical splits marked by a series of prominent, raised, irregular rings that almost appear as steps.

Leaves Costa-palmate, petiole extends several inches into the leaf fan; circular in outline, 3–4 feet across; divided more than halfway to the costa; segments with strongly pendulous apices; petiole 5–6 feet long, broad at the base; petiole with fine dark recurved teeth that are especially prominent towards the base.

Notes The Australian fan palm has been cut extensively for its tasty palm hearts and is now protected in its native habitat. It is one of the hardier species of the genus. The species name *australis* means southern.

Locations Several trees at East Beach near the Cabrillo Pavilion Arts Center; an individual in East Alameda Plaza. Others on the Anacapa Street side of the County Courthouse. Two specimen trees at a business in the 100 block of East Anapamu Street opposite the County Courthouse.

Livistona australis, *with high rounded crown displaying drooping leaf tips and dark stem with irregular step-like rings.*

Livistona chinensis
Chinese fan palm, Chinese fountain palm

Native to open woodlands of southern Japan and Taiwan, where it is endangered.

Habit A solitary fan palm; to 30 feet tall (shorter in Santa Barbara).

Inflorescence Emerging from within the leaves; branched several times along a central rachis; flowers in clusters of 6. Flowers in spring and summer.

Fruit Oblong, 3/4 x 1/2 inch, shiny, blue-green.

Stem Wrinkled, light gray, swollen at the base.

Leaves Costa-palmate; roundish, but more broad (3–5 feet) than long; divided about halfway into noticeably drooping segments with tips split into slender filaments; blade with a prominent undivided central area; petiole 6 feet x 6 inches, triangular in cross section, with small recurved spines that are larger towards the base, 1 1/2–1 3/4 inches apart.

Notes This is is one of the hardier palms of the genus. The species name *chinensis* means from China.

Locations One tree in the Sunken Garden of the County Courthouse; others at Santa Barbara Cemetery.

Stout stem and crown with noticeably drooping leaf tips of Livistona chinensis.

Livistona decipiens
Ribbon fan palm, weeping cabbage palm

Found only in a geographically limited area along the coast of southeastern Queensland, Australia.

Habit A graceful solitary fan palm with a dense hemispherical crown; to 50 feet tall.

Inflorescence Emerging from within the leaves, to 6 feet long; branched several times along a central rachis; flowers in clusters of 6. Flowers in June.

Fruit Globose, 1/2 inch in diameter, black.

Stem Wrinkled, light gray, somewhat swollen at the base.

Leaves Costa-palmate, roundish; divided almost to the costa or petiole into noticeably drooping segments with tips deeply split into slender filaments, deep- to bluish-green above, glaucous gray-green below; petiole 6 feet x 4 inches, triangular in cross section, with small recurved spines that are larger towards the base, 1 1/2–1 3/4 inches apart, with a purple-brown splash near the base.

Notes Because it is uncommon in its restricted native habitat, *L. decipiens* was not recognized as a separate species until 1910. When observed in the field, it had been considered to be *L. australis* which was described 60 years earlier. It was once incorrectly known in France as *Copernica cerifera*. The species name *decipiens* means deceptive, resembling another species.

Locations Two trees in the Sunken Garden of the County Courthouse.

Hemispherical crown with drooping leaf tips and light gray stem of Livistona decipiens.

Phoenix

Phoenix is a genus of 17 species from tropical and subtropical Africa and Asia. Among the palms in Santa Barbara, it is the only genus whose lower leaflets become hardened into stout sharp spines. Species within the genus hybridize freely, and likely most specimens in horticulture today contain some mixed lineages. The name comes from the Greek, *phoenix* (date palm), but it may also originate from the Egyptian bird of myth or from Phoenicia, where date palms were grown abundantly as a food source.

Phoenix canariensis
Canary Island date palm

Endemic to the Canary Islands.

Habit   A stout feather palm, very tropical in appearance; leaves erect initially and then arching increasingly with age to give an overall global appearance to the dense crown of about 200 leaves; to 75 feet tall.

Inflorescence   Dioecious; emerging from within the leaves, much-branched, 4–6 feet long, bright orange and conspicuous. Flowers December to April.

Fruit   Bright orange, ovoid, 1 inch long, very fleshy; seed 3/4 inch long, somewhat wrinkled, with a deep groove.

Stem   Stout, to 3 feet in diameter; covered with persistent leaf bases which have usually been pruned.

Leaves   Pinnate, 15–20 feet long; with 150–200, one-foot-long leaflets on each side, deep, glossy green; petiole short with long, stout spines.

Notes   Although of naturally restricted origin, this date palm is planted widely throughout the world. It is probably the most commonly used palm in Palm Sunday celebrations. A hybrid, found at the County Courthouse, *P. canariensis* x *reclinata* has the overall habit of *P. canariensis* but with distinctly blue-gray foliage. A recent fungal attack by *Fusarium oxysporum* has killed numerous individuals in Beverly Hills. The species name *canariensis* means from the Canary Islands.

Locations   Common throughout town. Trees in East and West Alameda Plaza; others at the County Courthouse and Mission Park. A lovely line of street trees on Las Palmas Drive in Hope Ranch. A double row of trees along the margins of Ambassador Park in the 100 block of West Cabrillo Boulevard remain today from the entrance to the original Potter Hotel.

Distinctive form of Phoenix canariensis *with swollen stem base, long pinnate leaves, and yellow-orange fruit held within the crown.*

Phoenix dactylifera
Date, date palm

Thought to be native to a small region of northern Africa or the Near East.

Habit A clustered feather palm, with a thin, globose crown of approximately 20–40 leaves; the leaves are erect at first and then increasingly drooping with age; to 75 feet tall.

Inflorescence Dioecious; emerging from within the leaves, 4 feet long, with white, fragrant flowers. Blooms February to March.

Fruit Borne in hanging hand-like masses; oblong-ovoid, 1–3 inches long, deep orange when ripe.

Stem Slender, 1½–2 feet in diameter, covered with persistent leaves which later drop leaving a recognizable pattern of leaf bases; may sucker from the base.

Leaves Pinnate, to 20 feet long; leaflets clustered along the lower portion of the rachis and regularly arranged above, forward-pointing and emerging from the rachis in several planes, each 18 inches long, rigid, sharp-pointed, grayish-blue, glaucous; the lower leaflets reduced to sharp spines.

Notes *P. dactylifera* is the commercial date palm that has been cultivated for over 8,000 years. Although it originated in a restricted region, ancient commerce spread the tree throughout the broader Middle East from Morocco to northwestern India. Commonly associated with desert regions through film and travelogue, this palm has a high water requirement and is always an indicator of near surface water. Although commercial date plantations have flourished in Southern California, the summer climate of Santa Barbara is too cold for successful production of fruit. Today, labor costs have severely limited date production in California, and much of the world's commercial date production occurs in Iraq. The species name *dactylifera* means bearing fingers, referring to the appearance of the fruit.

Locations One tree in East Alameda Plaza. Single street trees in the first block of East Quinto Street and the 3200 block of Calle Piñon.

Grayish-blue leaves, open crown, and persistent leaf bases of Phoenix dactylifera.

Phoenix reclinata
Senegal date palm

Found along rivers and streams in tropical and southern Africa.

Habit A clustered feather palm with slender, frequently leaning trunks and an open crown; to 40 feet tall.

Inflorescence Dioecious; emerging from within the leaves, 3 feet long, much-branched, covered by boat-shaped spathes; petiole stout, flattened, orange. Blooms in June.

Fruit Ovoid, 3/4 inch long, orange, turning brown or reddish-black, astringent.

Stem Multiple; to 25 feet tall, 4–7 inches in diameter; roughened by persistent leaf bases; often leaning at an angle; light-colored.

Leaves Pinnate, 10–20 feet long, the apex strongly recurved, with 80 or more leaflets on each side arranged in a single plane; leaflets 10–15 x 1 inches, sharp, stiff-pointed, with white wool on the under surface of young plants, scales underneath on older plants; lower leaflets reduced to strong spines.

Notes The trunks of this palm are used in its native land for construction, while the leaves provide thatching and weaving materials. Seeds are ground into flour. The species name *reclinata* means leaning.

Locations Trees in East and West Alameda Plaza, on the grounds of the County Courthouse, and around the Cabrillo Pavilion Arts Center at East Beach.

Clump of curved stems with small crowns and additional sprouts growing from the base of Phoenix reclinata.

Phoenix roebelenii
Pigmy date palm

Native to the rain forests of Laos, Thailand, and Vietnam, usually found in river beds that are often flooded during heavy rain.

Habit   Solitary or sometimes clustered feather palm; dwarf, to 10 feet tall.

Inflorescence   Dioecious; emerging from within the leaves, 18 inches long, the large woody peduncular bract persistent, flowers pale yellow. Flowers in August.

Fruit   Ovoid, 1/2 x 3/16 inch, blackish.

Stem   Six inches in diameter, dark brown-black, with triangular knobs from residual leaf bases.

Leaves   Pinnate, 3–5 feet long with about 50 leaflets on each side in a single plane; leaflets 10 x 3/8 inches, soft, green, with prominent yellowish or grayish scales along the midrib beneath, reduced to spines towards the base, rachis flattened vertically towards the apex; leaf bases with considerable fibrous hair which eventually sloughs off to reveal the clear stem.

Notes   The species was named from a specimen purchased in an English nursery in 1889. In cultivation, it is often maintained as a single-stemmed individual; however, in the wild it is always a clumped palm. This has led to the speculation that the single-stemmed specimens are in fact a hybrid between the true *P. roebelenii* and other species of *Phoenix*. The species name *roebelenii* honors Carl Roebellen (1855–1927), botanical collector, especially of orchids and palm seeds.

Locations   An individual in the Palm Garden of East Alameda Plaza; several others at East Beach near the Cabrillo Pavilion Arts Center, others in sidewalk planters and foundation plantings in the 400 to 1200 blocks of State Street.

Top: Short stem and lacy crown of Phoenix roebelenii. *Bottom: Inflorescence of pale yellow flowers with persistent large woody bract.*

Phoenix rupicola
Cliff date palm, wild date palm, India date palm, East Indian wine palm

Native to mountainous forests of the Himalayan region of India.

Habit A graceful solitary feather palm of medium stature; to 35 feet tall.

Inflorescence Dioecious; interfoliar, 2 feet long on a three-foot peduncle. Blooms March to April.

Fruit Oblong-ovoid, 3/4 inch long, shiny yellow to deep purplish-red.

Stem Clear of leaf bases, with triangular knobby leaf base scars, to 10 inches in diameter.

Leaves Pinnate, 10–18 feet long, twisted towards the apex to an almost vertical plane, especially on younger leaves, with up to 80 leaflets on each side arranged in a single plane; leaflets 18 inches, soft, appearing limp, bright green, with lines of grayish peltate scales on central ridges beneath; lower leaflets reduced to spines.

Notes This is the least spiny of all the species of *Phoenix*. It is unique in not having persistent leaf bases on the trunk and is the only *Phoenix* with flat leaflets in a single plane. The species name *rupicola* means a dweller of rocky places.

Locations A single stem along the eastern boundary of Plaza Vera Cruz. Two trees labeled *P. rupicola* on the Anacapa Street side of the County Courthouse seem large and have persistent leaf bases. They may well be hybrids within the *Phoenix* complex.

Tall slender stem and irregular crown of pinnate leaves of **Phoenix rupicola.**

Rhopalostylis

Rhopalostylis is a genus of three species native to New Zealand, Norfolk Island, and Roul (Sunday) Island. Its name is derived from the combination of the Greek words *rhopalon* (club) and *stylis* (a small pillar) and refers to its club-shaped flower spike.

Rhopalostylis baueri
Norfolk Island palm, broom

Native to Norfolk Island (Australia).

Habit A solitary feather palm; to 35 feet tall.

Inflorescence Monoecious; emerging from the base of the crown sheath, to 20 inches long, with 50–60 branches, flowers creamy white. Blooms October to January.

Fruit Red, ellipsoid, to 3/4 inch inch long, with a dull brown seed.

Stem Greenish, turning brownish-gray, with closely spaced leaf scars, to 6 inches in diameter.

Leaves Pinnate, unarmed, 6–12 feet long, ascending and somewhat arching; leaflets 18–24 x 2 inches, found along the full length of the rachis; crown sheath to 16 inches long, swollen.

Notes The species name *baueri* honors Franz (1758–1840) and Ferdinand (1760–1826) Bauer, Austrian brothers and botanical artists of little known, but exquisite, talent.

Locations East Beach, on the north side of the Cabrillo Pavilion Arts Center, and in the 1800 block of Santa Barbara Street.

Top: *Upright foliage crown of pinnate leaves and swollen crown shaft of* **Rhopalostylis baueri**.
Bottom left: *Inflorescence emerging from a woody bract at the base of the crownshaft.*
Bottom right: *Branches of inflorescence with individual creamy white flowers.*

Rhopalostylis sapida
Naikau palm, feather duster palm, shaving brush palm

Native to Norfolk Island (Australia) and New Zealand.

Habit A solitary feather palm; to 25 feet tall.

Inflorescence Monoecious; emerging from the base of the crown, less than 2 feet long, branched to 3 times, usually 2–3 on a tree at one time; flowers tightly packed on the cream-colored spike, in groups of 3 with a female sandwiched between 2 male flowers, purplish to lilac. Blooms October to January.

Fruit Elliptic, 1/2 inch long, bright red; ripening in one year and frequently still held when the next year's flowers emerge.

Stem Ringed with closely spaced, obvious leaf scars; green between the scars when young, 4–5 inches in diameter.

Leaves Pinnate, 4–8 feet long, 12–14 on a tree, ascending in a shaving brush crown; leaflets 3 feet long, 1 1/2 inches broad, forward pointing, many and densely set on an unarmed rachis; crown sheath strongly swollen.

Notes *R. sapida* is unique in having the most southern natural distribution of any palm in the world. The Maori gathered and ate the tender growing tip of this species. The species name *sapida* means savory, tasty.

Locations An individual in the Sunken Garden of the County Courthouse. Others at Lotusland.

Top: Strongly upright crown of **Rhopalostylis sapida** *with swollen crown shaft.*
Bottom: Purplish flowers on branched spikes; bright red fruit.

Sabal
Palmetto

The palmetto palms consist of 16 species distributed around the Caribbean Sea. The generic name *Sabal* is possibly the native name for this palm.

Sabal causiarum
Puerto Rican hat palm

Found in sandy soils of coastal plains from sea level to 300 feet in Haiti, the Dominican Republic, and Puerto Rico.

Habit A solitary fan palm of medium dimensions with a stout appearance; to 30 feet tall.

Inflorescence Emerging from the axils of the leaves, to 12 feet long, branched 3 times, flowers small (1/4 inch), white. Blooms in June.

Fruit Globose, 1/3–1/2 inch in diameter, purple-black.

Stem Clear of leaf bases, leaving a gray, smooth trunk; 15–30 inches in diameter.

Leaves Costa-palmate, to 12 feet long; costa extending far into the blade and having an arching character, giving the blade a three-dimensional appearance; blade large, about 6 feet across, divided 1/2–2/3 to the base into 60–120 somewhat droopy leaflets with threads along the margins, usually bright green, may be glaucous; petiole unarmed.

Notes The Puerto Rican hat palm was once used extensively for making hats, baskets, and mats; however, many native uses seem to have declined with the advent of plastic. The species name *causiarum* means of broad-brimmed hats.

Locations Individuals in East Alameda Plaza and on the Anacapa Street side of the County Courthouse.

Stout stem and three-dimensionally-curved leaves with long costa extending into the blade of Sabal causiarum.

Syagrus

Syagrus is a genus of 32 species from tropical South America. Its name is Latin for wild pig (*syag-rus*) and was used by Pliny for a palm.

Syagrus romanzoffiana
Arecastrum romanzoffianum
Cocos plumosa

Queen palm

Found from central and southern Brazil to Uruguay in a variety of habitats from seasonally dry forests to swamps.

Habit A graceful feather palm with a solitary stem; to 50 feet tall.

Inflorescence Monoecious; emerging from the base of the crown, to 4 feet long with 80-280 flowering branches; flowers about 3/8 inch long, yellow. Flowers February to May.

Fruit In pendulous bunches; ovoid, 1–1 1/2 inches long, yellow to orange.

Stem Light to dark gray, smooth, without persistent leaves, with faint annular rings from deciduous leaf bases, 15–20 inches in diameter.

Leaves Pinnate, 7–15 in the open crown; 8–14 feet long, arching; leaflets 3 feet x 1 1/4 inches, 150–250 per side, yellow-green to deep green, the tips bent and hanging; petiole unarmed, but with fibrous hairs along the margin.

Notes Along with *Jubaea chilensis,* this species is the southernmost of the American palms. The fruit and palm hearts are edible, and in its native locations the durable stem is used for pilings in salt water. It is usually short-lived, 35–40 years. The species name *romanzoffianum* honors Prince Nicholas Romanzoff of Russia, who financed a round-the-world expedition in 1816–1817.

Locations Common throughout town. Street trees along much of Santa Barbara Street, in the 1300–1900 blocks of State Street, and along Cabrillo Boulevard near the Harbor. The old trees near the corner of Mission and Garden Streets persist from the earliest plantings of the species in 1912.

"Feather duster" crown of Syagrus romanzoffiana *with inflorescence emerging from the base and clear stem.*

Trachycarpus

Trachycarpos is a genus of six small- to medium-sized species from the Himalayan region, only one of which is planted in Santa Barbara. Its name combines the Greek words *trachys* (rough) and *karpos* (fruit), referring to the fruit of some of its species.

Trachycarpus fortunei
Windmill palm, Chinese windmill palm, hemp palm, Chusan palm

Native to the mountainous regions of northern Myanmar (Burma), and central and eastern China.

Habit A solitary fan palm; to 35 feet tall.

Inflorescence Emerging from among the leaves, repeatedly branched but small and inconspicuous; flowers pale yellow, fragrant. Blooms June to August.

Fruit Three-lobed, kidney-shaped, 1/2 inch long, bluish when mature.

Stem Covered by a thick mat of black fibers from which persistent leaf bases extend, to 6 inches in diameter.

Leaves Palmate, circular, 3–4 feet across, dull green, divided at least to the middle into stiff (becoming drooping) segments; petiole 1 1/2 feet x 3/4–1 inch, thin, with minute teeth along margins, base covered with long brown fibers.

Notes As suggested by its native distribution, the windmill palm is the most cold-hardy of cultivated palms. The seeds are used medicinally and are believed to have cancer-fighting properties. The species name *fortunei* honors Robert Fortune (1812–1880), Scottish horticulturist and botanical collector who lived in China for 18 years.

Locations Street trees on Junipero Plaza are among the oldest in the city. Those on Haley Street from Chapala to Milpas Streets were planted in 1974 by the Men's Garden Club of Santa Barbara. Individuals in East and West Alameda Plaza, on the campus of the University of California, Santa Barbara, and on the County Courthouse grounds.

Slender stem with persistent leaf bases and mat of black fibers, and palmate leaves with somewhat drooping leaflets of Trachycarpus fortunei.

Trithrinax

Trithrinax is a relatively primitive genus of three species from subtropical South America. Its species are among the most cold-tolerant and drought-resistant of the American palms. The genus is relatively new and was created as a result of splitting of three species from the genus *Thrinax;* hence, *tri-thrinax.*

Trithrinax brasiliensis
Trithrinax acanthecoma

Brazilian needle palm, *caranda,* spiny fiber palm

Found in open, dry inland areas of southern Brazil.

Habit A solitary or occasionally clustered fan palm with a dense crown of 5–35 leaves; to 45 feet tall.

Inflorescence Emerging from among the leaves, to 24 inches long, covered with several boat-shaped bracts, 6 inches long. Flowers in early winter.

Fruit Globose to ellipsoid, 2/3–1 inch across, yellowish.

Stem To 15 inches in diameter; covered with persistent fibrous leaf sheaths and vicious-looking spines that are 4–5 inches long.

Leaves Palmate, 3–4 feet across, deep green; leaflets somewhat flexible, pointed at the apex and divided halfway to the base; petiole unarmed, 2–2 1/2 feet long.

Notes The species name *brasiliensis* means from Brazil.

Locations Several trees in the palm garden of East Alameda Plaza, two in a planting on the corner of Anacapa and Anapamu Streets, and an individual tree on the Anacapa Street side of the County Courthouse.

Top: Trithrinax brasiliensis, *with persistent leaf bases and dark fibrous mats along stem and stout palmate leaves.* Bottom: *Needle-like spines and dense cluster of yellowish fruit.*

Washingtonia

Washingtonia is a genus of two species from the arid southwestern United States and northwestern Mexico. Its name honors George Washington (1732–1799), first President of the United States.

Washingtonia filifera
California fan palm, desert fan palm, petticoat palm

Found around streams and springs, especially along geological fault lines, in the border region of the Colorado Desert in Southern California, southwestern Arizona, and northwestern Mexico.

Habit A tall, stout fan palm with an open crown of ascending leaves; to 70 feet tall.

Inflorescence Monoecious; emerging from the lower leaves, 6 to 12 feet long with multiple branches, becoming incorporated in the skirt of dead leaves after seed dispersal; flowers small, numerous, white. Blooms June to August.

Fruit Ovoid, 1/3 inch long, black.

Stem 2–3 feet in diameter; if not pruned, covered with a dense "shag" of persistent dead leaves; if pruned, the persistent leaf bases form no obvious pattern; if exposed, the gray surface of the lower trunk is marked with vertical fissures that are more prominent than the leaf scars.

Leaves Palmate, 6 feet or more across, divided more than halfway to the base; segments noticeably drooping, with many long, hanging, filamentous threads, light green, not glaucous; petiole 6 feet long x 6 inches broad near the base, armed with prominent light tan teeth that become smaller towards the base, without a tawny brown spot on under side near the base.

Notes This species is well-adapted to drought and heat, but is not as tolerant of coastal conditions as *W. robusta*. The species name *filifera* means bearing threads.

Locations Trees intermixed with *W. robusta* in the first to 300 blocks of West Cabrillo Boulevard. Street trees in the 1700 block of Bath Street, the 300 block of Santa Barbara Street, and the 200 block of Palm Avenue. Others in East Alameda Plaza, De la Guerra Plaza, and the Desert Section of the Santa Barbara Botanic Garden. A planting in Carpinteria on Linden Avenue adjacent to 7th Street.

Stout stem of Washingtonia filifera, *upright crown of living leaves, and pendulous "skirt" of dead leaves.*

Washingtonia robusta
Mexican fan palm, Mexican Washington palm

Native to Mexico in a small portion of the state of Sonora and the southern half of Baja California.

Habit A tall, graceful palm with a dense, oblong crown; to 80 feet tall.

Inflorescence Monoecious; emerging from the lower leaves, 6–12 feet long with multiple branches, becoming incorporated in the skirt of leaves after seed dispersal; flowers small, numerous, white. Flowers May to June.

Fruit Ovoid, 1/3 inch long, black.

Stem Base expanded; if not pruned, covered with a dense "shag" of persistent dead leaves; if pruned, the persistent leaf bases form a distinctive cross-hatched pattern; if exposed, the surface more brown than gray, vertical fissures reduced, and less prominent than the leaf scars.

Leaves Palmate, 3 feet across, divided less than halfway to the base, shiny bright green; segments somewhat stiff, not strongly drooping; filamentous threads present only in young leaves; petiole 6 feet long x 6 inches wide near the base, armed with prominent reddish-brown teeth that become smaller towards the base, reddish-brown, with a large distinctive purplish spot on the under side near the base.

Notes The Mexican fan palm is the most widely planted palm in Santa Barbara. It is perhaps misnamed in that it is much less robust and is more graceful than *W. filifera*. It is more tolerant of coastal conditions and excess moisture than *W. filifera;* however, it is also more sensitive to cold winter temperatures. The species name *robusta* means stout, strong.

Locations Extensively planted along Cabrillo Boulevard from the Bird Refuge to Leadbetter Beach. A planting in Carpinteria on 7th Street adjacent to Linden Avenue.

Slender stems of Washingtonia robusta *with oblong crown of living and dead leaves and persistent leaf bases that form a distinctive cross-hatched pattern on stems.*

Asphodelaceae

The Asphodel Family consists of 17 genera and 750 species found throughout the Eastern Hemisphere, from Europe to central Asia to South Africa. The family was originally placed in the much larger Liliaceae, the taxonomy of which remains fluid. Recent revisions have recognized the distinct differences of this family, including succulent, non-fibrous leaves and inflorescences in spikes or panicles. Contributing to the confusing taxonomic history, the following genus was at one time placed in its own family, the Aloeaceae.

Aloe

Aloe is a genus of about 365 species that are concentrated in South Africa, Madagascar, Arabia, and the Canary Islands. *Aloe* has been a well-recognized component of many cultures. It is mentioned in Babylonian texts and has been used as a purgative and for skin infections. Today, extracts of *Aloe vera* are used in many cosmetics and as a home remedy for burns. Although most of its species can not be classified as trees, several are clearly arborescent. These "tree" aloes are of two forms: those with a main stem that branches into a clearly defined "canopy," and those with a single stem that poses as a pedestal to support the foliage. The genus name is derived from the Arabic name for these succulent plants.

Aloe barberae
Aloe bainesii
Tree aloe, *boomaalwyn*

Native to the humid, subtropical regions of southeastern South Africa from Cape Province to Swaziland. The species grows in dense bush lands and low forest in which it can reach above the shade-producing canopy.

Habit An evergreen succulent tree with dichotomous branching and a well-developed rounded crown; to 30 feet tall.

Inflorescence Upright terminal racemes, usually 3 in a single vertical plane, each 8–12 x 3–4 inches, on an eight- to twelve-inch peduncle; flowers composed of a tubular perianth with 6 shortly spreading lobes, about 1 1/2 inches long; rose- to orange-pink, greenish at the spreading tips, with 6 exserted stamens, 1/2 inch long; producing large amounts of nectar. Blooms in November.

Left: Upright crown of Aloe barberae *with succulent leaves held at the ends of the branches and upright racemes of flowers.*
Right: Racemes of orangish-pink flowers and channeled succulent leaves.

Fruit Erect capsules.

Twigs Stout, 1–2 inches across at the base of the leaves, smooth, dull gray, showing scars from many previous leaves as thin lines.

Bark Light gray showing tannish-brown underneath, slightly roughened by paper-thin peeling flakes.

Leaves Clustered at the ends of the ultimate branches; sword-shaped, thickly succulent, 24–36 inches long, 3–4 inches across at the base, deeply channeled in a U-shape above, convex below; dull green overall; margins with hardened dull white teeth with brownish tips, less than 1/8 inch long.

Notes This is the largest of the tree aloes in South Africa. It has been used extensively as a horticultural complement in the region. The species name *barberae* honors Mary Elizabeth Barber, plant collector in the former Transkei region of eastern South Africa.

Locations One tree at Alice Keck Park Memorial Gardens near the corner of Garden and Arrellaga Streets. Another at Lotusland.

Dracaenaceae
Agavaceae

The Dragon Tree Family includes two genera and approximately 160 species. The family is found almost exclusively in arid habitats of the tropical and subtropical regions in the Eastern Hemisphere, although one species occurs in Central America.

Dracaena

Dracaena is a genus of about 60 species primarily from the Old World and Canary Islands. Two species are found in the New World tropics. The name has been ascribed to the Greek *drakaina,* a female dragon, in reference to the blood-red color of the sap of the following species. It has also been suggested that the name honors Sir Francis Drake.

Dracaena draco
Dragon tree

Native to Madeira and the Canary Islands.

Habit An evergreen tree with branches forking in equal pairs; to 45 feet tall.

Inflorescence Terminal panicles, to 24 inches long; flowers 1/3 inch long, creamy white, fragrant. Blooms in August.

Fruit A fleshy capsule 1/2 inch across, ripening reddish-orange.

Stem Initially bulbous between nodes, becoming flattened vertically.

Bark Smooth, creamy gray, initially marked with thin reddish-brown lines that outline the leaf scars, becoming scaly, grayish-brown on larger stems and branches.

Leaves Clustered in terminal rosettes, sword-shaped, 12–24 x 1/2–1 2/3 inches, the base flared and clasping, bluish-green becoming brownish, leathery and very fibrous, not succulent, margins smooth, apex rounded.

Notes *D. draco* has been the source of much fanciful myth and legend dating to Pliny who detailed its magical qualities. Early commerce recorded its use for medicinal purposes, painting, and jewelry crafts. It was also used by 17th-century Italian violin makers in their final varnish and may have contributed to the long-lasting qualities of these instruments that are so appreciated today. Although the species has been recorded to attain massive size (70 feet tall and 25 feet in diameter at ground level), excessive human pressures and grazing have led to its near extinction in its native habitat. The species name *draco* means dragon.

Locations A large tree in West Alameda Plaza near Santa Barbara Street, another in the parking lot of the Old Mission, and a third in the inner courtyard of El Paseo. Street trees in the first block of East Arrellaga. A large and striking grove of trees in Lotusland.

Top: Distinctive dense crown of bluish-green succulent leaves of Dracaena draco *with distinctive swollen trunk and primary branches.*
Bottom left: Branched inflorescence of creamy white flowers and sword-shaped leaves.
Bottom right: Reddish-orange fruit and individual flowers.

Glossary

Abaxial - Located on the side away from the main axis of the organism.

Abscission - The separation of a fully developed organ (fruit, leaf, etc.) by the formation of a layer of corky cells, which protect the stem.

Acuminate - Having a long tapering tip with concave sides.

Acute - Having a short, sharp tip with parallel or convex sides.

Adaxial - Located on the side, towards the main axis of the organism.

Alternate - Arranged singly along an axis, not in pairs.

Anther - The pollen-bearing portion of the *stamen*.

Anthesis - The time of flower expansion.

Apex - The top or tip of a structure, usually the leaf.

Apophysis - The swelling of the ends of cone scales, typically in the Pinaceae.

Appressed - Pressed against.

Areole - The space between the finest veins on the blade of a leaf.

Aril - A fleshy structure on a seed, developing from the point of attachment.

Axillary - Pertaining to the upper angle between a leaf and a *twig* or between a *twig* and a branchlet.

Banner - The uppermost, often erect, *petal* of pea-like flowers of the Fabaceae.

Beak - A prolonged narrow tip.

Berry - A fleshy fruit in which there is usually more than one seed not encased in a *stone*.

Bipinnate - Said of a *pinnately compound* leaf in which the leaflets are further divided into secondary leaflets.

Bract - A small leaf-like structure, usually subtending an *inflorescence* or cone.

Calyx - The outermost *whorl* of flower parts made up of sepals, which are usually green and encase the remainder of the flower.

Capsule - A dry, usually many-seeded fruit with a distinct opening to enable release of seeds.

Catkin - A *spike* of flowers of the same sex without obvious perianths.

Claw - The narrow stalk-like base of some sepals or petals.

Compound - Divided into two or more parts, creating a repeated structural pattern.

Conflorescence - A *compound inflorescence* consisting of two or more *simple* inflorescences.

Cordate - With a heart-shaped base.

Corolla - The *whorl* of flower parts immediately above and inside the *calyx,* usually large and brightly colored.

Corymb - A flat or slightly convex flower *head* created by a *raceme* in which the lower flowers are on proportionately longer pedicels.

Costa - In the fan palms, the extension of the *petiole* as a rib into the fan-like leaf.

Costa-palmate - A fan palm leaf characterized by the extension of a *costa* into the *lamina*.

Crenulate - A leaf margin with small, shallow rounded teeth.

Crown shaft - The cylinder formed by the *sheath* of a palm leaf *petiole* extending around the stem.

Cyathium - An *inflorescence* of unisexual flowers surrounded by a cluster of bracts.

Cyme - A branched *inflorescence* in which the central or upper-most flowers open first.

Decussate - Occurring in opposite pairs that alternate at right angles to one another.

Dehisce - Splitting open at maturity to release the contents.

Deltoid, deltate - Generally equilaterally triangular with rounded basal corners.

Dentate - Said of leaf margins with relatively coarse teeth pointed outward.

Dichotomous - A branching pattern in which each branch supports equal branching above it.

Dioecious - Said of a species in which male and female flowers occur on separate plants.

Disc - A plate or rim of tissue derived from the *receptacle* of a flower on which the *ovary* and/or stamens are attached.

Discolorous - Of two different colors, as on two sides of a leaf.

Dorsal - Relating to the back of an organ.

Downy - Covered with fine hairs.

Drupe - A fleshy fruit with a single seed enclosed in a hardened *stone*.

Elliptic(al) - In the shape of an ellipse.

Entire - Having continuous margins without teeth or lobes.

Epicormic - Said of new growth occurring on old wood of trees.

Epimatium - A fleshy structure covering seeds in some gymnosperms, derived from the ovule-bearing scales.

Exserted - Said of flower and fruit parts *(stamens, pistils,* and *valves)* that extend beyond

the surrounding parts.
Falcate - Scythe-shaped; curved, flat and gradually tapering.
Fascicle - A bundle or cluster.
Filament - The threadlike structure of the *stamen* which supports the *anther*.
Follicle - A dry, generally many-seeded fruit opening along a single suture.
Glabrous - Without hairs, smooth.
Glandular - Containing a small body exuding a sticky substance, often held at the end of a short hair.
Glaucous - Covered with a whitish or bluish powder or film, often easily rubbed off to expose the green color of a leaf or *twig*.
Globose - Round, spherical.
Head - A dense, round *inflorescence* of *sessile* flowers.
Hydathode - A specialized structure for the exudation of water, usually found on leaves.
Hypanthium - The base of a flower to which the *stamens, petals,* and *sepals* are attached.
Inflorescence - An entire cluster of flowers and associated structures.
Inserted - Said of flower or fruit parts that are contained within the surrounding parts.
Intramarginal vein - In the Myrtaceae, a vein that parallels the margin of the leaf, but is often distinct from it.
Keel - A ridge or crease on the surface of a structure.
Kino - The thickened or frequently brittle gum or sap of some tropical trees, which is dark reddish-brown and is sometimes used in native medicines.
Lamina - The blade of a leaf.
Lanceolate - Lance-shaped; narrowly elongate, widest in the basal half and tapering towards the tip; said of a leaf shape.
Leaflet - A leaf-like unit of a *compound* leaf.
Leaf scar - The scar left on a *twig* after the *abscission* of a leaf.
Lenticel - A spongy area or pore, found on the surfaces of twigs and fruits.
Lenticellate - Said of branches and twigs with numerous *lenticels*.
Linear - Elongate with parallel sides; longer than *oblong*.
Lobe - A significant expansion or bulge, usually along the margin of a leaf.
Mallee - A growth form of *Eucalyptus* consisting of several stems rising from a tuber; often a large shrub.

Monoecious - Said of a species in which separate male and female flowers occur on the same plant.
Monotypic - Said of a genus or family containing a single species.
Nerve - A *simple* or unbranched vein.
Nut - A dry, indehiscent fruit in which the seed is encased in a hard shell.
Oblong - Longer than broad with parallel sides; shorter than *linear*.
Obovate - Said of a two-dimensional structure (leaf) that is widest above the middle; egg-shaped.
Obtuse - Said of a leaf with a short, blunt point and parallel or convex sides converging at an angle greater than 90°.
Operculum - A lid or cap on a flower, formed from the fused *perianth* segments and falling as a unit; found in *Eucalyptus*.
Opposite - Arranged in pairs along an axis.
Ostiole - A small opening or pore; usually applied to the opening of the fig in *Ficus* that allows pollinating wasps to enter the *receptacle* and fertilize the individual flowers.
Ovate - Said of a two-dimensional leaf structure that is widest below the middle; egg-shaped.
Ovary - The ovule-bearing portion of the *pistil* which develops into the fruit.
Ovoid - Said of a three-dimensional fruit structure that is widest below the middle; egg-shaped.
Palmate - Radiating from a common point.
Panicle - A branched *inflorescence* in which the lateral or lower-most flowers open first.
Pedicel - The stalk of an individual flower.
Peduncle - The stalk of an entire *inflorescence*.
Pendulous - Hanging or declined.
Perianth - The floral envelope consisting of the *calyx* and *corolla*.
Petal - One member of the *corolla*, evolved from a modified leaf.
Petiole - The stalk of a leaf connecting the blade to the stem.
Phloem - The tissue in plants through which organic metabolites are transported.
Petiolule - The stalk of a *leaflet* in a *compound* leaf.
Phyllychnia - Longitudinal ribs on the branchlets of *Casuarina*.
Pinna(e) - A primary division of a pinnately *compound* leaf.
Pinnate - A feather-like arrangement with two

rows of structures along opposite sides of a central axis.

Pinnule - The secondary division in a bi-pinnately *compound* structure.

Pistil - The female reproductive structure of a flower, consisting of an *ovary*, a *stigma*, and an interconnecting *style*.

Pith - The spongy, hollow, or diaphragmed center of a *twig*.

Pod - A dry, several-seeded fruit that generally dehisces along two sutures, usually applied to the Fabaceae.

Pome - A fleshy, indehiscent fruit such as an apple or pear, usually applied to the Rosaceae.

Prickle - A superficial, sharp projection derived from the bark.

Puberulent - With minute hairs normally only visible with magnification.

Pubescent - Covered with visible hairs.

Pulvinus - An area of swollen tissue at the base of the stalk of a leaf or *leaflet*, which is often involved in leaf movement.

Raceme - An unbranched *inflorescence* of pediceled flowers that open from bottom to top (see *spike*).

Rachis - The main stalk of an *inflorescence* or a *compound* leaf.

Recurved - Gradually curved downward or back.

Reflexed - Abruptly bent or curved downward or back.

Receptacle - The structure to which flower parts are attached or, in *Ficus*, the structure on which flowers are attached.

Reticulate - Networked or netveined.

Revolute - Rolled backward from the margin or *apex*.

Rim - In the fruit of *Eucalyptus*, the scar left behind from the attachment of the *operculum* and *stamens*.

Samara - A dry, one-seeded, *winged* fruit.

Scabrous - Rough or sand papery to the touch.

Scalloped - A leaf margin characterized by shallow, rounded teeth.

Sclerenchyma - Cells that have thickened walls and often serve to strengthen plant tissue.

Seedcase - The portion of a dried fruit which encloses the seed.

Sepal - A single member of the *calyx*, evolved from a modified leaf, usually green.

Serotinous - Said of a pine cone that is slow to open and release its seed, usually requiring heat of a fire to open. A *serotinous* cone may remain unopened on a tree for several years.

Serrate - Having a margin with sharp, forward-pointing teeth.

Sessile - Without a *petiole, pedicel,* or other kind of stalk.

Sheath - A structure that surrounds another structure, as in the *sheath* about a bundle of pine needles.

Simple - Composed of a single part, undivided.

Sinus - The recess between two lobes of a leaf.

Spathe - A single *bract* enclosing an *inflorescence*.

Spike - An unbranched *inflorescence* of *sessile* flowers, usually opening from bottom to top.

Spine - A sharp point derived from a leaf.

Spur shoot - A stubby *twig* with densely crowded leaves and *leaf scars*.

Stamen - The male reproductive structure of a flower consisting of the pollen-bearing *anther* and the *filament* upon which it is borne.

Stigma - That part of the *pistil* upon which the pollen lands to initiate fertilization.

Stipule - A leaf-like appendage at the base of a leaf *petiole*, usually in pairs.

Stomate - A pore in a leaf or stem through which gas exchange occurs.

Stone - The very hard shell and single seed in a fleshy *drupe*.

Style - The stalk-like portion of a *pistil* that connects the *stigma* to the *ovary*.

Submarginal vein - A vein that is immediately inside and parallel to the margin of a leaf, usually found in the Myrtaceae.

Succulent - Having fleshy stems or leaves, often in plants from arid regions.

Taxon - A unit of classification of taxonomic similarity (family, genus, species, etc.).

Tepal - A division of a *perianth* in which the sepals and the *petals* are indistinguishable.

Terminal - At the end of a structure.

Thorn - A sharp point derived from a *twig* or branch.

Tomentose - Covered with densely interwoven and matted hairs.

Trifoliate - Having leaves in threes.

Twig - The current or most recent year's growth of a stem segment in woody plants.

Umbel - An *inflorescence* in which three or more flowers emerge from a common point.

Umbilicus - A depression, as in the fruit of *Ficus*.

Umbo - A projection (sometimes sharpened) arising from the center of an object; applied to the *prickle* usually at the ends of cone scales in *Pinus*.

Urn-shaped - Hollow, cylindrical, or *ovoid*, but strongly contracted at the mouth.

Valve - One of the parts into which a *capsule* splits.

Velvet - Even more densely covered with matted hairs than *tomentose*.

Venation - The pattern of veins in a leaf.

Whorl - A grouping of three or more structures of the same kind at a node on a stem.

Wing(ed) - 1) Containing a thin appendage on the surface or margin of an organ. 2) One of the lateral petals in many members of the Fabaceae.

Xerophyte - A plant adapted to very dry habitats.

Bibliography

Much of the information provided in this book came from what is known as the "primary literature." This encompasses the results of original research on individual species or genera frequently published in scientific journals. Because this information is so diffuse, it is unfeasible to present a comprehensive bibliography. The following list of materials is offered as sources of additional information regarding many of the trees growing in Santa Barbara.

Allen, O. N. and E. K. Allen. 1981. *The Leguminosae: A Source Book of Characteristics, Uses and Nodulation.* University of Wisconsin Press. Madison. 812 pp.

Backer, C. A. and R. Van Den Brink. 1965. *Flora of Java,* Vol. 1–3. N.V.P. Noordhoff-Groningen. The Netherlands.

Bean, W. J. 1976. *Trees and Shrubs Hardy in the British Isles,* Vol. 1–4. J. Murray, London. 8th Edition.

Beentje, H. 1994. *Kenya Trees and Shrubs.* National Museums of Kenya, Nairobi. 722 pp.

Boland, D. J., M. I. H. Brooker, G. M. Chippendale, N. Hall, B. P. M. Hyland, R. D. Johnston, D. A. Kleinig and J. D. Turner. 1984. *Forest Trees of Australia.* Nelson-CSIRO, Melbourne, Australia. 687 pp.

Brandis, D. 1906. *Indian Trees.* Archibald Constable & Co., London. 767 pp.

Brooker, M. I. H. and D. A. Kleinig. 1990. *Field Guide to the Eucalypts,* Vol. 1–3. Inkata Press Proprietary Limited, Melbourne, Australia.

Chippendale, G. M. 1988. *Eucalyptus, Angophora (Myrtaceae), Flora of Australia,* Vol. 19. Australian Government Publishing Service, Canberra, Australia. 542 pp.

Condit, I. J. 1969. *Ficus: The Exotic Species.* University of California, Berkeley. 363 pp.

Corner, E. J. H. 1952. *Wayside Trees of Malaya,* Vol. 1–2. Government Printing Office, Singapore.

Dirr, M. A. 1990. *Manual of Woody Landscape Plants.* Stipes Publishing Company, Champaign, Illinois. 1007 pp.

Elliot, W. R. and D. L. Jones. 1980. *Encyclopaedia of Australian Plants Suitable for Cultivation,* Vol. 1–8. Lothian, Port Melbourne, Australia.

Farjon, A. 1984. *Pines: Drawings and Descriptions of the Genus Pinus.* E. J. Brill, Leiden, The Netherlands. 220pp.

Farrar, J. L. 1995. *Trees of the Northern United States and Canada.* Iowa State University Press. Ames, Iowa. 502 pp.

Hansell, D. E. 1970. Handbook of Hollies. *The American Horticultural Magazine* 49:150–331.

Harden, G. J., ed. 1993. *Flora of New South Wales,* Vol. 1–4. New South Wales University Press, Kensington, Australia.

Hickman, J. C. 1993. *The Jepson Manual: Higher Plants of California.* University of California Press, Berkeley. 1400 pp.

Hunt, D., ed. 1998. *Magnolias and their Allies.* Proceedings of an International Symposium, University of London, 12–13 April, 1996. International Dendrology Society and the Magnolia Society. 304 pp.

Jones, D. L. 1995. *Palms Throughout the World.* Smithsonian Institute Press, Washington, D.C. 410 pp.

Krukoff, B. A. and R. C. Barneby. 1974. Conspectus of species of the genus *Erythrina. Lloydia* 37:332–459.

Krüssmann, G. 1978. *Manual of Cultivated Broad-Leaved Trees & Shrubs,* Vol. 1–3. Timber Press, Oregon.

Krüssmann, G. 1985. *Manual of Cultivated Conifers.* Timber Press, Oregon. 361 pp.

Li, H. L. 1963. *Woody Flora of Taiwan.* Livingtson Publishing Company, Narbeth, Pennsylvania. 974 pp.

Mitchell, A. 1974. *A Field Guide to the Trees of Britain and Northern Europe.* Collins, London. 415 pp.

Moore, L. B. and E. Edgar. 1970. *Flora of New Zealand.* A. R. Shearer, Government Printer, Wellington, New Zealand.

Ohwi, J. 1965. *Flora of Japan.* Smithsonian Institution, Washington, D.C. 1067 pp.

Palgrave, K. C. 1988. *The Trees of Southern Africa.* Struik Publishers, Capetown, South Africa. 959 pp.

Palmer, E. and N. Pitman. 1972. *Trees of Southern Africa.* A. A. Balkema, Cape Town, South Africa. 2235 pp.

Perry, J. P. 1991. *The Pines of Mexico and Central America.* Timber Press, Portland. 231pp.

Riffle, R. L. and P. Craft. 2003. *An Encyclopedia*

of Cultivated Palms. Timber Press, Portland. 528 pp.

Salmon, J. T. 1980. *The Native Trees of New Zealand.* A. H. and A. W. Reed, Ltd., Wellington, New Zealand. 384 pp.

Sleumer, H. O. 1980. Flacourtiaceae. *Flora Neotropica: Monograph 22.* 499 pp.

Stanley, T. D. and E. M. Ross. 1983. *Flora of South-eastern Queensland,* Vol. 1–3. Queensland Department of Primary Industries, Misc. Pub. 81020. Brisbane, Australia.

Wagner, W. L., D. R. Herbst, and S. H. Sohmer. 1990. *Manual of the Flowering Plants of Hawai'i,* Vol. 1–2. Bishop Museum, Honolulu.

Whibley, D. J. E. 1980. *Acacias of South Australia.* Government Printer, South Australia. 240 pp.

Wolf, C. B. and W. W. Wagener. 1948. The new world cypresses. *El Aliso* 1:1–444.

Wrigley, J. W. and M. Fagg. 1979. *Australian Native Plants.* Collins, Sidney, Australia. 448 pp.

Additional accounts of individual species can be found in various issues of periodicals such as Allertonia, The American Horticultural Magazine, Curtis's Botanical Magazine, Journal of Arboriculture, Journal of the Arnold Arboretum, and Lloydia.

Finally, considerable material is now available on the World Wide Web. However, much of this is of conflicting value. The web sites that are offered here are noted for their scientific accuracy.

Flora of China
http://flora.huh.harvard.edu/china/mss/treatments.htm

Flora of North America.
http://hua.huh.harvard.edu/FNA/

Gymnosperm Database
http://www.botanik.unibonn.de/conifers/index.html

Kew Royal Botanic Garden, electronic Plant Information Centre (ePIC).
http://www.kew.org/searchepic/searchpage.do

Kirstenbosch National Botanical Garden, South Africa, National Botanical Institute, Plants of Africa.
http://www.plantzafrica.com/

Missouri Botanical Garden, W^3 Tropicos.
http://mobot.mobot.org/W3T/search/vast.html

USDA, Agricultural Research Service, Germplasm Resources Information Network (GRIN).
http://www.ars-grin.gov/cgi-bin/npgs/html/index.pl

Latin/Common Name Index

Page numbers in **bold** *indicate a primary reference for the entry within the species profiles. Species names within parentheses are synonyms. The symbol "x" in front of a species or genus name indicates that the taxon is a product of hybridization.*

Abarema sapindoides **182**
Abies
   bracteata (venusta) 12, **49**
   concolor **50**, 51
   grandis **51**
   lowiana **50**
   pinsapo **52**
Acacia
   arabica 139
   Bailey **140**
   baileyana **140**
   binervia (glaucescens) **141**
   Black **148**
   cultriformis **142**
   dealbata **143**, 144, 147
   decurrens **144**, 147
   farnesiana 17, **145**
   longifolia **146**
   mearnsii (decurrens var. mollis) 143, 144, **147**
   melanoxylon 11, 13, **148**
   Pearl **150**
   pendula **149**
   podalyriifolia **150**
   pycnantha **151**
   Shoestring **152**
   Silky **156**
   stenophylla **152**
   Sweet **145**
   verticillata var. *verticillata* **153**
Acca sellowiana **259**
Acer
   buergerianum **87**
   japonicum **86**
   macrophyllum **83**, 84
   negundo **84**
   oblongum **85**
   palmatum **86**
   paxii **87**
   rubrum **88**
   saccharinum 12, 14, **89**
   saccharum 88, 391
Aceraceae **83–89**
Acmena smithii **260**
Acrocarpus fraxinifolius **154**

Acronychia baueri **370**
Aesculus
   californica 12, 13, **210**, 212
   x *carnea* **211**
   hippocastanum 211, **212**
   pavia 212
African fern pine 11, **77**
African tulip tree **116**
African wattle **184**
Afrocarpus gracilior 11, 12, 18, **77**
Agathis robusta **20**
Agavaceae **408–409**, 439
Agonis flexuosa **261**
Ailanthus
   'Vilmoriniana' **389**
   altissima 10, 16, **389**
Akeake **381**
Alamo cottonwood **374**
Albizia
   chinensis **155**
   Chinese **155**
   julibrissin 155, **156**
   lophantha (distachya) **157**
   Plume **157**
Alder
   California **108**
   White **108**
Alectryon excelsus **379**
Aleppo pine **63**
Aleurites moluccana **133**
Alligator pear **223**
Allocasuarina verticillata **124**
Almond 1, 2, 354, **358**
Alnus rhombifolia 16, **108**
Aloe barberae (bainsii) **438**
American elm 177, **401**
Anacardiaceae **90-97**, 380
Angiosperms 10, 13, 14, 19, **83–439**
Angophora costata **262**, 281
Annona cherimola 9, **98**
Annonaceae **98**
Apocynaceae **99-100**, 226
Apple
   Argyle **275**
   Long-leaved Argyle **274**
   Mexican **366**
   Red-barked **262**
   Rose **323**
   Smooth-barked **262**
Apple box **272**
Apple gum **272**

Apricot 1, 48, **354**
Aquifoliaceae **101–103**
Araliaceae **104–107**
Araucaria
 bidwillii 11, **21**
 columnaris **22**
 cunninghamii **23**
 heterophylla **24**
Araucariaceae **20–24**
Arbor-vitae
 Chinese **46**
 Oriental **46**
 Western **47**
Arbutus
 'Marina' 9, **132**
 menziesii **131**, 132
 unedo 9, 131, **132**
Archidendron **182**
Archontophoenix cunninghamiana **410**
Arecaceae 9, **410–437**
Arecastrum romanzoffianum **433**
Argyle apple 274, **275**
Arizona ash **330**
Armeniaca vulgaris **354**
Arroyo willow **377**
Ash
 Arizona **330**
 California **327**
 Chinese **328**
 Foothill **327**
 Japanese **328**
 Shamel **329**
 Velvet **330**
Ashleaf maple **84**
Asphodelaceae **438**
Athel tree **398**
Atlas cedar **53**
Australian banyan **247**
Australian beech **294**
Australian dammar pine **20**
Australian fan palm **422**
Australian tea-tree **306**
Australian willow **369**
Avocado 218, **223**
Bailey acacia **140**
Baloghia inophylla (lucida) **134**
Bangalay **271**
Banksia
 Coast **344**
 Granite **345**
 integrifolia 18, **344**
 verticillata **345**
Banyan fig **242**

Bauerella simplicifolia **370**
Bauhinia
 blakeana **158**
 forficata **159**
 variegata **160**
Bay
 California 1, 5, **225**
 Madeira **224**
 Sweet **222**
Bebe tree **371**
Beefwood **125**
Beilschmiedia miersii **218**
Bell-flowered cherry **355**
Bellota **218**
Belmore sentry palm **419**
Benjamin tree **243**
Betula
 nigra **109**
 pendula (verucosa) **110**
Betulaceae **108–110**
Bigcone Douglas-fir **75**
Big-cone pine **61**
Bigcone spruce **75**
Bigleaf maple **83**
Bignoniaceae **111–119**, 121
Birch
 European white **110**
 Red **109**
 River **109**
 Silver **110**
 Weeping **110**
Bischofia javanica **135**
Bishop pine 31, **66**
Black acacia **148**
Black bean **164**
Black cottonwood **373**, 374
Black locust **186**
Black Sally **301**
Black walnut 215, **216**
Black wattle 144, **147**
Blackwood **148**
Blue-berry elder **122**
Blue elder **122**
Blue elderberry **122**
Blue gum 2, **285**
Blue hesper palm **411**
Blue mahoe **232**
Blue oak **195**
Blue palo verde **166**
Boer-bean
 Bush **189**
 Karoo **187**
 Weeping **188**

LATIN/COMMON NAME INDEX 447

Bombacaceae 120, 234
Boomaalwyn 438
Boraginaceae 121, 213
Boree 149
Bottlebrush
  Pink 312
  Red 263
  Weeping 265
  White 264
  Willow 264
Bottle-tree
  Kurrajong 393
  Scrub 391
Bougainvillea goldenrain tree 383
Box
  Apple 272
  Brush 307
  Peppermint 293
  Queensland 307
  Red 294
  Victorian 341
Box-elder 84
Bracelet honey-myrtle 308
Brachychiton
  acerifolius 14, 390, 391, 394
  discolor 390, 391
  gregorii (populneus x occidentalis) 392
  populneus 392, 393, 394
  x *roseus (populnea-acerifolius)* 3, 394
Brahea
  armata 411
  brandegeei 412
  edulis 413
Brassaia actinophylla 106
Brazilian cedarwood 5, 236
Brazilian coral tree 172
Brazilian needle palm 435
Brazilian orchid tree 159
Brazilian pepper tree 97
Bride of India 385
Bristlecone fir 49
Broad-leaved coral tree 174
Broad-leaved ironbark 284
Broad-leaved lucky bean tree 174
Broad-leaved paperbark 313
Bronze loquat 351
Broom 430
Brush box 307
Brush cherry 321
Bull bay 229
Bunya-bunya tree 21, 24
Burdekin plum 93
Bush boer-bean 189

Bushy yate 288
Butia capitata 414
Buttonwood 137
Buxton gum 280
Cabbage tree
  New Zealand 408
Cabbage tree palm 422
Cadaga 270
Caesalpinia
  pluviosa var. *peltophoroides (peltophoroides)* 161
  spinosa 162
California alder 108
California ash 327
California bay 1, 5, 225
California black oak 198
California black walnut 215
California buckeye 12, 210
California fan palm 2, 436
California juniper 38
California laurel 225
California mountain cypress 34
California nutmeg 82
California pepper tree 96
California white oak 200
Callery pear 362
Callicoma serratifolia 139
Callistemon
  citrinus 263
  salignus 264, 313
  viminalis 265
Callitris rhomboidea 25
Calocedrus decurrens 26
Calodendrum capense 365
Calyptranthes syzygium 321
Cambuca 318
Camel hoof 158
Camphor tree 5, 219
Canary Island date palm 425
Canary Island pine 11, 59
Candelabra tree 136
Candlenut-tree 133
Canyon live oak 194
Cape chestnut 365
Cape fig 244
Cape pittosporum 342
Cape wattle 157
Caprifoliaceae 122–123
Caranda 435
Carob 165, 189
Carolina cherry-laurel 356
Carrot wood 380
Carya illinoensis 14, 214
Caryota

gigas 415
urens 416
Casimiroa edulis 366
Cassava 138, 409
Cassia leptophylla 17, **163**
Cassipourea gummiflua var. *verticillata*
   (*verticillata*) 350
Castanospermum australe 2, **164**
Casuarina
  cunninghamiana 125
  glauca 18, **126**
  stricta 124
Casuarinaceae 124–126
Catalpa
  bignonioides 111, 112
  speciosa 17, **111**
Cedar
  Atlas 53
  Deodar 54
  Himalayan 54
  Incense 26
  Japanese 27
  Pink 154
  Port Orford 33
  Western red 47
  Yellow 94
Cedrela
  fissilis 5, **236**
  odorata 236
  sinensis 239
Cedrus
  atlantica **53**, 54
  deodara **54**
  libani 53
Ceiba
  insignis 120
  pentandra 120
  speciosa 17, **120**
Celastraceae 127
Ceratonia siliqua 14, **165**, 189
Cercidium floridum **166**
Chamaecyparis
  funebris **30**
  lawsoniana **33**
  nootkatensis 37
Chamaerops humilis **417**
Chaste tree **406**
  New Zealand 407
Cheese tree 137
Cheesewood 336
Cherimoya 9, **98**
Cherry
  Bell-flowered 355

Brush 321
Holly-leaved 1, **359**
Taiwan 355
Cherry-laurel **356**, 360
Cherry plum 357
Chestnut
  Cape 365
  Moreton Bay 164
Chilean wine palm 2, **421**
Chilopsis linearis **112**
China doll tree 115
Chinaberry tree 238
Chinese albizia 155
Chinese arbor-vitae 46
Chinese ash 328
Chinese elm **402**
Chinese fan palm **423**
Chinese fountain palm 423
Chinese fringe tree 326
Chinese hibiscus 233
Chinese juniper 39
Chinese lantern tree **383**
Chinese magnolia **231**
Chinese mahogany 239
Chinese parasol tree **397**
Chinese pistache 91
Chinese scholar tree 190
Chinese sumac 389
Chinese weeping cypress 30
Chinese windmill palm **434**
Chionanthus retusus **326**
Chir pine 71
Chiranthodendron pentadactylon 14, **395**
X *Chitalpa tashkentensis* 112
Chorisia speciosa 120
Cigartree 111
Cinnamomum
  camphora 5, **219**
  japonicum 220
Citrus
  aurantifolia 367
  aurantium 367
  limon 367
  maxima 367
  medica 367
  x *paradisi* 367
  reticulata 367
  sinensis 367
Cliff date palm **429**
Coarse-leaved mallee 287
Coast banksia 344
Coast live oak 11, **193**
Coast myall

Coast redwood 43, 258
Coast tea-tree 306
Cocculus laurifolius (bariensis) 9, **240**
Cockspur coral tree 171
Cocos
   australis 414
   campestris 414
   plumosa 433
Common fig 245
Common horsechestnut 211
Common myrtle 317
Common wild fig 252
Cootamundra wattle 140
Copernica cerifera 424
Coral gum 303
Coral tree
   Brazilian 172
   Broad-leaved 174
   Cockspur 171
   Dwarf 173
   Flame 170
   Naked 170
   Sykes' 176
Cordia myxa 223
Cordyline australis 408
Cork oak 1, 6, **203**
Corkscrew willow 378
Corymbia
   calophylla **266**, 268
   citriodora 11, **267**, 269
   ficifolia 266, **268**, 271
   maculata **269**
   torelliana **270**
Cotinus 399
Cottonwood
   Alamo 374
   Black **373**, 374
   Fremont **374**
Coulter pine 61
Cow hoof 158
Cow-itch tree 234
Crape myrtle 227
Crepe flower 227
Crinodendron patagua **130**
Cryptocarya alba (rubra) 6, 18, **221**
Cryptomeria japonica **27**
Cuban bast 232
Cupaniopsis anacardioides **380**
Cup gum 278
Cupressaceae 25–47
X *Cupressocyparis leylandii* 37
Cupressus
   abramsiana **28**

arizonica 18, **29**
funebris **30**
goveniana **31**
guadalupensis **32**
lawsoniana **33**
macrocarpa **34**, 37
sargentii **35**
sempervirens 28, **36**
X *Cuprocyparis leylandii* **37**
Cussonia spicata **104**
Cypress
   California mountain 34
   Chinese weeping 30
   Gowen 31
   Guadalupe 32
   Italian 28, 36
   Lawson false 33
   Leyland 37
   Mediterranean 36
   Mexican swamp 45
   Monterey 34
   Montezuma bald 4, 45
   Mourning 30
   Santa Cruz 28
   Sargent 35
   Smooth-bark Arizona 29
Dais cotinifolia 15, **399**
Date 426
Date palm 410, 415, 425, **426**
Dawn redwood 42
Deep yellow wood 94
Del Mar pine 74
Deodar cedar 54
Desert *kurrajong* 392
Desert willow 112, **338**
Devil's hand tree 395
Diamond leaf pittosporum 339
Diospyros
   kaki **128**
   virginiana **129**
Dodonaea viscosa 'Purpurea' **381**
Dombeya cacuminum **396**
Douglas-fir 76
Dracaena draco 1, **439**
Dracaenaceae 439
Dragon's claw willow 378
Dragon tree 1, **439**
Drooping she oak 124
Duranta repens (erecta) **405**
Dwarf coral tree 173
Dwarf lucky bean tree 173
Dypsis decaryi **418**
Early black wattle 144

East African yellow wood 77
Ebenaceae 128–129
Ehretia anacua 121
Elaeocarpaceae 130
Elder
   Blue 122
   Blue-berry 122
   Yellow 119
Elm
   American 177, 401
   Chinese 402
   Lacebark 402
   Siberian 403
Engelmann oak 196
English holly 101
English laurel 360
English oak 201
English walnut 217
English yew 81
Enterolobium cyclocarpum 167
Ericaceae 9, 131–132, 344
Eriobotrya
   deflexa 18, 351
   japonica 352
Erythea
   armata 411
   brandegeei 412
   edulis 413
   elegans 412
Erythrina
   abyssinica 168
   americana 170
   caffra 169, 175, 176
   coralloides 170
   crista-galli 171
   falcata 172
   humeana 173
   latissima 9, 169, 174
   lysistemon 5, 18, 169, 175, 176
   poianthes 170
   speciosa 176
   x *sykesii* 176
Eucalyptus
   amygdalina 44
   botryoides 271
   bridgesiana 272
   calophylla 266
   camaldulensis (rostrata) 273
   cephalocarpa 18, 274
   cinerea 18, 274, 275
   citriodora 267
   cladocalyx 276
   cornuta 4, 277

   cosmophylla 278
   crebra (racemosa) 279
   crenulata 280
   deglupta 281
   diversicolor 282
   erythrocorys 283
   fibrosa subsp. *fibrosa* 284
   ficifolia 268
   globulus 210, 271, 285
   grandis 286
   grossa 287
   lehmannii 288
   leucoxylon 289
   macrandra 290
   maidenii 285
   megacornuta 291
   nicholii 292
   odorata (fruticetorum) 293
   polyanthemos 294
   punctata 295
   robusta 296
   saligna 297
   sideroxylon 298
   spathulata 299
   steedmanii 300
   stellulata 301
   tereticornis 302
   torelliana 270
   torquata 303, 305
   viminalis 304
   woodwardii 305
Eugenia
   jambolana 322
   Willow-leaved 318
Euodia daniellii (hupehensis) 371
Euphorbia ingens 136
Euphorbiaceae 133–138, 409
European fan palm 417
European horsechestnut 211
European white birch 110
Evergreen maple 87
Evergreen pear 363
Evodia hupehensis 371
Fabaceae 139–191
Fagaceae 192–205
False Brazilwood 161
Feather duster palm 431
Feijoa sellowiana 259
Ficus
   auriculata (roxburghii) 241
   benghalensis 242
   benjamina 243
   capensis 244

    carica 241, **245**
    gnaphalocarpa **246**
    macrophylla 4, 247, **250**, 254
    microcarpa var. *nitida* 243, **248**
    microphylla **250**
    mysorensis **249**
    palmata **245**
    rubiginosa 4, 247, **250**
    rumphii **251**
    thonningii (petersii) **252**
    vogelii **253**
    watkinsiana **254**
Fig
    Banyan **242**
    Benjamin tree **243**
    Cape **244**
    Common **245**
    Common wild **252**
    Laurel **248**
    Moreton Bay 4, **247**
    Mysore **249**
    Port Jackson **250**
    Roxburgh **241**
    Rumphius **251**
    Rusty-leaf 4, **250**
    Sandpaper **246**
    Vogel's **253**
    Watkins **254**
    Weeping **243**
Fir
    Bigcone Douglas- **75**
    Bristlecone **49**
    Douglas- 75, **76**
    Goddess of mercy **27**
    Grand **51**
    Santa Lucia **49**
    Spanish **52**
    White **50**
Firmiana simplex (platanifolia) **397**
Five-veined paperbark **313**
Flacourtiaceae **206**
Flame coral tree **170**
Flame *kurrajong* **390**
Flame tree 116, **390**
    Pink **391**
    Sexton 3, **394**
Flamegold **384**
Flaxleaf paperbark **311**
Flooded gum **286**
Floss silk tree **120**
Flying moth tree **85**
Foothill ash **327**
Foothill pine **72**

Forest red gum **302**
Fortunella margarita **368**
Four-leaved pinyon pine **69**
Frangipani **335**
Fraxinus
    dipetala **327**
    latifolia **330**
    malacophylla 327, **328**
    uhdei **329**
    velutina 329, **330**
Fremont cottonwood **374**
Geijera parviflora 338, **369**
Giant honey-myrtle **308**
Giant sequoia **44**
Giant Thai mountain palm **415**
Giant yucca **409**
Ginkgo biloba 12, **48**
Ginkgoaceae **48**
Gleditsia triacanthos f. *inermis* **177**
Glochidion ferdinandii **137**
Glossy privet **331**
Goddess of mercy fir **27**
Gold medallion tree **163**
Golden cup oak **194**
Golden trumpet tree **117**
Golden wattle **151**
Goldenrain tree **385**
Gowen cypress **31**
Grand fir **51**
Granite banksia **345**
Gray goddess blue palm **411**
Gray gum **295**
Gray pine 1, **72**
Grecian laurel **222**
Green dracaena **408**
Green wattle **144**
Grevillea robusta **346**
Guadalupe cypress **32**
Guadalupe palm **413**
Guaje 180, **181**
Guanacaste **167**
Guava
    Pineapple **259**
    Strawberry **319**
Gum
    Apple **272**
    Blue 2, 285, 289, 297, **302**
    Buxton **280**
    Coral **303**
    Cup **278**
    Flooded **286**
    Forest red **302**
    Gray **295**

Lemon-flowered 305
　　Lemon-scented 267
　　Manna 304
　　Mindanao 281
　　Red 262, 273
　　Red cap 283
　　Red-flowering 268
　　Ribbon 304
　　River red 273
　　Rose 286
　　Silver 280
　　Spotted 269
　　Sugar 276
　　Sydney blue 297
　　Tasmanian blue 2, 285
　　Water 324
　　Yellow 289
Gummy onionwood 350
Gymnocladus dioica 178
Gymnosperms 12, 19, 48, 20–82
Hakea sauveolens 347
Hamamelidaceae 207–209
Hand tree
　　Devil's 395
　　Monkey's 395
Handflower tree 395
Harpephyllum caffrum 90, 169
Harpullia arborea 382
Henkel's yellow wood 78
Hibiscus
　　Chinese 233
　　elatus 18, 232
　　Norfolk Island 234
　　rosa-sinensis 17, 233
Himalayan cedar 54
Himalayan pittosporum 337
Hindu laurel 9, 240
Hippocastanaceae 210–212
Holly
　　English 101
　　Lusterleaf 102
Holly-leaved cherry 102
Holly oak 197
Holm oak 197
Honeylocust 177
Hong Kong orchid tree 158
Hoop pine 23
Horsechestnut
　　Common 211
　　European 211
　　Red 212
Howeia
　　belmoreana 419

　　forsteriana 420
Hydrophyllaceae 213
Hymenosporum flavum 335
Ice cream bean 179
Ilex
　　aquifolium 101
　　latifolia 102
　　vomitoria 103
Illyarrie 283
Incense cedar 26
Indian-bean 111
Indian laurel 248
Indian snakeroot 100
Indian walnut 133
Inga pilosula (affinis) 18, 179
Ipe 118
Ironbark
　　Broad-leaved 284
　　Narrow-leaved 279
　　Red 298
　　White 289
Ironwood
　　Persian 209
　　Santa Cruz Island 353
　　White 372
Island oak 204
Islay 359
Italian cypress 28, 36
Italian poplar 375
Italian stone pine 67
Jacaranda
　　acutifolia 113
　　mimosifolia 113
Jaggery palm 416
Jambolan plum 322
Japanese ash 328
Japanese black pine 73
Japanese cedar 27
Japanese maple 86
Japanese pagoda tree 190
Japanese persimmon 128
Japanese pittosporum 340
Japanese podoberry 79
Japanese zelkova 404
Javan plum 322
Jeffrey pine 64
Jelly palm 414
Jerusalem thorn 183
Jornate 235
Jubaea chilensis 2, 421, 433
Juglandaceae 214–217
Juglans
　　californica 215, 217

LATIN/COMMON NAME INDEX   453

nigra 216
regia 17, 217
Juniper
  California 38
  Chinese 39
  Utah 41
  Western 40
Juniperus
  californica 12, 38
  chinensis 39
  occidentalis 40
  osteosperma 41
Ka'a oveti 400
Kaki 128
Kamarere 281
Kanooka 324
Kara 282
Karo 336
Karoo boer-bean 187
Karree 95
Kasuur 342
Kentia palm 419, 420
Kentucky coffee-tree 178
Khaya nyasica 237
King palm 410
Kinsel oak 199
Kite tree 226
Knife-leaf wattle 142
Knob-cone pine 58
Knock-away 121
Koelreuteria
  bipinnata 14, 17, **383**, **385**, 391
  elegans (formosana) 383, **384**
  paniculata 385
Kumquat 368
Kuro-matsu 73
Kurrajong
  Desert 392
  Flame 390
Kurrajong bottle-tree 393
Lacebark elm 402
Lacebark tree 391
Lagerstroemia indica 227
Lagunaria patersonii 234
Lauraceae 218–225
Laurel
  California 225
  Common cherry- 360
  English 360
  Grecian 222
  Hindu 9, 240
  Indian 248
Laurel fig 248

Laurus nobilis 222, 225
Lawson false cypress 33
Lemon-flowered gum 305
Lemon-flowered mallee 305
Lemon-scented gum 267
Leptospermum laevigatum 306
Leucaena
  esculenta 180
  leucocephala subsp. *glabrata* 181
Leyland cypress 37
Ligustrum lucidum 18, 331
Lillipilli 260
Lily-of-the-valley tree 130
Liquidambar
  orientalis 207
  styraciflua 11, 16, 86, **208**, 391
Liriodendron tulipifera 8, 11, **228**
Lithocarpus densiflorus 192
Livistona
  australis **422**, 424
  chinensis 423
  decipiens 424
Locust
  Black 186
  Yellow 186
Loganiaceae 226
Lombardy poplar 1, 375
Long-flowered marlock 290
Long-leaved Argyle apple 274
Long-leaved Indian pine 71
Long-leaved yellow wood 78
Lophostemon confertus 4, 13, **307**
Loquat 352
  Bronze 351
Lucky bean tree
  Broad-leaved 9, **174**
  Dwarf 173
Luehea divaricata 400
Lusterleaf holly 102
Lyonothamnus floribundus
  subsp. *aspleniifolius* 353
Lythraceae 227
Macadamia integrifolia (ternifolia) 348
Maclura pomifera 255
Madagascar three-sided palm 418
Madeira bay 224
Magnolia
  Chinese 231
  denudata 230
  grandiflora 6, **229**
  liliifera 230
  Saucer 230
  x *soulangiana* 230

Southern 6, 229
Magnoliaceae 228–231
Mahogany
   Chinese 239
   Red 237
   Southern 271
   Swamp 296
Maidenhair tree 48
Mallet
   Steedman's 300
   Swamp 299
Mallet flower 107
Malvaceae 120, **232**–**235**, 390, 400
Manihot
   carthaginensis 138
   esculenta 138
Manioc 138
Manitoba maple 84
Manna gum 304
Maple
   Ashleaf 84
   Bigleaf 83
   Evergreen 87
   Japanese 86
   Manitoba 84
   Oblong 85
   Oregon 83
   Red 88
   Silver 12, **89**
   Water 89
Markhamia lutea (hildebrandtii) 114
Marri 266
Maul oak 194
Mayten tree 127
Maytenus boaria 16, **127**
Mealy stringybark 274, 275
Mediterranean cypress 36
Melaleuca
   armillaris **308**, 310
   decora (genistifolia) **309**, 314
   ericifolia 310
   leucadendra 313
   linariifolia 311
   nesophila 312
   quinquinervia 313
   Rigidleaf 314
   styphelioides 309, 311, **314**
Melia azedarach 1, **238**
Meliaceae **236**–**239**
Menispermaceae **240**, 241
Mesquite 185
Metasequoia glyptostroboides 42
Metrosideros excelsa 315

Mexican apple 366
Mexican fan palm 1, 5, **437**
Mexican nut pine 60
Mexican palo verde 183
Mexican stone pine 60
Mexican swamp cypress 45
Michelia
   doltsopa 231
   figo 231
Mimosa 113, **156**
Mindanao gum 281
Mock orange 341
Mock privet 333
Molle 96
Monkey's hand tree 395
Monk's protector 406
Monterey cypress 34
Monterey pine 70
Montezuma bald cypress 4, **45**
Moraceae **241**–**256**
Moreton Bay chestnut 164
Moreton Bay fig 4, **247**
Moreton Bay pine 23
Morinda spruce 57
Morus
   alba 17, **256**
   nigra 256
Mountain ebony 160
Mourning cypress 30
Mugga 298
Myall 149
   Coast 141
   Weeping 149
Myoporaceae **257**
Myoporum
   laetum 257
   sandwicense 257
Myrciaria edulis 318
Myrica californica 258
Myricaceae **258**
Myrobalan plum 357
Myrrhinium atropurpureum var. *octandrum*
   (salicinum) 316
Myrtaceae **259**–**325**
Myrtle
   Bracelet honey- 308
   Common 317
   Giant honey- 308
   Showy honey- 312
   Wax 258
   Willow 261
Myrtus communis 317
Mysore fig 249

Nagami kumquat 368
Naikau palm 431
Naked coral tree 170
Narrow-cone pine 58
Narrow-leaved black peppermint 292
Narrow-leaved ironbark 279
Narrow-leaved pittosporum 338
Needle bush 347
Neodypsis decaryi 418
Nerium oleander 99
New Caledonian pine 22
New Zealand cabbage tree 408
New Zealand chaste tree 407
New Zealand Christmas tree 315
New Zealand oak 379
Ngaio 257
Norfolk Island hibiscus 234
Norfolk Island palm 430
Norfolk Island pine 24
Northern acorn 218
Northern red oak 202
Norway spruce 55
Nut
   Macadamia 348
   Queensland 348
Nut pine 62
Nuxia floribunda 6, 226
Oak
   Blue 195
   California black 198
   California white 200
   Canyon live 194
   Coast live 1, 11, 193
   Cork 1, 6, 203
   Engelmann 196
   English 201
   Golden cup 194
   Holly 197
   Holm 197
   Island 204
   Kinsel 199
   Maul 194
   New Zealand 379
   Northern red 202
   River 125
   Silky 346
   Southern live 205
   Swamp 126
   Tan 192
   Tanbark 192
   Valley 193, 200
Oblong maple 85
Octopus tree 106

Olea europaea 6, **332**
Oleaceae 326–333
Oleander 99
Olive 1, 2, 6, 99, **332**
Ombu 334
Orange 1, 367
Orchid tree
   Brazilian 159
   Hong Kong 158
Oregon maple 83
Oreopanax capitatus 105
Oriental arbor-vitae 46
Osage orange 255
Oyster Bay pine 25
Pacific madrone 131
Palm
   Australian fan 422
   Brazilian needle 435
   Belmore sentry 419
   Blue hesper 411
   Cabbage tree 422
   California fan 2, 436
   Canary Island date 425
   Chilean wine 2, 421
   Chinese fan 423
   Chinese fountain 423
   Chinese windmill 434
   Cliff date 429
   Date 410, 415, 425, 426
   European fan 417
   Feather duster 431
   Giant Thai mountain 415
   Gray goddess blue 411
   Guadalupe 413
   Jaggery 416
   Jelly 414
   Kentia 419, 420
   King 410
   Madagascar three-sided 418
   Mexican fan 1, 5, 437
   Naikau 431
   Norfolk Island 430
   Paradise 420
   Piccabeen 410
   Pigmy date 428
   Pindo 414
   Puerto Rican hat 432
   Queen 5, 433
   Ribbon fan 424
   Sago 416
   San José hesper 412
   Senegal date 427
   Sentry 419, 420

Shaving brush 431
Triangle 418
Weeping cabbage 424
Wild date 429
Windmill 434
Wine 416
Palma negra 412
Palo verde
  Blue 166
  Mexican 183
Paperbark
  Broad-leaved 313
  Five-veined 313
  Flaxleaf 311
  Pineleaf 310
  Prickly leaved 314
  Swamp 310
Paradise palm 420
Pararchidendron pruinosum 182
Parkinsonia
  aculeata 17, **183**, 185
  florida 166
Parota 167
Parrotia persica 209
Parry pinyon pine 69
Pataqua 130
Paulownia tomentosa 388
Peach 1, 354, **361**
Peacock pine 27
Pear
  Alligator 223
  Callery 362
  Evergreen 363
Pearl acacia 150
Pecan 214
Peltophorum africanum 184
Pepper tree 96
  Brazilian 97
  California 96
  Peruvian 96
Peppermint
  Narrow-leaved black 292
  Western Australian 261
  Willow 261
  Willow-leaved 292
Peppermint box 293
Persea
  americana 223
  indica 224
Persian ironwood 209
Persian lily 238
Persian walnut 217
Persimmon 129

  Japanese 128
Peruvian pepper tree 96
Peumo 6, 221
Phillyrea latifolia 333
Phoenix
  canariensis 425
  canariensis x *reclinata* 425
  dactylifera 426
  reclinata 427
  roebelenii 410, **428**
  rupicola 429
Phytolacca dioica 334
Phytolaccaceae 334
Piccabeen palm 410
Picea
  abies **55**, 57
  sitchensis 56
  smithiana (morinda) 55, **57**
Picon 105
Pigeonberry 405
Pigmy date palm 428
Pinaceae 49–76
Pindo palm 414
Pine
  African fern 11, 77
  Aleppo 63
  Australian dammar 20
  Big-cone 61
  Bishop 31, **66**
  Bunya-bunya 21
  Canary Island 11, **59**
  Chir 71
  Coulter 61
  Del Mar 74
  Foothill 72
  Four-leaved pinyon 69
  Gray 1, **72**
  Hoop 23
  Italian stone 5, **67**
  Japanese black 73
  Jeffrey 64
  Knob-cone 58
  Long-leaved Indian 71
  Mexican nut 60
  Mexican stone 60
  Monterey 70
  Moreton Bay 23
  Narrow-cone 58
  New Caledonian 22
  Norfolk Island 24
  Nut 62
  Oyster Bay 25
  Parry pinyon 69

Pinyon 60
Ponderosa 68
Queensland kauri- 20
Santa Cruz Island 66
Singleleaf pinyon 65
Soledad 74
Star 24
Torrey 74
Two-needle pinyon 62
Umbrella 67
Western yellow 68
Yew 79
Pineapple guava 259
Pineleaf paperbark 310
Pink bottlebrush 312
Pink box 307
Pink cedar 154
Pink flame tree 391
Pink trumpet tree 118
Pinus
   attenuata 58
   canariensis 11, 59, 71, 73
   cembra 60
   cembroides 60, 62
   coulteri 61
   edulis 62, 65
   halepensis 63
   jeffreyi 64, 68
   longaeva 44
   monophylla 65, 69
   muricata 66
   nigra 73
   pinea 5, 63, 67
   ponderosa 64, 68
   quadrifolia 65, 69
   radiata 58, 70
   roxburghii 59, 71, 73
   sabiniana 1, 72
   saponis 52
   thunbergii 73
   torreyana 61, 74
Pinyon pine 60
Pissard plum 357
Pistache
   Chinese 91
Pistachio
   Wild 92
Pistacia
   chinensis 86, 91
   khinjuk 92
   terebinthus 97
Pithecellobium pruinosum 182
Pittosporaceae 335–342

Pittosporum
   Cape 342
   colensoi 339
   crassifolium 336
   Diamond leaf 339
   floribundum 337
   Himalayan 337
   Japanese 340
   Narrow-leaved 338
   phylliraeoides 338
   Queensland 339
   rhombifolium 339
   tenuifolium 336
   tobira 340
   undulatum 18, 341, 372
   viridiflorum 342
   Weeping 338
Platanaceae 343
Platanus
   x *acerifolia* 343
   occidentalis 343
   orientalis 343
   racemosa 14, 343
Pleiogynium timorense (solandri) 93
Plinia edulis 18, 318
Plum 354
   Burdekin 93
   Cherry 357
   Jambolan 322
   Javan 322
   Myrobalan 357
   Pissard 357
   South African wild 90
Plume albizia 157
Podalyrius 150
Podocarpaceae 77–80
Podocarpus
   elongatus 77
   gracilior 77
   henkelii 78
   macrophyllus 79
   totara 80
   Yew 79
Pohutukawa 315
Pompon tree 399
Ponderosa pine 68
Poplar 373
   Italian 375
   Lombardy 1, 375
   Tulip 228
   Yellow- 228
Populus
   balsamifera subsp. *trichocarpa* 373, 374

fremontii 374
nigra 'Italica' 1, 375
Port Jackson fig 250
Port Orford cedar 33
Possomwood 129
Prickly leaved paperbark 314
Prickly Moses 153
Primrose tree 234
Princess tree 388
Privet
   Glossy 331
   Mock 333
Prosopis glandulosa var. *torreyana*
   (*juliflora* var.*torreyana*) 183, **185**
Proteaceae 344–349
Prunus
   armeniaca 354
   campanulata 355
   caroliniana 356
   cerasifera 'Atropurpurea' 357
   dulcis (*amygdalus*) 358
   ilicifolia 1, 359
   laurocerasus 360
   persica 361
Pseudotsuga
   macrocarpa 12, 75
   menziesii 76
Psidium cattleyanum 319
Puas 382
Puerto Rican hat palm 432
Puriri 407
Purple hop-bush 381
Pyrus
   calleryana 362
   communis 362, 363
   kawakamii 363
Queen palm 5, **433**
Queensland box 307
Queensland fire-wheel tree 349
Queensland kauri-pine 20
Queensland nut 348
Queensland pittosporum 339
Queensland silver wattle 150
Quercus
   agrifolia 11, **193**
   chrysolepis 194
   douglasii 195
   dumosa 199
   engelmannii 196
   ilex 101, **197**
   kelloggii 198
   x *kinseliae* 199
   lobata 193, 199, **200**

robur 193, **201**, 205
rubra **202**
suber 1, 6, **203**
tomentella **204**
virginiana **201**, **205**, 229
Quicuio 246
Quillaja saponaria 18, **364**
Radermachera sinica 16, 115
Rain tree 137, 184
Rauwolfia samarensis 100
Red-barked apple 262
Red birch 109
Red bottlebrush 263
Red box 294
Red cap gum 283
Red-flowering gum 268
Red gum 262, 273
Red horsechestnut 212
Red-hot-poker tree 168
Red ironbark 298
Red mahogany 237
Red maple 88
Redwood
   Coast 43
   Dawn 42
Rhizophoraceae 350
Rhodosphaera rhodanthema 94
Rhopalostylis
   baueri **430**
   sapida **431**
Rhus lancea 95
Ribbon fan palm 424
Ribbon gum 304
Rigidleaf melaleuca 314
River birch 109
River oak 125
River red gum 273
River she oak 125
River yate 290
Robinia pseudoacacia 10, **186**
Robinsonella cordata 235
Roble serrano 118
Rosaceae 351–364
Rose apple 323
Rose-bay 99
Rose gum 286
Roxburgh fig 241
Rumphius fig 251
Rusty-leaf fig 4, **250**
Rutaceae 365–372
Sabal causiarum 432
Sago palm 416
Salicaceae 373–378

Salix
   babylonica 376, 378
   lasiolepis 377
   matsudana 'Tortuosa' 378
Sallee 301
Sallow wattle 146
Sambucus
   caerulea 122
   mexicana 14, 122
San José hesper palm 412
Sandpaper fig 246
Santa Cruz cypress 28
Santa Cruz Island ironwood 353
Santa Cruz Island pine 66
Santa Lucia fir 49
Sapindaceae 379–388
Sapindus
   rarak 386
   saponaria 387
Sarcomelicope simplicifolia 370
Sargent cypress 35
Satinash 260
   Weeping 325
Saucer magnolia 230
Schefflera
   actinophylla 13, 106
   pueckleri 107
Schinus
   molle 1, 10, 96
   terebinthifolius 97
Schotia
   afra var. *angustifolia* 187
   brachypetala 188
   latifolia 189
   Weeping 188
Scrophulariaceae 388
Scrub bloodwood 134
Scrub bottle-tree 391
Scrub yellow-wood 370
Seaforthia elegans 410
Senegal date palm 427
Sentry palm 419, 420
Sequoia sempervirens 43
Sequoiadendron giganteum 43, 44
Sexton flame tree 3, 394
Shamel ash 329
Shaving brush palm 431
She oak 125
   Drooping 124
   River 125
Sheep bush 369
Shingle tree 154
Shiny xylosma 206

Shoestring acacia 152
Showy honey-myrtle 312
Siberian elm 403
Silk oak tree 346
Silk tree 156
Silky acacia 156
Silky oak 346
Silver birch 110
Silver gum 280
Silver maple 12, 89
Silver wattle 143
Simaroubaceae 389
Singleleaf pinyon pine 65
Sitka spruce 56
Smooth-bark Arizona cypress 29
Smooth-barked apple 262
Snowwood 182
Snowy fleece tree 309
Soapbark tree 364
Soapberry 386, 387
Soledad pine 74
Sophora japonica 18, 190
South African wild plum 90
Southern live oak 205, 229
Southern magnolia 6, 229
Southern mahogany 271
Spanish fir 52
Spathodea campanulata 13, 116
Spotted gum 269
Spruce 55
   Bigcone 75
   Morinda 57
   Norway 55
   Sitka 56
   West Himalayan 57
St. John's bread 165
St. Paul's tree 213
Star pine 24
Steedman's mallet 300
Stenocarpus sinuatus 349
Stenolobium stans 119
Sterculiaceae 390–397
Stinkwood 182
Strawberry guava 319
Strawberry snowball tree 396
Strawberry tree 132
Sugar gum 276
Sugarberry 121
Sula 71
Swamp mahogany 296
Swamp mallet 299
Swamp messmate 296
Swamp oak 126

Swamp paperbark 310
Swamp wattle 157
Sweet acacia 145
Sweet bay 222
Sweet pecan 214
Sweet viburnum 123
Sweetgum 208
   Turkish 207
Sweetshade 335
Syagrus
   capitata 414
   romanzoffiana viii, 5, 410, **433**
Sydney blue gum 297
Sydney golden wattle 146
Sykes' coral tree 176
Syncarpia glomulifera (laurifolia) 320
Syzygium
   aromaticum 321
   australe 321
   cumini 322
   floribundum 325
   jambos 3, 323
   paniculatum 321
Tabebuia
   chrysotricha 17, **117**
   impetiginosa (avellanedae) **118**
Taiwan cherry 355
Tamaricaceae 398
Tamarix aphylla 10, **398**
Tan oak 192
Tanbark oak 192
Tapioca 138
Tara 162
Tarco 113
Tasmanian blue gum 2, 285
Taxaceae 81–82
Taxodium mucronatum 4, **45**
Taxus
   baccata 81
   brevifolia 81
Tea-tree
   Australian 306
   Coast 306
Tecoma
   ipe 118
   stans 119
Tetradium daniellii 371
Thuja
   occidentalis 46
   orientalis 46
   plicata 47
Thymelaeaceae 399
Ti kouka 408

Tiliaceae 400
Tipu 191
Tipuana tipu **191**
Titoki 379
Tobira 340
Toog 135
Toona sinensis 239
Torrey pine 74
Torreya californica **82**
Totara 80
Trachycarpus fortunei **434**
Tree aloe 438
Tree-of-heaven 389
Triangle palm 418
Tristania
   conferta 307
   laurina 324
Tristaniopsis laurina 324
Trithrinax brasiliensis (acanthecoma) **435**
Trumpet tree
   Golden 117
   Pink 118
Tsuga 75
Tuckeroo 380
Tulip poplar 228
Tulip satinwood 94
Tulip tree 11, 228
Tupidanthus calyptratus **107**
Turpentine tree 320
Two-needle pinyon pine 62
Ulmaceae 401–404
Ulmus
   americana 401
   parvifolia 402
   pumila 403
Umbellularia californica 1, 5, **225**
Umbrella pine 67
Umbrella tree
   Queensland 106
Umbu 334
Utah juniper 41
Valley oak 193, **200**
Velvet ash 330
Vepris undulata 372
Verbenaceae 405–407
Viburnum
   awabuk 123
   japonicum 123
   lantanum 123
   odoratissimum 123
Victorian box 341
Vitex
   agnus-castus 18, **406**

    lucens 407
    negundo 84
Vogel's fig 253
Walnut 214, 215
    Black 216
    California black 215
    English 217
    Persian 217
Warted yate 291
Washingtonia
    filifera 2, 436, 437
    robusta 1, 5, 412, 436, 437
Water gum 324
Water maple 89
Waterhousea floribunda 325
Watkins fig 254
Wattle 139
    African 184
    Black 147
    Cape 157
    Cootamundra 140
    Early black 144
    Golden 151
    Green 144
    Knife-leaf 142
    Queensland silver 150
    Sallow 146
    Silver 143
    Swamp 157
    Sydney golden 146
    Weeping 184
Wax myrtle 258
Weeping birch 110
Weeping boer-bean 188
Weeping bottlebrush 265
Weeping cabbage palm 424
Weeping fig 243
Weeping myall 149
Weeping pittosporum 338
Weeping schotia 188
Weeping wattle 184
Weeping willow 376
West African rubber tree 253
West Himalayan spruce 57
Western arbor-vitae 47
Western Australian peppermint 261
Western juniper 40
Western red cedar 47
Western sycamore 343
Western yellow pine 68
Wheel of fire 349
Whip-horse 400
White alder 108

White bottlebrush 264
White elder 6, 226
White fir 50
White ironbark 289
White ironwood 372
White mulberry 256
White sapote 366
Wigandia caracasana 213
Wild date palm 429
Wild pistachio 92
Willow 373, 376
    Arroyo 377
    Australian 369
    Corkscrew 378
    Desert 112, 338
    Dragon's claw 378
    Weeping 376
Willow bottlebrush 264
Willow myrtle 261
Willow peppermint 261
Willow rhus 95
Willow-leaved eugenia 318
Willow-leaved peppermint 292
Windmill palm 434
Wine palm 416
Xanthocyparis 37
Xylosma congesta 206
Yabunikkei 220
Yate 4, 277
    Bushy 288
    River 290
    Warted 291
Yaupon 103
Yellow aspen 370
Yellow bignonia 119
Yellow cedar 94
Yellow elder 119
Yellow gum 289
Yellow locust 186
Yellow wood 78
    Deep 94
    East African 77
    Henkel's 78
    Long-leaved 78
Yellow-poplar 228
Yew pine 79
Yew podocarpus 79
Yucca
    elephantipes 409
    Giant 409
Zelkova serrulata 404

THE AUTHORS

Robert N. Muller is a native Santa Barbaran and has returned to join the Santa Barbara Botanic Garden as Director of Research. Bob received his Ph.D. from Yale University in plant ecology and spent four years at Argonne National Laboratory where he conducted research in air pollution and biological transport of radio-nuclides. Subsequently, he spent 24 years in the Department of Forestry at the University of Kentucky where he taught dendrology, forest ecology, and ecosystem analysis to forestry undergraduate and graduate students. Dr. Muller's research interests have led to numerous publications on the dynamics of old-growth forests.

J. Robert Haller is a native of Los Angeles and a resident of Santa Barbara since 1957. Bob received his Ph.D. from the University of California at Los Angeles, where he studied the systematic relationships of California's yellow pines. From 1957 to 1993 he served on the faculty of the Department of Biological Sciences at the University of California at Santa Barbara and continued his studies of western conifers. His classes trained generations of California botanists and were well-known among students for their exquisite slide shows of the California flora. Since retiring from UCSB, Bob has continued teaching as Travel Botanist at the Santa Barbara Botanic Garden, where his class field trips to Figueroa Mountain, the Sierras, and Chile have been in popular demand.

Grevillea robusta

www.ingramcontent.com/pod-product-compliance
Lightning Source LLC
Chambersburg PA
CBHW040736300426
44111CB00026B/2965